THE COMPLETE SCRIPTS

Mad Movies

With the

L.A. CONNECTION

THE COMPLETE SCRIPTS

Mad Movies

With the

L.A. CONNECTION

Foreword by Kent Skov

BearManor Media

2022

Mad Movies With the L.A. Conection: The Complete Scripts
Foreword © Kent Skov

All rights reserved.

No portion of this publication may be reproduced, stored, and/or copied electronically (except for academic use as a source), nor transmitted in any form or by any means without the prior written permission of the publisher and/or author.

Published in the United States of America by:

BearManor Media
1317 Edgewater Dr #110
Orlando FL 32804
bearmanormedia.com

Printed in the United States.

ISBN—978-1-62933-896-5

CONTENTS

Introduction 1

Beneath the 12-Mile Reef 3

Captain Scarlett 31

Decameron Nights 61

Divorce of Lady X 93

D.O.A. 123

Doll Face 151

Inspector General 179

Little Princess 209

My Favorite Brunette 239

Nothing Sacred 269

Night of the Living Dead 295

The Outlaw 317

Outpost In Morocco 345

Perils of Pauline 373

Sante Fe Trail 401

Sherlock Holmes 427

Shock Pt. 1 455

Shock Pt. 2 479

A Star Is Born 503

The Stranger 529

This Is the Army 557

Under California Stars 587

Zorro's Fighting Legions 615

FOREWORD

My time spent making *Mad Movies with the L.A. Connection* gave me some of the most exciting and wonderful memories I will always cherish. I thank all our fans for their unwavering support through the years. In particular, I want to personally thank Ben Ohmart for commissioning the first book about *Mad Movies* and now a new book, a composite of the original scripts to all 26 episodes. When you watch an episode and compare it to the original scripts in this book, you may notice some of the words or lines may be different. These were either altered from the script purposely for better lip sync or the improv recording was funnier than the original script and so we kept the take. Maybe you can find those changes when you match up our scripts with the actual TV show.

Ben's desire to write the first book was apparent from the start. His regular persistence over the last couple of years to get all of the content was flattering. He was relentless in his pursuit and *Mad Movies With the L.A. Connection* would never have been published without him. Thus, when Ben approached me for this second book containing the scripts to all 26 episodes, I knew it would be futile to ignore him. He would just persist until he got them all so I sent them to him and forgot about it. A couple years later, out of the blue, Ben emailed me a digital pre-print of his new book, complete with all 26 episodes. I was surprised and elated at the news. It was then that I asked Ben if I could write the Foreword.

If it weren't for Ben, neither the *Mad Movies* series nor our movie dubbing history would have ever been told. Thanks to Ben for being *Mad Movies*'s biggest fan, a personal friend of mine, and for keeping our series alive. Who knows? Maybe theatre companies and comedians may start dubbing our scripts live all over the world. That way a new generation can enjoy *Mad Movies with the LA Connection* all over again.

– Kent Skov, 2021

INTRODUCTION

A Word (of Warning) from the Editor

Hi, folks. Ben Ohmart here, owner of BearManor Media and 46-year-old HUGE fan of *Mad Movies*. I grew up with this series, short lived though it was, in the 1980s. I was delivering newspapers every day in high school on my bike, so I could afford two, count them, *two* VCRs, back when they were expensive and the average person didn't own *two*.

One of the perks being that I could dub tapes for myself of all the best things in life. One of these being a "greatest hits" compilation of *Mad Movies* for my best friend, Britt Henderson, and myself to watch over and over and over and over again, along with our favorite scenes from *Airplane!, Hardware Wars,* and *Airplane 2.*

To this day, he and I still quote some of these great lines from *Mad Movies*: "R!", "You think I look like Dean Martin?" "Is this a pencil?" "Sorry, didn't mean to spit on ya!" If you don't know what I'm talking about, *you should not be reading this book*!

I applaud Kent Skov for not only coming up with the hilarious concept of debunking old flicks, and going the hard road toward getting the series on TV—but also for allowing me to put **two** books out on this fantastic, groundbreaking series. The first book was a wonderful history of the series by Mike White. This is the second book. But, a word of warning.

In editing these scripts (and all of the typos are mine, I'm totally to blame—plus, I tried to keep the scripts as close to the originals as possible, which might make them look weird sometimes), I found that… they are really quite visual. It might be like reading the script of a Rifftrax or *Mystery Science Theatre 3000* cast member. These are clearly scripts that were meant to be read to the screen, not in the privacy of your own Kindle. So, for the best enjoyment, I strongly suggest reading these along with what you can buy off www.laconnectioncomedy.com or their YouTube Channel. That way, you'll see the little things that got changed, and the brilliant comedy that remained the same. And you'll laugh your ass off, just as I did three decades ago…

– Ben Ohmart
February 2021

BENEATH THE 12-MILE REEF

With the

SHORT RUNDOWN FOR SHOW # 117 BENEATH THE 12-MILE REEF

DESCRIPTION	IN	OUT	SEGMENT TIME
SHOW OPEN	00:00	02:12	02:12
COMMERCIAL BREAK #1	02:12	04:13	02:01
ACT I	04:13	12:32	08:19
COMMERCIAL BREAK #2	12:32	14:33	02:01
ACT II	14:33	21:04	06:31
COMMERCIAL BREAK #3	21:04	23:05	02:01
ACT III/SHOW CLOSE	23:05	28:00	04:55

MAD MOVIES WITH THE L.A. CONNECTION

RUNDOWN SHOW # 117 BENEATH THE 12-MILE REEF

All times are in minutes and seconds	IN	OUT	DURATION
Four Star Logo	00:00	00:05	00:05
Clip Tease #1	00:05	00:21	00:16
Opening Montage	00:21	00:50	00:29
Host Intro and Preview Clip	00:50	02:13	01:23
Commercial Black #1	02:13	04:14	02:01
Bumper #1	04:14	04:18	00:04
Movie Segment #1 (includes Host Toss)	04:18	11:51	07:33
Host and Preview Clip	11:51	12:32	00:41
Commercial Black #2	12:32	14:33	02:01
Bumper #2	14:33	14:36	00:03
Movie Segment #2	14:36	21:02	06:26
Bumper #3	21:02	21:05	00:03
Commercial Black #2	21:05	23:05	02:00
Bumper #4	23:05	23:08	00:03

RUNDOWN, Pg 2

MAD MOVIES WITH THE L.A. CONNECTION

SHOW # <u>117 BENEATH THE 12-MILE REEF</u>

	IN	OUT	DURATION
Movie Segment #3	23:08	25:19	02:11
Host Intro to Home Movie	25:19	25:44	00:25
Home Movie (includes Billboard at tail)	25:44	26:45	01:01
Host Wrap-up	26:45	27:35	00:50
Clip Tease #2	27:35	27:40	00:05
Closing Montage (includes L.A. Connection Logo)	27:40	27:55	00:15
Four Star Logo	27:55	28:00	00:05

BENEATH THE 12 MILE REEF SHOW #117

CLIP TEASE

WAGNER
You know I was the star of "Hart to Hart."

CROWD
OHHH, ohhh...pretty impressive...

GRAVES
I was the lead in Mission Impossible.

CROWD
Oohhh, yeah...

MOORE
But I'm the co-host this week on Mad Movies.

CROWD
Ohhh, wow...

WAGNER
You?!

MOORE
Sure, let's go watch it.

MUSIC THEME

ACT I

SHOW INTRO

EXT. BOAT AT SEA

HOST
Hi, I'm Kent Skov and welcome to Mad Movies with the L.A. Connection. That clip you just saw is from our version of tonight's movie, "Beneath the 12 Mile Reef." Originally it was an action packed adventure about undersea diving. As you saw, some of the stars are actors from some well know TV series. The lovely young woman in the film happens to be our guest tonight...Miss Terry Moore.

HOST
Hi, Terry.

MOORE
Hi, Kent. Are you alright?

HOST
I think so, are you?

MOORE
Oh, I'm fine. You know that the only actors who didn't get seasick on Beneath the 12 Mile reef were the sponges.

                    HOST
Well listen, if you happen to get sick tonight we have water all around us.

                    MOORE
I'll just lean over the edge. I can't wait to see how you've rewritten this film.

                    HOST
Well, now it's about Jacques Cousteau trying to save the undersea world.

                    MOORE
Sponge divers?

                    HOST
Well, in our show, they're no longer sponge divers. We've turned these sponges into sea brains.

                    MOORE
I love it...sea brains.

CLIP TEASE

                    MAN
Hey Lucky, what is it?

                    MAN
Jacque, I just won 200 sea brains in the lottery. Imagine what great whoopee cushions these will make.

                    MAN
You can make a lot of whoopee.

                    MAN
When I get home I'll put it under my pillow and when my wife kisses me good night...wo-hoo...woooo...woo...

                    MOORE
Are they smart?

                    HOST
There's one way to find out.
                    (TO CAM)
We'll be right back with a bizarre undersea adventure.

COMMERCIAL #1

                    HOST
Well Terry, here's Act one of Beneath the 12 Mile Reef.

OVER TITLES

                    (V.O.) JACQUES
My name is Jacques Cousteau and welcome to another underwater oddity.

                    MALE (V.O.)

Ah, Jacques, that's odyssey.

JAC
Oh, odyssey.

(EXT. BOAT LONG SHOT)

JAC
It was a beautiful day for our ecological expedition.
We were...ow, get this thing off me. Idiot.

(EXT. BOAT DECK)

JAC
Hey, you're twisting my chest hairs.

(SFX: TWIST SQUEEKS)

Go the other way.

AL
This way?

JAC
Fine. You should do this professionally.

AL
Hey Jacques, what did Falco do to your pipe?

FALCO
Oh, when I pulled off this hair net, the big part of his pipe broke off.

AL
You know when I was in the little submarine today, I saw a mermaid. She swam right up to the window then she swam away. Then I swam after her. Soon as I got there, she swam the other way. She had a tail as wide as this boat.

JAC
I saw her. First she was on this side of the boat, then the other.

AL
The one with two big dorsal fins, right?

4.

(EXT. SHOT BOAT)

JAC
We were hired by the Environmental Protection Agency to return endangered sea brains that were stolen from the ocean floor. I was accompanied by my friend Falco with whom I always shared cigars and Alexander Tuesday with whom I always shared a hat. Diving is very dangerous. I always protect my head with a hair dryer.
(MUMBLES)
Ouch! It's too tight, it's too tight.

(UNDERWATER SCENE)

JAC (V.O.)
The dangerous barracuda watches me wherever I go, waiting to attack, just like my mother-in-law. I went about my business returning the sea brain to their natural halibut.

VOICE
That's habitat, Jacque.

JAC
Oh, habitat. They had been taken by fiendish fisherman, and sold on the black fish market as everything from paper weights to party favors. The best thing about running on the ocean floor is that when you fall, you don't skin your knees. Here in the red sea we see a school of fish. Swimming seems to fit them just fine. Here in the blue sea, we see a school of boys whose swim suits seem to fit them just fine.

(EXT. SHOT DOCKS)

JAC (V.O.)
As I enjoyed the ocean bottoms, little did I suspect what was happening back on shore.

(INT. DOCK BUILDING)

PHELPS
Well, Cassette, on a scale of one to ten, how would I score?

CASS
Maybe a two, on a good day, Mr. Kelps.

PHELPS
How could I raise it up?

CASS
You're a grown man...you should know. Say wait a minute, Jim, you are a grown man, aren't you?

PHELPS
I'm still growing.

CASS
Ooo. You're rocking my boat, Jimmy Boy.

PHELPS
Let me touch your rudder.

CASS
Ah-choo. You'll have to excuse me. I have a very bad cold.

PHELPS
(O.C.)
Let me take your temperature.

CASS
Aren't you afraid you'll catch my cold?

PHELPS

I'm with Fishin' Impossible, I'm not afraid to catch anything.

                    R.B.

Hey, stole another load of sea brains.

                    PHELPS

Groovy.

(EXT. UNDERWATER)

                    JAC

Now I'm going to show you the proper way to replant sea brains. First you...hey!

                    TURTLE
                    (Belch)

                    JAC

Everyone tries to get into the act, as I was saying. I said get out of the way. There's nothing worse than a turtle who's a ham, except for an air hose between your legs.

(EXT. SHIP DECK)

                    FALCO

Hey Alexander, you caught something. Pull it in.

                    JAC
                    (Mumbles)

Quit pulling. Ow, ow.

                    FALCO

Hey, we got the Loch Ness Monster.

                    AL

No, it's Jimmy Hoffa.

                    FALCO

Oh wait, it's just Jacques. He's not happy. Get him on board and I'll tell him a joke to cheer him up.

(EXT. SHIP DECK)

                    FALCO

And then the bartender says, I was talking to the duck...

                    AL

What's so funny?

                    FALCO

Well I was just telling him a joke and he really liked it. Watch this. And the bartender said, I was talking to the duck. See, go tell everyone. Go on. They'll love it, talkin' to the duck.

                    VARIOUS (V.O.'S)

The bartender said, "I was talkin' to the duck." Ha, ha, ha.

                    FALCO

Wait till I tell you the one about the penguin and the dishwasher.

(INT. HOUSE)

       HOWARD
       (Hums)
Do De Do Do. Excuse me, sir. I'm a stranger in town, and I was just passing by, feeling kinda frisky, thought I'd ask for your daughter's hand in marriage.

       R.B.
What do I get?

       HOWARD
I was fixin' to trade you a dead mule.

(SFX: SCREAM-FALL)

I should have warned her I left it on the porch.
       (OR)

(EXT. DOCKS)

       JAC (V.O.)
We returned to Port for lunch, with half the brains we started out with on our ship, "The Ugly."

       AL
We're almost in Port. We'll need a ride. I'll call a taxi. Taxi! Hey, taxi!

       GIRL
Hi sailors, I'll give you a ride.

       JAC
Okay, wait a minute, that's my daughter. She doesn't have a driver's license. The police would write me the ticket.

       AL
Hey Jacques, look, another load of sea brains has been taken.

       JAC
We must stop everything and return them to the ocean floor because the ecological balance of the world depends on us. Ahhhhh.

       GIRL
Yoo-hoo. Ugly. Ugly.

       AL
Who you calling ugly?

       V.O.
       (Hit by rope)
Ahhhhh.

       JAC
Catch me, darling, you're as beautiful as a sea elephant.

GUS
That'll be five cents for twirling those women.

JAC
What are you talking about? This is my daughter and this is my lovely, get out of the way, my lovely wife, Madame Cousteau. She is beautiful in every way, except of course for the hair on her chest.

MADAME
Oh Jacques.

FISHERMAN
Hey, you just can't take that. What are the magic words?

AL
Let go or I'll break your arm.

FISHERMAN
Those are the words.

AL
Jacques, look, I saved this one. They're shipping the rest out for a party.

FALCO
They made a whoopee cushion out of it.

AL
They make people sit on them.

JAC
Pitiful.

AL
Let's go.

MADAME
Jacques, wait, I made your favorite lunch, marshmallows and beans.

JAC
Uh, well, I, that is, it's just that I'm on a diet. Goodbye.

AL
Bye.

AUCTIONEER
The winning lottery number is 7, 7, 5, 1, 5.

JAC
Lucky, what is it?

LUCKY
Jacques, I won 200 sea brains in the lottery. Imagine what great whoopee cushions these will make.

AL

You can make a lot of whoopee.

LUCKY
When I get home, I'll put it under my pillow. Then when my wife kisses me goodnight, ya hoo!

AL
You're not going to return them to the ocean? Don't you think that's shellfish?

LUCKY
Oh clam up, mon ami. These are the best noise makers available. I don't have to give them back and you can't make me.

FALCO
Don't you care about ecology? You're making Jacques cry. And for what porpoise? Whoopee cushions!

AUCTIONEER
I'm tall and lonely and I'm looking for a 9 ft. woman to date.

AL
(O.C.)
If he fell down, he'd be
(ON C)
out of town.

GUS
Hey, you guys still owe me 5¢.

FALCO
Leave us alone, or I'll come back and get your nose.

AL
It takes more than the likes of you to get my money.

GUS
That's a switch. Speaking Hart to Hart usually It takes a Thief.

AL
Grrrrrrrr.

JAC
Alexander, forget it let's go to Lime Street.

(EXT. NIGHT ON BOARD SHIP)

P.G.
Look at all these sea brains. We can turn them into bagels.

SAILOR
Hey, where did you get that shirt?

P.G.
I got it at Sears, Barney, Paris, Willie.

WILLIE

Jim, we shouldn't be taking these brains. It's against the law. By the way, nice shirt.

PARIS
We're not moving till the police get here.

P.G;
This ship will self-destruct in five seconds.

BARNEY
Last one off's a dead man.

(SFX: TICK, TICK, TICK)

MIDDLE WRAP

HOST AND GUEST ON BOAT

HOST
Well, Terry, what do you think so far, huh?

MOORE
I hate to say it Kent, but this is more fun than when I made the original movie.

HOST
How's that?

MOORE
Well, I don't have to get wet, I don't have to learn lines.

HOST
Well, you know in Act Two, we'll be putting quite a few more words in your mouth.

MOORE
Oh, I look forward to that. I can't wait to see how Jacques Cousteau defeats Fishin' Impossible. He does, doesn't he?

HOST
Well, stick around,
(TO CAM)
and you guys stick around too, because when we come back with our Mad Movie we hope to answer that for you.

CHYRON OVER
"We'll be right back".

AL
You look sick.

CASS
(up chuck noises)

AL
Gee, you shouldn't hold your hands so close to your face. Let me show you the proper way to do it.
(UP CHUCK NOISES)

COMMERCIAL #2

EXT. NIGHT NEAR SHIP

                    OFFICER
This better be important. I was changing my oil.

                    FALCO
Gipetto, Gipetto.

                    AL
Gipetto, tell him what happened.

                    GIPETTO
Well, I was carving Pinocchio and I turned around and he came to life.

                    FALCO
No, no. What happened to the boat?

                    GIPETTO
Oh, the boat. Fishin Impossible Force came and turned it into an ash hull.

                    FALCO
Wait a second, Gipetto, can you act it out with hand puppets?

                    GIPETTO
(Mumbles)

                    OFFICER
He's burned up just like Jacques' boat.

                    AL
I've got to have a garage sale to raise money.

                    OFFICER
Well, I'll give you a dollar for that hat you got there.

                    AL
Okay, Falco wrap it up for him.

(INT. DINING ROOM)

                    CASSETTE
Look what followed me home. Can I keep him?

                    RICHARD BOONE
I don't know. Are you house broken?

                    AL
Uh, ummm...

                    BOONE
Well, that answers that.

                    AL

I was wondering if I could say there. I like your house. I like your family. I like your daughter. I like your shadow. I like your moustache. I won't be any trouble. I'll sleep in the piano.

CASS
(WHISPER)
Listen, don't anybody look, but the boogyman's at the back door. I said don't anyone look.

AL
I'm so upset I've squished this bowling ball.

(EXT. DOCK DAY)

AL
(THOUGHT)
Wow, look at that girl.
(speaks)
Hey baby, oh Gus, I thought you were a girl.

GUS
That'll be five cents for touching my rump, my friend. But I'll make you a deal. I'll let you touch it all you want just for a quarter.

AL
What kind of a deal is that? I've got a deal. Give me a dollar or I'll cut your throat.

(INT. BAR)

FALCO AND LUCKY
(singing)
You wonder why we dance alone
And why we leave our wives at home.
They nag and whine
And then they pout.
They tease us with their chests stuck out.
Don't touch there, they always cry.
That's why we would rather dance with guys.

(EXT. BOAT)

AL
Who fixed up the boat?

CASS
I did, it was going to be a surprise.

AL
It is a surprise. It used to be a sailboat. Where's the sail?

CASS
I put it in the dryer and it shrunk.

AL
You what! How could you do such a stupid thing? How's the boat supposed to get around.

                    CASS
Well...you have a paddle, don't you?

                    AL
If I did, I'd use it on you.

                    CASS
Ahhhhh...

                    JACQUES (V.O.)
Now we shall witness the underwater mating ritual of two humans. Unfortunately, they are interrupted by a giant blueberry pancake floating on the bottom.

                    CASS
Look out. Look out.

                    JACQUES (V.O.)
Witness the ability of the female to send out a warning signal to her mate, much like the porpoise.

                    CASS
              (MUMBLES W/UNDERWATER EFFECT)
The pancake has a gun.

                    JACQUES (V.O.)
The male responds by swimming in circles. This creates a diversion and makes him dizzy.

                    CASS
              (OVER STINGRAY/PANCAKE)
Over there, idiot!
                    (UNDERWATER EFFECT)

(EXT. ON BOAT DECK)

                    JACQUES (V.O.)
They catch the giant pancake and with it they patched this tire and made a delicious pancake stew.

                    CASS
There's only one spoon and I'm using it.

                    AL
                (SLURPS)
This tastes like old sneakers.

                    CASS
Really, I've never tasted old sneakers before, let's see.
                    (SLURPS)

                    AL
You look awful.

                    CASS
Really?

AL
You're breaking out in a cold sweat, your eyes are bulging out. You're foaming at the mouth. I may be wrong, but you look like your about to...

CASS
(Up chuck noises)

AL
Gee, you shouldn't hold your hands so close to your face. Let me show you the proper way to do it.
(UP CHUCK NOISES)

FALCO
Is that a light beer? The other day a guy walks in here, he had a light beer. He says to me, "Hey it's less filling." I said, "No, it tastes great." and he said, "No, it's less filling." So I pounded his head into the pavement.

(EXT. BOAT)

JAC
Alexander, I'm going to sing you my favorite sea chanty.
Oh to be a sailin' man,
You got to love the ocean.
And if the sea air dries your hands,
You use a lot of lotion.
Well, well...
Oooooooooooooooooooooo,
Oh to be a sailin' man,
You got to think fast.
You got to have a tattoo,
And you put it on your arm.
Then you'll be a sailin' man

(SFX: CAR SCREECHES)

(EXT. DOCKS)

CASS
Darn, put those sea brains back or I'll choke you.

BOONE
That hurts.

AL
Hey Jacques, I'm sorry about spilling that pancake stew on your hands but at least it removed your barnacles.

JAC
Forget it, I think they're using crossword puzzles and Trivial Pursuit questions for brain bait. We've got to find out where they keep them.

V.O. WOMAN
Ahhhhhhhhhh. This is the lady's room.

FALCO
Jacques, I have something to tell you that could change the whole world and effect our lives as we know it. Hey...

JAC
Leave me alone, Falco, I have a lot on my mind. You've been following me all day. You go back to the ship while Alexander and I wait here.

FALCO
Huh? No! You two wait here and I'll go back to the ship.

AL
Wait, I need to get a long sleeve shirt.

JAC
Well, go to Sears. Follow us.

FALCO
That reminds me, I'm out of Old Spice.
(Whistles)

(INT. BAR)

JAC
Madame Cousteau tells me that one of you was watching her through the kitchen window as she was warming her buns. Who was it?

CROWD REACTS

BARTENDER

(SFX: PHONE RING)

Hello, Santa Claus, is it really you?

AL
Say, anybody want to hear me sing?

JAC
I taught him a sea chanty, all three verses so he'll sing two verses on his own. Then everyone else join in. It'll be fun don't you think?

R.B.
Why not? We come in on the third verse.

MAN
I'll get my tuba.

CHYRON OVER PIX: "NEXT: The Sea-Brain Showdown"

(EXT. PARK)

JAC (V.O.)
Once again, in the spring, the mating ritual of the young homosapiens is performed, this time on land. The female moves

from side to side to avoid having her head smashed in. Sometimes this is called playing hard to get.

                         CASS
Was it good for you?

                         AL
Not really.

                         CASS
You gave me sand fleas.

                         AL
So what?

                         CASS
I don't think you really like me.

                         AL
Sure I do. Let's try it again.

                         CASS
Maybe later.

                         AL
How about now? I'm ready.

                         CASS
Later!

                         AL
Cassette, so you mean this much later? Is that what you're talking about?

                         CASS
Listen, oh Alexander, I'd never kiss you, even if your name was Robert Wagner.

                         AL
I didn't mean to be so pushy. How about now?

                         CASS
Alright.

                         P.G.
Hey, kiss this!

                         JACQUES
Hey, nobody's hit Alexander since he was this tall.

                         P.G.
I slipped.

                         JAC
That's okay then.

                         P.G.

I like your shirt, slipped again.

(BATMAN WORDS EFFECT DURING FIGHT—POW, ZAP, BIFF, BRASSIERE)

CASS

Alexander, do something, they'll get grass stains all over their clothes.

AL

They'll come out.

JAC

Falco, hide my hat where Kelps won't get it. That will teach you to steal sea brains, Mr. Kelps. Your fishin' is impossible.

CASS

Ah-choo. Excuse me.

JACQUES

You should cover your mouth. You got germs on my sausage. I don't want it now. You can have it. Eat this sausage. Eat this sausage.

P.G.

I'm a vegetarian.

JAC

All this excitement has made me drool. We can't stay any longer. Let's say goodbye.

CASS

Owww, you're biting my nose. You're biting my nose.

AL

Sorry, I meant to suck your eyeball out.

AL
(SINGS)

Oh, to be a sailin' man....

JAC, AL FALCO
(SINGS)

....it impresses all the ladies
But you end up out at sea
with no one but your maties.

(EXT. SHIP)

JAC. (V.O.)

And so our mission accomplished, we set sail, owww...
Get that thing off of me.
I'm surrounded by impulses.

FALCO (V.O.)

That's imbeciles, Jacque.

JACQUE (V.O.)

Oh, imbeciles.

###

(INT. BOAT, HOST AND GUEST)

HOST

Well, that's our Mad Movie.

MOORE

Pretty crazy.

HOST

Thanks, but it's not any crazier than our Home Movies our viewers sent us. See, what we do is re-edit them, and add a whole new story.

(PRESSES TAPE MACHINE)

MOORE

That's neat.

TAPE (V.O.)

Good afternoon, Mr. Skov and Miss Moore. Your mission, should you decide to accept it, is to watch this home movie. It was sent in by John Lusitana of San Diego. It's called The Rainmaker.

FOUR SECOND TEASE OF BABY FROM RAINMAKER WITH CHYRON "THE RAINMAKER"

RAINMAKER

After twenty years of draught, these three high school students were hired to make it rain. They tried to create a thunderstorm by blowing little smoke puffs, but all they created were birds—thousands of dry birds. Then the wise old gardener said he'd make it rain for five thousand dollars. He called out to the thunder gods, using a unique plastic trumpet and wearing a pre-moistened hood made from a polar bear's hide. Then he locked himself in a sound proof chamber, looked up to the heavens and began to scream with all his might for rain.

(SCREAMS RAIN)

He went to the driest parts of town, performing the dance of the Great Sea Otter, finishing up with something he called a Rainy-Go-Round. But still the land was dry. He had all but given up when suddenly... a flash of lightning... then another. And voila—upside down rain. He was able to create water in any location at any time, but some of it was very cold. And the water was delicious. Mmmmmm. But instead of paying him, the grateful town gave him a bath.

(INT. HOST AND GUEST)

BOAT

HOST

If you'd like your home movies made into Mad Movies, send them to the L.A. Connection, 6464 Sunset Blvd., Suite 820

(OVER ADDRESS)

Hollywood, California, 90028.

HOST
Well, I'd like to thank our guest, Terry Moore, for joining us. It's been a real pleasure, Terry.

MOORE
Oh, I've enjoyed it Kent. I really like that red and white sweater you're wearing.

HOST
Well, I tell you what, I'm going to give it to you. What do you think?

(TAKES OFF SWEATER)

GUEST
Oh, I'd love it,
(LAUGHS)
Thank you.

HOST
You know I'd do anything for a guest on this show.

CREDIT ROLL

GUEST
You know I really like those pants you're wearing.

HOST
Well, I'd give them to you, but we're on TV right now.

GUEST
Oh, I'll wait.

HOST
Hey, do you have any other movies you're in, you'd like to see us dub?

GUEST
Actually I'd like to see you dub all of them, but I also have some pretty interesting home movies. We could send them to you.

HOST
Oh, please do...and goodnight.

GUEST
Goodnight. And thank you.

HOST PUSHES TAPE MACHINE, SHOT OF TAPE MACHINE AND V.O. (Goodnight)

HOST V.O. OVER CREDIT ROLL (ADDITIONAL VOICES BY TODD TUREK)

12 MILE REEF SCENE OVER CREDIT:

AL
Boy that was great.

CASS

It was magical, let's do it again.

                              AL

Whoops, we missed.

                              CASS

Let's not miss Mad Movies next week.

                              AL

ONLY a week.

                              CASS

Oh yes.

OPENING CRAWL*

SNOW # <u>117</u>

SHOW NAME <u>BENEATH THE 12 MILE REEF</u>

*Each numbered item as a single page...
Items 1-5 Centerframe
Items 6-10 Lower third of page

1   FOUR STAR
        in association with
        KENT SKOV

2   Presents
        an L.A. Connection
        production of

3   MAD MOVIES WITH THE L.A. CONNECTION

4   Tonight's Feature   BENEATH THE 12 MILE REEF

5   Starring
        the
        Voices
        of

6   Bob Buchholz

7   Connie Sue Cook

8   Stephen L. Rollman

9   Steve Pinto

10   Kent Skov

GENERIC BUMPERS*

SNOW # 117

SHOW NAME <u>BENEATH THE 12 MILE REEF</u>

*Each numbered item as a single page...

1   We'll be right back...

2   Coming Up
         More Mad Movies

3   Stay Tuned for
         "Your Home Movies"

4   Send Your Home Movies to...
         L.A. Connection Productions
         6464 Sunset Blvd., #820
         Hollywood, CA 90028
         (Include a self-addressed, stamped envelope for return of films)

5   Rainmaker   (Home Movie Title)

6   The Sea-Brain Show Down

CLOSING CRAWL*

SHOW   117

SHOW NAME BENEATH THE 12 MILE REEF

*Each numbered item as a single page...

1   Directed by
           Rent Skov

2   Written by
           Bob Buchholz
           Stephen L. Rollman

3   Produced by
           Randal W Ridges

4   Featuring
           Bob Buchholz
           Connie Sue Cook
           Steve Pinto
           Stephen L. Rollman
           Kent Skov

5   Associate Producers   (each name single page)
           Martha Whitney

6   Kent Weishaus

7   Music Composed and arranged by
           Richard Baker
           Mary Newland
           For Panda Productions

8   Music recorded by
           Richard Baker

9   Theme performed by.
           Mary Newland

CLOSING CREDIT CRAWL (CONT'D)

10   Research by
      Bob Petrella
      Ken Segall
      April Winchell
      Ted Hardwick

11   Talent Coordinator
      Martha Whitney

12   Associate Director/Stage Manager
      Randal W Ridges

13   Assistants to the Producers:
      Bob Buchholz
      Connie Sue Cook
      Steve Pinto
      Stephen L. Rollman

14   Facilities Provided by
      Hy-Tone Video

15   Lighting and Camera
      Bill Sheehy

16   Production Sound
      Mark Panes

17   Gaffer
      Jim Drewry

18   Production Assistants
      Lisa Gougas
      Ted Hardwick

19   Make-Up
      Lora Sanders

20   Wardrobe
      Annie Vicari

21   Production Secretary
      Eloise Gonzalez

22   Post-Production Coordinated by
      Monti Santilli Rainbolt

23   Post-Production Facilities
      Complete Post, Inc.

24   Post-Production Audio by
      Michael Perricone

Michaele Hogan
For Interloc Prod. Studios

CLOSING CREDIT CRAWL (CONT'D)

25 "Your Home Movies" submitted by
    John Lusitana
    San Diego, CA

26 Location provided by

27 Executive in Charge of Production for Four Star Television
    Bob Bosen

28 Special Thanks to:
    Susan Lenti
    Budget Films
    Richard Holiday
    Dennis Condon
    Snaggelpuss

29 Promotion by
    Dan Acree

30 Opening Title Montage by
    Homer & Associates

31 Opening Title Photography by
    Abe Perlstein

32 Post-Production Supervised by
    Randal W Ridges

33 Executive Producer
    Kent Skov

34 "Celebrity Voices and Appearances Impersonated"

35 Copyright 1985 Four Star International, Inc.
    All Rights Reserved

MAD MOVIES WITH THE L.A. CONNECTION

RUNDOWN SHOW #120 CAPTAIN SCARLETT

All times are in minutes and seconds	IN	OUT	DURATION
Four Star Logo	00:00	00:05	00:05
Clip Tease #1	00:05	00:26	00:21
Opening Montage	00:26	00:55	00:29
Host Intro and Preview Clip	00:55	01:56	01:01
Commercial Black #1	01:56	03:57	02:01
Bumper #1	03:57	04:00	00:03
Movie Segment #1 (includes Host Toss)	04:00	11:13	07:13
Host and Preview Clip	11:13	11:44	00:31
Commercial Black #2	11:44	13:45	02:01
Bumper #2	13:45	13:48	00:03
Movie Segment #2	13:48	19:46	05:58
Bumper #3	19:46	19:50	00:04
Commercial Black #2	19:50	21:51	02:01
Bumper #4	21:51	21:54	00:03

MAD MOVIES WITH THE L.A. CONNECTION

RUNDOWN, Pg 2   SHOW #120

Movie Segment #3	21:54	25:14	03:20
Host Intro to Home Movie	25:14	25:47	00:33
Home Movie (includes Billboard at tail)	25:47	27:10	01:23
Host Wrap-up	27:10	27:30	00:20
Clip Tease #2	27:30	27:55	00:25
Closing Montage (includes L.A. Connection Logo)	27:55	28:00	00:05
Four Star Logo			

CAPTAIN SCARLETT
SHOW NUMBER 120

(EXT. WOODS)

FIRST MUSTACHE MAN
Hey, I hear you're on Mad Movies this week.

CAPT. SCARLETT
I'm the star.

MAID MARIAN
He's the star, but it's not his voice, it's dubbed.

FIRST MUST. MAN
Hey, what about my voice…I…

SECOND MUSTACHE MAN
What about me? We look the same. I wonder if the same person is dubbing our voices.

CAPT. SCARLETT
I know of a sure way to find out. Let's watch it. There's a tv in the back of my van.

MUSIC THEME

(EXT. WOODS)

HOST
Hi, I'm Kent Skov and welcome to Mad Movies with the L.A. Connection. The clip you've just seen is from our version of Capt. Scarlett. Originally an adventurous sword fighting film about a man, coincidentally called Capt. Scarlett. But we've changed all the dialogue and now it's a sequel to Robin Hood.

FILM INSERT

Robin Hood has replaced the sheriff of Nottingham and has become equally corrupt.

HOST
Our hero, Will Scarlett is now a former member of Robin Hood's gang, who has broken off and formed his own band of merry men. He and Robin are fighting for the hand of Maid Marian. Take a look at some of the changes we've made in the original plot.

(INT. HOUSE)

ROBIN HOOD
Will Scarlett's behind this. I want him eliminated.

RED RIDING HOOD
I shall see to it, my brother, that Will Scarlett is well-hanged.

ROBIN HOOD
Hm-Hm.

RED HIDING HOOD
Take a look at what I found in the cat box.

ROBIN HOOD
Hmmm.
(SNORTS)
Why are you looking at me like that?

(EXT. WOODS)

HOST
I wonder what the merry men did all day in the forest. In a moment, we'll be back to find out.

(POINTS BOW AND ARROW AT CAMERA)

COMMERCIAL #1

(EXT. WOODS)

HOST
With all new dialogue, here's Capt. Scarlett.

TITLES…

(INT. HOUSE)

(SFX: LOUD KNOCK)

WILL
Let me in. Open the door.

MRS. SCARLETT
It's unlocked.

WILL
Sorry dear, I forgot my key. I've been at work all day with Robin Hood and the rest of the married men.

MRS. SCARLETT
How did things go?

WILL
It's been dull since Robin Hood was made sheriff of Nottingham.

MRS. SCARLETT
I have a special treat for you, Will.

WILL
Don't tell me. You finally took a bath.

MRS. SCARLETT
No, Will, I wouldn't do a thing like that. I made dinner.

WILL
Whoopie dingus! What're we having?

MRS. SCARLETT

I fixed clam chowder sludge.

WILL

Clam chowder sludge, that's the fourth time this week and it's only Monday. Is it the red or the white?

MRS. SCARLETT

It's the green.

(ESTABLISH CASTLE) CHYRON-NOTTINGHAM CASTLE

(INT. CASTLE)

RED RIDING HOOD

Well Robin, things aren't going too well. There's a lot of dissent. You've gained twenty pounds and you're balding.

ROBIN

And I'm only twenty-nine. You're happy, aren't you?

RED RIDING HOOD

Mmmmmmmm… yes, I am.

ROBIN

Will Scarlett's behind this. I want him eliminated.

RED RIDING HOOD

I will do my duty.

ROBIN

Just don't do it on my porch, after all, you are my brother, Red Riding Hood.

RED RIDING HOOD

I'll see to it, my brother, that Will Scarlett is well-hanged. Look what I found in the cat box.

ROBIN

Hmm.
(Sniff)
Why are you looking at me like that?

(INT. HOUSE)

WILL

Mmm… clam chowder.

MRS. SCARLETT

How is it?

WILL

There's too many bones. I keep having to pick my teeth. You'll hear from my orthodontist.

MRS. SCARLETT
Hmmm. Well! I've never been so insulted in my life. I'm going to my Mother's and never coming back.

WILL
Again.

(O.C.)
You're dragging your feet.

MRS. SCARLETT
(B, T, C,) These aren't my feet.

(INT. HOUSE)

MRS. SCARLETT
Take off your hat.

RED RIDING HOOD
Sorry, I forgot my manners. I'm Red Riding Hood, Robin Hood's brother.

MRS. SCARLETT
What do you want?

RED RIDING HOOD
Not too much. I'd like to meet a nice woman and settle down.

MRS. SCARLETT
No, with me?

RED RIDING HOOD
Your husband's head.

MRS. SCARLETT
Going bowling?

RED RIDING HOOD
No, my brother, Robin thinks he's a trouble maker and wants him out of the way.

MRS. SCARLETT
And what, pray tell, will I get for helping you?

RED RIDING HOOD
Anything.

MRS. SCARLETT
Well, I'd like to meet a nice woman and settle down but I'll take a bag of potato chips.

RED RIDING HOOD

(SFX: POTATO CHIPS BEING POURED THEN CRUNCHED)

Hmmm...here. Hey, watch it, you're breaking them into little bitty pieces.

(EXT. HOUSE)

RED RIDING HOOD

I'll whip this out. You've set him up, Mrs. Scarlett, now I'll take a stab at it. Aye-ya.

WILL

Hey, you've killed my coat rack, Red and next time use the door. You nearly stepped on the dog.

DOG

Yelps, barks, growls.

WILL

(B, T, C,) Bowser, get off me. Sit, Bowser, sit. Now you've stabbed my seat. I won't stand for that. Hey, there's a spider on your vest.

RED RIDING HOOD

I hate spiders.

WILL

I'll get it.

RED RIDING HOOD

Aaaaaagh.

(INT. CASTLE)

LITTLE JOHN

I'm sorry, Robin, the deli was out of the corned beef so I got you a head cheese sandwich.

(SFX: DOOR OPENS O.C. LOUD MUSIC)

ROBIN

Ah, Maid Marion, close the door will you. Ah, well, help her take her hands out of her back pockets.

(SFX: POP)

Thanks, Bruce. Dear, I brought you up from the dungeon for a reason. You see, our marriage isn't working out too well. We never seem to talk anymore.

MARIAN

It's very hard to talk, fatty, when you're gagged and stretched on a rack.

ROBIN

Picky picky, besides I've only gained thirty pounds. You need to spend two more weeks in the dungeon with the lizards, and the spiders and the rats. Oh my…

LITTLE JOHN

I think what Robin means to say is that you need more time alone to reflect on how you can improve your marriage. Isn't that right, my liege?

ROBIN
No, Little John, you idiot. I meant what I said. She should spend more time with the rats.

(EXT-INT OF CASTLE WALL)

MUCH
(Starts O.C.)
C'mon Friar Tuck, Will wants to see you.

FRIAR TUCK
You know, Much, there's something about Will that just doesn't grab me. Yeeoow! Hi, Will. You two stretched out my robe.

WILL
You got a good head start, already.

FRIAR TUCK
So tell me, Will, why'd you want to see me?

WILL
Robin Hood had locked Maid Marian in the dungeon, she's down there with the rats and the rats don't like it.

FRIAR TUCK
And you want me to risk my life and rescue her.

WILL
Yes, will you?

FRIAR TUCK
Stuff it! Oh that reminds me, I got a goose cooking in the oven.

(EXT. CASTLE GATE)

SOLDIER #1
Stop, stop, stop, whoa, whoa, or we'll shoot. You can't pass here unless you pass this test.

WILL
I'm ready, go ahead.

SOLDIER #1
Where's your nose?

SOLDIER #2
Lucky guess. What do you want?

WILL
(O.C.)
I'll show you where my cheeks are. Ow, wrong cheeks.

SOLDIER #2
Crockett stabbed you.

SOLDIER #1
No I didn't, it was Tubbs.

WILL
You two stop fighting. Now kiss and make up. Hey, I said just kiss. Stop that!

(INT. BEDROOM)

WILL
I can't believe I made it past the guards disguised as a bag of cement.

MARIAN
Will Scarlett, what are you doing here in the dungeon?

WILL
Hmmm, this is a dungeon. I expected to find you strapped to a bed of nails.

MARIAN
I have to wear a giant doily on my head. Isn't that torture?

WILL
Only for those who have to look at you.

MARIAN
Be careful with those sheets, they're rubber.

WILL
Now that's torture. But I can use a new cape.

MARIAN
They'll laugh at you. They'll call you captain bed sheet.

WILL
I guess it's lucky for me that I brought some red crayons.

(INT. HALLWAY)

GUARD #1
(STARTS O.C.)
Sorry I'm late, I just got a haircut.

CAPTAIN OF THE GUARD

(SFX: KNOB JIGGLES)

Wait a minute, I'm the officer, you guys jiggle the knob.

(INT. BEDROOM)

CAPTAIN SCARLETT
Those red crayons really did the trick, don't you think? C'mon, I'll throw you out the window.

MAID MARIAN
Can't we just climb down?

CAPTAIN SCARLETT

No, it's only a matter of time before they realize the door's not locked. Don't worry, the trash cans will break your fall.

(INT. HALLWAY)

MAID MARIAN
(O.C.)

Aaaaaaaagh.

(SFX: BODY HITTING BIKE RACK)

(EXT. COURTYARD)

MRS. SCARLETT

You're late again.

CAPTAIN SCARLETT
(O.C.)

I was saving a damsel in this dress.

MRS. SCARLETT

What about this damsel in this dress?

MAID MARIAN

You're barely in that dress.

MRS. SCARLETT
(STARTS O.C. ENDS ON C.)

Maid Marian! Well Will, what does she have that I don't have?

CAPTAIN SCARLETT

For one, she's got a couple of…of course you've got those…

MRS. SCARLETT

Forget it. I have eyes.

MAID MARIAN

That's about it.

M.S.

You have to choose between us. I just made you new curtains.

MAID MARIAN

Pick one, the fox or the curtains?

C.S.

How can I leave you, you're my wife. Good bye.

MAID MARIAN

How could you stand that woman? I'd hate to be in her family.

C.S.

Her sister, Bovine, is a real cow.

(EXT. COURTYARD)

GUARD #1

C'mon Bovine, we're going to go ride the bumper cars. I'll let you steer.

M.S.
Wait, you can't take my sister out, it's a school night. You have to take her to the barn dance on the weekend.

GUARD #2
I can see the family resemblance.

(EXT. WOODS)

HOST
While I was here, I thought I'd practice my archery.

FIRE ARROWS, ONE HITS BETWEEN THE ROCKS, ANOTHER A TREE AND A THIRD A RUBBER CHICKEN.

Eh. I seemed to be missing the target. But you won't want to miss what's happening next with our Mad Movie. I'll, uh…give it one more try.

FIRES ARROW OFF CAMERA. SOUND OF YELL.

(EXT. MOUNTAINSIDE)

(SOUND OF HORSES)

MUCH
Robin sure has a lot of soldiers, doesn't he?

WILL
Yeah, you'd think they grow on trees?

(EXT. FOREST)

WILL
Here's a couple ready to pick.

MUCH
I don't think that they're quite ripe.

CHYRON—"WE'LL BE RIGHT BACK."

COMMERCIAL #2

WILL
Well Marian, now that you're free from Robin, what are you going to do now?

MARIAN
I don't know, Will, how about you?

WILL
Beats me, it's just the two of us here in this cave.

MARIAN
What do you have in mind?

WILL
When two people are alone, they should do whatever comes naturally. Don't you agree?

MARIAN
You wait here, I'll get the checker board.

(INT. SITTING ROOM)

PAINTER
(O.C.)
Let's see, all the threes are brown and the fives are grey.

MESSENGER
Maid Marian's run off with Will Scarlett and there's dirt on your chin.

ROBIN
Well, call out the guards and get me a wash cloth.

MESSENGER
Yes, my liege.

ROBIN
Alright, who will help me round up that scoundrel, Will Scarlett?

CROWD
I hear my mother calling. My horse is double parked.

PAINTER
Can I go too?

ROBIN
Oh get out and take that pizza with you.

(SFX: FLY) (SFX: SWACK, SWACK) (SFX: FLY)

MAN ON DESK

You missed.

(EXT. TOWN SQUARE)

CRIER
Hear ye, hear ye. Hence forth anyone reading a scroll in public will be hung.

(EXT. CAVE)

WILL
(SFX: MOTORCYCLE)
(O.C.)
Much, Much, it's good to see you.

(SFX: HAND BUZZER)

MUCH
Aaaaaaaa.

WILL
The hand buzzer gets him every time.

MUCH
That's very clever of you Will, but my horse and I always prefer the egg on the sleeve trick.

(SFX: EGG ON SLEEVE)

(O.C.)
I'm gonna lead my horse to water.

MAID MARIAN
I bet he can't make him drink.

WILL
Mmm, I'll take that bet.

MAID MARIAN
Alright then, I'll bet you can't put your hands in your cummerbund.

WILL
Bet I can.

MAID MARIAN
You lose, those are your thumbs.

WILL
Mmmm, hey what's that on your back?

MUCH
Oh, I have a buried treasure under my coat.

(EXT. ROAD)

SOLDIERS
C'mon Dasher, c'mon Donner, c'mon Prancer and Vixen. On Cupid, on Comet, on Dancer and Nixon.

MUCH
Hey Will, Robin sure has a lot of men, doesn't he?

WILL
And they're all looking for us, too. I wonder where he gets them all.

MUCH
You'd think that they grow on trees.

(EXT. FOREST)

WILL
You were right, here's a couple ready to pick.

MUCH
No, I don't think that they're quite ripe.

MAID MARIAN
Don't wait too long. I don't like 'em soft.

MUCH
(O.C.)
If you pick 'em early, they'll ripen on the window sill.

WILL
No let's wait.

SOLDIERS
We're ripe, we're ripe.

(EXT. WOODS)

WILL

(W/BACK TO CAMERA)

Say, Much, did you put this itching powder on my saddle? Well, did you?

MUCH
You put the crazy glue on my sword.

WILL
Now, that's funny.

MARIAN
(Fast)
About as funny as when you put that feather duster down the back of my pants.

WILL
So.

MARIAN
(O.C.)
A rooster chased me halfway to town.

WILL
You know, Marian, I don't think you know how to have fun anymore.

MARIAN
Maybe I should go back to Robin.

WILL
Suit yourself. Make like a shepherd and get the flock out of town.

(EXT. BY THE FIRE)

MUCH
(B.T.C.) Will, I cooked a pot of Cheerios for you. Any luck finding Maid Marian?

WILL
Not at all.

MUCH
Too bad.

WILL
I've got to get Marian back.

MUCH
Because you love her, right, Will?

WILL
No, because I hate your cooking.
(LAUGHS)

(INT. CHAPEL)

FRIAR TUCK
A mini skirt on your shoulders, how very trendy.

WILL
(B.T.C.) So's dieting.

FRIAR TUCK
You calling me a fat friar?

WILL
Depends. Can you help me rescue Maid Marian?

FRIAR TUCK
Oh I suppose you want me to risk my life again by climbing up the castle wall in my cassock, then shimmy down a tree on the other side and knock out the guard with my staff.

WILL
That's right.

FRIAR TUCK
Then after I've done all the dirty work you come in and get the woman. Now why would I want to do a thing like that?

WILL
'Cause you like me, Friar Tuck. Or because you're stupid.

(INT. BEDROOM)

MAID MARIAN
(Humming)

WILL
(O.C. in mirror)
Marian, I was worried about you.

MAID MARIAN
You were. Then prove it.

WILL

I'm losing hair, I missed you. I love you more than the flowers in spring (O.C.) and the leaves in autumn.

                    MAID MARIAN

Why?

                    WILL
                   (Shrugs)

Mmmmm. Return with me.

                    MAID MARIAN

Can you give me one good reason why I should?

                    WILL

As a matter of fact, Maid Marian, I can give you a very big reason why you should come back with me.

                    MAID MARIAN

You're not talking about…?

                    WILL

Yes, I am.

                    MAID MARIAN

Oh well, in that case I'll go to get the checker board.

                    WILL

Good, but don't be surprised if I jump you and make you king me.

(EXT. GATE)

                    GATE GUARD #1

Close the gate. Goodbye Robin, have fun at the sheriff's convention. Open the gate. Open it up, open it up. They're coming back. What'd we got here?

                    CARRIAGE DRIVER

We forgot our toothpaste.

                    GATE GUARD #1

Oh, idiots. Close that gate. Close it. Bring it around. Bring the gate around. Wait…what…open up. Open the gate up. Open up the gate.

                    CARRIAGE DRIVER

We got it, thanks.

                    GATE GUARD #2

Open the gate, close the gate, open the gate, close the gate.

(EXT. TOWNSQUARE)

                    TOWNSPERSON

What did I do wrong? All I did was ask you to open the gate.

                    CAPTAIN HORNDOG

Yeah, you and two thousand other yahoos.

(EXT. LONG SHOT TOWNSQUARE)

       CAPTAIN HORNDOG
Whoa, whoa, whoa there. Say there, old woman. Where do you think you're going upon this old rig?

       HARRIET
To market to market to buy a fat pig.

       CAPTAIN HORNDOG
Can you stay a while and have some eggnog?

       HARRIET
No, I'm off to market to buy a fat hog.

       C.H.
Hey, let me see your hand.

       HARRIET
Why?

       C.H.
I like women with hairy knuckles. My mom used to have 'em. I think I wanna marry you.

       HARRIET
Well, wait marry this.

(SFX: PUNCHES)

       OLD WOMAN
C'mon Harriet, let's boogie.

       HARRIET
Yahoo, I'm back in the saddle again.

       CAPTAIN HORNDOG
Ah, there goes my future bride. Bring her back.

       SOLDIER
C'mon, let's get him.

       OLD WOMAN #2
He was kinda cute.

       HARRIET
Yeah, but I wanna play hard to get.

       SOLDIER #1
Any of you guys untie the horses?

       SOLDIERS
Not me. Not me. I didn't.

CHYRON—"WILL IS HUNG OUT TO DRY."

COMMERCIAL ##

(EXT. WOODS)

                CAPTAIN OF THE GUARD
Which one's Captain Scarlett?

                CAPTAIN SCARLETT
Hmmm, depends. Who wants to know?

                CAPTAIN OF THE GUARD
I want to know.

                CAPTAIN SCARLETT
What would you do if I was?

                CAPTAIN OF THE GUARD
I'd chain you up in a dungeon with Don Rickles.

                CAPTAIN SCARLETT
In that case, I'm not him. Wooo hoo.

                CAPTAIN OF THE GUARD
How about you, my weasel like friend? Are you he?

                MUCH
The correct term is; are you him? Ow.

(SFX: SLAP)

                CAPTAIN OF THE GUARD
Take him away.

                CAPTAIN SCARLETT
Boy, I can't stand him.

                MUCH
Yeah, he has bad grammar.
                (O.C.)
Hey, what if they torture me?

                CAPTAIN SCARLETT
Whatever you do, don't tell 'em I'm Captain Scarlett.

(INT. DUNGEON)

                MUCH
Way to go. You had to go and open your big mouth.

                CAPTAIN SCARLETT
Look at the bright side. Rickles is in Vegas.

                MUCH
Fortunately for us though, your band of married men will soon be here to rescue us.

                CAPTAIN SCARLETT
You seem to be forgetting one thing, Much, you are my band of men.

                        MUCH
Oh yeah, that's right.

(INT. CASTLE CHAMBER)

                        ROBIN
You made a mistake trying to rescue Will.

                    BRUCE THE GUARD
                        (O.C.)
I'll tie her to the chair 'cause I used to be a boy scout.

                        ROBIN
You know, you have chocolate on your chin.

                      LITTLE JOHN
I'm not going to let her use my hanky.

                        ROBIN
Oh chill out. I've got some treats. Over there on my desk.

                    JOSE THE GUARD
Frank, hold your finger here in this knot.

                        ROBIN
Ohh, I can't believe this. Somebody ate my head cheese sandwich. There's nothing but a few crumbs.

                        ROBIN
Why don't you people like me?

                        SONG
                        (SLOW)
When people talked of Robin Hood,
I was a good guy and a hero.
But now they laugh and jeer at me,
I'm a loser and a zero.
Why is that? I'll tell you why,

CHANGE OF TEMPO

I rob from the poor, I rob from the rich,
Greedy is what I am.
I'm the meanest evilest son of a gun,
I'm the sheriff of Nottingham.

                    SOLDIER'S CHORUS
He's the meanest evilest son of a gun,
The sheriff of Nottingham.

(INT. CASTLE)

                        WILL
Sorry I'm late. Much and I were just hanging around.

                        ROBIN

If we're gonna have a fight, be careful of the furniture. Hey, that chair's one of a kind.

                    WILL
(B.T.C.) You don't mind if I have a seat do you?

                    ROBIN
Put that chair down, you'll ruin it.

                    WILL
                    (O.C.)
You're the one chopping it up.

                    ROBIN
How'd you escape from the shackles in my dungeon?

                    WILL
                    (O.C.)
I guess you didn't know I am a chain smoker.

                    ROBIN
The surgeon general says smoking is bad for your health.

                    WILL
So are knives.

                    ROBIN
You're right.

                    MUCH
                    (O.C.)
Say, Will I...

                    MAID MARIAN
Get lost.

                    MUCH
Oh wow.

                    MAID MARIAN
Ow!

                    WILL
(B.T.C.) C'mon let's go, Marian. We'll escape off the balcony.

                    MAID MARIAN
(B.T.C.) Wait a minute Will, you're not going to throw me out again, are you?
                    (ON C.)
Won't you...let me climb down with you?

                    WILL
                    (B.T.C.)

(SFX: MONKEY KISS)

Watch out for trash cans.

                    MAID MARIAN
                      (O.C.)
          Aaaaaaagh!

(EXT. WOODS)

                    HOST
          That was quite a story. You know, Robin Hood and his band of
          merry men always had a stout stick. We're not sure why. But we
          believe it was used to balance yourself when crossing a river on a
          fallen log. Now, uh, this stout stick is just a little too stout.

(STARTS CHAINSAW AND CUTS LOG)

          Well listen, while I get my stout stick together, why don't you guys
          watch tonight's home movie. Like our feature, we edit them and
          add new dialogue.

CHYRON OVER PIX OF LADY—"ODDITIES II."

(V.O.)

          From the flatlands…the oceans, to the mountains, white with
          foam…these are nature's oddities. The world's youngest stand-up
          comedian, so young, he can't stand up. This break-dancing elephant
          demonstrates the moon walk. He was trained by the man, who uses
          complex hand signals to get his dog to eat water, starting first with
          handfuls…and finally working up to this. Here's the annual toilet
          paper harvest of Two Ply, Texas. Now this is the toughest thing in
          the world to do…hitting a piñata *without* a blindfold. This is the
          world's shortest tunnel…see what I mean. It leads to Jo-Jo, the
          rubber-faced boy of Akron, Ohio. He can stretch his face into over
          a million geometric shapes. Look, an isosceles triangle,
          dodecahedron, and a perfect rhombus. The Satellite Twins, one
          signals with his ear, and the other revolves…until the end of time.
          This man lost over 300 pounds, by eating only ostrich food. His
          wife is a model for a TV network. And finally, a drum roll please…
          Uh, no, uh, uh. Don't look at…I'm too nervous. I'm not ready, no,
          no, no.

(EXT. WOODS)

                    HOST
          If you'd like your home movies made into Mad Movies, send them
          to the L.A. Connection,

(OVER ADDRESS)

          6464 Sunset Blvd., Suite 820, Hollywood, California 90028.

(EXT. WOODS)—CREDIT ROLL—

                    HOST
          Uh, this isn't as hard as I thought. Well, we'll see you next time for
          Mad Movies.

(FALLS INTO WATER)

          Oh, oh, well,
                              (laugh)

at least I still have my stout stick. Oh, oh.

(EXT. FOREST)

                        RED RIDING HOOD
Say, did you watch Mad Movies?

                        CAPT. SCARLETT
Yes, I was the star.

                        MAID MARIAN
It still wasn't your voice.

                        CAPT. SCARLETT
So? By the way, you know someone's been dubbing your voice as well.

                        MAID MARIAN
I don't mind someone doing my voice.

                        CAPT.
Mmm, someone should also do your hair. He-Ha-ha.

                        MAID MARIAN
                (DISGUSTED, RIDES AWAY)

                        HOST (V.O.)
Additional voices by Ted Harwick.

OPENING CRAWL*

SHOW #<u>120</u>

SHOW NAME <u>CAPTAIN SCARLET</u>

*Each numbered item as a single page…
Items #1-5 Centerframe
Items #6-10 Lower third of page

1   FOUR STAR
in association with
KENT SKOV

2   Presents
as L.A. Connection
production of

3   MAD MOVIES WITH THE L.A. CONNECTION

4   Tonight's Feature   CAPTAIN SCARLET

5   Starring
the
Voices
of

6   Bob Buchholz

7   Connie Sue Cook

8   Stephen L. Rollman

9   Steve Pinto

10   Kent Skov

GENERIC BUMPERS*

SHOW #<u>120</u>

SHOW NAME   <u>CAPTAIN SCARLET</u>

*Each numbered item as a single page…

1   We'll be right back…

2   Coming Up
            More Mad Movies

3   Stay Tuned for
            "Your Home Movies"

4   Send Your Home Movies to…
            L.A. Connection Productions
            6464 Sunset Blvd., #820
            Hollywood, CA 90028
            (Include a self-addressed, stamped envelope for return of films)

5   ODDITIES II   (Homemovie Title)

6   Next…
            Will hung out to dry

CLOSING CRAWL*

SHOW #<u>120</u>

SHOW NAME   <u>CAPTAIN SCARLET</u>

*Each numbered item as a single page…

1	Directed by Kent Skov
2	Written by Bob Buchholz Stephen L. Rollman
3	Produced by Randal W Ridges
4	Featuring Bob Buchholz Connie Sue Cook Steve Pinto Stephen L. Rollman Kent Skov
5	Associate Producers (each name single page) Martha Whitney
6	Kent Weishaus
7	Music Composed and arranged by Richard Baker Mary Newland For Panda Productions
8	Music recorded by Richard Baker
9	Theme performed by Mary Newland

2-2-2-2

CLOSING CREDIT CRAWL (CONT'D)

10	Research by	Bob Petrella Ken Segall April Winchell Ted Hardwick
11	Talent Coordinator	Martha Whitney
12	Associate Director/Stage Manager	Randal W Ridges
13	Assistants to the Producers:	Bob Buchholz Connie Sue Cook Steve Pinto Stephen L. Rollman
14	Facilities Provided by	Hy-Tone Video
15	Lighting and Camera	Bill Sheehy
16	Production Sound	Eric Zeehandelaar
17	Gaffer	Jim Drewry
18	Production Assistants	Lisa Gougas Ted Hardwick
19	Make-Up	Lora Sanders
20	Wardrobe	Annie Vicari
21	Production Secretary	Eloise Gonzalez
22	Post-Production Coordinated by	Monti Santilli Rainbolt
23	Post-Production Facilities	Complete Post, Inc.
23a	Editor	Brent Carpenter
24	Post-Production Audio by	Michael Perricone Michaele Hogan

CLOSING CREDIT CRAWL (CONT'D)

25 "Your Home Movies" submitted by
    Alanna Velasquez
    Downey, CA

26 Location provided by
    George Waters
    Claremont, CA

27 Executive in Charge of Production for Four Star Television
    Bob Bosen

28 Special Thanks to:
    Susan Lenti
    Budget Films
    Richard Holiday
    Dennis Condon
    Snaggelpuss

29 Promotion by
    Dan Acree

30 Opening Title Montage by
    Homer & Associates

31 Opening Title Photography by
    Abe Perlstein

32 Post-Production Supervised by
    Randal W Ridges

33 Executive Producer
    Kent Skov

34 "Celebrity Voices and Appearances Impersonated"

35 Copyright 1985 Four Star International, Inc.
    All Rights Reserved

DECAMERON NIGHTS

With the

SHORT RUNDOWN FOR SHOW # <u>DECAMERON NIGHTS #119</u>

DESCRIPTION	IN	OUT	SEGMENT TIME
SHOW OPEN	00:00	01:53	01:53
COMMERCIAL BREAK #1	01:53	03:56	02:03
ACT I	03:56	11:35	07:39
COMMERCIAL BREAK #2	11:35	13:37	02:02
ACT II	13:37	21:00	07:23
COMMERCIAL BREAK #3	21:00	23:03	02:03
ACT III/SHOW CLOSE	23:03	28:00	04:57

RUNDOWN

MAD MOVIES WITH THE L.A. CONNECTION

SHOW #<u>119 DECAMERON NIGHTS</u>

TIMES ARE IN MINUTES AND SECONDS	IN	OUT	DURATION
FOUR STAR LOGO	00:00	00:05	00:05
OPENING CLIP TEASE	00:05	00:24	00:19
OPENING MONTAGE	00:24	00:52	00:28
OPENING WRAP	00:52	01:19	00:27
CLIP #2	01:19	01:32	00:32
TOSS TO COMMERCIAL	01:32	01:54	00:32
COMMERCIAL #1	01:54	03:55	02:01
BUMPER #1	03:55	03:58	00:03
TOSS TO FEATURE	03:58	04:04	00:06
FEATURE SEGMENT #1	04:04	10:54	06:50
TOSS TO CLIP #3	10:54	11:19	00:25
CLIP #3	11:19	11:35	00:16
COMMERCIAL #2	11:35	13:36	02:01
BUMPER #2	13:36	13:40	00:04
FEATURE SEGMENT #2	13:40	20:57	07:17
BUMPER #3	20:57	21:00	00:03

MAD MOVIES WITH THE L.A. CONNECTION

RUNDOWN   SHOW #119 DECAMERON NIGHTS

COMMERCIAL #3	21:00	23:02	02:02
BUMPER #4	23:02	23:04	00:02
FEATURE SEGMENT #3	23:04	25:25	02:21
HOME MOVIE INTRO	25:25	25:45	00:20
HOME MOVIE	25:45	26:55	01:10
CLOSING WRAP/CLOSING CREDITS	26:55	27:50	00:55
L.A. CONNECTION LOGO	27:50	27:55	00:05
FOUR STAR LOGO	27:55	28:00	00:05

DECAMERON NIGHTS
SHOW #119

CLIP TEASE

(EXT. FOREST)

          PRINCE CHARMING
I bet you're excited about Mad Movies coming on.

          COLLINS
Oh, I've never seen it.

          CHARMING
What do you mean, you've never seen it?

          COLLINS
They don't have it where I come from.

          CHARMING
Sounds pretty dull. What do you do for fun?

          COLLINS
Well, we do each other's nails and then we talk about boys.

          CHARMING
TV's better.

MUSIC THEME

(INT. GARAGE/ATTIC)

          HOST
Oh, Hi, I'm Kent Skov and welcome to Mad Movies with the L.A. Connection. The clip you've just seen is from our version of *DeCameron Nights*, originally a romantic medieval story. But we've revoiced all the dialogue and expanded the tale to follow the lives of Cinderella and Prince Charming. Did you ever really wonder if Prince Charming and Cinderella lived happily ever after? Well, this week on our show we hope to provide the answers.

CLIP

(INT. DAY—CHURCH)

          CHARMING
What is it Cinderella, I'm in a hurry.

          CINDERELLA
It's our wedding day.

          CHARMING
Yeah, so what?

          CINDERELLA
We're supposed to celebrate with a feast and gifts.

          CHARMING

Have a chew stick, from me to you.

(INT. GARAGE)

          HOST
You know this old trunk reminds me a lot of my childhood. A lot of sentimental things are in here. Uhhh
          (OPENS TRUNK)
Oh, how did you get in there? I been looking for you since I was twelve. Well, I wonder what happened to Cinderella and Prince Charming after they got married. In a moment, we'll find out.
          (LOOKS AT DOG)
Hmmm, what do you think? Hmmm.

COMMERCIAL #1

(INT. GARAGE)

          HOST
With all new dialogue, here's the L.A. Connection's rendition of "Decameron Nights."

TITLE

(EXT. DAY—TOWNSQUARE)

          GIRL ON LAP
So you're Prince Charming, huh?

          PRINCE
Uh-huh.

          DAD
Knock it off. Did you hear me, son?

          PRINCE
Yeah, Dad. So what?

          DAD
          (O.C.)
You can't chew gum with other women anymore.

          PRINCE
Why?

          DAD
Cause you're marrying Cinderella tomorrow, that's why. You royal pain.
          (OFF CAM)
Mellow out, King!

          PRINCE
Relax, pop. Let me enjoy my last day of gum chewing freedom. I'm Prince Charming, let me charm you. Sit down and park it. Let me buy you a margarita or something.

          DAD
You're as charming as a pair of old gym socks.

                    PRINCE
I don't make fun of you for wearing a lunch sack on your head.

                    DAD
It's not a lunch sack…it's a crown cover your mother made.

                    MAN AT TABLE
Let the kid chew gum.

                    DAD
Blow it out your…

(SONG STARTS)

(EXT. DAY—COURTYARD)

SONG

                    MALE V.O. #1
Hey, the beer keg's gonna explode. Take it over to the reception hall.

                    MALE V.O. #2
Hey, isn't that Kareem Abdul Jabar?

                    WOMAN V.O.
And Wilt Chamberland. Who invited them?

                    MALE V.O. #2
I think they're friends of Cinderella.

(SFX: WEDDING BELLS)

                    WOMAN V.O.
I heard they hired the Mushroom Blues band.

(MUSHROOM BAND PLAYING POST WEDDING MUSIC ON WEIRD INSTRUMENTS-BLUES)

(EXT. DAY—COURTYARD)

                    CROWD V.O.
Short wedding, where's the food?

(INT. DAY—CHURCH)

                    DAD
Well, congratulations, son, Cinderella. Since the beer keg exploded there's no reason for me to stay. Besides, I gotta go to the cleaners and see if they can get these kids off my robe.

                    PRINCE
Well, I can't stay either. I'm going out to get a drink with the boys. Bye.

                    CINDERELLA
Huh? Wait a minute.

PRINCE
What is it, Cinderella, I'm in a hurry.

CINDERELLA
It's our wedding day.

PRINCE
Yeah, so what?

CINDERELLA
We're supposed to celebrate with a feast and gifts.

PRINCE
Have a chew stick, from me to you. They were on sale at the Mini-mart.

CINDERELLA
Wait! What about our honeymoon? Our appearance on the Newlywed Game?

PRINCE
Are you going to nag?

CINDERELLA
Well, no, Darling, but it's just that…

PRINCE
We'll go to Beirut as soon as I get back. Oh and, you left your slipper on the steps again.

CINDERELLA
Prince, honey…how will I know when you're coming back?

PRINCE
Umm. According to my Rumplestilskin Pinkie watch, I'll be back by seven.
(V.O.)
Maybe.

(INT. BEDROOM)

PRINCE
(Snores)
(Louder when hat's removed)

CINDERELLA
Prince, Darling, Honey.
(Thought)
Oh, fine, drinks all evening with the boys and then passes out. What a wonderful wedding night this is. This is the happily ever after part?

PRINCE
(Snores/Burps)

(EXT. DAY—MARKET)

CINDERELLA

I thought we were going to Lebanon.

            PRINCE
But Tijuana is less crowded this time of year.

            CINDERELLA
Why did we come here?

            PRINCE
            (O.C.)
It was cheaper. Aren't you happy?

            CINDERELLA
Not really. I thought this would be…romantic.

            PRINCE
I got you that nice clown hat.

            CINDERELLA
Well, I want something expensive.

            PRINCE
Maybe you think I ought to buy this table full of jewelry.

            CINDERELLA
Yes I do. Wrap it up.

            PRINCE
You drive a hard bargain, Cindy. Here, have some rock candy.

            CINDERELLA
Oh, boy.

            PRINCE
            (O.C.)
Like it?

            CINDERELLA
Oooooo. Sweetest thing you ever gave me.

            PRINCE
            (O.C.)
Wait, I need ten bucks to pay for that.

            CINDERELLA
            (Mumbles)

(INT. HOTEL)

            PRINCE
What's on your head?

            CINDERELLA
It's a Grecian urn.

            PRINCE
What's a Grecian urn?

CINDERELLA
About 2.50 an hour.

PRINCE
That killed vaudeville.

(EXT. CASTLE GARDEN)

PEARL
The honeymooners are going to be returning.

SNOW WHITE
I just love Jackie Gleason and Art Carney.

DEBBIE
Snow White thinks you're talking about the TV show.

PEARL
Oh that was on ages ago.

SNOW WHITE
You would know.

(EXT. DAY—ROAD)

BAKER
Mobil homes for sale. This one comes complete with a maid. Step up, take a look. Eight point eight financing.

(INT. CASTLE BEDROOM)

STEP MOM
That porter potty would look better over in that corner. You know it took me a long time to find a gift that both you and the prince would enjoy.

CINDERELLA
Thanks, Mom.

STEP MOM
By the way, I'm moving in forever.

CINDERELLA
Well, why don't you go tell the Prince.

STEP MOM
Alright, oww!

(SFX: CRACK)

My knee!

(EXT. BALCONY/COURTYARD)

STEP MOM
Hey, frog brain!

PRINCE

Huh?

STEP MOM
(O.C.)

I'm living here now.

PRINCE
(O.C.)

Talkin' to me?

STEP MOM
(Start on camera)

You see
(O.C.)
anyone else dressed like Red Ridinghood? And I'll need an allowance.

PRINCE
(Groans)

For facials?

STEP MOM

Eat flies.

(EXT. NIGHT—BALCONY)

OMAR

What's up?

CINDERELLA

Oh, Omar, I don't know what to do. My marriage just isn't working out.

OMAR

Let us consult the stars.

CINDERELLA

I did. I asked Art Carney and Jackie Gleason. They think the Prince and I are perfectly compatible.

OMAR

Not those stars, these stars. Ah, a giant ink blot will appear and change your life.

CINDERELLA

Ink blot?

OMAR

Yeah, you go find him, show him this chart and point out the spots on your moon. He'll love you for it.

CINDERELLA

Are you sure?

OMAR

Wellllllll.

(EXT. DAY—SEA)

                    FISH
Help, help me. Oh help me, oh help me.

                    OMAR
               (Groans of strain)
He put up quite a fight, three hours.

                    CINDERELLA V.O.
                    (O.C.)
Yoo-hoo.

                    OMAR
Cinderella!

                    CINDERELLA
               (Long shot)
Have you seen my husband?

                    MYRON
It's my turn to find him.

                    OMAR
You looked last time. And take off that ridiculous bathing cap, Myron. He's behind you.

                    CINDERELLA
What did he say?

                    PEARL
Something about our behinds.

                    OMAR
                    (O.C.)
Turn around!

                    PEARL
Oh, behind us.

                    CINDERELLA
There he is…paddle faster.

                    PRINCE
                 (Thought)
Why does she follow me?

BLACK

(EXT. DAY—SEA)

                    PRINCE
You paddle fast. I told you not to bother me at the office. It's embarrassing.

                    PEARL
We brought lunch.

PRINCE
I can't take anymore pumpkin quiche. Get out.

PEARL/CINDERELLA
Well!

PRINCE
Bye, bye. Alright men, let's polish our planks.

(EXT. CAFÉ PATIO)

DENNY
Hey King, try the chef's special.

DAD
Thanks, Denny. I usually don't dine out, but Cinderella is a lousy cook. What is the chef's special anyway?

DENNY
It's Pumpkin quiche.

DAD
Oh, do I get free desert with this thing?

DENNY
Sure, cream puff.

DAD
Call me your highness.

TO-TOO
Boss, boss, can I have a bite?

DAD
No, To-Too.

TO-TOO
I can't take Cinderella's cooking anymore.

DAD
Listen pal, you were hired to eat it cause no one else would.

DENNY
Don't you think that's kinda cruel?

DAD
No, I don't.

TO-TOO
I need to be alone, come with me.

DAD
(Thought)
I wish this lemonade came in a glass.

TO-TOO V.O.
(O.C.)

Boss, boss the boat, the boat.

                DAD
              (Burps)

              DENNY
Look, there's your son.

              TO-TOO
What's his fantasy, boss? What's his fantasy?

              DAD
To see you hang from the ship's mast.

              DENNY
Careful of your blood pressure, your highness.

              DAD
Yeah, well, I'm sorry, To-Too. Here, have some lemonade.

              TO-TOO
It makes my lips pucker.

              DAD
It's alright, Cinderella didn't make it. Suck it up sailor.

(EXT. DOCK/SHIP)

              PRINCE
Genie, how did you get out of the bottle?

              GENIE
Somebody rubbed me the wrong way, I got so mad I blew my cork.

              PRINCE
You know, it would just tickle me to sit on your hat.

(INT. GARAGE)

              HOST
           (WITH DOG)
Well, Cinderella's life is turning into a night-time soap opera. Besides my dog here and this book, I found some pretty interesting things in this trunk. A glass slipper,

(PULLS OUT AND HOLDS UP RESPECTIVE OBJECTS)

    a pair of mice, and this old wand. I wonder if magically, I can find out what's happening next with our Mad Movie.

WAVES WAND INTO CLIP…

(INT. BEDROOM)

CINDERELLA SNORING

                    PRINCE
Cinderella, Oh Cindy.

                    CINDERELLA
                      (O.C.)
Oh, well you stop that Dracula stuff, and get out of there. Come to bed.

                    PRINCE
                    (Thought)
Mmmhh. My butt's stuck.

(SFX: POP)

CHYRON—OVER PRINCE LINE—"COMING UP...DRACULA?"

COMMERCIAL #2

                    TO-TOO
I'll race ya to the bottom, boss.

                    DAD
Okay, but watch out for open manholes.
                    YELL
Arrarrhhh.

EXT: SHIP

                    DAD
Oh, boy, that guy gave me a run for my money. I'm out of breath.

                    GENIE
Your son was just telling me how you were so long-winded.

                    DAD
What? Why you...

                    PRINCE
It just slipped out, Dad.

                    DAD
His brain slipped out. It slipped out the day he married Cinderella.
                    (O.C.)
That girl's trying to kill me. And I think she ground up those glass slippers in the pumpkin quiche.
                    (ON C.)
I oughta open up my own restaurant before I starve to death.

                    PRINCE
What are ya gonna call it? Mel's Diner?

                    DAD
Good idea. I think I will.

                    CINDERELLA

Well, kiss my grits.

(OFF CAM)

Ground glass, indeed.

DAD
Cinderella, I said you made good all around bass.

CINDERELLA
Prince, does your Dad have to die for you to become King?

GENIE
Do you want me to make her disappear?

DAD
Not yet, but stick around. Let's make up. How 'bout a kiss?

CINDERELLA
Forget it, whale breath.

DAD
King whale breath to you.

(SFX: CRACK)

Oh, I just broke my heel. Now how about that kiss?

CINDERELLA
He's lost his marbles.

DAD
I have not. I carry them with me everywhere in these two big bags.

CINDERELLA
Why don't you get off the thrown? He should let someone else use it once in a while.

(INT. BEDROOM)

CINDERELLA
Have you seen the Prince, Mom?

STEP MOM
He's playing hide-and-seek again, eh?

CINDERELLA
Yes, last time he hid in the moat.

STEP MOM

(SFX: CRACK)

Ow, my knee.

CINDERELLA
(O.C.)
It's a shame those alligators are such fussy eaters.

STEP MOM
Well, if he's hiding in a cooking pot, I'll shove it in the oven. Good night.

CINDERELLA
(Snores)

PRINCE
Cinderella, Cindy.

CINDERELLA
(O.C.)
What? Don't start that Dracula stuff again. Get out of there and come to bed.

PRINCE
(Thought)
Oh my butt's stuck.

(Grunts)

CINDERELLA
(O.C.)
You're such a wacko.

PRINCE
(Thought)
Oh wow, is her Mom ugly!

CINDERELLA
(O.C.)
What are you doing now?

PRINCE
Cindy, try and find me.

(EXT. GARDEN)

SNOW WHITE
Hi.

PRINCE
Hello, Snow White, what's happening with my favorite flake?

SNOW WHITE
Wanna chew gum with me?

PRINCE
What did you say?

SNOW WHITE
Prince, you heard me.

PRINCE
Cinderella won't let me chew gum.

SNOW WHITE

Well you know that I would and it wouldn't be sugarless.

                PRINCE

That'd be kinda neat. But someday your Prince will come.
                (O.C.)
And you'll have your own Dynasty.

                CINDERELLA

What's going on here?

                SNOW WHITE

Oh Cinderella, the Prince was telling me about dwarves.

                CINDERELLA
                (O.C.)

They're short.

                SNOW WHITE
                (O.C.)

Is this one?

                CINDERELLA
                (O.C.)

No!
                (ON C.)
They're Sleepy and Dopey, like him!

                SNOW WHITE

Yes, no, well, ah, bye.

(INT. LAB)

                PRINCE

Hey!
                (O.C.)
What are you doing in the wizard's lab?

                CINDERELLA

Nothin'.

                PRINCE
                (O.C.)

Forget it.

                CINDERELLA

Okay I lied. I'm inventing a love potion.

                PRINCE

You spend too much time in this laboratory inventing. The only good thing you ever made was this flexible brandy snifter for the bed ridden.

                CINDERELLA

What about your bath robe?

                PRINCE

The sleeves are too long.

CINDERELLA
You can sweep the floor, can't you?

PRINCE
I keep tripping on the cuff-links.

CINDERELLA
Please, let's take this love potion together.

PRINCE
I can't, I never drink and drive.

(EXT. SERVANTS YARD)

SNOW WHITE
Mom, Cinderella's here looking for her husband.

MRS. WHITE
Thanks, Snow. What you want?

CINDERELLA
I thought he might be here.

MRS. WHITE

(SFX: KNEE CRACK)

We leave the gates wide open, all the time, anything could crawl in. I mean walk in. You can look around. C'mon up.

(INT. SNOW WHITE'S BDRM)

MRS. WHITE
You can see he's not in Snow's room. Eeech.
    (O.C.)
Snow White let me see your apple.
    (ON C.)
Get away from that scum…
    (O.C.)
right now.
    (At Prince)
Why you rotten…

CINDERELLA
No! Use this.

MRS. WHITE
Get out! Get out.

PRINCE
Missed me. You missed me. Now you have to kiss me.

MRS. WHITE
Excuse me.

CINDERELLA
That's okay. I only get 2 out of 3 myself. I just don't know what to do.

MRS. WHITE
About what?

CINDERELLA
My husband, the Prince.

MRS. WHITE
You wouldn't really care what I think.
(O.C.)
Would ya?

CINDERELLA
Well, no I wouldn't.

MRS. WHITE
(O.C.)
Good, first I'd take
(ON C.)
those stupid sheets off my head and put them on the bed where they belong. 'Course I'm just an uneducated peasant woman, myself.

CINDERELLA
Yes, you are. But I like you anyway. And I'll try that sheet thing. Maybe that will put a spark in my marriage.

MRS. WHITE
Spark, eh? Why don't you try standing out in a rain storm. With a lightening rod between your horns.

CINDERELLA
Thank you, take this.

MRS. WHITE
Oh, I couldn't accept money for my advice.

CINDERELLA
This isn't money, Mrs. White. These are magic beans.

MRS. WHITE
What do you do with them?

CINDERELLA
You can make a nice soup or serve them with magic franks.

(EXT. LEAVING ROOM)

CINDERELLA
(Thought)
Phew! Mrs. White was right. That lightning rod trick made the Prince stand up and take notice. I scorched my hand and burned my hair, but it was worth it.

(INT. BEDROOM)

PRINCE

She knocked my boots off.

(EXT. GARDEN)

SNOW WHITE

Maybe it isn't fair to want the prince for my own, but who said life was fair.

SUSIE

That was me.

S.W.
(O.C.)

You live in a fairy world.

(ON C.)

Someday I'll be Queen and then I'll blow this pop stand then I won't have to be one of the ladies-in-waiting anymore.

LINDA

And no one ever bothered to tell us what we were waiting for.

LADIES-IN-WAITING
(O.C. RESPONSE)

Yeah!

(INT. LIVING ROOM)

STEP MOM

It's a message from your husband.

CINDERELLA

Thanks, mom.

STEP MOM

You won't like it, I already read it.

CINDERELLA
(Reading)

I have to work late again tonight.
P.S. I'm leaving you.

MOM

It's written in crayon and he spelled your name wrong.

CINDERELLA

I thought things were better. He's probably with Snow White. He should be shot. I'll need practice. Hold this target and I'll go get my bow and arrow.

STEP MOM

Oh.

(EXT. SNOW WHITE'S BALCONY)

PRINCE

Let's go.

SNOW WHITE
Forget it. You'll dump me like you dumped your wife.

PRINCE
Look at this?

SNOW WHITE
Oh my gauze.

PRINCE
I hurt myself, fighting for your honor. Which is more than you ever did.

S.W.
Mom.

(SFX: FOOT STEPS)

MRS. WHITE
(O.C.)
You again.

PRINCE
Nice day, huh?

MRS. WHITE
Not for you. Grumpy, Doc, Happy, Sneezey, Skecky, all of you, throw this bum out. This wolf treats my daughter like she's one of the three pigs. Kick him in the crown jewels.

CROWD OF MEN
Punch him in the pumpkin. Clean his clock, break his scepter, etc.

PRINCE
(THOUGHT)
Good thing I landed on my head.

(OFF CAMERA VOICE)

THOUGHT
Turn the hogs loose on 'em.

DOCTOR
Been feeling nauseous? And gaining weight?

CINDERELLA
Yes doctor, that's true.

NURSE
(MAN)
Have you been eating those golden eggs?

DOCTOR
Let's see your waist. It could be a guess, but you might have a bun in the oven.

CINDERELLA

Are you sure, Doctor?

> NURSE
> (O.C.)

Do an E.B.T., Early Bun Test.

> DOCTOR

I saw your reflection in the knife, you're expecting. Congratulations.

> CINDERELLA

Oh, thank you.

COMMERCIAL #3

(EXT. MOTEL YARD)

> MALE V.O. #1

Why does he always ride the horse?

> MALE V.O. #2

When is it my turn?

> MALE V.O. #1

Wait 'til your birthday.

> SOLDIER

Prince (with echo effect)... Prince.

> PRINCE
> (In shadows)

I'm doing the dishes. What do you want?

> SOLDIER

Cinderella sent me to get you. For some reason she wants you back.

> PRINCE

After the way I treated her. Well, I'll be glad to go back 'cause there's nothing but guys here at the Y.

> SOLDIER

What's that you're drinking?

> PRINCE

Swill.

> SOLDIER

Not how it is. I asked you what it is.

> PRINCE

Pig swill.
> (Splashed cup)

Aw! I drooled in it. Want it?

> SOLDIER

It was an accident.

(EXT. CASTLE ENTRANCE)

        PRINCE
        (Thought)
After being away for a year, my castle sure looks different.

        PEASANTS V.O.
Hurry. Run for your life. Get out.

        PRINCE
Where are you going?

        PEASANT V.O.
Cinderella offered to make us dinner.

        PRINCE
Well, some things never change.

(INT. CASTLE HALL)

        PEARL
Now keep your hands off the prince or you'll be sent to the tower with Rapunzel.

        CINDERELLA
Right.
        (Gasps on seeing Prince)

        PRINCE

(SFX: VELCRO)

  Arg!
        (Yells in pain)

        CINDERELLA
What happened?

        PRINCE
I thought I was wearing a hat.

        CINDERELLA
Meet me in my room later.

        PRINCE
Still can't resist me, huh? Are they invited too?

        CINDERELLA
No, it's not what you think.

(INT. BEDROOM)

        PRINCE
        (Long Shot)
What do you want to tell me? Mmmm…
        (five times)
Hey, where'd this thing come from? What the heck is it?

                    CINDERELLA
It's a baby.

                    PRINCE
How can I be sure it's mine?

                    CINDERELLA
Just listen.

                    BABY
Hi, Papa.

                    PRINCE
When did this happen?

                    CINDERELLA
Well…let's just say I call him lightening boy.

                    PRINCE
Does Dad know?

                    CINDERELLA
Your father had to be locked away for showing his marbles.

                    PRINCE
Well, what do you know about that? Guess I'm King.

                    CINDERELLA
Notice anything else?

                    PRINCE
You have bubble gum in your hair. Let me chew it.

                    BABY
Guess her weight, papa.

                    PRINCE
Good idea. About 175 in the summer.

(INT. GARAGE)

                    HOST
Well, things turned out alright for our couple.

(HOLDING FIGURES CAUSING MONKEY KISS)

But you know our feature isn't the only thing we've redubbed tonight. Tisha Farrington of South Norwalk, Conn. sent us her home movie, and as always, we give them the L.A. Connection treatment by adding new dialogue. Voila.

(WANDS CAUSES FILM REEL TO APPEAR.)

And here's the L.A. Connection's home movie entitled, Baby-Robics.

<u>BABY ROBICS</u>

MAN:	Feeling listless? Wanna lose that baby fat? Then come on down to Teensy Fitness World and train the baby-robics way!
WMN:	Roll, and 2 and 3 and 4 and on your back, let's go! And 1 and 2 and 3 and over, c'mon, work it out.
MAN:	You'll learn how to do push-ups!
WMN:	And paddle, and paddle.
MAN:	Do the swim!
WMN:	And rest. And stay with it, now kick it out. And kick and swim and kick and swim and rest.
MAN:	Try our new state of the art jumping equipment!
WMN:	And bounce and bounce, c'mon. Feel the burn and bounce.
MAN:	Now available in our newer centers; the latest European teething system!
WMN:	And bite! C'mon, c'mon, work those gums, get ready, we're gonna do it again, and bite, and teethe.
MAN:	Trained pediatricians are available to wait on you hand and foot, making sure you keep your nose to the fitness grindstone. So come on by for your free introductory visit. You'll feel so good, you'll want to dance all night long!
WOMEN:	And dip and dance. And dip and dance.

(INT. GARAGE)

HOST
If you'd like your home moves made into Mad Movies, send them to the L.A. Connection
(OVER ADDRESS)
6464 Sunset Blvd., Suite 820, Hollywood, California 90028.

(BACK TO HOST INSIDE GARAGE)

Well, that was our show. Of course we all realize that Cinderella is just a fantasy,
(OVER CREDITS),
a figment of our imagination. But Prince Charming.

(LOOKS AT WAND, WAVES IT AND TURNS INTO FROG)

Hmmm. Wait a minute. This isn't what I had in mind. It's all backwards. Well, see you next time with more Mad Movies. Well, I hope I'm back to normal. Are there any women out there who want to kiss me?

(INT. ROOM)

PRINCE
I'm glad you came over to watch Mad Movies with me, but do you have to leave so soon?

CINDERELLA
YES.

PRINCE
But I have dinner all ready for us, Cinderella.

CINDERELLA

Well, like what?

PRINCE

Well, to start with, I've got seaweed cooler in this bendover beaker, a jar of refried beans, and a bottle of burgers. Shall we eat in here?

CINDERELLA

I'll have it to go.

HOST (V.O.)

Additional voices by April Winchell.

OPENING CRAWL*

SHOW #<u>119</u>

SHOW NAME Decameron Nights

*Each numbered item as a single page…
Items #1-5 Centerframe
Items #6-10 Lower third of page

1	FOUR STAR in association with KENT SKOV
2	Presents as L.A. Connection production of
3	MAD MOVIES WITH THE L.A. CONNECTION
4	Tonight's Feature Decameron Nights
5	Starring the Voices of
6	Bob Buchholz
7	Connie Sue Cook
8	Stephen L. Rollman
9	Steve Pinto
10	Kent Skov

GENERIC BUMPERS*

SHOW #<u>119</u>

SHOW NAME <u>Decameron Nights</u>

*Each numbered item as a single page…

1. We'll be right back…

2. Coming Up…
   Dracula?

3. ~~Stay Tuned for~~
   ~~"Your Home Movies"~~

4. Send Your Home Movies to…
   L.A. Connection Productions
   6464 Sunset Blvd., #820
   Hollywood, CA 90028
   (Include a self-addressed, stamped envelope for return of films)

5. BABY-ROBICS

6. Next…
   Royal Baby Rumors

CLOSING CRAWL*

SHOW #119

SHOW NAME Decameron Nights

*Each numbered item as a single page…

1	Directed by Kent Skov
2	Written by Kent Skov
3	Produced by Randal W Ridges
4	Featuring Bob Buchholz Connie Sue Cook Steve Pinto Stephen L. Rollman Kent Skov
5	Associate Producers (each name single page) Martha Whitney
6	Kent Weishaus
7	Music Composed and arranged by Richard Baker Mary Newland For Panda Productions
8	Music recorded by Richard Baker
9	Theme performed by Mary Newland

CLOSING CREDIT CRAWL (CONT'D)

10 Research by
    Bob Petrella
    Ken Segall
    April Winchell
    Ted Hardwick

11 Talent Coordinator
    Martha Whitney

12 Associate Director/Stage Manager
    Randal W Ridges

13 Assistants to the Producers:
    Bob Buchholz
    Connie Sue Cook
    Steve Pinto
    Stephen L. Rollman

14 Facilities Provided by
    Hy-Tone Video

15 Lighting and Camera
    Bill Sheehy

16 Production Sound
    Eric Zeehandelaar

17 Gaffer
    Jim Drewry

18 Production Assistants
    Lisa Gougas
    Ted Hardwick

19 Make-Up
    Lora Sanders

20 Wardrobe
    Annie Vicari

21 Production Secretary
    Eloise Gonzalez

22 Post-Production Coordinated by
    Monti Santilli Rainbolt

23 Post-Production Facilities
    Complete Post, Inc.

23a Editor
    Brent Carpenter

24 Post-Production Audio by
    Michael Perricone

3-3-3-3

CLOSING CREDIT CRAWL (CONT'D)

25   "Your Home Movies" submitted by
Laticia Farrighton
S. Norwalk, CT

27   Executive in Charge of Production for Four Star Tel.
Bob Bosen

28   Special Thanks to:

Susan Lenti	Dennis Condon
Budget Films	"Ruby Rubato" The Pup
Richard Holiday	"Prince" The Frog
	Snagglepuss

29   Promotion by
Dan Acree

30   Opening Title Montage by
Homer & Associates

31   Opening Title Photography by
Abe Perlstein

32   Post-Production Supervised by
Randal W Ridges

33   Executive Producer
Kent Skov

34   "Celebrity Voices and Appearances Impersonated"

35   Copyright 1985 Four Star International, Inc.
All Rights Reserved

DIVORCE OF LADY X

With the

SHORT RUNDOWN FOR SHOW #123 DIVORCE OF LADY X

DESCRIPTION	IN	OUT	SEGMENT TIME
SHOW OPEN	00:00	01:44	01:44
COMMERCIAL BREAK #1	01:44	03:47	02:03
ACT I	03:47	11:55	08:08
COMMERCIAL BREAK #2	11:55	13:59	02:04
ACT II	13:59	29:46	06:47
COMMERCIAL BREAK #3	20:46	22:49	02:03
ACT III/SHOW CLOSE	22:49	28:00	05:11

MAD MOVIES WITH THE L.A. CONNECTION

RUNDOWN   SHOW #<u>123 DIVORCE OF LADY X</u>

All times are in minutes and seconds	IN	OUT	DURATION
Four Star Logo	00:00	00:05	00:05
Clip Tease #1	00:05	00:23	00:18
Opening Montage	00:23	00:50	00:27
Host Intro and Preview Clip	00:50	01:44	00:54
Commercial Black #1	01:44	03:47	02:03
Bumper #1	03:47	03:51	00:04
Movie Segment #1 (includes Host Toss)	03:51	11:16	07:25
Host and Preview Clip	11:16	11:55	00:39
Commercial Black #2	11:55	13:59	02:04
Bumper #2	13:59	14:01	00:02
Movie Segment #2	14:01	20:42	06:41
Bumper #3	20:42	20:46	00:04
Commercial Black #2	20:46	22:49	02:03
Bumper #4	22:49	22:53	00:04

MAD MOVIES WITH THE L.A. CONNECTION

RUNDOWN, Pg 2   SHOW #<u>123</u>

	IN	OUT	DURATION
Movie Segment #3	22:53	24:55	02:02
Host Intro to Home Movie	24:55	25:16	00:21
Home Movie (includes Billboard at tail)	25:16	26:26	01:10
Host Wrap-up	26:26	26:57	00:31
Clip Tease #2	26:57	27:10	00:13
Closing Montage (includes L.A. Connection Logo)	27:10	27:55	00:45
Four Star Logo	27:55	28:00	00:05

DIVORCE OF LADY X
SHOW NUMBER 123

(INT. ROOM)

                        OLIVIER

1, 2, 3…

                        LADY X

Don't peek.

                        OLIVIER

4…

                        LADY X

I'm hiding in here.

                        OLIVIER

Oh, you're not supposed to tell me. Now we have to start over.

                        LADY X

I'm not playing. I'm watching Mad Movies.

                        OLIVIER

Fine. I'll play by myself. Ready or not, here I come. Geee, I wonder where I'm hiding.

(INT. HOTEL)

                        HOST

Hi, I'm Kent Skov and welcome to Mad Movies with the L.A. Connection. The clip you've just seen is from our version of *Divorce of Lady X*, originally a romantic comedy. However we've revoiced all the dialogue and now our story is simply about extra-marital affairs.

(INT. OFFICE)

                        OLIVIER

I'm cruising, because tonight Lady Z and I are going to get together and do this. Of course, not with so many legs, if you get my meaning. Tonight I'll be crossing her latitude with my longitude.

(INT. HOTEL LOBBY)

                        HOST

You know, when experiencing their affairs, many people like to come to a hotel. I mean, it's a lot more secretive, than say, a nightclub. And chances are absolutely no one will know you. Excuse me…would you have an affair here? GENTLEMEN, SMILES NERVOUSLY, WALKS OUT OF FRAME. We'll be right back with Divorce of Lady X…soap opera style.

COMMERCIAL #1

(INT. HOTEL LOBBY)

HOST
With all new dialogue, here's our rendition of *Divorce of Lady X*.
(RINGS BELL)

TITLE

(INT. BEAUTY SHOP)

LADY Z
Lady Y, are you reading "Divorce of the Month" magazine too?

LADY Y
Mr. X is the centerfold.

LADY Z
After spending the last fifteen years in a nunnery, I'm dying to go out with a man.
(O.C.)
And I'd like to start with Mr. X.

LADY Y
What a stud!

LADY Z
I'm going to go look him up as soon as my hair grows back.

LADY Y
That'll take a month, Lady Z.

LADY Z
Not really, the beautician's turning the hair knob on the back of my neck right now.
(O.C.)
It makes it sprout instantly.

LADY Y
I wish I had one.

(INT. OFFICE)

MR. X
Maps! And I've got to refold them again.
(O.C.)
Oh no, Mr. B, not more maps to refold.

MR. B
Yep. You did 'em wrong again.

MR. X
I don't know what's the matter.

MR. B
If you don't stop thinking about your divorce, Mr. X, our map business is gonna fold.

MR. X
That's right. Then we'll be up against that wall.

MR. B
It's wet paint.

(INT. HALL)

OPIE
You're Lady Y and Lady Z.

LADY Y & LADY Z
Why yes, we are.

OPIE
Here to have an affair?

LADY Z & LADY Y
That's right. But I saw him first!

LADY Z
But you're married.

LADY Y
So? Have you ever seen my husband?

LADY Z
Well, c'mon, I'll flip you for him.

LADY Y
Okay.
(giggles)

(INT. OFFICE)

(SFX: (O.C.) BODY GETTING SLAMMED TO GROUND & SCREAM)

MR. X
What was that?

OPIE
Some lady getting flipped to the ground.

(INT. OFFICE)

MR. X
What are you here for?

LADY X
The settlement.
(O.C.)
I'm not happy with it.

MR. X
But you
(O.C.)
got everything but my holey underwear.

LADY X
I want them too.

MR. X
(O.C.)

What would you do with them?

LADY X

I'm out of coffee filters.

MR. X

Can't I have them back when you're done?

LADY X
(O.C.)

Absolutely not!

MR. X

What am I supposed to wear?

LADY X

After the way you acted during our marriage, I don't care if you wear a rope around your neck.

MR. X

You don't really mean that, do you?

LADY X
(O.C.)

Of course not. I'm not so cold hearted that I'd like to see you hang. I'd prefer to throw you out the window.

MR. X

That would mess up my hair.

(INT. HOUSE)

LORD Z

Dear, is it true you're having an affair…with a married man?

LADY Z

No, papa. He's recently divorced and now I'm waiting for a chance to dink his dirigible.

LORD Z

I'll have you know your mother and I never fooled around.

LADY Z

Ooh sure, I've heard this story. You and mom were sitting on the porch when the baby truck drove by, it hit a bump, and that's when I popped out.

LORD Z

That's right. MMM-MMM.

LADY Z

Then you cooked me in the oven 'til I was 21.

LORD Z

Did you know that you're on fire?

LADY Z

Yes, I do, papa, I'm on fire with burning passion. I feel just like a sizzlin' griddle of love.

LORD Z
(O.C.)

No, I mean you're on fire.

(INT. OFFICE)

MR. X

Who burned my tree? And who are you?

LADY Z
(O.C.)

I'm Lady Z and I brought you some fish. I boned them for you.

MR. X
(STARTS BTC)

What makes you think I like fish?

LADY Z

Well, it said in the magazine that you are fond of sturgeon and collect herring.

MR. X

No! You read it wrong. I want to be a surgeon and correct hearing.

LADY Z

Huh. Ooooh.

MR. X

SONG

I'm not like any ordinary man,
I've got athlete's foot on my hands.
So if you have some qualms about a man with itchy palms,
I think perhaps that you had better scram.

LADY Z

No thanks.

MR. X
(O.C.)

You mean you still wanna stay?

LADY Z

Yeah, sure…Is there anything else I should know?

MR. X
(START O.C.)

Did I mention I love warts,
And I'm very bad at sports.
I'm afraid of the dark, and the swings in the park,
And I eat onion dip by the quart.

> LADY Z
> Oh, I prefer gallons.

(INT. DINING ROOM)

> LORD Z
> (Slurp, burp)
> Jeeves, I've told you a million times…to make good coffee…you need to use bathwater…chili beans and brown shoe polish.

(SFX: GONG SOUND) (BURPS)

This egg is so hard my fist couldn't break it.

> JEEVES
> (Mumbles)

Try sitting on it.

(INT. OFFICE)

> LADY Z
> So without even realizing it I had ripped off the lips of my pet lizard, and that's my story.

> MR. X
> Somehow I don't think you're quite the woman for me.

> LADY Z
> Why not?

> MR. X
> For one, I don't care for women who stuff prunes up their noses or pluck their eyebrows out with a hedge clip.
> (END O.C.)

> LADY Z
> Oh, have you ever tried it?

> MR. X
> No, I have a gardener.

> LADY Z
> Kiss me, fool.

> MR. X
> No…I…okay.

(SFX: MOTOR KISS)

Your kisses remind me of my '56 Ford.

> LADY Z
> That's why you were squeezing my bumpers.

> MR. X
> Listen…you get your hedge clippers and I'll get a box of prunes. Okay?

(O.C.)
Meet ya for dinner tonight.

(INT. OFFICE)

MR. Y
Good day, are you Mr. X? Bang!

MR. X
(Laughs)
You missed. Get lost, Mr. B.

MR. Y
I'm Mr. Y. I read about you in "Divorce of the month" magazine. I love that centerfold with you, the shaved lamb and the box of fruit. I'm dissatisfied with my marriage; I want to find a woman to do this with. I want to have an affair.

MR. X
(START O.C.)
Why?

MR. Y
Gee, I forgot. It's been just too long.

MR. X
Tell me…

MR. Y
Well, it all started 30 years ago…I was on my…

MR. X
Is this going to be a long, boring story? If so, I think I'm going to have a cigarette.

MR. Y
If you read the package, you'll see those things are bad for you. I, myself smoke laundry markers.

MR. X
Laundry markers? What do they taste like, Mr. Y?

MR. Y
Have you ever licked an old doll leg?

MR. X
Of course, but not for years. What about the smell?

MR. Y
Yes, tantalizing, isn't it? Just like the stock yards in spring, when all the steam is rising from the cow blossoms.

(INT. RESTAURANT ENTRANCE)

LADY Z
I need to powder my nose.

MR. X
Wait, wait, wait, hey, hey, hey, that's the men's room.

LADY Z
Yes, I know.

MALE V.O.
Hey!

MR. X
Here, throw these away for me.

(INT. BEDROOM)

MRS. Y
(Thought)
Gee, I wish this dress was tighter.

MR. Y
(O.C.)
Honey?
(ON C.)
I'm back to stay.

(SFX: MONKEY KISS ON CHEEK)

Dear, when do you think we can start kissing on the lips?

MRS. Y
What kind of woman do you think I am?

MR. Y
But we've been married 30 years.

MRS. Y
So what!

MR. Y
Don't you want to?

MRS. Y
Well, I just had my nails done. Besides, women need a certain amount of time to warm up. Not like men!

MR. Y
Sit on a stove!

(INT. RESTAURANT)

LADY Z
Don't bite your nails.

MR. X
I'm hungry.

LADY Z
Well, didn't you order dinner?

                    MR. X
These are the appetizers.

                    LADY Z
I hope we're not having finger sandwiches.

                    MR. X
I just noticed that…there are
                    (O.C.)
no straps on your...

                    LADY Z
Yes.

                    MR. X
                    (O.C.)
You mean just those two small bumps are holding up that big dress.
                    (ON C.)
Wow, I wish I'd met you sooner. I could have used this as a science project on anti-gravity in high school, or something. I, uh…
                    (GASPS)…(BEHIND MENU)
Isn't that Jimmy Hoffa.

                    HOFFA
Ha, Uh…Ha, Uh…

(EXT. REST. NIGHT STREET)

                    MR. X
Well, thanks for the affair.

                    LADY Z
We haven't had it yet, silly.
                    (To Driver)
A big hotel, please.

                    MR. X
Well, should I get a room there, too?

                    LADY Z
Same one.

                    MR. X
Wait, shouldn't I be in the car with you?

                    LADY Z
You should have been, idiot!

                    MR. X
                    (Thought)
This is working out better than my honeymoon did.

(INT. RESTAURANT)

                    HOST

Things seem to be getting hot and heavy for our leading lady. I'm here at a fine restaurant, another place where one might have an affair.
(O.C. ON MEEK GENTLEMAN)
After all, it is a perfect place. It's quiet and romantic.
(ON CAM)
And most who have affairs are very subtle and don't want to draw any attention to themselves.

(MEEK GENTLEMAN KNOCKS OVER GLASS)

You okay? Uh…

(GENTLEMAN RUNS OUT OF FRAME)

Well, some people are just so rude. Here's a clip of what's coming up next with Divorce of Lady X.

(INT. BEDROOM)

MR. X
Front desk, check the lobby, see if there's a woman there waiting to have an affair.

(INT. HALLWAY)

HOTEL MGR.
Wait here, I'll see if he prefers blondes, brunettes, or bimbos.
(LADIES LAUGHING)

HOST
We'll be right back…

COMMERCIAL #2

(INT. OFFICE)

MR. Y
Ah, Mr. X, congratulate me, I think I just had an affair.

MR. X
Did you take the first thing that came in outta the rain?

MR. Y
Your ex-wife.

MR. X
Lady X?

MR. Y
Yes and I owe it all to my umbrella.

MR. X
Umbrella?

MR. Y
I met her on the avenue. She said I'd like to be havin' you.

MR. X
What's that got to do with your umbrella?

MR. Y
I'll tell you.
She wanted the company of a fella,
With an expandable umbrella.
But when I began to stall,
She grabbed for my parasol.
We did a horizontal dance,
And I may have split my pants,
Mind checking for me, old man.

MR. X
No! Uh-huh. No!

MR. Y
Are you sure you can't see my skivvies? There was a lot of action.

MR. X
No, no.

MR. Y
Now I'll continue on my route, remembering her hand on my bumbershoot.

(INT. OFFICE)

MR. B
Excuse me, but your ex-wife is here and she set off all the metal detectors.

MR. X
Did she try to hit you when you frisked her for weapons?

MR. B
I don't think she'd hit a man with glasses.

MR. X
Yeah, but I don't have any.

MR. Y
Mr. X, this man needs no introduction, so I won't give him one. Sit down.

MR. X
Would you like to buy a map to the movie stars homes in Boise?

MR. Y
No, we're not here about that.
(O.C.)

MR. X
(Mumbles)
What do you want custody of now?

LADY X

Put down that map. I can't understand you.

MR. X
(O.C.)
What do you want now?

LADY X
(Ends O.C.)
Well, we'd like the electric toilet seat.

MR. X
Fine, take it!

MR. Y
Dear, what about…the…uh…

LADY X
Well…
(O.C.)
I don't know.

MR. Y
Go on, ask him.

LADY X
Don't get pushy, I'll hit you so hard, your brother will hurt.
(PAUSE)
That's exactly why I divorced Mr. X.

MR. X
Ha, that's a lie.

LADY X
(O.C.)
It is not!

MR. X
You left me because I refused to whistle through a duck's bladder. Admit it.

LADY X
Well, yeah but…

MR. X
What is it, Mr. B?

MR. B
Your car got sucked into a vortex.

MR. X
What do you mean?

MR. B
Well, now, you're going to have to hitchhike home.

MR. X

Oh, I well, ah…

(EXITS)

…oh…

(INT. OFFICE)

PHONE V.O.

Pssst, hey, over here. It's me, the phone talkin' to ya. Pick me up. Now shake me. Shake me hard.

OPIE
(Coughs)

MR. X

Nothin'

OPIE

I won't tell.

DESK V.O.

Hi…it's me your desk, I love you. Look in my drawers.

P.J. V.O.

Hey it's me, your pajamas. How you doin! Pick me up. Smell me. Fresh, huh? Hey, hey, watch it buddy. Take it easy, you're pinching my buttons.

MR. X
(Thought)

I'd better call for some help.

PHONE V.O.

Get your hands off my receiver.

(INTO OFFICE)

MR. Y

Listen old man, take better care of yourself.
(O.C.)
Get the Dom de Luis workout tape. Improve your diet.

MR. X

Should I eat more lard?

MR. Y
(O.C.)

That's good, but maybe it's your hormones that are out of whack. Have that affair with Lady Z. Wet your eyebrows and go wild.

MR. X
Well, I'll try, but I don't think it will do any good.
Say, how did you score?

MR. Y

SONG

I was an insecure fella, now I'm making it with your ex.
When she twirls my umbrella, it's almost as good as sex.
Shuns of a pie or a ham and cheese on rye.
And a...

MR. X
Yeah, I got the picture. I'll call her.

(INT. OFFICE)

MR. X
(Mumbles)

Umbrella.

(Mumbles)

LADY Z
That's not what it's for.

MR. X
(Mumbles)

Dom de Luis.

LADY Z
Why Mr. X!

MR. X
(Mumbles)

Lard...

LADY Z
I think you mean oil.

MR. X
Does that mean yes?

(INT. OFFICE)

MR. B
Good morning, Mr. X.

MR. X
Good morning, Mr. B, throw these away for me, L.B.

MR. E
Blood sucking alien? Do you believe in life on other planets?

LADY Z
I have an uncle who watches Bonanza reruns without a television.

                    MR. E
I don't think that counts.

                    V.O.
Blood curdling screams.
                    (O.C.)

                    MR. E
Well it looks like they found it.

(INT. HOTEL ROOM)

                    VALET
Anything else, sir?

                    MR. X
                    (NASAL)
I have a prune stuck up my nose, could you get me some tweezers or some salad tongs?

                    VALET
Not another one.

                    MR. X
                    (NASAL)
There goes your tip.
                    (ON PHONE)
Listen, front desk, could you check the lobby, see if there's a woman waiting to have an affair, thanks.

NO COMMERCIAL

(INT. HALL)

                    HOTEL MANAGER
Wait here. I'll see if he prefers blondes, brunettes or bimbos.

(INT. HOTEL ROOM)

                    HOTEL MANAGER
I'm not cleanin' that up. I got a woman for ya.

                    MR. X
Oh good.

                    HOTEL MANAGER
Matter of fact, I've got 37 of 'em, outside in the hall. I'm kinda partial to the one…how do you say…with legs up to her neck.

                    MR. X
I've never said that.

                    H.M.
That doesn't matter. Oh and by the way, there's a tiny little one with big picnic baskets.

MR. X
I want one with a certain dress on.

H.M.
You'll only—take it off.

MR. X
(Laughs)
That's a good idea, I was just going to sit her down in a chair and give her a glass of wine. Then let her stuff my hors d'eou. And they say I don't know how to show a girl a good time.

H.M.
Well, if you don't want those ladies in the hall, I'll take at least four of them.

MR. X
Why don't you take an even nine and you can start your own softball team.

(INT. ROOM)

MR. X
(ON PHONE)
Gee, Dad, I tried that already but I think I was just a little too rough with it. And now it just seems to be floppin' around. I'm having a professional come over and wire it to the ceiling, 'cause I don't think I can get it to stand up on its own again.

LADY Z
Ahem!

MR. X

(SFX: PHONE HANG UP)
(O.C.)
I was just telling my dad about my broken t.v. antenna.

LADY Z
We're meant for each other. It's destiny. I was given a sign.

MR. X
Come here.

LADY Z
Well, why?

MR. X
I'll tell ya. You're standing on the part of the floor that suck people into the fourth dimension.

LADY Z
Why should the floor have all the fun?

MR. X

SONG
Well uh…that is,

you're a girl who likes to have fun I see,
No wonder you left the nunnery.
But I have no strength for folding maps,
when you wear dresses without straps.
                    (Pause)
You'd like to find out what you're missing.

LADY Z
Oh shut up, and let's start kissing.

MR. X
Kissing's a start, that's true. I'm just not sure what else to do. Perhaps you could give me a hint.

LADY Z
Please be my clothes brush, and remove my lint. What do I have to do, draw you a picture?

CHYRON…NEXT…ONCE UPON A MATTRESS…

COMMERCIAL #3

MR. X
Have I been boring you?

LADY Z
(Yawns)
Yes, just a little.

MR. X
Well, what do you think about going in the other room and dressing up like a duck?

LADY Z
Oh, how exciting, carry me.

MR. X
No, I meant you should go in by yourself.

LADY Z
Oh, alright. Quack, quack, quack.

MR. X
YEEEOOOOWW!
(O.C.)
My thumb!

LADY Z
Just a minute.

MR. X
What?

LADY Z
Hey, I'm not going to put this on. The bill's broken and one of the webbed feet is missing.

MR. X
Well...Mmmmm...

LADY Z
Besides that, I don't think we'll both fit on this couch.

Mr. X
Why don't we try it on the floor?

LADY Z
(O.C.)
Someone might look in the window.

MR. X
So what!?

LADY Z
We need to be comfortable.

MR. X
Now I'll just put this mattress down. It'll be like camping. We'll set a chair on fire, toast marshmallows, maybe
(O.C.)
even sing Kumbaya.
(ON CAMERA)
There, go ahead try it out.

LADY Z
No. You first.

MR. X
No. After you.

LADY Z
No. Go ahead.

MR. X
Doesn't this excite you?

LADY Z
Not really, sorry.

LADY Z
Boy, these pajamas are loud.

MR. X
(O.C.)
Did they say something to you too?

LADY Z
(LAUGHING)
Oh no!

MR. X
(O.C.)
Don't pinch the buttons.

                    LADY Z
What do you say we trade clothes? It'll be fun, huh?

                    MR. X
I don't think your panty hose will fit.

                    LADY Z
One size fits all.

                    LADY Z
Try it on.
                    (O.C.)
Forget it. I'm wild with passion, yearning for you.
                    (ON C.)
But first, brush your teeth.

                    MR. X
                    (MUMBLES)
I'll be back in a minute.

                    LADY Z
Gargle.
                    (V.O.—READING)
Using position "1", insert tab "A" into slot "B", then your glider is ready to fly.

                    LADY Z
                    (O.C.)
Mr. X, I've changed my mind, I'm too tired now. I need some sleep.

                    MR. X
OH, NO!

(CRIES)

THE END

(INT. RESTAURANT)

                    HOST
Woo, boy...that was some ending. But that soap opera we just presented via our redubbing process isn't the only thing we changed. Athena Marie of Los Angeles, California sent us her home movie. And as always, we edit them and add dialogue. It's called the Fable. Here it is. Check.

FOUR SECOND CHYRON OVER RACE CARS...THE FABLE...

Once upon a time in a big castle made of rocks and sugar, there lived the Princess Athena, who wore a plate on her head and carried a bag made of licorice. When Princess Athena wanted to go somewhere, she crawled on a grownup's back and said Giddyap.

(LITTLE GIRL'S VOICE: Giddyap.)

But sometimes she said it backwards...

(L. GIRL'S VOICE: Yapdigig.)

> That's Giddyap backwards. She made a law that every day was her birthday. And she was even involved in some controversial anti-gravity experiments which enabled her to be the first female astronaut in a big orange ship. (See, here's a picture of the orange ship…It's pretty). Athena's circle of royal friends all traveled in the fast lane. And if she didn't like what was for dinner, she'd just put on her prettiest dress and ate dessert instead…with her hands. If she didn't feel like going to bed, she didn't. She'd stay up all night reading the race results from Belmont Park. But even though it seemed like an ideal life, Princess Athena was denied one thing… she wasn't supposed to get on the coffee table.

(INT. RESTAURANT)

> If you want your home movies made into Mad Movies, send them to the L.A.

(OVER ADDRESS)

> Connection, 6464 Sunset Blvd., Suite 820, Hollywood California 90028.

(INT. OFFICE)

HOST
We thought we'd close our show at another place where one might have an affair, the business office. I mean, when you think about it, it's a perfect place, especially after everyone's gone home. And that's where I'm going right now…home. It doesn't look like anyone here is going to have an affair tonight.

WALKS OVER TOWARD CLOSET TO DISCOVER MEEK GENTLEMAN WITH LADY COMPANION IN HOT EMBRACE…

> Oh,

GENTLEMAN CLOSES DOOR…

> I'll see ya next time.

GENTLEMAN OPENS DOOR TO SURVEY AREA, LADY'S HAND PULLS HIM BACK IN.

(INT. DINING ROOM)

OLD MAN
I never seen one of those. What's it for?

LADY
Pouring coffee.

OLD MAN
Pouring coffee?

LADY
See, it's a coffee pot. You pour the coffee into the cup and then you drink it from the cup. I'm going to drink it.

                    OLD MAN
Ohh, ahh, what'd they think of next?

CREDITS

                    HOST V.O.
Additional voices by Nancy Van Anders.

OPENING CRAWL*

SHOW #<u>123</u>

SHOW NAME <u>DIVORCE OF LADY 'X'</u>

*Each numbered item as a single page…
Items #1-5 Centerframe
Items #6-10 Lower third of page

1   FOUR STAR
in association with
KENT SKOV

2   Presents
as L.A. Connection
production of

3   MAD MOVIES WITH THE L.A. CONNECTION

4   Tonight's Feature   DIVORCE OF LADY 'X'

5   Starring
the
Voices
of

6   Bob Buchholz

7   Connie Sue Cook

8   Stephen L. Rollman

9   Steve Pinto

10   Kent Skov

GENERIC BUMPERS*

SHOW #<u>123</u>

SHOW NAME   <u>DIVORCE OF LADY 'X'</u>

*Each numbered item as a single page…

1.   We'll be right back…

2.   Coming Up
    More Mad Movies

3.   ~~Stay Tuned for~~ [more to come…(lower ⅓ of page]
    ~~"Your Home Movies"~~

4.   Send Your Home Movies to…
    L.A. Connection Productions
    6464 Sunset Blvd., #820
    Hollywood, CA 90028
    (Include a self-addressed, stamped envelope for return of films)

5.   [The Fable (some font as #4 on previous page)]

[6   A Star is Born (same as #4)]

CLOSING CRAWL*

SHOW #<u>123</u>

SHOW NAME <u>DIVORCE OF LADY 'X'</u>

*Each numbered item as a single page...

1	Directed by Kent Skov
2	Written by Bob Buchholz Stephen L. Rollman
3	Produced by Randal W Ridges
4	Featuring Bob Buchholz Connie Sue Cook Steve Pinto Stephen L. Rollman Kent Skov
5	Associate Producers (each name single page) Martha Whitney
6	Kent Weishaus (single page)
7	Music Composed and arranged by Richard Baker Mary Newland For Panda Productons
8	Music recorded by Richard Baker
9	Theme performed by Mary Newland

CLOSING CREDIT CRAWL (CONT'D)

10	Research by	Bob Petrella Ken Segall April Winchell Ted Hardwick
11	Talent Coordinator	Martha Whitney
12	Associate Director/Stage Manager	Randal W Ridges
13	Assistants to the Producers:	Bob Buchholz Connie Sue Cook Steve Pinto Stephen L. Rollman
14	Facilities Provided by	Hy-Tone Video
15	Lighting and Camera	Bill Sheehy
16	Production Sound	Mark Hanes
17	Gaffer	Jim Drewry
18	Production Assistants	Lisa Gougas Ted Hardwick
19	Make-Up	Lora Sanders
20	Wardrobe	Annie Viccari
21	Production Secretary	Eloise Gonzalez
22	Post-Production Coordinated by	Monti Santilli Rainbolt
23	Post-Production Facilities	Complete Post, Inc.
23a	Editor	Brent Carpenter
24	Post-Production Audio by	Michael Perricone Michaele Hogan

3-3-3-3

CLOSING CREDIT CRAWL (CONT'D)

25   "Your Home Movies" submitted by
Athena Marie
Los Angeles, CA

26   Location provided by
Hotel Hollywood
5825 Sunset Blvd., Hollywood CA.

27   Executive in Charge of Production for Four Star Television
Bob Bosen

28   Special Thanks to:
Susan Lenti   Dennis Condon
Budget Films   Snagglepuss
Richard Holiday

29   Promotion by
Dan Acree

30   Opening Title Montage by
Homer & Associates

31   Opening Title Photography by
Abe Perlstein

32   Post-Production Supervised by
Randal W Ridges

33   Executive Producer
Kent Skov

34   "Celebrity Voices and Appearances Impersonated"

35   Copyright 1985 Four Star International, Inc.
All Rights Reserved

D.O.A.

With the

SHORT RUNDOWN FOR SHOW # <u>114 D.O.A.</u>

DESCRIPTION	IN	OUT	SEGMENT TIME
SHOW OPEN	33:00	34:54	01:54
COMMERCIAL BREAK #1	34:54	36:57	02:03
ACT I	36:57	44:01	07:56
COMMERCIAL BREAK #2	44:01	46:04	02:03
ACT II	46:04	52:49	06:45
COMMERCIAL BREAK #3	52:49	54:52	02:03
ACT III/SHOW CLOSE	54:52	01:00	05:08

MAD MOVIES WITH THE L.A. CONNECTION

RUNDOWN   SHOW # <u>114 D.O.A.</u>

All times are in minutes and seconds	IN	OUT	DURATION
Four Star Logo	33:00	33:05	00:05
Clip Tease #1	33:05	33:19	00:14
Opening Montage	33:19	33:47	00:28
Host Intro and Preview Clip	33:47	34:54	01:07
Commercial Black #1	34:54	36:57	02:03
Bumper #1	36:57	37:00	00:03
Movie Segment #1 (includes Host Toss)	37:00	43:24	06:24
Host and Preview Clip	43:24	44:01	00:37
Commercial Black #2	44:01	46:04	02:03
Bumper #2	46:04	46:07	00:03
Movie Segment #2	46:07	52:45	06:38
Bumper #3	52:45	52:49	00:04
Commercial Black #2	52:49	54:52	02:03
Bumper #4	54:52	54:55	00:03

MAD MOVIES WITH THE L.A. CONNECTION

RUNDOWN, Pg 2   SHOW # <u>114 D.O.A.</u>

	IN	OUT	DURATION
Movie Segment #3	54:55	58:14	03:19
Host Intro to Home Movie	58:14	58:37	00:23
Home Movie (includes Billboard at tail)	58:37	59:40	01:03
Host Wrap-up	59:40	2:00:15	00:35
Clip Tease #2	2:00:15	2:00:30	00:15
Closing Montage (includes L.A. Connection Logo)	00:30	00:55	00:25
Four Star Logo	00:55	01:00	00:05

D.O.A.
#114

CLIP TEASE

RICO
Mad Movies is on, they're dubbing my voice.

MARY JANE
Are they dubbing my voice too?

RICO
Yeah, but for only one scene.

MARY JANE
Why only one, is it the way I look, the way I wear my hair?

RICO
No, I think it's that stupid blouse you made out of coasters.

MARY JANE
Well...

MUSIC THEME

ACT I

SHOW INTRO

EXT. MOTEL BALCONY

HOST
Hi, I'm Kent Skov and welcome to Mad Movies with the L.A. Connection. What you've just seen is a clip from our version of D.O.A., originally about a desperate man with only 24 hours to live. But our actors changed the dialogue completely. We thought the star

(OVER CLIP OF RICO)

looked like a famous Latin bandleader from an old tv sitcom.

(BACK TO HOST)

So we decided to write a whole new episode that you can't see anywhere else.

CUT TO CLIP TEASE

RUCY
Let's go to Rico's club. He'll put us in the show.

REAGAN
That's a great idea. If I don't get a job soon, I may have to run for president.

WELK
If you do, I'll throw this in Rico's face.

RICO
I can't promise any of you a number in the show.

RUCY
Oh Rico, you can't promise a number for us? Well, I got a number for you…immigration.

HOST
If you recall, Rico was a bandleader who worked in a nightclub called the Tropicana. We thought wouldn't it be a gas if we went to the Tropicana. But of course there isn't one, there never was one. So instead we came to the Tropicana Motel. So don't go away, we'll be right back with our Mad Movie. I wonder if Ethel ever took any towels from here.

KNOCKS ON DOOR

COMMERCIAL #1

EXT.—HOTEL BALCONY

HOST
Well, as I promised, here's the L.A. Connection's version of D.O.A.

D.O.A.

INT. APT.

JERRY
(O.C.)
Mr. Ricardo?
(Enters)

RICO
That's dinner? I ordered steak, baked potatoes, okra and a burrito.

JERRY
Well, all we had was a glass of cheese.

RICO
What about my pudding surprise?

JERRY
I ate that on the elevator. Surprise? Anyway, it's bad for your teeth.

RICO
How would you know?

JERRY
I'm also a dentist on the "Dick Van Dyke Show." Well, excuse me, Mr. Welk.
(exits)

WELK
Hey Rico, I was wondering if I could use your telephone. We're having a party across the hall and my bubble machine is broken. Say, why don't you join us? Bring your bongos.

RICO

Ok.

WELK

I've got to call Bobby and Sissy. Operator, get me a one and a two and a three.

(INT. APT.)

WELK

I'm back, folks. Please hold your applause. Rico here decided to join us. Rico, I'd like you here to introduce Nancy and Ronald Reagan.

RICO

Nice to meet you.

REAGAN

I'm an actor. Nancy tells me what to do.

WELK

A wonderful, a wonderful.

RUCY

When it comes to the polka, I can't keep up with Fred Astair.

ASTAIR

I can't dance, don't ask me.

WELK

You know your wife, Rucy, and this is Fred Astair.

ASTAIR

You've got quite a wife, we were dancing pretty well 'til she hit me in the head with that hat.

RUCY

Rico, you'll need a napkin.

RICO

Aw, that's okay, I'll use my fingers.

RUCY

Oh, he always puts on a show.

ASTAIR

Show?! I'll call Ginger.

NANCY

Show?! I can get a hold of the Beach Boys. It'll be great.

STACY

I could show you my act, but there's not room enough in here for the giraffes and the Frank Zappa blow-up doll.

RUCY

Well, let's all go down to Rico's club, The Tropicana and he'll put us all in the show.

REAGAN
That sounds great. If I don't get a job soon, I'll have to run for president.

WELK
You do, and I'll throw this in Rico's face.

CROWD
Ha, ha, ha.

RICO
Wait, I can't promise any of you a number in the show.

RUCY
Aw Ricky, you can't promise a number for us? Well, I've got one for you…Immigration.

CROWD
Ha, ha, ha.

INT. CLUB

RUCY
Rico, your club's too small.

RICO
Thanks, you don't have to tell anyone.

RUCY
Rico.

INTO BEDROOM

RUCY
(MUMBLE)
Rucy, Rucy.
(THOUGHT)
I shouldn't have drank that whole glass of cheese.
(MUMBLE)
Rucy.
(THOUGHT)
Where's that pain in the neck, what if she left me?
(CRY)
Babba loo hoo hoo.
(THOUGHT)
Boy, is my hair greasy. I'd better get dressed.

(INT. LIVING ROOM)

(SFX: PHONE RING)

RICO
Rucy?!

                          ETHEL
                        (mumbles)

                          RICO
Oh, it's you, Ethel. I was hoping it was Rucy. She's disappeared.

                          ETHEL
Ed's gone too, along with the refrigerator, our shower curtain and worst of all, a box of pancake mix.

                          RICO
Ed must have run away with Rucy. How could they do such a thing? Running off and leaving us with nothing for breakfast.

CHYRON—"ONE WEEK LATER"—OVER PICTURE.

(INT. POLICE STATION)

                          RICO
Listen McGarrett, I need the police's help.

                         MCGARRETT
Park it.

                          RICO
My wife Rucy is missing. I think she ran off with Ed Nertz. I've looked in every cran and nookie, and you're my last hope.

                         MCGARRETT
This wouldn't be Rucy Bicardo, 5'7", 115 lbs, red hair?

                          RICO
Jess.

                         MCGARRETT
Never heard of her. Danno, take this order down to Wo Fat's World of Won Ton and make sure I get a fortune cookie this time. So, Mr. Bicardo, you want to tell us your story? Or do you want to sit there with your mouth hangin' open.

                          RICO
I'd like to sit here with my mouth open, but the flies will get out. My life began to go down the toilet last week.

(SFX: TOILET FLUSH)

(INT. RICKY'S OFFICE)

                          RICO
                          (V.O.)
I was in my office showing my secretary pictures of my little Rico. Then Ethel came in…

                          ETHEL
Rucy's on the phone.

RICO
…and here is Little Rico in his sombrero. Tell Rucy I'll be late, Ehtel.

ETHEL
Alright, Rico.

RICO
And here he is bare on a naked rug.

STACY
He's so cute, I could just hold him and squeeze him.

RICO
…like tooth paste.

ED
Hey Rico, I'm taking Rucy's car to Mexico to fix the windshield-wiper.

STACY
Adios, Ed.

RICO
Hey, wait a minute. What's Rucy gonna drive?

ED
She's going with me.

(EXT. STREET)

RICO
(V.O.)
I should have been suspicious when I remembered that we don't even own a car. That reminded me, I got to change my own oil. I decided to check with my neighbors to see if they'd heard from Rucy.

(SFX: DOOR KNOCKS)

(INT. HALL)

RICO
Mrs. Trumole. I know you're in there. I hear you branding cattle. Have you seen Rucy or Little Rico?

MRS. TRUMPLE
Well, no it's just that…

RICO
Do you know where they are?

MAID
Hey pal, little Rico's 32 years old and you owe Mrs. Trumple $30,000 in babysitting fees.

RICO
I do.

MRS. TRUMPLE
Well, if it's too much trouble.

RICO
I'll check for change…nope!

(EXT. STREET)

CROWD
Aaaaaaa-wee

RICKY
Rucy, here Rucy.

(INT. DR. OFFICE)

RICO
I'm looking for Rucy.

NURSE #1
Oh, it's Rico Bicardo.

NURSE #2
I want his shirt.

NURSE #1
And I want his tie.

NURSE #2
I want his wallet.

DOCTOR
Who the heck do you think you are?

RICKY
Rico Bicardo, famous Cuban bandleader.

DR.
Oh, in that case, come on in.

(INT. DR'S OFFICE)

RICO
(thought)
Darn those nurses, they couldn't resist rumpling me to bits.

DOCTOR
Care for some coffee? It's my own special blend.

RICO
Coffee!? How can you think of coffee at a time like this?

DR.

Times like these were made for tasting coffee. This was brewed in a nuclear powered coffee machine.

                        RICO

Fill it to the rim.

                        DR.

Geez, he never has a second test tube at home.

(EXT. LIQUOR STORE)

                        HOST

We've moved on to the Tropicana Liquor Store. I doubt very much whether this place has a floor show. Anyway, we'll be right back with our Mad Movie in a minute. But first, take a look at what happens when Little Rico goes crazy after he gets his driver's permit.

(TURNS TO L. STORE)

I wonder if this place has a two drink minimum.

CLIP TEASE

(EXT. IN CONVERTIBLE CAR)

                        LITTLE RICO

I don't have a license, Dad. So if anything happens, it's you who's responsible.

(SFX: CAR HITTING BODY)

                        O.C. VOICE
                        (SCREAMS)

CHRYON OVER PICTURE—"WE'LL BE RIGHT BACK"

                        LITTLE RICKY

That's one.

(SFX: ASST. BODIES BEING HIT)

COMMERCIAL NUMBER TWO

ACT TWO

<u>D.O.A.</u> (SCENE GOES IN AFTER DR. W/COFFEE IN TEST TUBE SCENE, COMES UP AFTER COMMERCIAL)

(INT. APT)

                        BUTLER

There's a Mister Ricardo here to see you, Miss Ramsey.

                        RICO

Betty, last time I saw you, you didn't have a butler.

BETTY
After I lost my husband, Ralph, in that bowling mishap, I didn't feel safe without a man around the apartment. So, I hired the first stud who came along. What's up, Rico?

RICO
I've been looking all over for Rucy.

BETTY
Checked with missing persons?

RICO
No, they were missing, but I've checked every ally and gutter.

BETTY
Oh Rico…
(Sobs)
(And blows her nose)

BUTLER
You shouldn't have brought up bowling.

(INT. HOTEL LOBBY)

HOTEL MANAGER
So you lost your wife. Take mine, please.

RICO
Thanks.

H.M.
Here's my keys. Go down and pick her up.

RICO
I don't care for bald women, but I'll see if anyone in the lobby wants her.

(SFX: PHONE RINGS)

H.M.
What!?

(INT. APT.)

RICO
Ethel, any word from Ed yet?

ETHEL
(mumbles)

RICO
Ethel, will you turn the phone around.

ETHEL
Is this better, Rico? So that's what the problem's been. I've always had trouble…

RICO

>   Will you stop talking and tell me what you called to say.
>
>   ETHEL
>   Well alright. I found this note. It says, "Darling, I miss you. I'm
>   sorry for anything I may have done…"
>
>   RICO
>   Be mine forever. I love you.
>
>   ETHEL
>   That's right. How'd you know?
>
>   RICO
>   Darn it, Ethel. I wrote that note. Put it back and stay out of my
>   apartment. Arg!

(INT. BLD. HALLWAY)

>   RICO
>   (thought)
>   Maybe the Mission Impossible Force can help me.

(INT. OFFICE RECP.)

>   RICO
>   I'd like to see Mr. Phelps.
>
>   BEVERLY
>   It's Phillips.
>
>   RICO
>   I have an impossible mission for him.
>
>   BEVERLY
>   I'll see if he's in. I'll use my secret Dick Tracy intercom.

(SFX: CATTLE MOOS)

>   We know you're in there. He's branding cattle. Go in.

(INT. OFFICE)

>   PHILLIPS

(SFX: COWS MOOING IN BACKGROUND)

>   Mr. Bicardo.
>
>   RICO
>   I need your help.
>
>   PHILLIPS
>   Sit—you're on my branding iron.
>
>   RICO
>   (YELLS)

(EXT. BLDG. STEPS)

RICO

Yeoooooow! Mi tostado. You're it! Tag, you're it. Tag, you're it! Tag, you're it. You're it! Tag, you're it!
(thought)
I'll hide behind the news stand. They'll never find me here. Aw, forget it.
(Yells)
Ollie, Ollie, oxen free.

(INT. RUCY JR'S APT.)

RICO

Junior, could you get this picture of Sean Penn autographed for me?

RUCY JR.

He dumped me for Madonna!

RICO

Maybe you should have worn your bra on the outside. Well, what about your Mother?

RUCY JR.

Mother? She doesn't wear a bra.

RICO

That's not what I meant. Have you heard from her or have you seen her? By the way, you have something there on your chin.

RUCY JR.

Oh yeah, that's the paint thinner.

RICO

Oh, trying to remove some of that make-up, huh?

RUCY JR.

You know how sensitive I am about that. You haven't had a kind word to say to me ever since I made "The Jazz Singer" with Neil Diamond. And you, you've got your hand in front of my face. That does it, give me your check book. Yey, you bought a weed-eater at Sears.

RICO

It's for the guys in the band. You shouldn't play with these things in the house. Checks are dangerous.

RUCY JR.

So are Poles and Swedes.

RICO

We're going to Little Rico's.

RUCY JR.

I'm not going over there. His house smells like a cat box.

RICO

You broke my frame and you're gonna pay for it.

INT. LITTLE RICO'S CASA

RICO
Little Rico, we've been waiting for you.

LITTLE RICO
Pop's here lookin' for Mom. But Mom ran away with Ed Nertz. Oh Mr. De Cordova, I've got the deed to the Nertz property.

RICO
Nertz property?

MR. DE CORDOVA
That's right. Ed sold the apartments and I'm raising your rent.

RICO
How can you raise the rent? I got bad plumbing.

LITTLE RICO
So do I, I think it's hereditary. But I'm not one to hold a grudge.
(laugh)

RICO
Then hold this.

LITTLE RICO
Why you...

(EXT. IN CONVERTIBLE CAR)

LITTLE RICO
I don't have a license, Dad. So if anything happens, you're responsible.

(SFX: CAR HITTING BODY)

O.C. VOICE
(screams)

LITTLE RICO
That's one.

(SFX: ASST. BODIES BEING HIT)

LITTLE RICO
Two, three, four, seven, ten.

RICO

(SFX: BRAKES SCREECH)

That's enough, that's enough. This is my stop. I gotta run.

(INT. BLDG. HALLWAY)

RICO
(thought)
Alright, they just waxed the floor.

(SFX: SLIDE WHISTLE)

Wheeeeeeeee.

                    UMPIRE V.O.
You're safe.

(SFX: CROWD GOING WILD)

(INT. PHILLIPS OFFICE)

                    RICO
Mr. Phelps.

                    PHILLIPS
It's Phillips. How many times do I have to tell you that? What is it, Rico?

                    RICO
I autographed a picture for you.

                    PHILLIPS
But this is a picture of Sean Penn.

                    RICO
Yeah, but it's my handwriting.

                    PHILLIPS
Are you sure?

                    RICO
Yeah, I was there when I wrote it.

                    PHILLIPS
There's scribble on the back.

                    RICO
Yeah, I know, my pen wouldn't write at first.

                    PHILLIPS
What's this for?

                    RICO
Payment.

                    PHILLIPS
Payment for what?

                    RICO
Another mission. It's dangerous, very. I'm afraid you'd be risking your life.

                    PHILLIPS
You want me to find the birds that messed up your suit, huh?

                    RICO
That's right, Mr. Phelps.

(INT. RICKY'S HOTEL RM)

                    RICO
Babaloo, Babaloo!
                    (O.C.)
                (Cuban yells and yips)

                    BELLBOY
Stop that.

                    RICO
Good!

                    BELLBOY
Can I please have Sean Penn's autograph?

                    RICO
Sure. Hey, I ordered bacon and eggs.

                    BELLBOY
All we had was a glass of ham.

                    RICO
Oh, great.

                    RICO
                    (mumble)
Wait!

                    BELLBOY
Yes, sir?

                    RICO
This glass is dirty.

                    BELLBOY
You didn't order a clean one.

(INT. RICKY'S OFFICE)

                    RICO
                    (enters)
Ethel, I love you. Fate has brought us together.

                    ETHEL
                    (sobs)
                    (sneezes)

                    RICO
Gesundheit!

                    ETHEL
Rico, I'm falling for you too, but I'm allergic to your hair cream. It stinks! What is it made from, pig grease?

                    RICO
Yes, as a matter of fact, it is.

> ETHEL

Aaa yuk ooo.

(INT. MR. DRUCKER'S BAR AND CAFE)

> MR. DRUCKER

Howdy, folks!

> ETHEL

Hi, Mr. Drucker. Hi, Renko.

> RICO

Renko, can we sit by you?

> RENKO

Sit over there and behave yourself.

> RICO

Let's sit over here.

> ETHEL

Thanks, Rico. Say, can I have one of those to tap? This is really a lot of fun.

> RICO

If you think that's fun, try lighting the wrong end.

> DRUCKER

Arnold Ziffel called.

> ETHEL

What did he say, Mr. Drucker?

> DRUCKER

Mr. Douglas shot Mr. Haney and Arnold got elected Mayor of Hooterville.

> RICO
> (MUMBLES)

> DRUCKER

Yeah, but you didn't order a clean glass.

> ETHEL

Chug it, Rico.

> RICO
> (GULPS AND BELCHES)

CHYRON—"RICO ON THE EDGE" OVER PICTURE

COMMERCIAL #3

(EXT. NIGHT, BUS AND CAR)

> MR. DECORDOVA
> (O.C.)

Hey, hey, that's Rico Bicardo. I know that guy. I met him earlier today. Hey, hey Rico. I know his kids, too. Hey, Rico, hey, Rico, over here, in the car. Say hi to my cousins here from Kansas City. Hey, Rico, Rico, hey, Rico. Hey, is that Rucy's mom sitting next to you? Hey, Mrs. McGillicutty. Hey, Rico. Forget it. Another stuck up movie star.

(SFX: CAR HONKING)

INT. APT. BALCONY

                            MARY JANE
I don't know where Rucy is. All I have is that note.

                            RICO
Are you talking about this note that's all crumpled and sweaty?

                            MARY JANE
Yeah, that's the one. I got it from Ethel. She said that she found it somewhere at home.

                            RICO
She found it in my apartment. I wrote it.

                            O.C. VOICES
Hey! Isn't that Rico Bicardo up there on that balcony? I know that guy. Hey, Rico.

(SFX: SLIDE WHISTLE)

                            RICO
Look, Betty, I don't care if you're one of Rucy's best friends. I gonna stuff you in a conga drum.

                            MARY JANE
Whatever you do, don't put me in the closet.

                            RICO
Good idea, and develop my pictures while you're in there.

EXT. BUSHES IN FRONT OF BUILDING

                            JACK
It's Rico, hey, Rico, gimme a piggy-back ride.

                            RICO
No!

                            JACK
Hey, everybody, it's Rico. Over here. Hey Rico, Rico, wait up for us. Sing Babaloo for us.

EXT. SIDEWALK, NIGHT

                            RICO
If Ed Nertz were here, I'd pound his papaya.

                            ETHEL

Rico, don't be mad at Ed and Rucy. If they hadn't run off, we'd never have fallen in love. I'm so happy, I could dance.

RICO

Oh, don't do that, Ethel.

ETHEL

(SFX: BONES)

Ah, Rico, my back.

RICO

Sorry, it was the only way I knew to stop you.

(SONG)

ETHEL

I love you so much Rico, so much that it hurts.
I was so very sicko, of being Mrs. Nertz.
I love the special feeling when your chin dents in my head.
Now my heart is reeling, for I am rid of Ed.
Oh, I'm so nuts about you, I love you to death.
Why won't you face me? Is there something on my breath?
When I grab your armpits, I can tell you'd be wise,
To buy an antiperspirant especially for guys.

RICO

In my search for Rucy, my energy was spent but Ethel, now you can see.

ETHEL
(HARMONIZE)

Yes, I see.

RICO

I stiffed you for the rent. Nice set of thighs.

ETHEL

Thanks.

(SFX: Monkey Kiss)

(INT. POLICE STATION)

MCGARRET

I'm sorry, Mr. Bicardo, the guys in the back were making faces and I wasn't paying attention. Could you repeat your story?

RICO

You weren't listening.
(sobs)

MCGARRET

Rico, don't lose that temper.

RICO
BUT...but...
(SOBS...CRIES)
Carama, ay chihuahua, que terible, ay Fernando, que verguensa, babaloo.

MCGARRET
What a baby.

DETECTIVE
What do we put on his report?

MCGARRET
Just use the initials for dreadfully over acting.

###

EXT. WRAP OUTSIDE COFFEE SHOP

(OFF CAM. HOST)
Well, that brings us to a close to another Mad Movie. As you can see
(PUSH IN TO HOST'S FACE)
We've moved on to the Tropicana Coffee Shop. You know, rewriting the plots of Hollywood movies is fun, but it's no more of a challenge than writing dialogue to your home movies. Tonight's was sent in by Melinda Philbrook of Norwalk, Conn., and it's the story of a lucky family that goes from Rags to Riches.

(Four Second teaser "Rags to Riches" over picture of "umbrella man")

HOME MOVIE

RAGS TO RICHES
Well, hello there. This is a story about me, my kids, and how we went from rags to riches. For years we were so poor we existed on watermelon alone. Pretend you're eating something else I told the kids. Most of the time they couldn't take it. Then one day, as we were leaving the supermarket, we were given our free Scratch N'Win game pieces. We were thrilled to discover we'd won a chance to compete in their talent contest. I don't want to brag, but we have talent. Some people would have given their eyeteeth to be in our position, but the competition was tough. There was the one man valet ballet, a skilled parking lot acrobat, and a man who could locate missing persons just like that. But were we scared? NO! We pulled out all the stops and created this magnificent living family portrait...seen here in progress. Well, you could've heard a pin drop as the judges emerged from their endless deliberations. This was the moment we've been waiting for. Had we really won? Well, their smiling faces told the whole story. When we got all of our prizes home, dad washed our brand new car while mom performed the baptism.

HOST, EXT. COFFEE SHOP

                    HOST
If you'd like your home movies made into Mad Movies,

(OVER ADD.)

send them to the L.A. Connection, 6464 Sunset, Hollywood,
California, 90028.

EXT. HOST NEAR HIGHWAY

                    HOST
Well, that's our show for this week. Our Tropicanarama has led us
to one last location. The Hollywood Tropicana Nightclub, but it's
quite a bit different

(HOST WALKS CLOSER TO NIGHTCLUB)

than the Tropicana Rico once played.

INTO FRAME WITH NIGHTCLUB IN BACKGROUND.

You see, at this particular Tropicana,

PUSH TO MARQUEE HIGHLIGHTING FESTIVITIES—FEMALE MUD WRESTLING

you see a lot more babaloo than you hear.
See you next time.

ENDING CRAWL…

CLIP TEASE

                    RICO
It was fun watching Mad Movies with you, but I really have to go
now.

                    OLD MAN
Listen to me, man. You're not really Rico Bicardo.

                    RICO
Of course I'm Rico Bicardo, what do you mean I'm not Rico
Bicardo? The L.A. Connection just did a whole show about me
being Rico Bicardo, and they wouldn't lie. If Rucy calls, tell her
I'm down at the club.

HOST V.O. OVER CRAWL

Additional voices by April Winchell.

OPENING CRAWL*

SHOW # <u>114</u>

SHOW NAME <u>D.O.A.</u>

*Each numbered item as a single page…
Items #1-5 Centerframe
Items #6-10 Lower third of page

1   FOUR STAR
    in association with
    KENT SKOV

2   Presents
    as L.A. Connection
     production of

3   MAD MOVIES WITH THE L.A. CONNECTION

4   Tonight's Feature D.O.A.

5   Starring
      the
     Voices
      of

6   Bob Buchholz

7   Connie Sue Cook

8   Stephen L. Rollman

9   Steve Pinto

10   Kent Skov

GENERIC BUMPERS*

SHOW #<u>114</u>

SHOW NAME <u>D.O.A.</u>

*Each numbered item as a single page…

1   We'll be right back…

2   Coming Up
         More Mad Movies

3   Stay Tuned for
         "Your Home Movies"

4   Send Your Home Movies to…
         L.A. Connection Productions
         6464 Sunset Blvd., #820
         Hollywood, CA 90028
         (Include a self-addressed, stamped envelope for return of films)

5   Rags To Riches   (Homemovie Title)

CLOSING CRAWL*

SHOW # <u>114</u>

SHOW NAME <u>D.O.A.</u>

*Each numbered item as a single page...

1	Directed by Kent Skov
2	Written by Bob Buchholz Stephen L. Rollman
3	Produced by Randal W Ridges
4	Featuring Bob Buchholz Connie Sue Cook Steve Pinto Stephen L. Rollman Kent Skov
5	Associate Producers (each name single page) Martha Whitney
6	Kent Weishaus
7	Music Composed and arranged by Richard Baker Mary Newland
8	For Panda Productions Music recorded by Richard Baker
9	Theme performed by Mary Newland

CLOSING CREDIT CRAWL (CONT'D)

10	Research by	Bob Petrella Ken Segall April Winchell Ted Hardwick
11	Talent Coordinator	Martha Whitney
12	Associate Director/Stage Manager	Randal W Ridges
13	Assistants to the Producers:	Bob Buchholz Connie Sue Cook Steve Pinto Stephen L. Rollman
14	Facilities Provided by	Hy-Tone Video
15	Lighting and Camera	Bill Sheehy
16	Production Sound	Mark Hanes
17	Gaffer	Jim Drewry
18	Production Assistants	Lisa Gougas Ted Hardwick
19	Make-Up	Lora Sanders
20	Wardrobe	Annie Vicari
21	Production Secretary	Eloise Gonzalez
22	Post-Production Coordinated by	Monti Santilli Rainbolt
23	Post-Production Facilities	Complete Post, Inc.
24	Post-Production Audio by	Michael Perricone Michaele Hogan For Interloc Prod. Studios

3-3-3-3

CLOSING CREDIT CRAWL (CONT'D)

25 "Your Home Movies" submitted by
   Melinda Philbrook
   Norwalk, CT

26 Location provided by
   Tropican Motel
   8585 Santa Monica Blvd.
   West Hollywood, CA

27 Executive in Charge of Production for Four Star Television
   Bob Bosen

28 Special Thanks to:
   Susan Lenti Dennis Condon
   Budget Films Snaggelpuss
   Richard Holiday

29 Promotion by
   Dan Acree

30 Opening Title Montage by
   Homer & Associates

31 Opening Title Photography by
   Abe Perlstein

32 Post-Production Supervised by
   Randal W Ridges

33 Executive Producer
   Kent Skov

34 "Celebrity Voices and Appearances Impersonated"

35 Copyright 1985 Four Star International, Inc.
   All Rights Reserved

DOLL FACE

With the

SHORT RUNDOWN FOR SHOW # <u>109 DOLL FACE</u>

Description	In	Out	Seg Time
Show Open	00:00	01:10	01:10
Commercial Break #1	01:10	03:13	02:03
Act I	03:13	09:59	06:46
Commercial Break #2	09:59	12:02	02:03
Act II	12:02	20:08	08:06
Commercial Break #3	20:08	22:11	02:03
Act III/Show Close	22:11	28:00	05:49

MAD MOVIES WITH THE L.A. CONNECTION

RUNDOWN   SHOW # <u>109 DOLL FACE</u>

All times are in minutes and seconds	IN	OUT	DURATION
Four Star Logo (slug Black)	00:00	00:05	00:05
Show Open: Clip Tease.	00:05	00:20	00:15
Opening Montage.	00:20	01:10	00:50
Commercial Black #1	01:10	03:13	02:03
Bumper #1	03:13	03:16	00:03
Wrap #1	03:16	03:46	00:30
Movie Segment #1	03:46	09:55	06:09
Bumper #2 (Next…Your Home Movie)	09:55	09:59	00:04
Commercial Black #2	09:59	12:02	02:03
Bumper #3	12:02	12:05	00:03
Man On The Street Intro. (as needed)	12:05	12:11	00:06
Man On The Street or Interview Segment.	12:11	12:58	00:47
Movie Segment #2	12:58	16:15	03:17
Home Movie Intro.	16:15	16:42	00:27
Home Movie	16:42	17:40	00:58
Movie Segment #3	17:40	20:04	02:24

MAD MOVIES WITH THE L.A. CONNECTION

RUNDOWN   SHOW # <u>109 DOLL FACE</u>

	IN	OUT	DURATION
Bumper #4	20:04	20:08	00:04
Commercial Black #3	20:08	22:11	02:03
Bumper #5	22:11	22:14	00:03
Movie Segment #4	22:14	25:49	03:49
Toss to Preview	25:49	25:54	00:06
Preview	25:54	26:24	00:30
Final Close	26:24	26:53	00:29
Closing Montage	26:53	27:50	00:57
L.A. Connection Logo	27:50	27:55	00:05
Four Star Logo (slug black)	27:55	28:00	00:05

DOLL FACE SHOW NUMBER 109

CLIP TEASE

CYRANO
I'm very excited. Mad Movies with the L.A. Connection is coming on in a minute. It's absolutely my favorite show. Every time I watch it, I laugh out loud. I go like this…ha, ha, ha, ha!

MUSIC INTRO

COMMERCIAL #1

KENT
Hi! I'm Kent Skov and welcome to Mad Movies with the L.A. Connection. Tonight's feature is called "Doll Face." The original story was all about… well, that's not important. Our story is about a great American institution; the beauty pageant, where women will do just about anything for the coveted title of Miss Doll Face.

CONNIE
And now, for the intelligence portion of the competition, I would like to recite the formula for hydrogen fusion in Spanish.

KENT
I think I'd rather watch the movie.

INT. SODA SHOP

SODA JERK
Gonna order?

VANESSA
First I'd like to meet this gentleman. How are ya?

BARRY GOMO
Fine, I'm Barry Gomo. I'm the emcee of the Miss Doll Face contest.

VANESSA
Gee, do you think you could slip me into that contest? I don't have any silicone implants and these are my real eyes.

BARRY GOMO
That's not bad, baby. That's what they look for.

VANESSA
And I had an operation to keep my ears from sticking out.

BARRY GOMO
I had that operation too but they screwed up and now I howl whenever there is a full moon.

VANESSA
It's been my life's ambition to win a beauty pageant. If you can't get me in, I'll shoot myself. I'll throw myself into the river or become a window washer.

BARRY GOMO

Well I'll try.

INT. BACKSTAGE

FLOYD

This is the fifth contestant you've picked up at that soda shop this week. What's this Vanessa like?

BARRY GOMO

She likes walks in the rain and young men about 18.

FLOYD

Well Barry, she'd better be at least five feet tall and a knock out.

BARRY GOMO

See you at the soda shop.

FLOYD

I'll be there as soon as I find myself a longer tie.

BLACK

INT. SODA SHOP

VANESSA

Burp.

BARRY

Don't be such a pig, Floyd.

FLOYD

What do ya mean?

BARRY

Vanessa's been sitting with you for over 13 minutes. Why don't you give me a chance with her?

VANESSA

Gee, it seems longer.

FLOYD

Well, you know you can stay here with me.

VANESSA

Oh no!

FLOYD
(Thought)

I wish I had that swing on my back porch, and she's not bad either. Harold!

HAROLD
(Thought)

Oh boy, not again.

FLOYD
I want you to make me a soda, with two scoops of ice cream in a glass, with some whipped cream and a cherry on top.

HAROLD
Gee Floyd, I never heard of such a thing.

FLOYD
I guess that's why they call you a soda jerk.

HAROLD
(Mumbles)

BLACK

EXT. STREET

BARRY
Congratulations, you made it into the preliminaries of Miss Doll Face contest. I think you can pass, that is, of course, if you're willing to follow the "rules." Are you?

VANESSA
I never heard anyone talk so slow in my entire life.

BARRY
I have some valium.

VANESSA
Well, that explains it.

BARRY
I haven't taken them yet.

BLACK

INT. STAGE

(SFX: TAPPING)

ZEKE
These women are ugly.

JACK
Good thing we screen 'em first.

ZEKE
Get rid of 'em. Next.

VANESSA
Hi I'm Vanessa Bumpis and my life's ambition is to be Miss Doll Face and win hundreds and thousands of prizes.

ZEKE
Do you have any naked pictures?

VANESSA
Oh yes, I have more than you can imagine. I have Suzanne Somers, Joan Collins, Madonna and Ed McMahon.

ZEKE
Are those your real eyes?

VANESSA
Yes they are, right, Amadeus?

PIANO PLAYER
Yeah.
(Laugh)

ZEKE
Well, what is your stand on world peace?

VANESSA
Well, I think kinda like this.

BLACK

INT. BOOKSTORE

BOOK CLERK
If you're getting a contestant rule book you should be aware of the changes...In the second chapter, rule seventeen now says every contestant must sleep with the judges in order to qualify for the finals.

FLOYD
That's not a new rule, we've been doing that for years.

BOOK CLERK
Huh.

INT. LIVING ROOM

VANESSA
Well Mr. Zeke I've read the rule book and I have a question.

ZEKE
You're probably referring to that new rule seventeen. We felt the rule about sleeping with the judges was necessary to weed out the girls who are just in this contest for the scholarships.

VANESSA
Well, I...oh.

KEN
Ever been involved in a scandal?

VANESSA
Well, no.

ZEKE
We'll soon fix that.

                        KEN

Are you ready?

                        VANESSA

For rule 43? I'll try it, Ken.

(SFX: KISS)

                        KEN

Wonderful, you broke the old record…I'll go get a trumpet and test you on rule 39.

INT. BACK STAGE

                        FLOYD

Now girls, on rule six, disregard the part about spaghetti, it's been replaced with ball-peen hammers.

(SFX: APPLAUSE)

                        SHARMIN

Floyd, I got sort of a dilemma.

                        FLOYD

What is it, Sharmin? If you've got a problem, I'm here to solve it.

                        SHARMIN

You gotta talk to the hairdresser. He cut my hair with his elbows. He made my hair look like parsley. And these tomatoes don't need garnish.

                        FLOYD

Well, what if I shoot him?

                        SHARMIN

Perfect.

(SFX: BOINK, BOINK, BOINK, BOINK)

INT. BACKSTAGE

                        BARRY

Barbie, how'd the bathing suit competition go?

                        BARBIE

I lost several points because I got caught wearing a foam rubber butt.

                        BARRY

I told you, you should have worn it inside your bathing suit.

                        BARBIE

I wasn't wearing a bathing suit.

                        BARRY

Oh, Barbie.

EDDIE
There's a note for you.

BARBIE
Thanks, Eddie. My goodness, it's an obscene note. Which one of you two clowns wrote this? It's filled with filthy words form a secret admirer.

BARRY
I got one too, Barbie, mine has a lot of heavy breathing in it. He said he had to write a note because his phone was temporarily disconnected.

KEN
What the hell happened to your hair, Sharmin? It looks like a tape cassette exploded on your head.

SHARMIN
Oooh, Ken, since my hairdresser is in the hospital recovering from shot gun wounds, I had to find someone else to do my hair. So, I hired my gardener, he's so wonderful with roots.

INT. DRESSING ROOM

FLOYD
To win, you gotta pay.

VANESSA
How much?

FLOYD
Well, first you just get a check, then you sign it. But, leave it blank.

VANESSA
All right. Do the other girls pay?

FLOYD
No, not with money.

VANESSA
Oh Floyd, you're a wonderful judge. If all the other judges were like you, I'd be sure to win. I want to be Miss Doll Face and take the cruise around the world. Am I cutting off your circulation?

FLOYD
Yes.

VANESSA
I'll resuscitate you.

FLOYD
I think I'm falling for Vanessa.

SHARMIN
Everyone likes Vanessa, she's got beautiful hair down to here. I had the jeweler do mine.

FLOYD
Well I've had him cut my hair too.

SHARMIN
But he didn't use your family jewels.

COMMERCIAL #2/BUMPER #1

KENT
(V.O.)
While the competition continues, let's find out what kind of "Miss" competition you'd like to see.

RESPONSES:
"I'd rather see a Mister pageant, probably."
"Probably the Miss Obeese contest."
"I think I'd like to see the Miss Management pageant. Then all the people who run the post office and the department of motor vehicles could get together."
"Actually, I think pageants are dumb."
"African pageant."
"Could it be like a guy pageant?"
"Miss Tee Meanor."
"Miss Animal pageant."
"Miss Nude pageant."
"Miss Future world."
"Miss Future Vice President of America and have Geraldine Ferraro as the Emcee. You could get Walter Mondale to come out of retirement and sing "Here she comes…""
"Miss Fit pageant."

EXT. BEACH

POPEYE
Looks like she's complying with rule seventeen.

FLOYD
Get up, Ken. So uh, you having fun with my girl?

STEVE
Vanessa, wake up.

VANESSA
What is it, Ken? I was dreaming I was Annette Funicello and you were a peanut butter sandwich.

FLOYD
When it comes time to vote, Vanessa—I'm not going to pull your lever.

VANESSA
What! But Floyd, you don't understand. We were just resting, we were tired from rehearsing a scene from "Blood Beach." I'm preparing for the talent competition.

FLOYD
I suppose you're gonna wear that outfit.

VANESSA

Oh no, at first I was going to do a scene from "I Love Lucy" but then I changed my mind.

FLOYD

Oh, I see. Hey Ken, if you're not gonna light that thing, can I have it?

VANESSA

But haven't you seen the warning labels by the Surgeon General?

FLOYD

I asked you nicely for that and you bent it.

STEVE

It's chalk.

BLACK

INT. BACKSTAGE

BARRY

Barbie, you better not be a sore loser 'cause I'm gonna strip search the runners up.

BARBIE

I'd like that.

BARRY
(Thought)

I can't believe that line worked.

FLOYD

Huh, huh, huh, huh? Sure Barry, they also fall for "Hey Baby, I know Wayne Newton personally."

BARRY

Wow—Hey Barbie!

INT. DRESSING ROOM

FLOYD

Knock, knock.

SHARMIN

Who is there?

FLOYD

I forget.

SHARMIN

Don't quit your day job.

FLOYD
(Mumbles w/cig in mouth)

SHARMIN

If you're not gonna light that, give it to me.

FLOYD

It's chalk, I found it on the beach.

SHARMIN

Listen Floyd, you're a judge. You shouldn't have fallen for one of us contestants.

FLOYD

But I love that Vanessa.

SHARMIN

You have got to tell her you are not her door mat, her whipping boy, the scavenger snail in her aquarium of life.

FLOYD

That's right. I don't have to take this from Vanessa.

SHARMIN

Why don't you tell her that Nashville is the place that she should be? And to pack up her bags and move to Tennessee, hills that is, and get a longer tie while you're there.

BLACK

INT. HALLWAY NIGHT

FLOYD
(Thought)

I don't know if I should knock or ring the bell. If I ring the bell with these sweaty hands, I run the risk of electrocution. I've got to stop smoking my hands. I'd better knock. Knock! Oh good, you're home, I…

VANESSA

What the hell are you doing? What's the idea of yelling in the hall? Don't you realize it's 2:00 am? People need their sleep around here and they don't appreciate all that noise. How can you be such a dorkbrain! All these…

FLOYD
(Whispers)

Oh, I'm sorry, I just…

VANESSA

Oh great! You're not only loud, but you're also impolite. You interrupted me right in the middle of a sentence. You know things I say are important too! And keep it down out here in the hall!

BLACK

INT. HOTEL LOBBY

FLOYD

Listen Sharmin, this is the last time I'm giving you a ride, until my car's out of the shop. You're giving me a bad back.

SHARMIN

They wouldn't let me on the bus.

FLOYD

What about a taxi? Or the subway?

SHARMIN

They all say my hair is too ugly. I can't get on any public transportation. I had to rip off part of my dress to hide my head. All the trouble I've had with the hairdresser, it will be a miracle if I win Miss Photogenic.

FLOYD

Or Miss Congeniality.

CONNIE
(SUNG)

Tonight's home movie is really a peach; we visited a place that we call Beer Beach. It was submitted by a fellow named Cecil Smith and it is with his permission that we do it with. Cecil is from Standford, Califor-ny-a. You can send us your home movie, any day. Ole!

ANNOUNCER

Next time you're out hiking or on a picnic, and you realize you're running out of cold drinks, don't waste your time searching for a grocery store when there's a whole delicious world of refreshment just waiting for you to find it. And how much does it cost? Nothing! It's never far away or hard to get to. All you have to do is follow your thirst buds to…Beer Beach! A sea of icy suds, some of it already in cans and just waiting for you to carry back to your home or campsite. Take as much as you like…there's plenty more where that came from. Beer Beach! Waves of frosty brew as far as the eye can see. Bubbly and refreshing as it washes right up to you and says, "Drink me!" Cheers! Enjoy it on the rocks or have a beer chaser. Bring your best girl and watch her try to stand up sideways. And when does all the beer run out? Never! Shimmering, thirst-quenching memories that last a lifetime. Sometimes it's hard to say goodbye, so stick around. In all the world, there's only one Beer Beach!

EXT. THEATRE

HUCKSTER

Step right up, see the bearded lady, the tattooed woman and the fat lady. Doll Face contest about to start.

BLACK

INT. STAGE

BARRY

Next in the talent competition, the incredible Sharmin. But before she comes on, I have a couple of things I'd like to say…

CROWD

(SFX: APPLAUSE)

Bring on Sharmin. Get off the stage.

                    SHARMIN

(SFX: BONGOS)

I had a cat imagine that,
She ran away from me one day,
I found her in the grass and I spanked her butt.

                 LADY IN AUDIENCE
This is bad.

BLACK

INT. BACK STAGE

                    HEAD JUDGE
I know it's the middle of the pageant, Vanessa, and it's not a good time to tell you this. But you've been disqualified because you did not sleep with the judges as stated in rule seventeen.

                    VANESSA
That's not true, I slept with all of them.

                    ZEKE
What are talking about? You didn't sleep with me.

                    VANESSA
Don't you remember the other night when I fell asleep on your shoulder?

                    ZEKE
Wait a minute, that's not what rule seventeen meant. We didn't do anything.

                    FAT JUDGE
What's happening?

                    ZEKE
Did she sleep with you?

                    FAT JUDGE
No Zeke, we took a nap on the pool table and that's all.

                    PAUL
She said I looked like Paul Newman and passed out.

                    ZEKE
Yeah and one of you go ask the rest of the judges if she complied with the rule regarding "Mr. Ed" and "Hula-Hoops."

                    FAT JUDGE
Let me do it.

                    PAUL

No, I'll do it.

                    FAT JUDGE

I said I'd do it.

                    PAUL

Let me do it.

INT. BACKSTAGE

                    BARBIE

Say Barry, what's that on your wrist?

                    BARRY

Spaghetti sauce.

                    SHARMIN

So Floyd, you ran out on my poem, because you were so emotionally moved, si?

                    FLOYD

Yeah, I wanted to cry.

                    SHARMIN

I thought so.

                    BARRY

What's with him?

                    SHARMIN

He thinks that I could be the next Rod McKuen.

INT. BACKSTAGE

                    FLOYD

That's my hat.
                    (Gasps)
What's this about you not following the rules?

                    ZEKE

That's right. She slept with all us judges but didn't get naked.

                    FLOYD

Is that true?

                    VANESSA

The rule said nothing about sex, just sleep. Your snoring sounds like a bull in heat.

                    ZEKE

None of the other girls made a big beef about it. Why are you?

                    VANESSA

Because I wanted to win on my sparkling personality, you bunch of horndogs!

                    ZEKE

We'll have to re-write that rule.

FLOYD
Hey Zeke, your fly's open.

ZEKE
Oh wow.

MAN W/HAT
Mine too.

OTHER JUDGE
Oh, me too.

VANESSA
I should win!

FLOYD
I love you and I know Wayne Newton personally.

VANESSA
Zeke, Zeke, Floyd says he knows Wayne Newton personally. Is that true or just a line he uses to impress people?

ZEKE
Wayne who?

COMMERCIAL #3/BUMPER #2

INT. BACKSTAGE

ZEKE
Hey pal, what's this crap you've been feeding Vanessa about Wayne Newton. You know damn good and well you've never met him in your life.

FLOYD
I did too.

ZEKE
Yeah, tell me when.

FLOYD
Saw him in Vegas.

VANESSA
Well, seeing someone perform is not the same as knowing them.

FLOYD
I think it is!

VANESSA
Well, I've seen Liberace, but that doesn't mean I can play the piano.

FLOYD
(O.C.)

> I'm telling you I had a ring-side table. We were this close.

> ZEKE
> The Liberace—Floyd, why don't you take me to Vegas and introduce me to Wayne Newton?

> VANESSA
> Go ahead—go on.

> ZEKE
> Or maybe Liberace.

> FLOYD
> Alright, maybe I will. I'll just walk up and say, "Hey Wayne." Nay, that's no good, I'll say, "Hey Wayne." Vanessa, you better get your butt out on that stage.

INT. STAGE

> BARRY
> Well, Vanessa, are you ready for your final question?

> VANESSA
> Well, alright.

> BARRY
> What is good grocery store etiquette?

> VANESSA
> Don't race shopping carts down the aisle.

INT. STAGE

> BARRY
> Here are the runners-up…
> They have at least D-cups.
> That's how they got into the competition.
> Listen to them giggle, watch their bodies wiggle.
> It's kind of like the worms when you go fishin'.
> Though their brains are tiny, take a good look at their hiney.
> We know what all you guys out there are wishin'.

> SAILOR
> Make my wish come true.

> VANESSA
> Thanks for my big break.

> FLOYD
> She had onions for lunch.

> SHARMIN
> I could tell. You know when she goes on her world cruise, I hope her boat sinks and takes her with it.

> FLOYD
> What are you going to do?

SHARMIN

I got a call from Ripley's Believe It or Not. They want to do a special on my hair.

FLOYD

Oh-huh.

BARRY
(O.C.)

Ladies and gentlemen, I give you the winner of this year's Miss Doll Face contest, Vanessa Bumpis.

CROWD
(Cheers, etc.)

Take it off. Hey baby, I'm yours. Let me see some skin. Do Mae West!

VANESSA

Thank goodness, I won, although goodness had nothing to do with it. Thanks, big boy.

BARRY
(SONG)

There she is, Miss Doll Face, standing there with a thing on her head.

FLOYD

You're standing on my foot.

BARBIE

I didn't want you to leave until I could talk to you.

FLOYD

All you had to do was ask me; you didn't have to break my instep.

BARBIE

I could grab your arm.

FLOYD

I'd grab your…

BARBIE

What!?

FLOYD

Never mind, that's rule four and I've already done that. If you're planning on coming back next year, here's the revised rules.

BARBIE

Did they change rule seventeen?

FLOYD

Yeah, you're gonna like it. It provides for a lunch break.

BARBIE

There aren't any pictures.

FLOYD
Vanessa.

VANESSA
What is it?

FLOYD
Come with me to Vegas.

VANESSA
And give up my chance to be a centerfold?

STAGE MANAGER
You two clowns get out there.

CLOWN
What do you mean by clown?

STEVE
Where's the S.S. Princess?

POPEYE
It sailed a week ago. They're doing a special Love Boat in Wyoming. They had a chance to get George C. Scott and Marilyn Chambers.

VANESSA
But I'm Miss Doll Face and I won a cruise around the world!

KEN
I'm Ken, her escort.

POPEYE
Oh, your ship is right over here.

KEN
Watch your step on the poop deck.

VANESSA

(LONG SHOT)

Are we taking this boat to the ship?

KEN
This is the ship!

VANESSA
This is my world cruise? And some scholarship, it turned out to be at Wally Thorpe's school of trucking.

KEN
You won that lovely outfit, Vanessa. Plus that radar-range. You can cook dinner and watch for enemy aircraft at the same time.

VANESSA
Yeah, well, someone should have warned me about washing this hat in hot water.

THE END

SHOW CLOSING

KENT
Will all the finalists please come forward, please? Say, what's going on here? Where are the other finalists?

CONNIE
I gave them my bananas to let say disappear.

KENT
That's not fair.

CONNIE
Hay, cacajuate! You think it's fair that I have to wear a fruit bowl on my head?

KENT
Well for once it's good we've run out of time. See you soon for more Mad Movies.

CONNIE
What about the winner? Doesn't anybody want to see my impression of a salad fork?

CLOSING CREDITS

PANDA PRODUCTIONS　　　　　　　　　　　　　MAD MOVIES
　　　　　　　　　　　　　　　　　　　　　　　　TITLE: DOLL FACE
　　　　　　　　　　　　　PAGE 1 of 3　　SHOW # 109　　DATE:10/26/85

CUE	TITLE	COMPOSER	SOC	PUBLISHER	USEAGE	TIME
BG4	CLIP TEASE	RICHARD BAKER AND MARY NEWLAND	ASCAP	SONGSYNC MUSIC	BACKGROUND INST.	:15
T 1	MAD MOVIES THEME				SHOW OPEN VOCAL/INST	:50
BG1	KENT's THEME				B.G. INST	:29
M 1	DOLL FACE : THEME					:38
103-M3	FIFTH CONTESTANT					:16
M 2	SODA SHOP					:53
M 3	CONGRATULATIONS					:37
M 4	THESE WOMEN ARE UGLY					:15
103-M21	CONTESTANT RULE BOOK					:20
M5	READ THE RULE BOOK					:44
M6	BATHING SUIT COMPETITION					:10
108-M5	WHICH ONE OF YOU CLOWNS					:29
105-M14	TO WIN YOU GOTTA PAY					:28
B B	MAD MOVIES BUMPER	R. BAKER/M. NEWLAND			COMM BUMP	:04
B A	MAD MOVIES				VOCAL/INST	:03
M 7	COMPLYING WITH RULE 17					:19
103-M5	I'M NOT GONNA PULL YOU'RE LEVER.				B.G. INST	:35
M 8	STRIP SEARCH					:08
103-M2	KNOCK KNOCK					:33
M 9	SHOULD I RING THE BELL					:39
103-M8	CHARMIN/FLOYD					:26
F 1	HOME MOVIE INTRO	COMPOSERS: R. BAKER/M. NEWLAND AUTHORS: KEN SEGAL BOB PETRELLA			FEATURED SONG	:26
HM1	"BEER BEACH"	R. BAKER/M. NEWLAND			B.G. INST	:58

PANDA PRODUCTIONS
MAD MOVIES
TITLE: DOLL FACE
SHOW # 109   DATE:
PAGE 2 of 3

CUE	TITLE	COMPOSER	SOC	PUBLISHER	USEAGE	TIME
F 2	"I HAD A CAT"	R. BAKER/M. NEWLAND AUTHORS: CONNIE COOK STEVE PINTO STEVE ROLLMAN BOB BUCHHOLZ KENT SKOV	ASCAP	SONGSYNC MUSIC	FEATURED SONG	:16
103-M8	LOOK VANESSA	R. BAKER/M. NEWLAND			B.G. INST	:35
104-M14b	THAT'S MY HAT					:14
104-M12	I LOVE YOU					:18
B B	MAD MOVIES BUMPER				COMM/BUMP VOC/INST	:04
B A	GET ON STAGE/TRANSITIONAL					:03
103-M10	"HERE ARE THE RUNNERS UP"				B.G. INST	:07
F 3		COMPOSERS: R. BAKER/M. NEWLAND AUTHORS: CONNIE COOK STEVE PINTO STEVE ROLLMAN BOB BUCHHOLZ KENT SKOV			FEATURED SONG	:23
M10	MAKE MY WISH COME TRUE	R. BAKER/M. NEWLAND COMPOSERS: R. BAKER/M. NEWLAND AUTHORS: CONNIE COOK STEVE PINTO STEVE ROLLMAN BOB BUCHHOLZ KENT SKOV			B.G. INST	:37
F 4	"MISS DOLL FACE"				FEATURED SONG	:06
M11	YOU'RE STANDING ON MY FOOT	R. BAKER/M. NEWLAND			B.G. INST	:39

PANDA PRODUCTIONS
MAD MOVIES
TITLE: DOLL FACE
SHOW # 109   DATE:
PAGE 3 of 3

CUE	TITLE	COMPOSER	SOC	PUBLISHER	USEAGE	TIME
M7	WHERE'S THE SS PRINCESS	R. BAKER/M. NEWLAND	ASCAP	SONGSYNC MUSIC	B.G. INST	:19
M5a	SOME WORLD CRUISE				B.G. INST	:23
109-F1	DOLL FACE: WRAP				SHOW CLOSE	:24
T 2	MAD MOVIES THEME				VOCAL/INST	1:08

OPENING CRAWL*

SHOW # <u>109</u>

SHOW NAME   <u>DOLL FACE</u>

*Each numbered item as a single page…
Items #1-4: Centerframe
Items #5-9: Lower third of page

1   FOUR STAR
        in association with
        KENT SKOV

2   Presents
        an L.A. Connection
        production of

3   Tonight's Feature

4   Starring

5   Bob Buchholz

6   Connie Sue Cook

7   Stephen L. Rollman

8   Steve Pinto

9   Kent Skov

GENERIC BUMPERS*

SHOW #<u>109</u>

SHOW NAME   <u>DOLL FACE</u>

*Each numbered item as a single page…

1   We'll be right back…

2   Don't Go Away

3   More Mad Movies
            Coming Up

4   Coming Up…
            More Mad Movies

5   Stay Tuned for
            "Your Home Movies"

6   Next…
            "Your Home Movies"

7   Write Us…
            L.A. Connection Productions
            6464 Sunset Blvd., #820
            Hollywood, CA 90028

8   Send Your Home Movies to…
            L.A. Connection Productions
            6464 Sunset Blvd., #820
            Hollywood, CA 90028
            (Include a self-addressed, stamped envelope for return of films)

9   Next…
            Mad Movies takes it to the streets

10   Next…
            The Envelope Please

CLOSING CRAWL*

SHOW # <u>109</u>

SHOW NAME   <u>DOLL FACE</u>

*Each numbered item as a single page…

1   Directed by
    Kent Skov

2   Written by
    Connie Sue Cook
    Steve Pinto
    Kent Skov

3   Produced by
    Randal W Ridges

4   Featuring
    Bob Buchholz
    Connie Sue Cook
    Steve Pinto
    Stephan L. Rollman
    Kent Skov
    with
    Rachel Lutjean

5   Associate Producers (each name single page)
    Martha Whitney

6   Kent Weishaus (single page)

7   Music Composed and arranged by
    Richard Baker
    Mary Newland

8   For Panda Productions
    Music recorded by
    Richard Baker

9   Theme performed by
    Mary Newland

CLOSING CREDIT CRAWL (CONT'D)

10 Research by
    Bob Petrella
    Ken Segall
    April Winchell
    Ted Hardwick

11 Talent Coordinator
    Martha Whitney

12 Associate Director/Stage Manager
    Randal W Ridges

13 Assistants to the Producers:
    Bob Buchholz
    Connie Sue Cook
    Steve Pinto
    Stephan L. Rollman

14 Facilities Provided by
    Hy-Tone Video

15 Lighting and Camera
    Bill Sheehy

16 Production Sound
    Stu Fox

17 Gaffer
    Jim Drewry

18 Production Assistants
    Lisa Gougas
    Ted Hardwick

19 Make-Up
    Lora Sanders

20 Wardrobe
    Annie Vicari

21 Production Secretary
    Eloise Gonzalez

22 Post-Production Coordinated by
    Monti Santilli Rainbolt

23 Post-Production Facilities
    Complet Post, Inc.

24 Post-Production Audio by
    Michael Pericone
    Michaele Hogan
    For Interloc Productions

3-3-3-3

CLOSING CREDIT CRAWL (CONT'D)

25   "Your Home Movies" submitted by
        Cecil Smith Jr.
        Stanford, CA

25a   Location Courtesy of
        The City of Bellflower & The William Bristol Civic Auditorium

26   Executive in Charge of Production for Four Star Television
        Bob Bosen

27   Special Thanks to:
        Susan Lenti
        Budget Films, Inc.
        Richard Holiday
        Dennis Condon
        Snagglepuss

28   Opening Title Montage by
        Homer & Associates

29   Opening Title Photography by
        Abe Perlstein

30   Post-Production Supervised by
        Randal W Ridges

31   Executive Producer
        Kent Skov

32   "Celebrity Voices and Appearances Impersonated"

33   Copyright 1985 Four Star International, Inc.
        All Rights Reserved

INSPECTOR GENERAL

With the

SHORT RUNDOWN FOR SHOW # 113 "INSPECTOR GENERAL"

Description	In	Out	Seg Time
Show Open	00:00	01:10	01:10
Commercial Break #1	01:10	03:13	02:03
Act I	03:13	10:25	07:12
Commercial Break 2	10:25	12:28	02:03
Act II	12:28	22:29	10:01
Commercial Break #3	22:29	24:32	02:03
Act III/Show Close	24:32	28:00	03:28

MAD MOVIES WITH THE L.A. CONNECTION

RUNDOWN SHOW # <u>113 INSPECTOR GENERAL</u>

All times are in minutes and seconds	IN	OUT	DURATION
Four Star Logo (slug Black)	00:00	00:05	00:05
Show Open: Clip Tease.	00:05	00:20	00:15
Opening Montage.	00:20	01:10	00:50
Commercial Black #1	01:10	03:13	02:03
Bumper #1	03:13	03:16	00:03
Wrap #1	03:16	03:49	00:32
Movie Segment #1	03:49	10:21	06:32
Bumper #2 (Next…Your Home Movie)	10:21	10:25	00:04
Commercial Black #2	10:25	12:28	02:03
Bumper #3	12:28	12:31	00:03
Man On The Street Intro. (as needed)	12:31	12:37	00:06
Man On The Street or Interview Segment.	12:37	13:59	01:22
Movie Segment #2	13:59	17:52	03:53
Home Movie Intro.	17:52	18:05	00:14
Home Movie	18:05	19:11	01:06
Movie Segment #3	19:11	22:26	03:15

MAD MOVIES WITH THE L.A. CONNECTION

RUNDOWN   SHOW # <u>113 INSPECTOR GENERAL</u>

Item			
Bumper #4	22:26	22:29	00:03
Commercial Black #3	22:29	24:32	02:03
Bumper #5	24:32	24:35	00:03
Movie Segment #4	24:35	26:59	02:24
Toss to Preview			
Preview			
Final Close	26:59	27:13	00:14
Closing Montage	27:13	27:50	00:36
L.A. Connection Logo	27:50	27:55	00:05
Four Star Logo (slug black)	27:55	28:00	00:05

CLIP TEASE

WATSON
Quiet, Ralph, Holmes doesn't like to be disturbed during Mad Movies.

SHERLOCK
This is Sherlock Holmes. I'm not in right now, but if you leave your name and number…I'll call back after Mad Movies. Now don't forget…wait for the tone.

WATSON
Holmes needs an answering machine.

MUSIC THEME

COMMERCIAL #1

ACT I

SHOW INTRO

(INT.—RECORD STORE)

HOST
Hi, I'm Kent Skov and welcome to Mad Movies with the L.A. Connection. Tonight's feature is "Inspector General." In our version, you'll be seeing a Rock 'N' Roll exclusive, the first video by one of the country's hottest acts. You may not recognize the face right away. I bet you've heard of some of his albums:
"Bored In The U.S.A."
"He's so Unusual"
and of course his biggest selling L.P., "Chiller." He also happens to be the star of tonight's Mad Movie. Here's our salute to the crazy world of Rock 'N' Roll.

(INT.—BOARDROOM)

CROWD
Mr. Mayor, Mr. Mayor, Mr. Mayor.

MAYOR
Ever since our two-headed chicken died, tourism has been down. Any suggetions?

MOM (MAN)
We could charge people to see my leg. I have a mole shaped like George Bush.

MAYOR
Be quiet, Mom. Leonardo.

LEONARDO
Well, I think we should have a theme park based on Italian food. There would be Lasagne Land, Pirates of the Cacciatore, the Haunted Manicotti.

MAYOR
That's real good, Leonardo, you keep thinking about it. Alan?

ALAN
Well, I've got a great idea for an opera. It's about seven people who go on a pleasure cruise and get caught in a storm, then they get shipwrecked.

MAYOR
So far so good.

ALAN
Let's see, the first mate was a mighty sailing man.

MAYOR
There was a skipper?

ALAN
Brave and sure.

MAYOR
They sailed one day.

ALAN
For a three hour tour. There was a millionaire and his wife, a movie star, a professor and Mary Tyler Moore.

MAYOR
All on Gilligan's isle?

ALAN
No, island.

MAYOR
That is…so stupid.

ALAN
I don't think so. As a matter of fact, I was thinking that I could play the part of the skipper. What do you guys think? Well?

MAYOR
Grrrrrrrrrrrrrrrr.

ALAN
Well.

(EXT. TOWNSQUARE)

MANAGER
And now…the Doobie Brothers.

DOOBIE BROTHERS
DOOBIE, DOOBIE, DOOBIE, DOOBIE, DOOBIE.

MANAGER
And now for our featured performer…Michael Johnson!

                    M.J.
You there, quit having so much fun. Kissing will make your hair restored. Kissing will make you six foot four. Kissing is the way to score. With kissing you'll hear things you've never heard before.

                    DEEF
Missing, missing?

                    M.J.
Kiiiiiissssssing.

                    DEEF
Sorry, I've got a spatula in my ear. Ha!

                    M.J.
Smooching will give you beauty. Smooching will give you class and if it does its duty, smooching will give you gas.
                    (Belch)
Who should you kiss? A person with a beard? No. That would be too coarse. Who should you kiss? A person with a sore throat? No, then you'll feel hoarse.

                    HORSE
Don't touch me, I'm a donkey.

                    M.J.
Necking is for lads and lasses. If you make out, you won't need glasses. So before more time passes, suck some face, you stupid... ahhhh.

                    CROWD
What's wrong with him, look.

                    M.J.
I need some Tabasco sauce.

                    M.J.
                (WEIRD SOUNDS)

                    MANAGER
Quick, bring back the Doobies.

                    M.J.

(SFX: NOISES)

I've got to get some tabasco sauce.

                    CROWD
Bring back the Doobie Brothers.

                    DOOBIES
Doobie, doobie, doobie.

                    M.J.
Excuse me ma'am, can I have that tabasco sauce?

> OLD WOMAN
> No, I need it.

> M.J.
> You don't understand, I'm hooked on it.

> OLD WOMAN
> But this has a street value of a dollar forty-nine.

> M.J.
> I'll pay you a dollar forty-nine plus tax. I've got to have this stuff at least 3 times a day cause if I don't I start going like this…and you wouldn't want me to do that, would you? Besides, this isn't your brand. I love it. But I don't think you would care for it. It's way too thin. Look, if you were to get hooked on this stuff at your age, there's no going back. You'll end up like the degenerates behind me.

(SFX: BOTTLE CRASH)

> Ahhhh. Thank you!

(INT.—FOYER)

> MAYOR
> What did you and the other guys think of playing "Name that tune" to increase revenue?

> ALAN
> It was okay, but we decided that it was a little too easy. After all, I could name that tune in 2 notes.

> MAYOR
> Alright, name that tune.

> ALAN
> We Are the World.

> MAYOR
> That's wrong.

> LONG JOHN
> I can name that tune, my friend, in 1 note.

> ALAN
> You think you're so smart, name that tune.

> LONG JOHN
> Purple Rain. I was sure.

> GUARD W/G.T.
> I can name that tune in no notes.

> LONG JOHN
> Okay, name that tune.

> GUARD W/G.T.
> Moon River.

SHEPARD
I can name that tune in one goat. I didn't even get a chance.

GOAT
Goats just wanna have fun.

SHEPARD
Wrong.

(EXT.—CAMPFIRE)

M.J.
Half the fun of camping out is making smores. Here's a bag of marshmallows but they melted together. Hey, aren't you going to wait until I get the graham crackers and the chocolate bars?

MANAGER
No, I don't like graham crackers. Real men in the woods eat marshmallows like this. Now get lost.

M.J.
We are lost. Besides, Moe, you're my agent, why don't you get me work?

MANAGER
You're washed up.

M.J.
I took a shower.

MANAGER
Your life is a shell.

M.J.
Abalone?

MANAGER
You're over the hill.

M.J.
I'll commute.

MANAGER
You're dead meat, pal.

M.J.
I'm a vegetarian. You never see me put that tabasco sauce on ribs or any…

MANAGER

(OVER TALK)

If I keep you as a client we'll starve to death.

M.J.
That's not true. I'll prove it to you. I've got half an Oreo cookie.

MANAGER
That's my cookie. Why you, I oughta rip your…

M.J.
Look, Moe, why don't you give me one more chance, I know I can do it. Hey, you've got a little cookie on your hand. There I got it. Listen, why do you always yell at me?

MANAGER
I own ten percent of that hair. You never listen to anything I say to you.

M.J.
What?

(EXT.—COURTYARD)

MESSENGER
The British are coming! The British are coming! The British are coming!

GUARD #1
Where's the fire, Pilgrim?

MESSENGER
I've got to be using your bathroom.

GUARD #1
Wait a minute, what about the British?

MESSENGER
Let them go in the woods. Bears do it, don't they?

GUARD #2
Hold it.

MESSENGER
I can't. I have a weak bladder.

LONG JOHN
You can't go in there, the toilet's backed up.

(INT.—CITY HALL)

LONG JOHN
You can't use the bathroom unless you buy something.

MESSENGER
This is city hall. What can I buy?

LONG JOHN
Almost any judge.

MESSENGER
Listen, I'm gonna tell everyone that you act out dirty jokes with hand puppets.

LONG JOHN

Go ahead.

MESSENGER

Hey, everybody.

LONG JOHN

I dare you.

MESSENGER

Guess what? Long John acts out dirty jokes with hand puppets.

LONG JOHN

Alright, alright. I'll show you the one about the duck and the lunch box.

(INT. MAYOR'S OFFICE)

MESSENGER

I've heard someone who can bring a lot of money to our town. All we've got to do is have a concert with this guy and we're sure to make a million dollars, more!

MAYOR

What's this guy's name?

MESSENGER

Michael Jackson. Haven't you heard of him? He's had a victory tour that's sold out everywhere, he's been in all the papers and he wears a sequined glove.

MAYOR

He wears just one?

MESSENGER

Yeah, I'm not sure, but I think he lost the other one on a ski lift.

JONATHON

I hear the train a comin'.

MESSENGER

Well, I've got to go. I'll try to find him. Wish me luck! Goodbye. I love you, goodbye. I love you, not you, Mom and Dad.

MAYOR

Thanks for coming.

MESSENGER

Do you validate?

MAYOR

Take some change for the parking meter, alright there you go.

MESSENGER

Thank you.

COMMERCIAL #2

ACT II

> **HOST**
> Have you ever been mistaken for a celebrity?

> **QUESTION**
> What star do people think you look like?

> **MAN ON THE STREET**
> "They tell me I look like Princess Di in the morning and by late afternoon or evening I look like Robert Redford."
> "Woody Allen, I hate it."
> "Um, Barbara Streisand, notice the nose."
> "Ringo Starr."
> "Diana Ross."
> "I've been told I look like Arnold Schwarzenegger, at times. He's built almost as big as me."
> "Shirley Jones."
> "Uh, the kid from 'My Three Son's.' Um, I used to wear glasses and when I put them on. I think his name was Ernie, the character."
> "Madonna or Cyndi Lauper."
> "Jerry Lewis, eh."

> **KENT**
> Can you do a Jerry Lewis face?
> "Grrrrehhh."
> "Tommy Smothers."
> "A year ago I use to be told I look like Doris Day."
> "Yeah, ah, well, when I was younger, I was told I look like Michael Jackson, before his nose job."
> "Probably Roger Daltry. I was just told, as it goes, not as a rule. Yeah, is that all I have to say?"
> "Grace Jones I guess, 'cause of the hair or something."
> "Well, someone thought I look like Al Pacino and some others like Dustin Hoffman."
> "Uh, someone said I look like Eddie Murphy, once."
> "Probably, Maxwell Smart."

(INT.—KITCHEN)

> **ELSA**
> Now, Michael Jackson's coming and everything must be perfect. The first thing you should do is very important. You make sure the food is hot and you wash your hands. Do you understand?

> **1st DOLT**
> Yes. I should put him in the pot.

> **2nd DOLT**
> And I should clap my pans.

> **ELSA**
> Close enough...oh, Billy Jean, that must be awfully heavy with your bad knees. Spread out. She's carrying toxic waste. You come with me. We'll trade underwear.

                            1st DOLT
I've seen his underwear. Boy, is she getting a raw deal.

(SFX: LOW FLYING PLANE)

                            CROWD
Michael Jackson's outside! Michael Jackson.

                            DRIVER
I have a bald spot.

                            MOM
Me, too.

                            DAD
Me, too.

                            MAYOR
Mine is bigger.

                            M.J.
I got my long pointing thing stuck in the carriage.

(INT.—DINING AREA)

                            MAYOR
Race you to the door, I win!

                            ELSA
Michael Jackson.

                            M.J.
Uh, it's Johnson.

                            MAYOR
This is Michael Jackson. Stand up. He's already seen the Grand Canyon.

                            ELSA
You look so different than in your videos…you're much taller.

                            MAYOR
Oh please, allow me here to take this out to the chicken so it's not so lonely. Michael, hey Leonardo, take his long pointy thing, his manager told me he's hooked on tabasco sauce. We have to keep him happy. Make sure there is plenty. Ladies, show him the springs in your shoes.

                            GIRL #1
Watch me.

                            ELSA
I read in Tiger Beat he just loves springs, look at this.

                            TOM

Oh, Mr. Jackson, I just love Beat It.

                    M.J.

It's Johnson.

                    MAYOR

Ah, tabasco sauce for everyone. I would like to propose a toast and while we're at it, everyone check your dress shields.

                    M.J.

Uh, Johnson.

(INT.—DINNER TABLE)

                    M.J.

I need more tabasco sauce.

                    TODD

Here, we were out of tabasco sauce, try this. It's turpentine.

(INT.—M.J.'s BEDROOM)

                    MANAGER

What's the matter with you? You've got a good thing going here. People think you're Michael Jackson. You're lucky you had your old band uniform. Now you have the chance to prove that you're a great entertainer.

                    M.J.

But I don't look like him.

                    MANAGER

So what, you're a little taller. People pray every night to have a chance to be in your shoes. Of course they're size 17 and a lot of people could be in your shoes, but that's not the point. Listen, all you have to do is get a pair of sequined socks like these, go out on stage with some dark glasses, twirl around, maybe do a couple of spins and then walk backwards. And if you do well, there's a soft drink company that's looking for a star to represent it.

                    M.J.

But…I…

                    MANAGER

Stay off the sauce and I'll get you another treasure for your sunken chest.

                    M.J.

If they catch me in this charade, they'll skin me alive and nail my lips to the wall. However, if I get away with it, I can do all kinds of albums and videos like the real Michael Jackson.

                    M.J.
                  (BEARD)

Don't do it.

                    M.J.
                (MUSTACHE)
Do it.

                    M.J.
                  (OLDIE)
Who cares?

                    M.J.
                (MUSTACHE)
You'll make lots of money.

                    M.J.
                  (BEARD)
You'll be punished.

                    M.J.
                   (OLD)
What's for lunch?

                ALL OVER TALK
Beard—Don't do it. You'll never get away with it. I'm telling you.
Mustache—Go ahead, take a chance. Think of all the groupies.
Oldie—I sure could go for a hamburger right about now with pickles and onions.

                    M.J.
Stop!

INT.—MAYOR'S OFFICE

                    ALAN
There's something strange about Michael that I don't understand. He doesn't wear a glove.

                    MAYOR
What of it?

                    ALAN
I think he's a fraud.

                    MAYOR
He eats flies.

                    ALAN
You're thinking of a frog and what the hell did you do to your hair? You look like Don King, little buddy.

                    MAYOR
But, I always use mousse.

(INT. BEDROOM)

                   MANAGER
I heard what you were saying to yourself. What did you decide?

                    M.J.

Well, I decided to go ahead with this. I'm going to change my image. Moe, have you ever thought about changing your image… like getting a second earring or how would you look without a mustache? Oh, not bad at all. You look like Morey Amsterdam. Not bad at all.

MANAGER

Really?

M.J.

Sure, why don't you come inside and shave it off?

MANAGER

My moustache. Me.

M.J.

Sure, you can use my razor.

MANAGER

Where's the mirror?

(SFX: KNOCK)

M.J.

Oh, I sold it at a yard sale, Moe. Come in, come in, come in.

MANAGER

Oh, Michael, I brought some curlers for my hair and I was hoping you could show me -

M.J.

Not now. Oh, maybe later.

HOME MOVIE

NARRATOR

Regular-sized food was boring to Uncle Lee. Even watching regular-sized women do *this* for a couple hours left kind of a bad taste in his mouth. But seeing this huge bird got him thinking about huge food. The next day, while everyone enjoyed themselves at a barbeque, Uncle Lee started carving a block of gelatin. Some curious onlookers were tuned away as he unveiled the first edible convertible. "Come and get it!" he shouted. Uncle Lee's work gave him such a kick! While some of the family wolfed down tasty pistons, others tried to digest cups of transmission fluid. But all in all, everyone left the table happy. Then Uncle Lee went shopping for powdered sugar, and began the most ambitious baking project ever seen. He ended up using over five million recycled pancakes. "Come and get it!" cried local officials. And they did, by the millions. From every corner of the globe, bakers flocked to the arena to view the results of Uncle Lee's monumental baking spree. They jockeyed for position to get a better look at *this*—the world's largest cocoanut chip and organic vanilla wedding cake. Needless to say, the groom was shocked.

(INT.—BEDROOM)

BILLIE JEAN

How do you like the dinner, Michael?

M.J.

It was delicious, Billie Jean.

BILLIE JEAN

Did it fit into your vegetarian diet?

M.J.

I loved the gray bumps. And those yellow things were very good. But what was in that yellow glowing casserole?

BILLIE JEAN

Toxic Waste.

M.J.

I guess I don't need a nightlight. Gee, I, uh, can't wait for dessert.

BILLIE JEAN

Oh, Michael, we're having melons.

(SFX: DRESS RIPS)

(SFX: FLY)

(INT. CROWD AROUND TABLE)

ALAN
O.C.

Oh, I missed. Here's the phone book. Call everyone and make sure they're coming to your concert.

WEASEL

Here, let your fingers do the walking.

MAYOR

I'll call those.

M.J.

Don't be so grabby! Where were you brought up?

MAYOR

Milwaukee.

M.J.

Gimme that, aha. How do you explain this?

(SFX: FLY)

MAYOR

Those are the unlisted numbers.

M.J.

Got it.

(EXT.—COURTYARD)

                                        CROWD

Oooo! Ah.

VISUAL: COACH RIDES UP WITH GIANT ORGAN ON A WAGON.

                                          M.J.

Can I have your attention please, I need someone to help me get my organ off and get it up on stage. Who wants to help?

                                          BILLIE JEAN

I'll help.

                                          M.J.

You're a woman.

                                          BILLIE JEAN

I know.

(SFX: DANCING MUSIC)

SQUARE DANCE CALLER

(INT. DANCE HALL)

Swing your partner to and fro. Swing her 'til her bloomers show. Do si so and promenade. Don't get caught in a panty raid.

                                          WOMAN

Oh, I shouldn't. Get me a dozen.

                                          M.J.

Billie Jean, I'd like to start soon. You can get the crowds' attention. Go toss your cookies.

                                          BILLIE JEAN

I will, Michael.

                                          ALAN

Hmmmmm.
                                      (Thought)
Nice rock star but oh that dandruff.

                                          M.J.

Hi.

                                        WEASEL

Look, I'll give you $100 dollars for those tickets.

                                        MAYOR

One hundred dollars.

                                        WEASEL

Okay…I'll give you $200 dollars for those Michael Jackson tickets.

MAYOR
Two-hundred dollars, are you crazy? This is the biggest event this town has ever seen.

WEASEL
Look, my final offer: $300 dollars and I'll throw in my wife.

MAYOR
I've seen your wife. Just give me the money.

(INT.—DANCE HALL)

M.J.

SONG

It's almost midnight, and I am looking somewhat like a star. And in this light, you're convinced that I could play the part. You start to scream, and throw all your clothes up on the stage. I'm not who I seem. BBBBut if you look right into my eyes, you'd be surprised. 'Cause I'm a filler, filler, right. And nothing's gonna change, that I'm not who you like. 'Cause I'm a not Martin Milner or Phyllis Diller or Jerry Stiller. I can't do the moonwalk, but I realize there's nowhere left to run. And I admit now that my name's not Michael Jackson. I'd like to do another one of my hits. Cola!

V.O.
Here's some cola.

M.J.
It's the cola generation.
(HIC)
It's a cola generation. I like it, yeah.

ALAN
You ripped us off. He wasn't the real Michael Jackson.

MANAGER
So, he made money for the town and you could make more by using special effects like the lasers and a mechanical spider that comes down on stage.

MAYOR
I don't know. A spider once bit me on the chin.

MANAGER
Don't be such a wimp. You could raise a lot more money and I've got other performers that could make you money, too.

MAYOR
How much?

MANAGER
Twenty-six dollars.

MAYOR
I can't believe that. That's a, that's almost a small fortune.

MANAGER
Sure, I can get Bruce Springberg and Huey, Dewey, Louie and the News.

(INT.—PARLOR)

ELSA
Oh Michael, your concert was so wonderful. I don't care that you're Michael Johnson and not Michael Jackson. I don't know if you've noticed but I have two very big influences in this town.

M.J.
I couldn't help but notice.

ELSA
And I'd appreciate a private performance right now.

M.J.
Alright.
(SING)
I.

ELSA
That's not the song. I've had enough.

M.J.
Okay.
(SING)
I.

ELSA
Oh that was wonderful, Michael. Would you like to do a duet with me?

M.J.
No.

ELSA
I love a man that takes charge. I could just melt.

M.J.
I better move then. Dry cleaning bills are murder.

ELSA
I hope you didn't notice that I haven't shaved my legs.

M.J.
It's alright, neither have I.

ELSA
Before you beat it, I wanna be starting something.

M.J.
Billie Jean is my lover.

ELSA
Michael, your long pointy thing is dragging on the stairs.

                              M.J.
   Thanks.

(INT.—MAYOR'S OFFICE)

   Take a look outside, the crowd is going wild. They like Michael
   Johnson better than Michael Jackson. Let's cash in and make
   Michael Johnson dolls and shirts and tabasco sauce.

                              DAD
   Sheese, Mom. We could get those sequined socks that come up to
   here. I'd buy some and I'd buy some for Mom.

(EXT. STREET CROWD)

                             CROWD
   Michael Johnson, Michael Johnson.

                            OLD MAN
   Ladies and gentlemen, I give you Michael Johnson.

                             CROWD
   Oooo nice hat. Hey Michael, you wanna trade hats?

                              M.J.
   Come on up here, you pretty young thing.

                         VOICE IN CROWD
   Oh, watch those things.

                              M.J.
   I got my pointy thing stuck again.

                          BILLIE JEAN
   Here, everybody sing along.

(SINGING FILLER)

THE END

END WRAP

                              HOST
   I can't wait to get home and listen to these albums…Geez! This
   music is terrible! Now, ah, this is more my style. See you next time.

ENDING CRAWL

PANDA PRODUCTIONS
6420 HAZELINE AVE #5
VAN NUYS, CAL. 91401

MAD MOVIES
TITLE: INSPECTOR GENERAL

PAGE 1 of 3   SHOW # 113   DATE:

CUE	TITLE	COMPOSER	SOC	PUBLISHER	USEAGE	TIME
T 1	MAD MOVIES THEME	RICHARD BAKER AND MARY NEWLAND	ASCAP	SONGSYNC MUSIC	SHOW OPEN VOCAL/INST	:50
B B	MAD MOVIES BUMPER				COMM/BUMP VOC/INST	:04
BG1	KENT'S THEME				B.G. INST	:32
M 1	INSPECTOR GENERAL: THEME					:11
M 2	SHIPWRECKED					:02
M 3	TOWN MEETING CLOSE					:07
M 4	DOOBIE-DOOBIE					:06
F 1	KISSING SONG	COMPOSERS: RICHARD BAKER MARY NEWLAND AUTHORS: CONNIE COOK STEVE PINTO STEVE ROLLMAN BOB BUCHHOLZ KENT SKOV			FEATURED SONG	:16
F 1a	SMOOCHING	COMPOSERS: R. BAKER M. NEWLAND AUTHORS: C. COOK S. PINTO S. ROLLMAN B. BUCHHOLZ K. SKOV			FEATURED SONG	:26
F 1b	NECKING	COMPOSERS: R. BAKER M. NEWLAND AUTHORS: C. COOK KENT SKOV S. PINTO S. ROLLMAN			FEATURED SONG	:13

PANDA PRODUCTIONS
6420 HAZELINE AVE #5
VAN NUYS, CAL. 91401

MAD MOVIES
TITLE: INSPECTOR GENERAL

PAGE 2 of 3   SHOW # 113   DATE:

CUE	TITLE	COMPOSER	SOC	PUBLISHER	USEAGE	TIME
M 4	DOOBIE-DOOBIE	R. BAKER/M. NEWLAND	ASCAP	SONGSYNC	B.G. INST	:06
M 5	TABASCO/BOTTLE SMASH					:02
M 6	NAME THAT TUNE					:09
M 6a						:06
M 6b						:06
M 6c						:04
M 7	SMORES					:07
M 8	THE BRITISH ARE COMING					:09
M 9	A LOT OF MONEY					:44
B B	MAD MOVIES BUMPER					:04
B A	MAD MOVIES BUMPER					:03
M 10	KITCHEN MUSIC					:34
02-M13	ROYALTY MUSIC/ARRIVAL	R. BAKER/M. NEWLAND	ASCAP	SONGSYNC MUSIC	B.G. INST	:05
02-M13	THE ENTRANCE					:05
M11	LOOK AT THIS					:27
08-M15	WHAT'S THE MATTER WITH YOU					:40
08-M15	WHAT DID YOU DECIDE					:40
HM108-	"UNCLE LEE'S BAKE-OFF					1:06
08-M7	DID YOU LIKE YOUR DINNER					:10
08-M7	GLOWING CASSEROLE					:10
08-M10	HERE'S THE PHONE BOOK					:22
M12	SWING YOUR PARTNER					:26
F 2	FILLER					:48
		COMPOSERS: R. BAKER M. NEWLAND AUTHORS: CONNIE COOK STEVE PINTO STEVE ROLLMAN BOB BUCHHOLZ KENT SKOV				

PANDA PRODUCTIONS
6420 HAZELINE AVE #5
VAN NUYS, CAL. 91401

MAD MOVIES
TITLE: INSPECTOR GENERAL
SHOW # 113   DATE:
PAGE 3 of 3

CUE	TITLE	COMPOSER	SOC	PUBLISHER	USEAGE	TIME
F 3	ONE OF MY HITS	R. BAKER/M. NEWLAND AUTHORS: CONNIE COOK STEVE PINTO STEVE ROLLMAN BOB BUCHHOLZ KENT SKOV	ASCAP	SONGSYNC MUSIC	FEATURED SONG	:05
F 3a	FINALE	COMPOSERS: R. BAKER/M. NEWLAND AUTHORS: CONNIE COOK STEVE PINTO STEVE ROLLMAN BOB BUCHHOLZ KENT SKOV				:10
B A	MAD MOVIES BUMPER	R. BAKER/M. NEWLAND			COMM/BUMPER VOCAL/INST	:03
B A	MAD MOVIES BUMPER					:03
M 9a	YOU RIPPED US OFF				B.G. INST	:35
102-M10	OH MICHAEL					:42
102-M13	MICHAEL JOHNSON					:05
F 4	INSPECTOR GENERAL: CLOSE FILLER/FINALE	R. BAKER/M. NEWLAND AUTHORS: C. COOK S. PINTO S. ROLLMAN B. BUCHHOLZ K. SKOV			FEATURED SONG	:16
BG5	BAD MUSIC	R. BAKER/M. NEWLAND	ASCAP	SONGSYNC MUSIC	B.G. INST	:10
T 2	MAD MOVIES THEME	R. BAKER/M. NEWLAND				:50

OPENING CRAWL*

SHOW #<u>113</u>

SHOW NAME <u>INSPECTOR GENERAL</u>

*Each numbered item as a single page…
Items #1-4: Centerframe
Items #5-9: Lower third of page

1	FOUR STAR in association with KENT SKOV
2	Presents an L.A. Connection production of
3	Tonight's Feature
4	Starring
5	Bob Buchholz
6	Connie Sue Cook
7	Stephen L. Rollman
8	Steve Pinto
9	Kent Skov

GENERIC BUMPERS*

SHOW #<u>113</u>

SHOW NAME   <u>INSPECTOR GENERAL</u>

*Each numbered item as a single page…

1   We'll be right back…

2   Don't Go Away

3   More Mad Movies
    Coming Up

4   Coming Up…
    More Mad Movies

5   Stay Tuned for
    "Your Home Movies"

6   Next…
    "Your Home Movies"

7   Write Us…
    L.A. Connection Productions
    6464 Sunset Blvd., #820
    Hollywood, CA 90028

8   Send Your Home Movies to…
    L.A. Connection Productions
    6464 Sunset Blvd., #820
    Hollywood, CA 90028
    (Include a self-addressed, stamped envelope for return of films)

9   Next…
    Mad Movies takes it to the streets

CLOSING CRAWL*

SHOW #113

SHOW NAME   INSPECTOR GENERAL

*Each numbered item as a single page…

1   Directed by
          Kent Skov

2   Written by
          Connie Sue Cook
          Steve Pinto
          Kent Skov

3   Produced by
          Randal W Ridges

4   Featuring
          Bob Buchholz
          Connie Sue Cook
          Steve Pinto
          Stephan L. Rollman
          Kent Skov

5   Associate Producers (each name single page)
          Martha Whitney

6   Kent Weishaus

7   Music Composed and arranged by
          Richard Baker
          Mary Newland

8   For Panda Productions
          Music recorded by
          Richard Baker

9   Theme performed by
          Mary Newland

2-2-2-2

CLOSING CREDIT CRAWL (CONT'D)

10	Research by Bob Petrella Ken Segall April Winchell Ted Hardwick	
11	Talent Coordinator Martha Whitney	
12	Associate Director/Stage Manager Randal W Ridges	
13	Assistants to the Producers: Bob Buchholz Connie Sue Cook Steve Pinto Stephan L. Rollman	
14	Facilities Provided by Hy-Tone Video	
15	Lighting and Camera Bill Sheehy	
16	Production Sound Mark Hanes	
17	Gaffer Jim Drewry	
18	Production Assistants Lisa Gougas Ted Hardwick	
19	Make-Up Lora Sanders	
20	Wardrobe Annie Vicari	
21	Production Secretary Eloise Gonzalez	
22	Post-Production Coordinated by Monti Santilli Rainbolt	
22a	Videotape editor Jill Stanton	
23	Post-Production Facilities Complete Post, Inc.	
24	Post-Production Audio by Michael Perricone Michaele Hogan For Interloc Prod. Studios	

CLOSING CREDIT CRAWL (CONT'D)

25   "Your Home Movies" submitted by
     Geoffrey Todd
     Philadelphia, PA

25a Location Provided by
     Record Retreat

26   Los Angeles, CA
     Executive in Charge of Production for Four Star Television
     Bob Bosen

27   Special Thanks to:
     Susan Lenti
     Budget Films, Inc.
     Richard Holiday
     Dennis Condon
     Snagglepuss

28   Opening Title Montage by
     Homer & Associates

29   Opening Title Photography by
     Abe Perlstein

30   Post-Production Supervised by
     Randal W Ridges

31   Executive Producer
     Kent Skov

32   "Celebrity Voices and Appearances Impersonated"

33   Copyright 1985 Four Star International, Inc.
     All Rights Reserved

LITTLE PRINCESS

With the

SHORT RUNDOWN FOR SHOW # 102 LITTLE PRINCESS

Description	In	Out	Seg Time
Show Open	00:00	01:10	01:10
Commercial Break #1	01:10	03:13	02:03
Act I	03:13	10:15	07:02
Commercial Break #2	10:15	12:19	02:03
Act II	12:19	20:14	07:55
Commercial Break #3	20:14	22:17	02:03
Act III/Show Close	22:17	28:00	05:43

MAD MOVIES WITH THE L.A. CONNECTION

RUNDOWN   SHOW #<u>102</u> Page one of two. "Little Princess"

All times are in minutes and seconds	IN	OUT	DURATION
Four Star Logo (slug black)	00:00	00:05	00:05
Show Open: Clip Tease	00:05	00:19	00:14
Opening Montage	00:19	01:10	00:51
Commercial Black #1	01:10	03:13	02:03
Bumper #1	03:13	03:16	00:03
Wrap #1	03:16	04:07	00:51
Movie Segment #1	04:07	10:11	06:04
Bumper #2	10:11	10:15	00:04
Commercial Black #2	10:15	12:18	02:03
Bumper #3	12:18	12:21	00:03
Man On The Street Intro.	12:21	12:31	00:10
Man On The Street	12:31	13:20	00:49
Movie Segment #2	13:20	15:49	02:29
Home Movie Segment Intro.	15:49	16:01	00:12
Home Movie	16:01	17:05	01:04

MAD MOVIES WITH THE L.A. CONNECTION

RUNDOWN   SHOW #102 "Little Princess" pg. 2 of 2

Movie Segment #3	17:05	20:10	03:05
Bumper #4	20:10	20:14	00:04
Commercial Black #3	20:14	22:17	02:03
Bumper #5	22:17	22:20	00:03
Movie Segment #4	22:20	25:21	03:01
Wrap #2	25:21	25:40	00:19
Comming Attractions	25:40	26:10	00:30
Final Wrap	26:10	26:14	00:04
Closeing Montage	26:14	27:50	01:36
L.A. Connection Logo	27:50	27:55	00:05
Four Star Logo	27:55	28:00	00:05

LITTLE PRINCESS SHOW NUMBER 102

CLIP TEASE

VINCENT PRICE
I have some good news and some bad news. The bad news is you have only 30 minutes to live.

ANABEL SHAW
What could possibly be the good news, doctor?

VINCENT PRICE
MAD MOVIES is on now, and you could watch the entire show.

COMMERCIAL #1

SHOW INTRO

HOST
Hi, I'm Kent Skov and welcome to Mad Movies with the L.A. Connection. Thanks. This little concoction here is called a Shirley Temple. It's totally non-alcoholic…just cherry juice, ginger ale, and one of these.

(CRASH SOUND EFX)

Now, I'm drinking this for a very good reason, and it's not because I like it. Actually it has to do with tonight's movie, entitled, "The Little Princess." Our version is about a little girl whose doll possesses her mind and makes her do very naughty things. It stars…um, I can't remember, it doesn't make any difference. Oh, well…Abdul, let me have another Shirley Temple.

SHIRLEY
Now here's the show.

(INT.—TRAIN)

ACT I

LITTLE PRINCESS

L.P.
I don't like this broccoli hat!

UNCLE
Your mommy said you have to wear it as punishment.

L.P.
I hope it's not because I set your house on fire.

UNCLE
Well, that's part of it. Plus the fact you've been levitating grandma's bed again. Grandma's afraid of heights.

                                                L.P.
Granny's just upset 'cause I spin my head at the dinner table. My dolly told me to do those things.

                                                UNCLE
Make sure you tell your doll that I'm her friend.

                                                L.P.
Where are we going, uncle?

                                                UNCLE
Your parents wanted me to take you to meet a very nice lady.

(EERIE MUSIC OVER LONGSHOT OF CARRIAGE & SEMINARY)

                                                MISS M.
It's hard to believe you're possessed, Lenore. Have you eliminated any other possibilities, are sure it's not psychological or just gas, maybe?

(UNCLE NOD AFFIRMATIVELY)

(INT.—MISS M'S OFFICE)

                                                MISS M.
Well in that case, we're prepared to take her in. I think you'll like it here. We have padded rooms with bars on the windows.

                                                L.P.
Does that mean I have to stay here?

                                                MISS M.
Well you can try to leave, if you like, but we'll pick you off from a guard tower.

                                                KARRAS
I'm an excellent shot.

                                                UNCLE
Here's some special instructions—they're very important.

KARRAS

No food after midnight.

MISS M.

Don't get her wet.

UNCLE

I hope all your beds are chained down, we've had trouble at home.

KARRAS

Oh, we're used to demons every day.

UNCLE

Are you used to having your under wear fly up in the sky and spell filthy words?

MISS M.

Father Karras doesn't wear under wear!

KARRAS

Tell everyone, you old bag.

MISS M.

His collar gives him a rash. Excuse me.

(INT.—MISS M.'S OFFICE)

UNCLE

How do you protect yourself in this dangerous job?

MISS M.

Well it's really simple, I have bloomers reinforce with cast iron.

UNCLE

I had a jock strap like that in my high school swim class. Be careful of Lenore. She has incredible powers.

(V.O. SHIRLEY W/COAT

That coat used to be our gardener.

MISS M.

I'll give it $2.00 if it mows the lawn.

L.P.

I heard what you said. You shouldn't have warned her about me. Now you must pay.

UNCLE
AAAAAGH, my neck, my neck, please Lenore you're hurting me. I won't tell anyone else.

L.P.
You've promised before, uncle.

UNCLE
I just lost my head, it's the last time, hon, it won't happen again.

L.P.
Too late, sucker.

UNCLE
AAAAAAAAAAAAAAAAAAAAA!

(INT.—BEDROOM)

DR. #1
Hello, Dr.

DR. #2
Hello.

NURSE
We found this man in a trash dump with neck bites. I also found a perfectly good pillow case.

DR. #1
Here's a list of the things we found.

DR. #2
I don't really need a broken toaster but I'll take the bird cage.

DR. #1
What about this man here with the bites all over his neck?

DR. #2
Let him get his own junk. After all, who do I look like? Santa Claus?

UNCLE
I want the toaster.

(INT.—MISS M.'S OFFICE)

MISS M.

Haven't you caused enough trouble? First, you break the toaster, then you bite your uncle. Now, now, you've given me this hang nail.

L.P.

Don't point that finger at me, it's very dangerous. You should know you could put someone's eye out with that thing.

MISS M.

How dare you lecture me about finger safety!

(SFX: WEIRD MUSIC)

L.P.

Well, you won this round, you little twerp

(INT.—BEDROOM)

L.P.

I hate you, you make me do those awful things. I can't get rid of you—you're worst than an insurance salesman.

DOLL

Your mother sews socks that smell.

L.P.

I hate you. I hate you, I hate you.

DOLL

Hey, this is my dress.

MISS M.

The new girl is demonically possessed, so everyone be nice to her.

YOUNG WOMAN

Here's the witch.

MISS M.

Oh Lenore, your head is on straight this morning. I hope you didn't do anything evil to the dog last night?

L.P.

No, just the cook.

V.O./YOUNG GIRL

I'm not having breakfast.

MISS M.

Don't sit in Lenore's chair, Charlotte, there's a stick of dynamite.

CHARLOTTE
Dynamite, I thought that was a carrot and I ate it.

(LADY-LIKE BELCH)

(INTERIOR—DINNER TABLE)

MISS M.
Lenore, why are you putting salt on your plate?

L.P.
It's not salt, it's ground up monkey eyes.

(EXTERIOR—STREET)

L.P.
Oh daddy, sorry what I did to uncle.

DAD
That's ok, he was just your mother's brother and he owed us money.

GRANDPA
What are you doing here with that rotten kid?

L.P.
Grandpa.

DAD
Hi, dad!

GRANDPA
What the heck do you mean by that, Sonnyboy?

DAD
Let me hide behind you.

GRANDPA
And after what you did to Grandma, you left Grandma floating on the ceiling.

DAD
That's not so bad.

GRANDPA
No, it's not—what—yes, it is.

DAD
You could always have her change a light bulb or paint while she's there.

MARIN
I had my brain removed.

L.P.
Oh!

GRANDPA
How are they going to do this exorcism?

DAD
By playing some Sonny Bono records—over and over again.

GRANDPA
This better work, 'cause I'm tired of wearing this armor-platted top hat.

DAD
Right, dad, you'll also be able to take off your bullet proof vest.

(SFX: TRASH CAN)

MARIN
Trade you this blanket for your brain.

L.P.
Tell Monty Hall.

GRANDPA
Now, I've gotta go toss some lunch up to Grandma.

(INT.—BEDROOM)

DOLL
Cut it off, cut it off.

L.P.
Oh, I don't wanna cut my foot off. This isn't fun. Please don't make me do this anymore. Besides, this knife is too dull. Isn't there anything else I can do to satisfy your heathen blood thirst?

DOLL
Yeah! Get me a cheese Danish and a cup of coffee.

                                                                    L.P.
You know for a doll, you really stink—Whew! I gotta open a window.

(EXT.—WINDOW SILL)

                                                                    L.P.
                                                              (AT WINDOW)
Hey, Marin, hey, whatcha been doing?

                                                                   MARIN
Not much, just took a shower and washed my hair.

                                                                    L.P.
Did you have your bird in there with you? They don't like to get wet, you know.

                                                                   MARIN
He scrubbed my back.

COMMERCIAL #2 BUMPER (Next…Your Home Movie)

(INT.—BAR)

ACT II

                                                                   HOST
We were wondering what the original "Little Princess" was all about? Weren't we?

                                                                 SHIRLEY
We sure, Mr. Mad Movies.

                                                           MAN ON THE STREET
In the movie "The Little Princess," what was Shirley "The Little Princess" of?

                                                                RESPONSES
"The Princess of what, what do you mean?"
"Movies, right?"
"It must be Maldavia."
"Bolivia."
"I think it was upper Solbobia, if I'm not mistaken."
"Outer Mongolia."
"Little Princess, how about an Extraterrestrial World?"
"Broken dreams."
"A mobster ring, wasn't it?"
"She was the princess of a number of people's hearts."
"I don't know."
"You got me."

"A circus."

                KENT

A circus.
"Yeah!"

                KENT

Are you sure?
"No I have no idea."

                KENT

You're making this up?
"Yeah, I'm making this up."
"Oh, I don't go back as far as Shirley Temple."
"Movies, right?"

(INT.—BEDROOM)

                L.P.

I don't know how these children's feet got under my bed. Would you throw them away for me please, Sarah?

                SARAH

But they're perfectly good feet.

(INT.—BEDROOM)

                DOLL

Our room is lovely, Lenore, it's so cheerful, um.

                L.P.
               (SNIFFS)

You still stink, don't you use deodorant?

                DOLL

Oh give me a break, I just got back from my aerobics class.

(EXT.—HOSPITAL)

             HOSPITAL GUARD

This is a hospital. No horns allowed.

                L.P.

Let me in or I'll put a curse on you.

             HOSPITAL GUARD

Go ahead, make my day.

                                                           L.P.

That does it, you're a frog.

(SFX: RIBBIT-FROG SOUNDS)

(INT. HOSPITAL)

                                                           L.P.

Oh, uncle, uncle, you're got to help me. Look at me, you lunkhead!

                                                       UNCLE

You're ruining my shirt. Where's that doll? Where's that horrible doll?

                                                           L.P.

I snuck away from it. It's in the coffee shop downstairs.

                                                     UNCLE

They have good egg salad.

                                                           L.P.

I don't care! I don't care! They say I need an exorcism!

                                                     UNCLE

Exorcism, what you need is a shave.

                                                           L.P.

You're no help.

(INT.—BEDROOM)

                                                     WHN

What's it like being possessed?

                                                           L.P.

Stuff it!

                                                     WHN

Why you little cretin! I only asked a simple question.

                                                           L.P.

It has its advantages and disadvantages, the good part is I could lift heavy objects.

                                                     WHN

Well, what are the disadvantages?

                                                           L.P.

Oh well, sometimes, when I lift them, I lose my balance. Oops!

(EXT. BARNYARD)

DAD
Mom and I brought Grandma to visit you today. She's not too pleased with what you did to her. She's over in the barn.

L.P.
Isn't she happy I got her off the ceiling?

DAD
Ah, go talk to her yourself, she's waiting.

L.P.
Alright!

DAD
Geez!

(EXT. BARN)

L.P.
Hi, Grandma. How are you today? Isn't it nice having chickens for friends? And everybody knows you're used to sleeping with an old goat.

(INTERIOR—FIELD HOUSE)

MOM
My hearing aid, it's not working.

(over shoulder)

DAD
You probably need new batteries.

(kiss)

MOM
No dear, we're out of cheddar cheese.

L.P.
(THOUGHT)
Dad was never good at wrestling.

(INTERIOR—BAR)

WRAP

SHIRLEY

It's time for the Home Movie! It was sent in by Helen Elak from Beaver Falls, PA and I think it's really gnarley.

HOME MOVIE

NARRATOR

After their tiny country was blown up by giant golf balls, the entire population of East Zontonia made their way across the ocean to find a new way of life. They dreamed of gigantic concrete women holding torches. The faceless millions envisioned discos. But when they turned around, they were on the street and jobless. Some men passed the time telling each others' fortunes using crude hand-symbols, which even *they* didn't understand. Others prepared themselves for executive decision making positions as best they could. Then a struggling American industry answered their prayers. The mashed potato farms of the Great Northwest, where acres of fluffy white spuds were waiting to be delivered to market...to feed a hungry world. Hardworking moms got their own gigantic mashers. Everybody was happy. The children of East Zontonia were assured of secure and productive futures in America...and it was all thanks to delicious, vitamin-enriched mashed potatoes.

(INTERIOR—LIVING ROOM)

DAD

Yes dear, don't misunderstand—but your hand stinks.

MOM

Oh no, it's this garlic, see, I wear it around my neck and sometimes my hand, it keeps away evil spirits, and most of my friends.

DAD

They must be superstitious.

MOM

No, it smells bad.

(SNIFF)

DAD

Oh! You're smart.

MOM

I was smart enough to marry you.

DAD

Let me tell you how I feel.

(MUMBLE ON CHEEK)

MOM

I didn't understand a thing you said, but that's what I love about you.

(MONKEY KISS)

(INT.—HALLWAY)

(SFX: L.P. MARCHING IN HALL—SOUND OF WATER SQUISHING IN BOOKS)

MISS M.

What!

L.P.

Nothing.

MISS M.

What, what, are you doing here?

L.P.

Uh, I was just breaking in some new feet. Uh, whatever you do, don't go in that room—ok. Just this one—surprise.

(OPENS DOOR TO ROOM)

MISS M.

Are you still here?

DAD

We want to find out about our daughter.

MOM

How much longer will Lenore have to stay?

MISS M.

She must stay here 'til she recites a nursery rhyme.

(INT.—SHIRLEY'S BEDROOM)

L.P.

This is the church, this is the temple, open the doors—and, um, oh throw in a hand grenade. I don't know why I'm trying to learn this rhyme. I don't know what possessed me to do a dumb thing like this.

CROWD
(V.O.)

Burn the witch, hang the witch, drown the witch, kiss the witch…

(SFX: SLAP)

L.P.

Heh!

CROWD
(V.O.)

Get it right. Stone the witch.

                              (RHYTHM BUILDS TO SOUSA MARCH) (SINGING)
Burn the witch, hang the witch, and drown the witch. It'll make us feel good in the morning.

                                                    L.P.
Oh, goodie, a parade. I can throw hot oil on them. Oh thank you, big dolly in the sky.

(INT.—HALLWAY)

                                                    L.P.
"Dear Lenore, drown yourself." Oh mommy, Grandma sends such nasty notes.
                                                 (KISS)

                                                    MOM
I know, darling.

                                                    L.P.
I didn't mean to be such a stinkin' slimeball. There they are.

                                                   CROWD
Chanting.

                                                    L.P.
Them again—they've been there for three weeks.

(EXTERIOR—GROUP—STREET)

                                                 MAN W/CAP
I'd like to take that witch, and really pop her one.

                                                  2ND MAN
I'd like to take that doll and knock the stuffin' out of it.

                                                  3RD MAN
I'd like a new hat.

                                                 MAN W/CAP
Yeah!

                                           JULIA CHILD/OLD WOMAN
I personally think she should be cooked in a nice white wine sauce with a dash of paprika.

(EXT.—CHASE)

                                                    L.P.
                                                 (RUNNING)
Whoop-whoop-whoop.

(SFX: BRAKES SCREECH—AS COP SLIDES IN WATER)

                COP

Narg-narg.

(EXTERIOR—TO INT. STAIRWELL)

                L.P.
               (PANTING)

I've got to hide.

               HALL COP

Come back here, the balcony's closed.

               (IN ROOM)

You can't to go in there.

                L.P.

I can go anywhere I want and you can go to hell-o your majesty.

               QUEEN

I'm sitting on a tomato.

COMMERCIAL #3 BUMPER—An Exercise In Exorcism

(INT. STAIRWELL & BEDROOM)

ACT III

               MISS M.

You had to break the elevator.

(MUSIC—SOMETHING CLOSE TO "TUBULAR BELLS" ON WALK)

                L.P.

Sorry.

               MISS M.

Well, Marin will be here for the exorcism. Ordinarily, this ritual involves using a holy book, some blessed water, and some incense. But in your case, he'll have to use the Sunday funnies, a vat of pudding and a squeegee—to avoid getting any pea soup on the party dress. Change into this. I'll send up Marin.

(INT.—BEDROOM SHIRLEY & MARIN)

               MARIN

To start the exorcism we must first rid your room of all foul creatures.

               PARROT

AAACK! Who are you calling foul? AAACK!

                                        MARIN

Look what this bird has done to your room.

                                          L.P.

Well, I don't have any newspapers, besides I don't mind and the bird's fun to play with. Why just yesterday I had it steal the lunch buckets from the entire third grade class. I can also make it bite your neck.

                                        PARROT

AAACK!

                                          L.P.

Well, making a parrot bite people isn't a very good display of my powers. Even though you have no brain, I could make you act like a bird. I could make you fly out the window!

                                        MARIN

AAAAAAAAAAAGH!

                                          L.P.

Here's your in-flight meal.

(INT. STAIRWELL UPSTAIRS)

(SFX: MAIL DROPPING)

                                      KARRAS
                                       (O.C.)

Oh no, more complaint mail about the evil Lenore.

                                      SARAH

Oh, ah, ah, she gives me such a headache I got to wear an ice pack on my head.

                                      KARRAS

I have one in my pants.

                                      SARAH

I understand why people complain, what with bodies flying out the windows, landing on their relatives, and blocking the driveway.

                                      KARRAS

I've been expecting these new instructions from Exorcisms-R-US.

                                      SARAH

Oh, granny will be so happy.

KARRAS
Ooops, you have a pimple on your cheek.

MAID
OW!!

KARRAS
Got it!

MAID
Thanks.

(INT.—DANCING)

KARRAS
(READING)
Walk like a jerk across the floor. This will summon the demon Lenore! Kick up your heels and lift your knees! Stay clear of soup that's made from peas! Look in the mirror, and straighten your tie, if you do it too tight you will die. Make her dance and then you yell, "Evil spirits go back to Cleveland."

(INT.—SHIRLEY & KARRAS)

KARRAS
Well Lenore, tell me, is it working? Is it working?

L.P.
I can feel it leaving…COUGH!

(INT.—GROUP)

L.P.
I feel all better, I'm all better.

KIDS
Huzzah, huzzah, huzzah!
(CHEER)
Hurrahs.

MISS M.
Wait, wait, wait, what about that evil doll?

L.P.
Oh, I threw it in the cabbage patch, out back.

                   KIDS
 Huzzah, huzzah, huzzah!
                   (CHEER)
 Hurrahs.

(INT.—KARRAS &SHIRLEY)

                   KARRAS
 I'm sorry you no longer have any toys. But maybe you might like this.

(PICTURE IN DOLL VOICE—HELLO, LENORE IT'S ME)

CLOSING WRAP

(INT.—BAR)

                   HOST
 Where's Shirley?

                   DOLL
 Take a wild guess, Slime ball.

                   HOST
                (PLAYING ALONG)
 That's *Mister* Slime Ball to you!

                   DOLL
 If Linda Blair were here, she'd punch you out!

                   HOST
 Well, if Gepetto were here, you'd be on strings.

                   DOLL
 That's it Buster!

                   V.O.
 Here's a preview of our next movie.

(INT.—BAR)

                   HOST
                (DOLL'S VOICE)
 See you next time, Slime Balls.

Little Princess • 231

PAGE 1 of 2　　　SHOW # 102　　　DATE: 9/14/85

CUE	TITLE	COMPOSER	SOC	PUBLISHER	USEAGE	TIME
BG3	CLIP TEASE	R. BAKER/M. NEWLAND	ASCAP	SONGSYNC MUSIC	B.G. INST	:13
T 1	MAD MOVIES THEME				SHOW OPEN VOCAL/INST	:50
B B	MAD MOVIES BUMPER				COMMERCIAL BUMPER VOCAL/INST	:04
BG1	KENT'S THEME				B.G. INST	:51
M 1	LITTLE PRINCESS: THEME					:45
M 2	HIS COLLAR GIVES HIM RASH					:51
M 3	I OUGHTA					:32
M 1	BREAKFAST TIME					:45
M 4	SORRY ABOUT UNCLE					:55
M 5	CUT IT OFF					:31
B B	MAD MOVIES BUMPER				COMM/BUMP VOCAL/INST	:04
B A	MAD MOVIES BUMPER	R. BAKER/M. NEWLAND	ASCAP	SONGSYNC MUSIC	B.G. INST	:03
M 6	OUR ROOM IS LOVELY					:22
M 7	UNCLE UNCLE					:38
M 8	BEING POSESSED					:20
M 9	GRAMA'S IN THE BARN					:06
02-M11	HOME MOVIE: WRAP					:11
HM1	MASHED POTATO FARMS					1:00
M10	YOUR HAND STINKS					:42
M11	NURSERY RHYME					:21
F 1	KILL THE WITCH	TRADITIONAL MARCH P.D. ADAPTED BY: R. BAKER/M. NEWLAND AUTHORS: CONNIE COOK STEVE PINTO STEVE ROLLMAN BOB BUCHHOLZ KENT SKOV			FEATURED SONG	:21

PAGE 2 of 2　　　　SHOW # 102　　　　DATE: 9/14/85

CUE	TITLE	COMPOSER	SOC	PUBLISHER	USEAGE	TIME
M12	COP CHASE	RICHARD BAKER AND MARY NEWLAND	ASCAP	SONGSYNC MUSIC	B.G. INST	:14
M13	ROYALTY MUSIC				COMM/BUMP	:02
B C	MAD MOVIES BUMPER				VOC/INST	:05
B B	MAD MOVIES BUMPER					:04
M14	INTO THE ATTIC				B.G. INST	:48
M15	START THE EXORCISM					:42
F 1	EXORCISM JINGLE	COMPOSERS: R. BAKER/M. NEWLAND AUTHORS: CONNIE COOK STEVE PINTO STEVE ROLLMAN BOB BUCHHOLZ KENT SKOV			FEATURED SONG	:29
M16	LITTLE PRINCESS: CLOSE	R. BAKER/M. NEWLAND			B.G. INST	:11
6-M6	LITTLE PRINCESS WRAP					:19
T 2	MAD MOVIES THEME				SHOW CLOSE VOCAL/INST	1:47

OPENING CRAWL*

SHOW #102

SHOW NAME   Little Princess

*Each numbered item as a single page…
Items #1-4: Centerframe
Items #5-9: Lower third of page

1   FOUR STAR
           in association with
            KENT SKOV

2   Presents
         an L.A. Connection
           production of

3   Tonight's Feature

4   Starring

5   Bob Buchholz

6   Connie Sue Cook

7   Stephen L. Rollman

8   Steve Pinto

9   Kent Skov

GENERIC BUMPERS*

SHOW #<u>102</u>

SHOW NAME   <u>Little Princess</u>

*Each numbered item as a single page…

1   We'll be right back…

2   Don't Go Away

3   More Mad Movies
          Coming Up

4   Coming Up…
          More Mad Movies

5   Stay Tuned for
          "Your Home Movies"

6   Next…
          "Your Home Movies"

7   Write Us…
          L.A. Connection Productions
          6464 Sunset Blvd., #820
          Hollywood, CA 90028

8   Send Your Home Moves to…
          L.A. Connection Productions
          6464 Sunset Blvd., #820
          Hollywood, CA 90028
          (Include a self-addressed, stamped envelope for return of films)

9   Next…
          Mad Movies takes it to the streets

CLOSING CRAWL*

SHOW #<u>102</u>

SHOW NAME   <u>Little Princess</u>

*Each numbered item as a single page...

1   Directed by
         Kent Skov

2   Written by
         Connie Sue Cook
         Steve Pinto
         Kent Skov

3   Produced by
         Randall W Ridges

4   Featuring
         Bob Buchholz
         Connie Sue Cook
         Steve Pinto
         Stephen L. Rollman
         Kent Skov

5   Associate Producers (each name single page)
         Martha Whitney

6   Kent Weishaus (single page)

7   Music Composed and arranged by
         Richard Baker
         Mary Newland

8   Theme Performed by
         Mary Newland

2-2-2-2

CLOSING CREDIT CRAWL (cont'd)

9   Research by
                Ken Segall
                Bob Petrella

10   Talent Coordinator
                Martha Whitney

11   Associate Director/Stage Manager
                Randall W Ridges

12   Lighting and Camera
                Steven Hirsh

13   Video Technician
                Bob Thorndike

14   Grips
                Scott Steele

15   Production Assistants
                Lisa Gougas
                Ted Hardwick
                Monti Satnilli Rainbolt

16   Make Up
                Lora Sanders

17   Wardrobe
                Annie Vicari

18   Production Secretary
                Eloise Gonzalez

19   Post-Production Facilities
                Comple Post, Inc.

20   Post-Production Audio by
                Interlok
                Michael Perricone
                Michaele Hogan

CLOSING CREDIT CRAWL (con't)

21	"Your Home Movie" submitted by Helen Elak Beaver Falls, PA
22	Executive in Charge of Production for Four Star Television Bob Bosen
23	Special Thanks to: Susan Lenti Robert E. Evans Sonja Bracy Tom Fortuin Molly De Hetre Budget, Films, Inc. Richard Holiday Dennis Condon Snaggelpuss
23a	Special Thanks to: Mort Borne Tom Spezze and The Chimney Sweep in Sherman Oaks
24	Post-Production supervised by Randall W Ridges
25	Executive Producer Kent Skov
26	"Celebrity Voices and Appearances Impersonated"
27	Copyright 1985 Four Star International, Inc. All Rights Reserved

MY FAVORITE BRUNETTE

With the

SHORT RUNDOWN FOR SHOW #111 MY FAVORITE BRUNETTE

Description	In	Out	Seg Time
Show Open	00:00	01:53	01:53
Commercial Break #1	01:53	03:56	02:03
Act I	03:56	10:21	06:25
Commercial Break #2	10:21	12:24	02:03
Act II	12:24	20:36	08:12
Commercial Break #3	20:36	22:39	02:03
Act III/Show Close	22:39	28:00	05:21

MAD MOVIES WITH THE L.A. CONNECTION

RUNDOWN   SHOW #<u>111 MY FAVORITE BRUNETTE</u>

ALL TIMES ARE IN MINUTES AND SECONDS	IN	OUT	DURATION
COMMERCIAL #3	20:36	22:39	02:03
BUMPER #4	22:39	22:42	00:03
FEATURE SEGMENT #3	22:42	24:47	02:05
HOME MOVIE INTO	24:47	25:10	00:23
HOME MOVIE	25:10	26:18	01:08
CLOSING WRAP	26:18	26:54	00:36
CLOSING CLIP	26:54	27:09	00:15
CLOSING MONTAGE	27:09	27:50	00:41
L.A. CONNECTION LOGO	27:50	27:55	00:05
FOUR STAR LOGO	27:55	28:00	00:05

(INT. ROOM)

                    WOMAN
Wake up, Mad Movies is on.

                    HOPE
Oh, Mad Movies. Hey, I'm on that show this week. Excuse me, I gotta go watch tv.

                    WOMAN
That's not your tv. That's a radio.

                    HOPE
No wonder I couldn't get a good picture.

CREDITS

(EXT. GARAGE)

                    HOST
Hi, I'm Kent Skov and welcome to Mad Movies with the L.A. Connection. The clip you've just seen is from "My Favorite Brunette." I'm sure you recognized one of the nation's most popular comedians.

(OVER CLIP)

In the original film, he plays a photographer who gets involved with mobsters. Now what we've done is simply change the dialogue and make our hero into the godfather of a one man organized crime family.

(CLIP)

                    MAITRE'D
How many in your party?

                    WAITER
I work here.

                    MAITRE'D
Oh, and you?

                    BOB
I'm not having a party. I just want dinner.

                    MAITRE'D
Well, how you'd like to sit where that guy is sitting?

                    BOB
Mmm, that's fine. My arm's asleep.

                    MAITRE'D
Go kick him out.

        WAITER
Right this way.

        BOB
Ah, wait a minute. Listen, here, give him a dollar so doesn't feel so bad.

(INT. GARAGE)

        HOST
We were wondering what kind of transportation a godfather comedian would have. So, we looked around and this is what we found. The world's first comedy limo. I'll be showing you this a later in the show, so don't go away, we'll be right back with our Mad Movie.

(SITS ON WHOPPEE CUSHION)

Ohhh,

(THROWS IT TOWARD CAMERA).

COMMERCIAL #1

(INT. CAR)

        HOST
As I promised, here's the L.A. Connection's version of "My Favorite Brunette."

"Godfather"

(EXT. PARKED CAR)

        BOB
Hey Dad, you left the radio on again. Wake up! What's this on your cheek? It can't be lipstick…it's not your color. Hey, this is blood. Where am I going to wipe my hand? You picked a fine time to die; I just washed the car. Hey, listen if you're not gonna use that gun, can I have it? I've always wanted this gun. It's got Hop-a-long Cassidy's picture on it. Yeow! It's hot! Someone must have stuck it in the cigarette lighter.

        COP #1
You can't park there. It's a red zone.

        BOB
Why not?

        COP #1
Not anymore.

        BOB
Now it's the dead zone.

                        COP #1
The godfather is dead.
                        (O.C.)
Where you going?

                        BOB
The end zone. Touchdown!

(SFX: GUNSHOTS)

                        COP #2
That's Don Perignon, Jr., son of the don.

                        COP #1
He's headin' down the alley. I'll get him with my bowling ball.

(SFX: BALL DOWN ALLEY)

                        COP #2
Seven—ten split. Nice going, Brunswick.

                        DON CORTIZONE
You did a good job wasting the godfather, Sonny.

                        SONNY
I didn't waste him, I killed him.

                        DON C.
Hey, clam up or I'll tear up your tickets to the Ice Capades.

(INT. OFFICE)

                        BOB
Oh, ah, hi, Shane. Hey, nice hat. Well listen, I got a new 45. I would have gotten the whole album, but it wouldn't fit in my holster, so I just got the single.

                        SHANE
                    (Reading Book)
G-spot run. Jane loves Dick.

                        BOB
I read that. Jane double-crosses Dick and runs off with Spot and Baby Sally to Louisville.

                        SHANE
Oh fine, you ruined it for me.

                        BOB
You should see the movie, it stars Meryl Streep and Nipsy Russel. Listen, I've become the head of the family after years of being the butt of the joke. So will you shoot my picture? I'll let you look through my nudie-scope. Hold it up and you can see a picture of a girl. Rub it and it takes her clothes off. Sometimes this technique works with a real woman too. So what do you say?

                        SHANE
No.

                        BOB
Hey, wait a minute. Come back, Shane, come back, Shane. Aren't you gonna shoot my picture?

                        SHANE
Oh yeah, well, alright.

                        BOB
Oh well, that's not exactly what I had in mind.

(INT. FOYER)

                        BOB
Hi, I'm here to see Don Cortizone.

(SFX: ECHO)

                        SONNY
He's busy. Would you like to talk to his daughter, Donna Cortizone?

                        BOB
She'll do.

                        SONNY
This place is so big you gotta hitchhike to the living room.

                        BOB
Take my coat, please.

(THROWS HAT SFX: GLASS BREAKS OR?)

                        SONNY
Don't mind if I do, but it's not my size. That's a nice suit.

                        SONNY
Polyester?

                        BOB
Thanks. It was Mom's.

                        SONNY
Ring around the collar! Ring around the collar!

                        BOB
Pre-soak your head.

                        SONNY
That's how I shrunk.
                        (Thought)
Hop-a-long Cassidy.

(INT. LIVING ROOM)

                        DONNA
Hello, gentlemen.

(SFX: KIDS PLAYING BAD PIANO)

BOB
Huh? What?

DONNA
Would you like to hear me sing?

BOB
No, not really, I wanted…

DONNA
Shhhh. Sonny, stop lurking so loud. And take your hands out of your pockets.

BOB
Ignore him, do a number.

DONNA
One. Two. Ten. Forty. Twenty-nine. One-hundred and four.

SONNY
(Thought)
That number gives me the chills.

BOB
You know one is the loneliest number?

DONNA
One? Listen, you shouldn't have come. It's very dangerous. My father's trying to kill you.

BOB
I'm the new Don. In fact, I'm the only one left in my family, unless you want to help me start a new one.

DONNA
You're lumping my lame.

BOB
You've got dandruff besides.

DONNA
Don't tell anyone. It came with the dress.

DON CORTIZONE
Hello, Don Perignon. Why do you come to me on the day of my daughter's piano lessons? That last man to do that now sleeps with the fishees.

DONNA
It means he had an aquarium in his bedroom, right?

BOB
Oh, well, I've got guppies in my waterbed.

DON C.

Oh, don't squish the fish.

(EXT. HOUSE DAY)

                BOB
            (Thought)
Gee, I have to use the bathroom. Should I go back in? No.

                MEN
           (Mumbling)

                BOB
           (Thought)
They're probably plotting against me and how to take over my territory.

         DON CORTIZONE
I walked into her bedroom and saw both of her…

                MEN
           (Mumbling)
Oooooo!

                BOB
Sonny's got my gun, I'll have to shoot them with this camera.
         (As window closes)
Hey!

                MEN

(SFX: MUMBLING PITCH RISES WITH SHADE)

                BOB
No fair. Ah! The keyhole. Gee, they look so small.

         DON CORIZONE
Then she showed me her leg. Ha, ha, ha.

                BOB
I would make this keyhole bigger if I had a knife.

              SONNY
            (Sighs)

                BOB
Thanks.

              SONNY
Cedar tree!

                BOB
What did I step in?

              SONNY
I love the smell of cedar wood. I'd like to shove a whole tree up my nose.

DON C.
Go ahead.

SONNY
Alright.

MICHAEL
He's getting away.

ALFREDO
That's my car.

(EXT. CAR CHASE DAY)

SONNY

(SFX: AUTO ENGINES)

Hurry up or I'll take back the steering wheel.

BOB
Where's Andy Granatelli when you need him?

SONNY
Put the pedal to the metal.

(EXT. STREET NIGHT)

BOB
I just remembered, I still have to use the bathroom. I guess I have enough time for a musical interlude.

(SFX: CALLIOPE)

(INT. FOYER)

(Sings)
"Old Mac Donald had a farm…E-I-E-I-O."
"And on this farm he had some ducks… E-I-E-I-O."
Anybody want a subscription to Time or People magazines?

VOICES
No! Get out!

BOB
How 'bout Sally Field and Stream?

VOICES
Alright, great, I want two subscriptions.

BOB
There's a centerfold of a halibut.

(INT. RESTAURANT)

MAITRE'D
Sit up straight. How many in your party?

                              WAITER
I work here.

                              MAITRE'D
Oh and you?

                              BOB
I'm not having a party, I just want dinner.

                              MAITRE'D
How'd you like to sit where that man is sitting?

                              BOB
That's fine. My arm's asleep.

                              MAITRE'D
Go kick him out.

                              WAITER
Right this way.

                              BOB
Wait a minute. Here, give him a dollar so he doesn't feel so bad.

                              WAITER
Big spender.

                              BOB
You owe me a buck.

(INT. CAR)

                              HOST
Well, as you can see, comedy is a pretty dangerous business. And that's why this comedy limo has the latest in security devices. Like seltzer proof glass.
                     (SELTZER SPRAYS AT WINDOW)
Ohh, well next up, ham to ham combat.

(INT. ROOM)

                              BOB
Ahh, I only came down for a midnight snack.

                              SONNY
It's twelve noon.

                              BOB
My watch is broken. Get me a ham sandwich.

                              CHIEF
Uh, here.

CHYRON—"WE'LL BE RIGHT BACK."

COMMERCIAL #2

(INT. DON C.'S HOUSE)

DON ABALONE
Have a seat. We called a meeting of the Dons.

BOB
I saw Don Johnson. But what about Don Knotts? Never mind.

DON A.
Since you're the only member of your family left, we're splitting up your territory, unless you can tell me who played Granny on the Beverly Hillbillies?

BOB
Oh, that's easy, it's a, don't tell me. Debby Boone. Right, wasn't it? Nolan Ryan, Irene Cara.

DON C.
No.

DON IRONSIDE
Don't look at me.

DON A.
The correct answer is Irene Ryan.

BOB
So what?

DON C.
Don Perignon, do you know what this means in Yiddish?

BOB
Uhh, loses something in the translation.

(INT. DON'S LIVING ROOM)

SONNY
Don't you know anything about fashion? Pockets are out this year.

BOB
I'm ticklish. Hee-hee.

SONNY
You've been messing around with my girl, Donna, so, I'm going to put you some place special.

BOB
Tell me what you're going to do, Sonny, don't leave me hanging.

SONNY
Hanging's too good for you.

BOB
You made my underwear creep up.

SONNY
We're going to put you in a hospital.

BOB
Alright, well, take my temperature, then.

(INT. HOSPITAL)

SONNY
If you're finished dressing, can I turn around?

BOB
Sure.

SONNY
It would have been a lot easier if you had just gone behind the screen.

BOB
It was occupied.

SONNY
Don't you know that cigarette smoking is bad for you? You should be ashamed.

DON IRONSIDE
Smoke this for me.

DON C.
Welcome to my hospital. I have dutch elm disease. What's wrong with you?

BOB
Nothing. I haven't been sick a day in my life. Okay, once.

(SFX: THWAP)

(Thwap)

Okay, twice.

DON C.
Sonny, no wonder the gardeners always quit. You keep chopping the hoses up. Why don't you go freshen up? You can use some of my aftershave.

(INT. HOSPITAL ROOM—DAY)

BOB
If I wasn't a prisoner here, we could party, party. Chief, girls love muscles.

CHIEF
I got your muscle.

BOB
Hey, who put this tea bag in my window?

CHIEF

I took the Nestea plunge.

                    BOB
No bars can hold me—unless they're open all night.

                    CHIEF
Girls, huh?

                    BOB
A strong guy like you could pick up girls real easy. They like it when you do this…

(SFX. MUSICAL HORNS)

But, not that. You're a tiger.

                    CHIEF
Listen. Pretend that you're the girl and let me try that out on you.

                    BOB
Alright.

(SFX: BAD MUSICAL HORNS)

Now say something romantic.

                    CHIEF
You're special.

                    BOB
That's good.

                    CHIEF
And you have an extra layer of fat.

                    BOB
Not so rough, Chief. Women like men who'll bend a little.

                    CHIEF
Oh, alright. Watch this.

(SFX: BARS BENDING)

                    BOB
That's great, now show her you got a brain, too.

                    CHIEF
I'll change the radiator in her car.

                    BOB
Hold it, Chief, you've seen Cuckoo's Nest one too many times.

(EXT. GARDEN—DAY)

                    SONNY
Can I get a new hose? Something happened to mine.

DON C.

You cut it up again, didn't you?

SONNY

Yes, I did.

DON C.

Put that away. Do you want all the other gardeners to start cutting up their hoses?

SONNY

Yes, I do.

DON C.
(O.C.)

Oh, Sonny. I picked up your class ring. The jeweler couldn't size it. So he—stuck some paper in it. If it's still too big, wear it on your thumb.

(INT. HOSPITAL ROOM—DAY)

DONNA

Don, Don Perignon.
(O.C.)
Did you get the nutcake I sent you?

BOB

Yes, but he moved to another room. Where are you?

DONNA

I'm talking through your knob. My father's took over your baseball card empire. Now he's going after your recycled cans.

BOB

No one's touching my can unless they're behind me. Where are all the godfathers?

DONNA
(O.C.)

They went out for pizza.

BOB

They did! How am I going to get this door open?

DONNA

I got a flea trained to be a locksmith. Here, I'll shove him under the door. You're lucky he works weekends.

BOB

I can't wait to see his bill.

DONNA

Yeah, well he already wrote it out. I got it right here in my hand. It's for $543.77.

(INT. KITCHEN—DAY)

BOB

I only came down for a midnight snack.

                SONNY
But it's twelve noon!

                BOB
So, my watch is broken. Get me a ham sandwich.

                CHIEF
Uh, here.

                SONNY
I'll slice it for you. You idiot, you forget the bread.

                SONNY
I stabbed the wrong ham.

(EXT. CAR—DAY)

                BOB
Say, my shoelace is untied. Does the loop go over or under?

                DONNA
It's the same way you do toilet paper. Look out.

(SFX: GUNSHOTS)

                CHIEF
Why don't you take the bullets out and throw them at 'im. You'd have better luck.

                SONNY
Oh, yeah.

                BOB
Goodbye. They think I'm a pawn. I'll fix them.

(EXT. PAWNSHOP—DAY)

                OWNER
You can't buy a Saturday night special, on Friday.

                DONNA
What about this Gabby Hayes hat?

                OWNER
Six bucks.

                BOB
Get Gabby's beard, too.

(INT. PLANE—DAY)

                DONNA
                (Thought)
I'm next to Lyndon Johnson.

STEWARDESS
Attention please. The inflight movie has been cancelled, but there will be arm wrestling in the main lounge upstairs. Please pick a partner at this time. I'm sure you've noticed the right side of the plane is missing, so those of you on that side will have a wonderful view of Oklahoma.

BOB
(BURP)

(INT. HOTEL LOBBY)

BOB
Can I talk to you for a second?

CLERK #1
You just did.

MAN
I'd like a room for the night.

CLERK #2
Do you have reservations?

MAN
Yes, but I'll stay here anyway. Here's a Pete Rose baseball card.

CLERK #2
No thanks, but I'll give you Reggie Jackson for Florence Henderson.

MAN
It's a deal.

BOB
He's hard to get.

CLERK #1
Don Perignon.

BOB
You're not supposed to call me that. I'm travelling incognito.

CLERK #1
I drive a Buick.

DON DE FORE
Somebody say Don Perignon.

DON O'MAN
Don Perignon.

BOB
No, I asked him if I should wear my girl's shoes, he said, "Don't, get a pair of your own."

GROUP
(Laughs)

BOB
Well, we'd better be going. Oh what's this, looks like Bob Hope's having another killer T.V. special with Joan Collins. Joan Collins, what a woman. She's got those two big dynasties. Well, gotta go. Big sale on horse heads.

DONNA
Yeah, gotta hurry, catch the tail-end.

BOB
Stay here and you boys compare your heaters. Take care. Bye-Bye.

(INT. LOBBY)

DONNA
This hotel's dangerous. There's a Dons convention.

BOB
It's safer than an EST seminar.

DONNA
That's right. Hey look, there's Don Pardo and Don Ironside.

IRONSIDE
Let's burn rubber. Park a wheely.

DONNA
And Don Duck.

BOB
If my plan to get these guys doesn't work, I'm Don of the Dead.

(INT. HOTEL ROOM)

DON CORTIZONE
I'm Don Cortizone.

SONNY
Hey boss, there's some chewing gum on your tush.

DON C.
Don't touch me there.

BOB
Oh, you need a hat to go in there. Oh…this will do.

(INT. HOTEL)

DONNA
(Thought)
Oh, there's an ant.

DON C.
Sounds like ants.

SONNY

I hate those little buggers.

DON C.

Well Donna, my own daughter, what are you doing wearing a diaper?

SONNY

She had her hands in my drawers.

DAD

Are you doing this because you love Don Perignon?

SONNY

What's that?

DONNA

Yes, I do love him and the horse he rode in on.

SONNY

But I loved you and your big soft hands, now you've gone and emptied my heart.

BOB

I'll fill it with lead.

(O.C.)

Get 'em up, I'm talkin' about your hands. You too, Sonny, let's see those underarms. Here, I can see you better without my glasses. Okay, Cortizone, handover all your baseball cards. I'll build my collection again, you'll see.

CORTIZONE

All I got is Florence Henderson.

BOB

That's good 'cause she's hard to get. Alright, move it. You guys will look better against a white wall in softer light. Nice hat, Donna.

CORTIZONE

Guys, don't you come in here. It's a trap.

DON DE FORE

What? Did you say something?

DON GIOVANNI

Huh?

CHIEF

What? Huh?

BOB

Get in here, all of you. C'mon. Alright, now stand together and sing five part harmony. Yeah, I'm taking a trip down the river.

GROUP OF DONS
(HUMS)

BOB
Come on, you're coming with me.

CHYRON—NEXT…THE DON'S LAST HOPE…

CROSBY
Phooey…We'll be right back.

COMMERCIAL #3

PICTURE WITH "SAN QUENTIN."

BOB V.O.
I said down the river, not up the river. I've got to get a better travel agent.

(INT. PRISON CELL)

PRISON GUARD #1
You didn't finish your matzah balls.

BOB
I don't like kosher day, warden. The bagel was good but I just picked at the lox. I want to complain to the chef.

WARDEN
You can't. He died this morning.

BOB
From what?

WARDEN
Food poisoning.

BOB
No! You sure? Good thing I didn't order dessert. How much longer do I have to stay here?

WARDEN
Till after breakfast tomorrow.

(SFX: STEAM WHISTLE)

(INT. PRISON CELL)

BOB
Here's my story, I had a mom, a woman.

MALE REPORTER #1
Gotta go. "Adam 12's" on.

REPORTER #2
Hey, Martin Milner.

BOB

My Dad, he was a German Shepard.

REPORTER #2

Forget it.

FEMALE REPORTER

That's disgusting.

BOB

No, he was a shepherd in Germany.

(INT. WARDEN'S OFFICE)

(SFX. ELECTRIC SHAVER)

BOB

Don't shave my lips. Donna, I love you, but you need a manicure. Hey, you're not Donna.

DON IRONSIDE

Hiya.

(LAUGHS)

IRONSIDES

That's right.

BOB

Donna has brown eyes. Where is she?

DON IRONSIDE

Over there.

BOB

Donna! Wait a minute. How come the Dons let me live?

DONNA

Because we got married.

BOB

Married? When? How? I...tell me, go ahead.

DONNA

When you were asleep. Here, look, here's our wedding picture. Look, you're the one in the horse-head pajamas.

BOB

I'll still need a bodyguard.

WARDEN

Harry. Don Perignon is going to be your boss.

BING

Boss! Phooey!

BOB

                        Will he sing?

(SFX: CRASH ON HAT)

                                        BING
                    Ba-boo, ba-boo…

                                        BOB
                    Nice song, thanks for the memory.

(SFX: MONKEY KISS)

                                        BOB
                    Hey!!

(SFX: MONKEY KISS)

(INT. CAR)

                                        HOST
                    Well, you just saw what we did to 'My Favorite Brunette." We can
                    do the same thing to your old home movies. Now in our Mad
                    Movie, the star was a gang of one. But in our home movie, sent in
                    by Elizabeth Bradley of Norwalk, Conn., the local town has to cope
                    with a gang of three—the shady Buck Brothers.

(GROUCHO MASK FALLS FROM ABOVE, HOST PUTS IT ON)

                    Roll the film.

FOUR SECOND CHYRON OVER CUB SCOUTS—THE BUCK BROTHERS

                                        NARRATOR
                    This is Rick and David…the notorious Buck Brothers. They came to take over a
                    peaceful town. They were packing guns and they knew how to use them. They tried to
                    break their little brother Bobby out of jail. But he was so bad, he broke out on his own.
                    When the shooting started,

(SFX: GUNSHOT)

                    he crawled like a weasel to freedom.

                                        (BOBBY
                    "Let's tear this town apart!")

                                        NARRATOR
                    The Buck Boys went on a rampage, eating off other people's plates and drinking
                    their beer. Then they made the mayor's wife cha-cha with a birthday cake.

                                        LADY
                    Oh, make 'em stop.

                                        NARRATOR
                    Townsfolk were in a frenzy. The state militia was called out, but
                    when they heard it was the Buck Boys they immediately turned
                    around, and hightailed it in over a thousand different directions.
                    Local police were dumbfounded.

(WOMAN
"No one can catch the Buck Brothers!")

NARRATOR
It finally took the Cub Scouts of America to bring those Buck Boys to justice, aided by some Formula One race car drivers. The Buck Boys reformed, learned table manners. David even joined the Texas Rangers. But Bad Bobby stayed bad and spent the rest of his days trying to break out of prison, but he couldn't escape the long arm of the law.

(BOBBY
"I'll be back!")

(INT. CAR)

HOST
You know, if you'd like your home movies made into Mad Movies, send them to the L.A. Connection,

(OVER ADD.)

6464 Sunset, Suite 820, Hollywood, California, 90028.

(BACK TO HOST IN CAR)

HOST
Well, that was our Mad Movie. Ah, excuse me for one second. I gotta make a very important phone call.
(DIALS MICKEY PHONE)
This will only take a second.
(RINGS)

V.O.
Thank you for calling Dial-A-Joke. A penguin and a chiropractor walk into a barber shop…

HOST
(OVER MUFFLED V.O.)
Uh, we've just run out of time. I'll see you next time with for more Mad Movies.

V.O.
How much would you give me for that casaba melon, and he says what, that's not a casaba melon…

(EXT. PARK)

BOB
Hey, I told you I was going to call the cops if you didn't watch Mad Movies.

SONNY
But wait, I…uh…I can explain, I didn't have a tv.

BOB
Ah, that's a poor excuse. I lent him my tv. Go ahead, ask him.

                    COP
Is this true?

                    SONNY
He only lent me his remote control.

CREDITS

                    HOST V.O.
Additional voices by David Leon.

OPENING CRAWL*

SHOW #<u>111</u>

SHOW NAME   <u>MY FAVORITE BRUNETTE</u>

*Each numbered item as a single page…
Items #1-5 Centerframe
Items #6-10 Lower third of page

1   FOUR STAR
            in association with
               KENT SKOV

2   Presents
            as L.A. Connection
              production of

3   MAD MOVIES WITH THE L.A. CONNECTION

4   Tonight's Feature MY FAVORITE BRUNETTE

5   Starring
                   the
                 Voices
                   of

6   Bob Buchholz

7   Connie Sue Cook

8   Stephen L. Rollman

9   Steve Pinto

10   Kent Skov

GENERIC BUMPERS*

SHOW #<u>111</u>

SHOW NAME   <u>MY FAVORITE BRUNETTE</u>

*Each numbered item as a single page...

1   We'll be right back…

2   Coming Up
    More Mad Movies

3   Stay Tuned for
    "Your Home Movies"

4   Send Your Home Movies to…
    L.A. Connection Productions
    6464 Sunset Blvd., #820
    Hollywood, CA 90028
    (Include a self-addressed, stamped envelope for return of films)

CLOSING CRAWL*

SHOW #<u>111</u>

SHOW NAME   <u>MY FAVORITE BRUNETTE</u>

*Each numbered item as a single page…

1   Directed by
            Kent Skov

2   Written by
            Bob Buchholz
            Stephen L. Rollman

3   Produced by
            Randal W Ridges

4   Featuring
            Bob Buchholz
            Connie Sue Cook
            Steve Pinto
            Stephen L. Rollman
            Kent Skov

5   Associate Producers (each name single page)
            Martha Whitney

6   Kent Weishaus

7   Music Composed and arranged by
            Richard Baker
            Mary Newland

8   For Panda Productions
            Music recorded by
            Richard Baker

9   Theme performed by
            Mary Newland

2-2-2-2

CLOSING CREDIT CRAWL (CONT'D)

10   Research by
Bob Petrella
Ken Segall
April Winchell
Ted Hardwick

11   Talent Coordinator
Martha Whitney

12   Associate Director/Stage Manager
Randal W Ridges

13   Assistants to the Producers:
Bob Buchholz
Connie Sue Cook
Steve Pinto
Stephen L. Rollman

14   Facilities Provided by
Hy-Tone Video

15   Lighting and Camera
Bill Sheehy

16   Production Sound
Mark Hanes

17   Gaffer
Jim Drewry

18   Production Assistants
Lisa Gougas
Ted Hardwick

19   Make-Up
Lora Sanders

20   Wardrobe
Annie Vicari

21   Production Secretary
Eloise Gonzalez

22   Post-Production Coordinated by
Monti Santilli Rainbolt

23   Post-Production Facilities
Complete Post, Inc.

24   Post-Production Audio by
Michael Perricone
Michaele Hogan
For Interloc Prod. Studios

3-3-3-3

CLOSING CREDIT CRAWL (CONT'D)

25   "Your Home Movies" submitted by
                 Elizabeth Bradley
                 Norwalk, CT

26   Location provided by
                 Edgewood Highschool
                 West Covina, CA

27   Executive in Charge of Production for Four Star Television
                 Bob Bosen

28   Special Thanks to:
                 Susan Lenti   Dennis Condon
                 Budget Films   Snagglepuss
                 Richard Holiday   Sam Hardwick

29   Promotion by
                 Dan Acree

30   Opening Title Montage by
                 Homer & Associates

31   Opening Title Photography by
                 Abe Perlstein

32   Post-Production Supervised by
                 Randal W Ridges

33   Executive Producer
                 Kent Skov

34   "Celebrity Voices and Appearances Impersonated"

35   Copyright 1985 Four Star International, Inc.
                 All Rights Reserved

NOTHING SACRED

With the

SHORT RUNDOWN FOR SHOW #107 NOTHING SACRED

Description	In	Out	Seg Time
Show Open	00:00	01:10	01:10
Commercial Break #1	01:10	03:13	02:03
Act I	03:13	09:40	06:27
Commercial Break #2	09:40	11:42	02:03
Act II	11:42	20:54	09:12
Commercial Break #3	20:54	22:57	02:03
Act III/Show Close	22:57	28:00	05:03

MAD MOVIES WITH THE L.A. CONNECTION

RUNDOWN   SHOW #<u>107 Nothing Sacred</u>

All times are in minutes and seconds	IN	OUT	DURATION
Four Star Logo (slug Black)	00:00	00:05	00:05
Show Open: Clip Tease.	00:05	00:20	00:15
Opening Montage.	00:20	01:10	00:50
Commercial Black #1	01:10	03:13	02:03
Bumper #1	03:13	03:16	00:03
Wrap #1	03:16	03:41	00:25
Movie Segment #1	03:41	09:36	05:55
Bumper #2 (Next…Your Home Movie)	09:36	09:40	00:04
Commercial Black #2	09:40	11:42	02:03
Bumper #3	11:42	11:46	00:03
Man On The Street Intro. (as needed)	11:46	11:56	00:10
Man On The Street on Interview Segment.	11:56	12:52	00:56
Movie Segment #2	12:52	16:30	03:39
Home Movie Intro.	16:30	16:40	00:10
Home Movie	16:40	17:42	01:02
Movie Segment #3	17:42	20:50	03:08

MAD MOVIES WITH THE L.A. CONNECTION

RUNDOWN   SHOW #<u>107 Nothing Sacred</u>

All times are in minutes and seconds	IN	OUT	DURATION
Bumper #4	20:50	20:54	00:04
Commercial Black #3	20:54	22:57	02:03
Bumper #5	22:57	23:00	00:03
Movie Segment #4	23:00	25:40	02:40
Toss to Preview	25:40	25:45	00:05
Preview	25:45	26:15	00:30
Final Close	26:15	26:50	00:35
Closing Montage	26:50	27:51	01:01
L.A. Connection Logo	27:51	27:55	00:04
Four Star Logo (slug black)	57:55	28:00	00:05

NOTHING SACRED SHOW NUMBER 107

CLIP TEASE

MAN #1
Yes I know, Mad Movies is about to start. But I have to do my laundry and, well, get new feathers for my hat.

MAN #2
Don't you ever miss Mad Movies?

MAN #1
I'll go watch it right now.

MUSIC INTRO

COMMERCIAL #1

KENT—SHOW OPENING

EXT. BALLOON

Hi, I'm Kent Skov and welcome to Mad Movies with the L.A. Connection. Our film tonight is "Nothing Sacred." But as always, we've re-cut all the scenes and dialogue in tribute to the world's favorite movie: "The Wizard of Oz." If you recall, in the movie, Dorothy made an attempt to return home via balloon. Well, today I've decided to balloon my way to Kansas. I know you're probably asking yourself why I'm doing this. Why not? Here's our Mad Movie.

ACT I

INT. BALLROOM

DOROTHY
So that's my story, Mr. Rockford. I'm very grateful to you for seeing me during your family reunion and oooh, I can't believe the size of your living room.

SFX (FLASH BLUE)

MR. ROCKFORD
Leonard!

DOROTHY
You'll attract bugs.

MR. ROCKFORD
There's no film in the camera. Leonard just likes to scare people. Now let me see if I have this straight, Dorothy. You want me to go to a place called OZ and find your friends. I don't know, from your description, I'd say they'd be better off lost.

DOROTHY
Oh please, help me. I've got to thank them and tell them I love them. I've got to get those two things off my chest.

WAITER
Good luck.

ROCKY
We've had a fabulous reunion here today but before we go… Grandpa would like to do his Frankenstein impression.

CROWD
Yea! Grandpa…Sock it to us, gramps…etc.

GRANPA ROCKFORD
I'm a big monster—I'm coming to get you. Did I scare the pants off of you? Bye, bye.

CROWD
Grandpa's losin' it—that was awful. But we haven't eaten yet. There's no food.

INT. POST OFFICE

MR. WOOL
(mumbles and chews)

MR. ROCKFORD
Thanks for telling me the witch runs the store.

MR. WOOL
(mumbles and chews)

MR. ROCKFORD
Oh, geez I didn't know you had a rubber hand, I'm sorry.

MR. WOOL
(mumbles and chews)
Witch—store.

MR. ROCKFORD
Is there a big demand for monkey wings?

MR. WOOL
(mumbles and chews)

MR. ROCKFORD
What about the wizard? I hear he makes air freshners somewhere in town.

MR. WOOL
(mumbles and chews)

MR. ROCKFORD
Thanks for the warning. Here's some gum.

MR. WOOL
Hmm gum! I never chew the stuff.

INT. STORE

MR. ROCKFORD
Hello witch.

WITCH
Hmmm.

MR. ROCKFORD
Monkey wing business is kind of slow, huh?

WITCH
Yup. They're more of a Christmas item.

MR. ROCKFORD
I bet they make a great little stocking stuffer. Mind if I sit down here?

WITCH
On your mark? It's a little game I play.

MR. ROCKFORD
Are you serious?

WITCH
Get set…go!

MR. ROCKFORD
Gee, that was fun.

WITCH
Yup.

MR. ROCKFORD
I'm working for Dorothy. I'm trying to find her friends.

WITCH
Dorothy! That little witch-buster.

MR. ROCKFORD
A little testy.

WITCH
I have every right to be. Dorothy, the Lion, the Tinman and whatever in hell that other thing was that cost me a bundle in plastic surgery. Thinking about it gets me so darn mad I could spit.

MR. ROCKFORD
Bull's eye…here, you want some gum?

WITCH
Well, long as it's sugarless.

MR. ROCKFORD
You're a credit to your race. But I think you may be starting to melt. Yup.

OLD WOMAN
Hmm, hmhmm.

MR. ROCKFORD
Hmm.

EXT. STREET

MUNCHKINS
We'd like to welcome you to Munchkin Land.

MR. ROCKFORD
Nothing worse than a wagonload of drunk Munchkins.

SINGLE MUNCHKIN
Welcome to Munchkin Land.
(Bites leg)
rrrrrrr.

MR. ROCKFORD
Ow…damn those things.

EXT. HOTEL

MR. ROCKFORD
'scuse me, I lookin' for Auntie Em.

EM
I'm Em.

MR. ROCKFORD
Oh—could you point out the Wizard to me? Dorothy told me you keep in touch with him.

EM
That's right, we're shackin' up together.

MR. ROCKFORD
Hmmm. Can I talk to him?

EM
Well, don't keep him too long. We got a handball tournament tonight.

MR. ROCKFORD
Hi Wiz, mind if I sit?

WIZARD
Sure, on your mark?

MR. ROCKFORD
Too late. I'm here to ask your help in locating Dorothy's friends.

WIZARD
Friends, you mean the Lion, the Tinman, and whatever in hell that other thing was. The mere mention of their names makes me

suicidal. I could just open the window and jump out. On second thought I'll open two windows and throw you out the other one.

WIZARD (con't)

Don't mention her name again, buster. That girl's been nothing but trouble. She hired me to take her back to Kansas and you know what I got for it? A rubber check, it bounced so high it went somewhere over the rainbow.

MR. ROCKFORD

This is drawn on the bank of Munchkin. They're always short on funds.

WIZARD

I don't want anything to do with Dorothy, and I mean it.

MR. ROCKFORD

So then, I can tell Dorothy you'll be happy to see her.

WIZARD

What? Alright, but only for a minute. Darn girl gave me a rubber door.

EXT. STREET

DOROTHY

So, the Wizard will see me?

MR. ROCKFORD

Yeah, but he's ticked off.

DOROTHY

Oh, he's probably mad about that bad check or maybe he's still bummed about Toto and that incident with his prize poppys. But I never felt it was…

(SFX) Birds chirping.

ROCKFORD

Better go see him know.

DOROTHY

And I'll go see the Wizard. Hurry, Toto, hurry!

INT. HOUSE

DOROTHY

Oh, Wizard, are you glad to see me?

WIZARD

I don't think you should ask me that when I have a straight razor in my hand. Did one of the Munchkins bite you? You're foaming at the mouth.

DOROTHY

Help me if you can, I'm feelin' down.

WIZARD

Oh alright, but I don't know where to find the Lion, the Tinman and whatever the hell that other thing was.

              DOROTHY
Let's try the Emerald City. That's the last place I saw them.

              WIZARD
Emerald City, huh? Traveling makes me irregular.

COMMERCIAL #2/BUMPER #1

              KENT
We're about t-minus five million or so…and counting. Meanwhile, who is your favorite "Wizard of Oz" character and why?

              RESPONSES:
"The wicked witch of the west because she had a perfectly evil time until her melt down."
"The scarecrow because he's full of hay."
"The flying monkeys."
 "Mitch's witch, which witch?"
"The wicked witch…I like her personality."
"She reminds me a lot of people I know."
"Dorothy…cause."
"The coroner of the Munchkin people."
"Dorothy."
"I haven't seen the movie so I can't say."
"I think it would have to be TOTO."
"Who's your favorite? Toto. You like Toto too?"
"Not Toto."
"The Munchkins as an ensemble group did a hell of a job. You can't pick out any particular Munchkin for doing an outstanding job. But the way they sang and danced…did me in. What can I say?"

ACT II

(SFX) Airplane Jet?

INT. PLANE

              DOROTHY
The creamed spinach was great. I still have a bone stuck in my teeth. Hey Wiz, how were your stewed prunes?

              WIZARD
I'll let you know in 20 minutes.

              ROCKFORD
We should be landing before that.

              DOROTHY
I'm happy as Anson Williams.

              ROCKFORD
Welp, there it is, the Emerald City. Gee, it's different than in the brochure.

(SFX) MUSIC BUILDS—STOPS IMMEDIATELY IN PLANE

                        (V.O.)
The pilot asked me to return this to you.

                        ROCKFORD
It's your check for our airline tickets, apparently it bounced. I don't mean to be telling you your business, but you run the risk of a bad credit rating. I'll take care of it this time. But now you'll owe me an extra 50 bucks, okay?

                        WIZARD
                    (Under his breath)
Good luck.

                        DOROTHY
I'll write you a check as soon as we land. I'm gonna change banks. You know, they've dipped their do-nuts in my coffee one too many times. Look! It's better than that the "Surrender Dorothy" I got last time. Wait a minute, they got the name wrong. That's an old maid!

(SFX) Toots, whistles, etc. New Year's Eve-like.

                        MAYOR
Welcome to Emerald City, Dorothy.

                        DOROTHY
Hi, hi, hi, hi.
                        (THOUGHT)
I've got an itch, I've got an itch—LEONARD.

(SFX) Fog Horn

                              (over pitch pipe)

                        MUNCHKINS
                         (sing)

TUNE: Battle Hymm of the Republic—chorus

        Dorothy, you're back in our city
        And we think it's such a pity
        Last time everything went wrong
        We hope you don't stay too long.
        Solo—We really mean it
                        (Music trails off)

INT. BOXING RING

                        ROCKFORD
Some fight, huh?

                        DOROTHY
You say the Lion's going to be here?

                        ROCKFORD
Yeah, that's him up there with the beard. He had to shave the rest of his body. Some rule about fleas and an unfair advantage. It wasn't easy to find him. There are a lot of lions in wrestling.

DOROTHY
The Lion was such a wonderful friend. I remember one day when the Tinman's arm was rusted and the Lion oiled him 'til his joint wasn't stiff anymore.

ROCKFORD
You oughta pick your friends more carefully. They're psychos. By the way, the Lion said he'd drop by later.

DOROTHY
Lion, Lion, I'm so glad to see you.

ROCKFORD
When he said he'd drop by I didn't take him literally.

DOROTHY
What's new, Lion?

LION
Can't talk now Dorothy. I've got a fist in my nose.

REFEREE
He's got my wallet!

INT. APT.

PIZZA MAN
Pizza Man!...Dorothy?

DOROTHY
(mumbles on phone)

PIZZA MAN
I delivered the pizza to your friend.

ROCKFORD
There's too much flour in it.

PIZZA MAN
They say there's too much flour in it, but I think it's just fine. Bye bye, Dorothy.

ROCKFORD
We oughta eat this thing or move it, Dad. I've got work to do. Dorothy may be built like a smokestack but it's a tough case…real tough.

ROCKY
Quit your whining, Jimbo.

ROCKFORD
Oh Dad…I've only found one of 'em. The Lion…

ROCKY
You still have to find the Tinman.

ROCKFORD
Yeah, I know, and whatever in hell the other thing was.

INT. OFFICE

PROF
I saw your son's ad in the paper. I looked all over this map, pulled all the strings I could. But I couldn't find Dorothy's friends. Would your son settle for The Three Stooges?

STOOGES
NNNEEEAAAAA.

PROF
Larry, Moe and Curly

STOOGES
Coitinly

KENT
Well, very soon I might be passing over your hometown, especially if it's Granada Hills, California. That's where our home movie comes from. It was sent in by Raquel Biaz.

ANNOUNCER
This is your target…Alexander Dorkoff, top enemy agent. We assigned one of our best men to eliminate him…but even the handshake of death didn't jar the sturdy master spy. When he realized we'd replaced his spare tire with an atom bomb, he didn't even flinch. This footage was shot from a mailbox a quarter mile away. It's almost as if Dorkoff knows exactly where we are all the time. This is the secret desert launch site of our new Rainbolt Missile. How Dorkoff found it, we'll never know. We think he has converted this limp, fuzzy cactus plant into a combination transmitter/anti-tank gun. We were getting ready to pick him off right here, but the crafty Communist surrounded himself with innocent American citizens and foiled our plans. Once again, the special agent assigned to Dorkoff attempted to liquidate him. Watch closely as he uses a little-known combination of ancient Chinese martial arts maneuvers…here he goes…but Dorkoff's superb physical conditioning once again saved his life. Nice view of the mountains, huh? Track this man down and neutralize him, before he either infiltrates the American dream or sits on it.

EXT. OCEAN

DOROTHY
(Thought)
I need more help finding my friends. I know, I'll call Flipper. Honk honk honk. Flipper…come here Flipper.

WIZARD
I feel like the Ty-d-bol man.

DOROTHY
(Quiet)
Honk.

FLIPPER
(Porpoise Sounds)

ROCKFORD
Knock it off.

FLIPPER
(Porpoise sounds)

Ow!

ROCKFORD
Oh no. Flipper's hurt.

DOROTHY
Ow!

POLICE
(Volga Boatmen)
"Old yo-yos"

Oo eee oo ooh ooh oo eee oo ooh ooh.
Oo eee oo ooh ooh oo eee oo ooh ooh.
Faster

ROCKFORD
Is Flipper okay?

DOROTHY
Yeah, my high heel was just stuck in his blow hole.

ROCKFORD
Hey, you've got green panties on.

DOROTHY
That's just seaweed.

ROCKFORD
Camptown ladies sing this song. Doo dah.

DOROTHY
Oh please.
(Over Rockford)
I hate that song.

ROCKFORD
So do I.

DOROTHY
Then why do you sing it?

ROCKFORD
Because I go crazy when I have trout in my trousers.

DOROTHY
Now see what you've done, Mr. Rockford. You've woken up all the neighbors with your lousy singing.

ROCKFORD

Nuts to them! Let's go back to my place…Here we are.

DOROTHY
Hey, the piano looks great in the corner. What a lovely chandelier, the carpet is so plush. Oh, excuse me for saying so but do you really think the pool table should be against the wall?

TINMAN
Hey, Bo Bo, go get my oil can. Not again.

ROCKFORD
Hey, you're the Tinman, aren't you? Dorothy, I found the Tinman. You owe me money. Pay up.

TINMAN
He didn't find me, I was just standing over there. Dorothy, it is you. You look great. Who does your hair? How's the weather in Kansas? Real talkative, ain't you?

ROCKFORD
Congratulations on becoming an honorary Tinman.

DOROTHY
Wait, Mr. Rockford. I owe so much for finding my friends. Thank you, thank you, thank you. A little rust.

ROCKFORD
I would have preferred cash, Dorothy.

INT. APT.

DOROTHY
What the…

PROF
Hello, Dorothy. I'm here to collect the reward, I found your friends.

ROCKFORD
But, Rockford already found all but one.

PROF
No, no, no, no, no, no, no, no, no, his Dad hired me to help him. Here they are. Here's your long lost friend, the Lion.

LION
Narg, narg, narg.

PROF
And I'm sure you recognize the Tinman.

TINMAN
Woop, woop, woop.

PROF
And finally whatever the hell that other thing is.

SCARECROW
Arf, arf, arf.

WIZARD
They're phonies. Get out, click your heels three times.

(SFX) (3 clicks)

STOOGES
Ooooooooooowh!

COMMERCIAL #3/BUMPER #2

INT. BEDROOM

ACT III

ROCKFORD
Dorothy.

DOROTHY
I dreamt I was back in OZ.

ROCKFORD
It wasn't a dream, you are back in OZ, and you owe me an awful lot of money.

DOROTHY
How can that be? I clicked my heels.

ROCKFORD
When you clicked your heels, you broke your ankle and passed out from the pain.

DOROTHY
What about my friends?

ROCKFORD
I'm still working on it. I feel like I'm getting close. With a couple extra hundred dollars I think I can wrap things up.

DOROTHY
(snores)

ROCKFORD
Am I boring you?

INT. OFFICE

ROCKY
Go in there and talk to my son and tell him what you told me.

MAX
The thing you been looking for is a scarecrow and he's my brother.

ROCKY
Jimbo, that's not the half of it, just wait'll you hear the rest.

ROCKFORD
Come on, Dad. Don't hold out on me. Tell me where to find him.

ROCKY
You don't want to know.

ROCKFORD
Sure I do, that's what Dorothy hired me to find out.

ROCKY
Alright, he's in state prison. The Scarecrow's serving 10 to 20 for arson, with no chance for parole.

ROCKFORD
That's just great!

ROCKY
This case gives me a headache.

MAX
You're leanin' on me.

ROCKY
Oh, sorry. This means we lose five hundred dollars and that's nothing to sneeze at.

MAX
(sneezes)

ROCKY
I should'a brought my umbrella.

ROCKFORD
If that bag of weeds were here right now, I'd feed him to a mule.

MAX
That bag of weeds is my brother.

(SFX) Junk breaking.

INT. APT.

DOROTHY
What's going on here? Why are you treating me like this?

MAYOR
We're sorry, Dorothy. All your checks have bounced. We've got Munchkins to feed, deadbeat. Nothing personal.

DOROTHY
Humph! That's the twelfth bank that's given me trouble. Here, take the key to my Corvair.

MAYOR
It's a rental.

WITCH

If you need a ride, give me a call and I'll come and get you, my pretty, and your little dog too.

                                        VOICES
                                         (O.C.)

Phew! P.U! Whooeee!

                                       DOROTHY
                                         (O.C.)

Which one of you clowns stole my ruby slippers?

                                         ROCKY

I did. I sold 'em to pay off your debts, Dorothy. We're investing the money in a fastfood restaurant that specializes in monkey wing nuggets.

                                       DOROTHY

Oh, that's peachy keen. Unless another tornado comes by, I have no way to get back to Kansas. I'll just have to take a boat!

EXT. ISLAND

                                       DOROTHY

It's sunset, you can take those off now.

                                       ROCKFORD

So can you. Now you'll have to give me mouth-to-mouth.

(SFX) Monkey kiss action.

                                         GLENDA
                                         (gasps)

                                       DOROTHY

Glenda, the good witch.

                                       GLENDA

Dorothy, remember all that stuff I told you about there being no place like home? It's a crock. I'm on my way to Hawaii to hula down and hang ten with Don Ho.

                                       KENT

Kansas, here I come. Here's a preview of our next Mad Movie. Thanks for joining us. Our next show will be coming to you from wherever I touch down. But don't worry, we'll be back for more Mad Movies. Okay guys, cut me loose…guys, anybody down there? Now how am I going to get down?

CLOSING CREDITS

PANDA PRODUCTIONS MAD MOVIES

TITLE: NOTHING SCARED

PAGE 1 of 2   SHOW # 107   DATE: 9/21/85

CUE	TITLE	COMPOSER	SOC	PUBLISHER	USEAGE	TIME
T 1	MAD MOVIES THEME	RICHARD BAKER AND MARY NEWLAND	ASCAP	SONGSYNC	SHOW OPEN VOCAL/INST	:50
B A	MAD MOVIES BUMPER				COMM/BUMP VOC/INST	:03
BG1	KENT'S THEME				B.G. INST	:21
M 1	NOTHING SACRED. THEME					:47
M 2	WITCH RUNS THE STORE/ MONKEY WING BUSINESS					1:17
M 3	MUNCHKINLAND					:21
M 4	LOOKING FOR AUNT EMM					:24
M 5	HI WIZ					:56
M 6	TO SEE THE WIZARD					:28
B B	MAD MOVIES BUMPER				COMM BUMP VOC/INST	:04
B A	EMERALD CITY				B.G. INST	:03
M 7	HELLO HAZEL					:07
M 8	GLORY HALLELUJIAH (TRADITIONAL)	P.D ADAPTED BY R. BAKER/M. NEWLAND				:13
M 9	PIZZA MAN	R. BAKER/M. NEWLAND				:18
M10	AD IN THE PAPER				B.G. INST	:30
M11	"SUPER SPY"					:17
HM1	ILL CALL FLIPPER	COMPOSER/AUTHOR STEPHEN FOSTER				1:00
M12	CAMPTOWN RACES	P.D. ADAPTED BY R. BAKER/M. NEWLAND	ASCAP			:31
M13		R. BAKER/M. NEWLAND				:03
M14	BACK TO MY PLACE				B.G. INST	:43
M15	HELLO DOROTHY					:43
B B	MAD MOVIES BUMPER				COMM/BUMPER VOC/INST	:04
B A	MAD MOVIES BUMPER					:03

PANDA PRODUCTIONS

MAD MOVIES

TITLE: NOTHING SCARED

SHOW # 107   DATE: 9/21/85

PAGE 2 of 2

CUE	TITLE	COMPOSER	SOC	PUBLISHER	USEAGE	TIME
M16	DREAMT I WAS BACK IN OZ	R. BAKER/M. NEWLAND	ASCAP	SONGSYNC MUSIC	B.G. INST	:35
M17	WHAT YOU TOLD ME					:47
M18	WHAT'S GOING ON HERE					:27
M16	HAVE TO TAKE A BOAT					:35
T 2	MAD MOVIES THEME				SHOW CLOSE VOCAL/INST	1:30

OPENING CRAWL*

SHOW #107

SHOW NAME   Nothing Sacred

*Each numbered item as a single page…
Items #1-4: Centerframe
Items #5-9: Lower third of page

1   FOUR STAR
        in association with
           KENT SKOV

2   Presents
        an L.A. Connection
            production of

3   Tonight's Feature

4   Starring

5   Bob Buchholz

6   Connie Sue Cook

7   Stephen L. Rollman

8   Steve Pinto

9   Kent Skov

GENERIC BUMPERS*

SHOW #<u>107</u>

SHOW NAME   <u>Nothing Sacred</u>

*Each numbered item as a single page…

1   We'll be right back…

2   Don't Go Away

3   More Mad Movies
    Coming Up

4   Coming Up…
    More Mad Movies

5   Stay Tuned for
    "Your Home Movies"

6   Next…
    "Your Home Movies"

7   Write Us…
    L.A. Connection Productions
    6464 Sunset Blvd., #820
    Hollywood, CA 90028

8   Send Your Home Movies to…
    L.A. Connection Productions
    6464 Sunset Blvd., #820
    Hollywood, CA 90028
    (Include a self-addressed, stamped envelope for return of films)

9   Next…
    Mad Movies takes it to the streets

CLOSING CRAWL*

SHOW #<u>107</u>

SHOW NAME   <u>Nothing Sacred</u>

*Each numbered item as a single page…

1	Directed by Kent Skov
2	Written by Connie Sue Cook Steve Pinto Kent Skov
3	Produced by Randal W Ridges
4	Featuring Bob Buchholz Connie Sue Cook Steve Pinto Stephen L. Rollman Kent Skov April Winchell
5	Associate Producers (each name single page) Martha Whitney
6	Kent Weishaus (single page)
7	Music Composed and arranged by Richard Baker Mary Newland For Panda Productions
7a	Music Recorded by Richard Baker
8	Theme performed by Mary Newland

CLOSING CREDIT CRAWL (con't)

9	Research by	Bob Petrella
		Ken Segall
		April Winchell
		Ted Hardwick
10	Talent Coordinator	Martha Whitney
11	Associate Director/Stage Manager	Randal W Ridges
11a	Assistants to the Producers:	Bob Buchholz
		Connie Sue Cook
		Steve Pinto
		Stephen L. Rollman
12	Facilities provided by	Hy-Tone Video
13	Lighting and Camera	Bill Sheehy
14	Gaffer	Jim Drewry
14a	Production Sound	Stu Fox
15	Production Assistants	Lisa Gougas
		Ted Hardwick
16	Make Up	Lora Sanders
17	Wardrobe	Annie Vicari
18	Production Secretary	Eloise Gonzalez
18a	Post-Production Coordinated by	Monti Santilli rainbolt
19	Post-Production Facilities	Comple Post, Inc.
20	Post-Production Audio by	Michael Pericone
		Michaele Hogan
		For Interlok Productions

CLOSING CREDIT CRAWL (con't)

21   "Your Home Movie" submitted by
Raquel Baiz
Granada Hills, CA

21a   Special Thanks to (single page)
Ronald Thronson and President G.T. Smith of
Chapman College, Orange California

22   Executive in Charge of Production
Bob Bosen

23   Special Thanks to:
Wesley Cornwell
Carole Fisher
Susan Lenti
Budget Films, Inc.
Richard Holiday
Dennis Condon
Snagglepuss

23a   Opening Title Montage by
Homer & Associates

23b   Opening Title Photography by
Abe Perlstein

24   Post-Production supervised by
Randal W Ridges

25   Executive Producer
Kent Skov

26   "Celebrity Voices and Appearances Impersonated"

27   Copyright 1985 Four Star International, Inc.
All Rights Reserved

NIGHT OF THE LIVING DEAD

With the

SHORT RUNDOWN FOR SHOW #106 "NIGHT OF THE LIVING DEAD"

Description	In	Out	Seg Time
Show Open	0:00	1:10	1:10
Commercial Break #1	1:10	3:13	2:03
Act I	3:13	9:07	5:54
Commercial Break #2	9:07	11:10	2:03
Act II	11:10	22:11	11:01
Commercial Break #3	22:11	24:14	2:03
Act III/Show Close	24:14	28:00	3:46

MAD MOVIES WITH THE L.A. CONNECTION

RUNDOWN   SHOW #<u>106</u> "<u>Night Of The Living Dead</u>"

All times are in minutes and seconds	IN	OUT	DURATION
Four Star Logo (slug black)	00:00	00:05	00:05
Show Open: Clip Tease.	00:05	00:20	00:15
Opening Montage.	00:20	01:10	00:50
Commercial Black #1	01:10	03:13	02:03
Bumper #1	03:13	03:16	00:03
Wrap #1	03:16	03:47	00:31
Movie Segment #1	03:47	09:03	05:16
Bumper #2	09:03	09:07	00:04
Commercial Black #2	09:07	11:10	02:03
Bumper #3	11:10	11:13	00:03
Interview	11:13	13:29	02:17
Movie Segment #2	13:29	17:21	03:52
Home Movie Intro	17:21	17:32	00:11
Home Movie	17:32	18:34	01:01
Movie Segment #3	18:34	22:07	03:33
Bumper #4	22:07	22:11	00:04

MAD MOVIES WITH THE L.A. CONNECTION

RUNDOWN SHOW #106 "Night Of The Living Dead"

All times are in minutes and seconds	IN	OUT	DURATION
Commercial Black #3	22:11	24:14	02:03
Bumper #5	24:14	24:17	00:03
Movie Segment #4	24:17	25:38	01:22
Toss to Preview	25:38	25:48	00:10
Preview	25:48	26:18	00:30
Final Close	26:18	26:40	00:23
Closing Montage	26:40	27:50	01:10
L.A. Connection Logo	27:50	27:55	00:05
Four Star Logo (slug black)	27:55	28:00	00:05

NIGHT OF THE LIVING DEAD SHOW NUMBER #106

CLIP TEASE

INT. HOUSE

WOMAN
Darn those neighbors. They're having a party and we weren't invited.

GIRL
Blow out the candles, dear. Then we'll watch Mad Movies with the L.A. Connection.

LITTLE GIRL
I'll blow them all out so then everyone can have a piece of my birthday cake.

GIRL
Hurry dear, there's a stick of dynamite.

SHOW MUSICAL THEME

COMMERCIAL #1

OPENING WRAP

INT. KITCHEN

KENT
I'm Kent Skov and welcome to Mad Movies with the L.A. Connection. As you can see, I'm preparing for a party to celebrate tonight's film, "Night of the Living Dead". One of our party guests is Harry Medved, the co-author of a book called "The Golden Turkey Awards". He's gonna drop by and talk about it with us. The original movie was about zombies who came back from the dead to eat the living. But our version is just a wild zombie party.

CHLORINE
It's a good thing we ran out of gas so close to the house.

JOHNNY
Why?

CHLORINE
The guests will be here soon for the party.

JOHNNY
Look, Chlorine, we've had so many parties before, why should this time be any different?

CHLORINE
But this time I sent out invitations.

JOHNNY
You should have decorated. Look at this place. You're supposed to use crepe paper and balloons, not just spray paint the cat.

CHLORINE
Well, Fluffy liked it.

MAN
Telegram.

JOHNNY
This is a great table decoration, I guess. But weren't we supposed to pick up some food?

CHLORINE
Johnny, I knew we forgot something.

JOHNNY
Great. Now I gotta walk back to the store and get it. Thanks a lot, cockerspaniel head. Go ahead and tell everybody when I get back I'll do my Buddy Holly impression.

CHLORINE
My cousin Duane's coming early to help.

JOHNNY
So what?

MAN
Telegram.

JOSH
It's a good thing we ran out of gas in this field.

DEXTER
Why?

JOSH
We're so close to the party.

DELBERT
Turn right, turn right, close enough. Let's get our dates. Come on, Willard.

EARL
Mine's got a fun coat.

MAN
Pull over! Pull over!

DEVON
Can my buddies and I get a ride to the party?
Alt: Did you take the road from town?

FELIX
Sure, ha-ha, ha-ha, ha-ha.
Alt: Why, is it missing?

DEVON
Somebody pick him off.
Alt: Somebody pick him off. That's an old Vaudeville joke.

DEVON
Anyone hungry? I have some sausages here.

MAN
Telegram.

(SFX RUNNING, PAINTING, JUNGLE NOISE & CRASHES)

CHLORINE
I've seen enough movies, I should've known I'd fall. Don't look up my dress. He'll want a tip. I'll pretend I'm not here. I'll invite Jimmy Carter, nobody talks to him anymore.

OPERATOR
The number you have reached is not in service at this time. And there is no new number—I said the number is not in service—Get away from this phone.

CHLORINE
I should've told Johnny to pick up some light bulbs, it's so dark in here.

MAN
Telegram.

CHLORINE
Oh, no, here come the Flintstones.

MAN
Ouch, this sunburn is killing me. Ooooo.

(HITS CHAIR, CAT YELLS)

Sorry, Fluffy.

CROWD
Surprise.

CHLORINE
It's not a surprise party…Duane.

MAN
Telegram.

DUANE
He'll want a tip, so lock the door.

CHLORINE
Johnny's not back with the food and we're out of ice.

DUANE
That's okay. I'll call for some.

CHLORINE
Don't go near the phone.

DUANE
(ON PHONE)
Hello, I'd like to order…

OPERATOR
Listen young lady—ah, Duane, is that you?

DUANE
Yeah hi,
(MUMBLING)
thanks, Ernestine.

DUANE
The operator said to look in the freezer for ice.

CHLORINE
Don't look in there, don't look in there.

DUANE
What the fu…

CHLORINE
The clothes hamper was full.

CROWD
Surprise.

DUANE
Hey! You kids get away from the car.

CHLORINE
(O.C.)
Look at me. Look at them. Look at me. Look at them.

DUANE
The guests are getting restless. There must be something to serve them. Nails! No, that's too tacky. Oh heck, these are a delicacy where I come from. Go get a platter and serve these outside.

CHLORINE
Damnit! Everybody's got one. We'll serve it on a bed of lettuce. Even hospital food looks good on lettuce. Do you have any?

CHLORINE
Yes.

DUANE
Where is it?

CHLORINE
Upstairs.

DUANE
Oh, wow, it's gone bad. I hope she doesn't have a rump roast in the bedroom.

COMMERCIAL#2/BUMPER #1

KENT
Harry Medved, the author of the Golden Turkey Awards, is a leading authority on bad movies. What would you say is the worst movie of all time?

MEDVED
It was Plan 9 From Outer Space, which is one of my favorites. This was voted the "Worst Movie of all Time" by our peoples' choice award. It's about zombies from outer space that land on earth. They have 8 plans to take over the world and all 8 plans fail. The 9th plan succeeds. It inspired "Night of the Living Dead". You can see that the zombies smell very bad and they smell bad in "Night of the Living Dead" too.

KENT
What makes you a leading authority on bad movies?

MEDVED
I think you have to be young and crazy like me to endure the kind of punishment I've gone through. I've seen 2000 bad films in part or in whole. The reason I say this is because some movies are just plain good or mediocre and not truly bad.

KENT
What makes a bad movie to you?

MEDVED
"Attack of the Killer Tomatoes" is not a bad movie to me. I like films that are unintentionally funny. In other words, "Attack of the Killer Tomatoes" is depressingly bad, but something like "I Dismember Mama" is wonderfully bad, it's entertainingly bad. Night of the Living Dead is actually a good movie with some bad performances.

KENT
What do you need to watch a good zombie movie?

MEDVED
I recommend some popcorn or some finger food. That way while watching the movie, the audience can identify a little with the zombies. When the zombies are munching away on the screen you can munch away at home. Kent, I gotta be going, I have a date.

KENT
Wait a minute, Harry, where are you going? I thought you were going to stay. I've got a beautiful blonde zombie for you.

MEDVED
I took a look at some of the zombies you have and they're not so pretty.

KENT
Do I still get my gift you were gonna give me?

MEDVED
Oh sure. This is a hero from a bad movie…this is Godzilla and he will wave goodbye and hope you enjoy the party.

KENT
Does he talk?

MEDVED
Ah, no.

KENT
I'm a little disappointed that you're not gonna stay. But a…

MEDVED
Next time get some better zombies. It's a really lousy party.

KENT
This has been Harry Medved. Now back to the movie.

DEVON
Hey! You're sitting on my lunch. Now go get me another one from the deli across the way. I had a pint of cole slaw in that bag.

EARL
Say, Devon, you seem a little tense.

DEVON
What of it?

EARL
Why don't you have some coffee?

DEVON
Thanks, Earl. You're what the expression "swell pal" is all about. I owe you one.
(WHERE CAN I THROW THIS AWAY?)

DUANE
First thing we gotta do is get rid of the table. If they don't see a table, they won't expect to eat.

CHLORINE
Good. We'll have room for the mud wrestling tub.

DUANE
You know something? This table has better legs than you do.

CHLORINE
Yes, but can it cha-cha?

DUANE
I just thought of something. We can take this table, make it into a raft, and sail it to the Caribbean.

CHLORINE
This was my mom's wedding dress. Funny, it looked better on the table.

DUANE
Help me with the table.
(GRUNTS & GROANS)

CHLORINE
What'd you say?

DUANE
Don't bother yourself, honkey.

CHLORINE
He said…then two people…maple syrup…

DUANE
This is no time to start crying.

CHLORINE
It's my party and I'll cry if I want to, cry if I want to, cry if I want to. You would cry too if it happened to you. I can hear more people coming.

CROWD
We're here. Surprise!

(ARMS THROUGH WINDOW)

DUANE
(O.C.)
It's not a surprise.

DOUG
They love sticks. Take these and share them. But don't give one to grandma; you know what she does with them.

DUANE
And stay away from my car!

LOU
I've gotta go.

DOUG
Wait a minute. My girlfriend's still in there.

(SFX: TOILET FLUSH)

DOUG
Christina, come on.

LOU
Man, PU! When are you going to get a regular lock on this door?

DOUG
(TALKING TO DOOR)
Don't use all the toilet paper. I need it too.
(MUMBLING)
Do you have someone in there with you? What's going on?
(MUMBLING)
Save that kinky stuff for your own home. Oh, your wife? Never mind.

MRS. LOU
I'm sorry I slammed the toilet seat on your forehead but you deserved it.

DOUG
Honey, are you having a good time?

CHRIS
No, not really.

DOUG
I have an idea. Let's play a wild party game. Hide and seek. I'll hide.

CHRIS
Oh, alright.

LOU
Wait for me. Don't start without me. Damn this lock. I love this game. I was great at this as a kid. Where should I hide?

CHLORINE
1…2…3…

DOUG
You better go hide—Well, I can tell this is your first time.

LOU
I'll hide in the trash.

KENT
I've got a home movie here that I was planning to show at the party, but since nobody is here…I'll show it to you. It was sent in by Betty and Cliff Bruton of Dallas, Texas.

ANNOUNCER
Eager, young, would-be magicians are taken by supersonic transport to the famous school of magic. Where they are instructed in the use of novelty gimmicks, such as a giant buzzer that squirts milk. If you want to pull a bunny out of a hat, you have to be able to think quickly. Moves like this require agility and strength. That's why the youngest students start by pulling full-grown adults across the lawn. Next, the amazing disappearing cake trick. It's not as easy as it looks, but by subtle finesse and total concentration, the skillful professional magician is able to perform the seemingly impossible. More difficult tricks include, how to create an earthquake. Only the most advanced students learn how to levitate an apple by keeping their mouth open, finally causing it to go into orbit around the magician's head. Newcomers must be careful, however, not to fall under their own spells. And so, their training complete, the magicians depart, with their hands on their heads to hold in all their new knowledge.

DOUG
I found the cat's saucer in the trash—all the milk's gone—Uncle Lou drank it. There were furballs everywhere. Want a dish of water?

CHRISTINA
I found your shorts in the car.

DOUG
The elastic is shot in these things.

CHRISTINA
How long are we gonna have to stay here?

DOUG
We've only been here an hour—we can't just get up and leave.

OUTSIDE
Surprise!

INSIDE
What? What? What?

CROWD
Surprise.

INSIDE
What? What?

DUANE
I can't hold them back much longer. Where's Johnny with the food?

(SFX GUN SHOT)

Ow, my head!

(SFX SECOND GUN SHOT)

LOU
I'm getting my slides, try and stop me.

CHLORINE
No, Lou.

DUANE
Anything but that.

CHLORINE
Johnny, you're back just in time.

JOHNNY
I've got the groceries.

CHLORINE
Everybody grab a bag. Oh, Johnny…be good.

DUANE
Can somebody give me a hand? One. One at a time.

MESSENGER
Telegram.

                              CROWD
    Duane, put some good music on the radio.
    Something we could dance to. Not that station.
    Come on, Duane!
    That's junk. Little bit country.
    Little bit rock'n'roll.
    That's good, turn it up.

                              DUANE
    What did I step in?

(SONG)
                Come on guys, grab your ghoul.
                Don't be shy, don't be a fool.
                Swing your baby round and round.
                Pick 'em up and throw 'em down.
                Poke 'em in the eye and kick 'em in the shin.
                And then you go and do it all over again.

                              CROWD
    Anybody want to go in the pool? I do. Who wants a drink? Make
    me a zombie.

COMMERCIAL #3/BUMPER #2

(SFX BONES BREAKING)

                              CHRISTINA
    Ow, Doug.

                              DOUG
    Sorry. I was wondering if I could get a kiss. I can tell this is your
    first time.

                              CROWD
                            (DANCING)
    Smack 'em in the nose and punch 'em in the chin. And then you go
    and do it all over again.

                              GIRL
    Great hors' deurves. And there still hot.

                              WOMAN
    Tasty ribs.

                              MAN
    Best finger sandwiches I ever had.

                              WOMAN
    I've got to get this recipe.

                              TV GUY
    This just in: Due to the success of Johnny and Chlorine's party,
    guests agreed to meet there same time tomorrow.

CHLORINE
They can't do this to me. There's no food left. I have nothing to wear.

KENT
Well it looks like this party turned out to be a real bomb and I made this great finger bowl. Hey, wipe your feet! Nothing worse than a messy zombie. See you next time.

CLOSING CREDITS

PANDA PRODUCTIONS

MAD MOVIES

TITLE: THE NIGHT OF THE LIVING DEAD

SHOW # 106　　DATE: 12/7/85

PAGE 1 of 2

CUE	TITLE	COMPOSER	SOC	PUBLISHER	USEAGE	TIME
T 1	MAD MOVIES THEME	RICHARD BAKER AND MARY NEWLAND	ASCAP	SONGSYNC MUSIC	SHOW OPEN VOCAL/INST	:50
B A	MAD MOVIES BUMPER				COMMERCIAL BUMPER: VOC/INST	:03
06-M2	NIGHT OF THE L.D. WRAP	R. BAKER/M. NEWLAND			B.G. INST	:31
M 1	NIGHT OF THE L.D.: THEME					:14
M 2	TELEGRAM					:31
M 3	TURN RIGHT					:13
M 4	SEE ENOUGH MOVIES					:21
M 5	TELEGRAM II					:32
M 6	COUSIN DWAYNE					:41
M 7	GOTTA GET SOME FOOD					:15
M 8	SURPRISE					:48
M 9	HEAD OF LETTUCE					:07
B B	MAD MOVIES BUMPER				COMM/BUMP VOC/INST	:04
B A	MAD MOVIES BUMPER					:03
M10	GET RID OF THE TABLE				B.G. INST	1:02
M11	THERE THEY ARE NOW					1:53
BG1	KENT'S THEME: HOME MOVIE INTRO					:10
HM1	"MAGIC SCHOOL"	R. BAKER/M. NEWLAND			B.G. INST	1:01
M12	UNCLE LOU'S SLIDE SHOW				B.G. INST	:40
M13	SURPRISE II				B.G. INST	:23
M14	GUN HITS FLOOR					:38
X1	GRAB YOUR GHOUL	COMPOSERS: R. BAKER/M. NEWLAND AUTHORS: CONNIE COOK STEVE PINTO STEVE ROLLMAN BOB BUCHHOLZ KENT SKOV			FEATURED SONG	:17

PANDA PRODUCTIONS MAD MOVIES

TITLE: THE NIGHT OF THE LIVING DEAD

PAGE 2 of 2　　SHOW # 106　　DATE: 12/7/85

CUE	TITLE	COMPOSER	SOC	PUBLISHER	USEAGE	TIME
B A	MAD MOVIES BUMPER	R. BAKER/M. NEWLAND	ASCAP	SONGSYNC MUSIC	COMMERCIAL BUMPER	:03
F 2	SWING YOUR BABY	COMPOSERS: R. BAKER/M. NEWLAND AUTHORS: CONNIE COOK STEVE PINTO STEVE ROLLMAN BOB BUCHHOLZ KENT SKOV			VOCAL/INST FEATURED SONG	:06
M 15	DIP IN THE POOL	R. BAKER/M. NEWLAND			B.G. INST	:31
F 3	SMACK 'EM IN THE NOSE	COMPOSERS: R. BAKER/M. NEWLAND AUTHORS: CONNIE COOK STEVE PINTO STEVE ROLLMAN BOB BUCHHOLZ KENT SKOV			FEATURED SONG	:09
M16	TASTY: PARTY MUSIC: CLOSE	R. BAKER/M. NEWLAND			B.G. INST	:36
106-M6	ZOMBIES WRAP					:18
T 2	MAD MOVIES THEME	R. BAKER/M. NEWLAND			SHOW CLOSE	1:20

OPENING CRAWL*

SHOW #<u>106</u>

SHOW NAME   <u>Night Of The Living Dead</u>

*Each numbered item as a single page...
Items #1-4: Centerframe
Items #5-9: Lower third of page

1   FOUR STAR
          in association with
          KENT SKOV

2   Presents
      an L.A. Connection
        production of

3   Night Of The Living Dead

4   Starring

5   Bob Buchholz

6   Connie Sue Cook

7   Stephen L. Rollman

8   Steve Pinto

9   Kent Skov

GENERIC BUMPERS*

SHOW #<u>106</u>

SHOW NAME   <u>Night Of The Living Dead</u>

*Each numbered item as a single page…

1   We'll be right back…

2   Don't Go Away

3   More Mad Movies
         Coming Up

4   Coming Up…
         More Mad Movies

5   Stay Tuned for
         "Your Home Movies"

6   Next…
         "Your Home Movies"

7   Write Us…
         L.A. Connection Productions
         6464 Sunset Blvd., #820
         Hollywood, CA 90028

8   Send Your Home Movies to…
         L.A. Connection Productions
         6464 Sunset Blvd., #820
         Hollywood, CA 90028
         (Include a self-addressed, stamped envelope for return of films)

9   Next…
         Mad Movies takes it to the streets

10   Next…
         Golden Turkey Expert

11   Next…
         The Party Continues

CLOSING CRAWL*

SHOW #<u>106</u>

SHOW NAME <u>Night Of The Living Dead</u>

*Each numbered item as a single page...

1 Directed by
  Kent Skov

2 Written by
  Connie Sue Cook
  Steve Pinto
  Kent Skov

3 Produced by
  Randall W Ridges

4 Featuring
  Bob Buchholz
  Connie Sue Cook
  Steve Pinto
  Stephen L. Rollman
  Kent Skov

4a Special Guest
  Harry Medved

5 Associate Producers (each name single page)
  Martha Whitney

6 Kent Weishaus (single page)

7 Music Composed and arranged by
  Richard Baker
  Mary Newland
  For Panda Productions

7a Music Recording by
  Richard Baker

8 Theme Performed by
  Mary Newland

CLOSING CREDIT CRAWL (con't)

9	Research by Bob Petrella Ken Segall April Winchell Ted Hardwick
10	Talent Coordinator Martha Whitney
11	Associate Director/Stage Manager Randall W Ridges
11a	Assistants to the Producers: Bob Buchholz Connie Sue Cook Steve Pinto Stephen L. Rollman
12	Facilities provided by Hy-Tone Video
13	Lighting and Camera Bill Sheehy
14	Gaffer Jim Drewry
14a	Production Sound Mark Hanes
15	Production Assistants Lisa Gougas Ted Hardwick Monti Santilli Rainbolt
16	Make Up Lora Sanders
17	Wardrobe Annie Vicari
18	Production Secretary Eloise Gonzalez
19	Post-Production Facilities Complete Post, Inc.
20	Post-Production Audio by Interlok Michael Perricone Michaele Hogan

CLOSING CREDIT CRAWL (con't)

21	"Your Home Movie" submitted by Bettye & Cliff Bruton Dallas, TX
21a	Location Courtesy of John & Joanne Singleton
22	Executive in Charge of Production for Four Star Television Bob Bosen
23	Special Thanks to: Susan Lenti Budget Films, Inc. Richard Holiday Dennis Condon Snagglepuss
23a	Opening Title Montage by Homer & Associates
23b	Opening Title Photography by Abe Perlstein
24	Post-Production supervised by Randall W Ridges
25	Executive Producer Kent Skov
26	"Celebrity Voices and Appearances Impersonated"
27	Copyright 1985 Four Star International, Inc. All Rights Reserved

THE OUTLAW

With the

SHORT RUNDOWN FOR SHOW #121 THE OUTLAW

DESCRIPTION	IN	OUT	SEGMENT TIME
SHOW OPEN	00:00	01:50	01:50
COMMERCIAL BREAK #1	01:50	03:54	02:04
ACT I	03:54	12:22	08:28
COMMERCIAL BREAK #2	12:22	14:25	02:04
ACT II	15:25	20:48	06:23
COMMERCIAL BREAK #3	20:48	22:51	02:03
ACT III/SHOW CLOSE	22:51	28:00	05:09

MAD MOVIES WITH THE L.A. CONNECTION

RUNDOWN   SHOW #<u>121 THE OUTLAW</u>

All times are in minutes and seconds	IN	OUT	DURATION
Four Star Logo	00:00	00:05	00:05
Clip Tease #1	00:05	00:24	00:19
Opening Montage	00:24	00:52	00:28
Host Intro and Preview Clip	00:52	01:50	0:58
Commercial Black #1	01:50	03:54	02:04
Bumper #1	03:54	03:57	00:03
Movie Segment #1 (includes Host Toss)	03:57	11:26	06:29
Host and Preview Clip	11:26	12:22	00:56
Commercial Black #2	12:22	14:25	02:03
Bumper #2	14:25	14:28	00:03
Movie Segment #2	14:28	20:45	06:17
Bumper #3	20:45	20:48	00:03
Commercial Black #2	20:48	22:51	02:03
Bumper #4	22:51	22:55	00:04

SHOW NUMBER 121 THE OUTLAW

(INT. CABIN)

DOC
Mad Movies is on. They're going to dub our voices. It'd sure help it you moved your lips once in a while. Hey, I got an idea.

(LOONEY TUNES SONG)

There, I moved your lips for ya.

CREDITS, OPENING TITLES

(EXT. RANCH)

HOST
Hi, I'm Kent Skov and welcome to Mad Movies with the L.A. Connection. The clip you've just seen is from our rendition of The Outlaw, originally one of the many Billy the Kid westerns. However we've changed all the dialogue. Now it's about three of the most famous gunslingers that ever roamed the West together, Billy the Kid, Bat Masterson and Doc Holiday.

(EXT. TOWN)

BILLY
What's up, Doc?

DOC
I've got a message for Bat.

BILLY
What is it?

DOC
He's looking for ya. He wants you and him to have a big hoedown.

BILLY
I think you're mistaken. I think you mean showdown.

DOC
No, Billy, I mean, hoedown. He wants to dance with ya.

(EXT. RANCH)

HOST
So, sit tight, we'll be right back with our…

(HORSE RIDES INTO FRAME WITH RIDER)

What the…
(READS MESSAGE)
Meet me at the end of Mad Movies—the Kid. Gee, I better get ready for a showdown of my own. We'll be right back with our Mad Movie.

COMMERCIAL #1

(EXT. RANCH)

                    HOST

With all new dialogue, here's the L.A. Connection's version of "The Outlaw."

(SIGN)

                    V.O.

(EXT—TOWN)

Our story takes place in Lincoln, Nebraska, but the state has been changed to protect the innocent. It's the story of Billy the Kid, Doc Holiday and Bat Masterson. It's the story of their legendary gun fight and it's the story of a lovely lady who was bringing up three very lovely girls.

(INT. BAR)

                    DOC
                   (B.T.C.)

Bat, Bat Masterson is that you? Come on back here and let me take a look at you. It's been a long time, Bat, you look like a horse's corral. And I see you're still chewin' tobacco.

                    BAT
                   (Gulp)

You made me swallow it, Doc.

                    DOC

That's something I owed you. For that time you set us up on that double date with the Rotunda sisters.

                    BAT

At least yours had teeth.

                    DOC

Just one and she was so ugly my horse gave her a carrot.
                   (B.T.C.)
Just thinking about her makes my hands sweat. What brings you here?

                    BAT

My big brown horse did. But that's not what I want to talk to you about. But I could sure use a drink first.

                    DOC

Yeah. Hey, you go back out and wait 'til we call for you. I hate pushy waiters.

                    BAT

You know that's not what we drink. You'd think someone was holding a gun on the bartender.

                    DRUNK

I'm not going to tell you again. I don't like a head on my beer.

BARTENDER
It can't hurt you. It's just foam.

DRUNK
I'm not talking about the bubbles, I'm talking about little bits of your head. You got a bad case of dandruff.

BAT
Well, what do you think? How do you like it?

DOC
I've never seen one that small.

BAT
It's still powerful and can do the job.

DOC
I wouldn't want to be caught in a tight jam with something as little as that.

BAT
It's new. They call it a derringer.

(EXT. STREET)

DOC
(Thought)
Hey, that looks like my girlfriend in front of that building. Naw, it's just my horse. That's right. My girlfriend doesn't have a saddle.

BILLY
Hi, partner.

DOC
Howdy, I see the dentist gave you a sucker.

BILLY
Yup, cherry.

DOC
Something stinks.

BILLY
I don't smell anything. What is it?

DOC
It smells kinda like a horse burning.

BILLY
I'm Billy the Kid.

DOC
So you're
(O.C.)
the fastest gun west of Lincoln.

BILLY
Ptui! Bad sucker. Who are you?

DOC
Well Billy…I'm Doc Holiday.

BILLY
So you're Doc Holiday, the fastest gun east of Lincoln.

DOC
What of it?

BILLY
If you're the fastest gun east of Lincoln and I'm the fastest gun west of Lincoln, who's the fastest gun in Lincoln?

DOC
Bat Masterson.

BILLY
I've heard of him. What's he like, Doc?

DOC
He likes you.

BILLY
That's good.

DOC
But he hates your hat.

BAT
Hi, I'm Bat Masterson, and I heard a lot about you.

BILLY
(O.C.)
Nobody says mean things about my hat.

DOC
Hey look, Bat, I got a real nice manicure today.

(INT. BARN)

HORSE
(B.T.C.)
Oh Wilbur.

BILLY
What's up, Doc?

DOC
I got a message from Bat.

BILLY
(B.T.C.)
What is it?

DOC
He's lookin' for ya. He wants you and him to have a big hoedown.

BILLY
I think you're mistaken, I think you mean show down.

DOC
No Billy, I mean hoedown, he wants to dance with you.

BILLY
How can I tell him no?

DOC
You have to stand up him and whatever you do, Billy, you have to be firm.

BILLY
Well when he expects me to show up I'll just send my horse.

DOC
I guess your horse don't dance.

(INT. HOUSE)

DOC
Listen Subpoena, after where Billy's horse kicked him, he's not going to be able to do any

(O.C.)
bronco bustin'. If you get my meaning. He's going to have to be left alone. That means no noise. Absolute quiet, understand?

(INT. HOUSE LATER THAT DAY)

(SFX: CLICK OF CHICKEN'S FEET)

SUBPOENA
Shut up! Quiet! You're making too much noise!

(SFX: WINDOW SLAM)

Who waxed his forehead?

BILLY
(O.C.)
Cigar smokin' stunts your growth.

KID #2
Hogwash. I've been smoking 'em for thirty years.

BILLY
I'll light it with my gun.

KID #2
Alright, thanks.

DOC
Say Billy, you know you haven't tried this trick in years.

BILLY
Don't worry, Doc. Hold it above your head.
(O.C.)
I said above your head. Close enough.

(SFX: GUN SHOT)

KID #2
Ow! He shot my finger off.

KIDS
Let me see...let me see.

DOC
My hemorrhoids are killing me.

BILLY
I'll take care of 'em.

DOC
How?

BILLY
Hold 'em above your head.

KID #2
Hey Billy, thanks to you I'll never smoke another cigar. I don't have enough fingers to hold it.

BILLY
You're welcome.

KID #2
Thanks.

(INT. HOUSE)

SADIE
(Hums.)
(B.T.C.)
Now Kitty, you stay outside 'til you've learned what kitty litter is used for.

(SFX: CAT YOWL)

WYATT
(O.C.)
Hey. Don't close that door, I'm Wyatt Earp and I'd like to sell you tickets to the sheriff's ball.

SUBPOENA
Oooooh.

SADIE
Aaah.

WYATT

Please.

          SUBPOENA
          (B.T.C.)
Never bought 'em, never will. Can't dance. So long, ciao, bye, adios, scram!

          SADIE
Sheriff's ball! I'll take two.

          WYATT
Great, now I win a trip to Disneyland.

          SADIE

(VISUAL: BIRD WALKING BETWEEN WYATT'S LEGS)

Congratulations!
          (O.C.)
Hey, that bird between your legs looks happy. I know a place for it to nest.

          WYATT
I bet you do.

          SADIE
I'll take care of your other animals, too.

          SUBPOENA
          (B.T.C.)
Sadie! Go to your room. Goodbye.

(EXT. PRAIRIE)

          BILLY THE KID
Look, wow, what is that?

          BAT
Beats, me Billy.

          BILLY
You ever see anything like that before?

          BAT
I don't even know what it is. I never come across one on the prairie before.

          BILLY
What do you think we should do, Bat?

          BAT
I think we should take off our hats.

          BILLY
Well, I think we should put 'em back on. Bat, this is stupid.

(INT. BACK ROOM)

                    GUNSLINGER
I've been gunnin' for you, Billy. You say draw.

                    BILLY
Alright, draw.

                    GUNSLINGER
                    (B.T.C.)
I'm warning you. I'm fast.

                    BILLY
                    (O.C.)
I'm over here.

(SFX: GUN SHOTS)

                    GUNSLINGER
Aaaagh.

                    MRS. KID
                    (O.C.)
Billy, wash up, your supper's ready.

                    BILLY
Comin', ma.

(INT. FRONT ROOM)

                    BILLY
How'd you like supper?

                    DOC
Pretty good.

                    BILLY
I'll think I'll leave ma a tip.

                    DOC
That's too much.

                    GUNSLINGER
Say Billy, you missed me. You want to try again?

                    BILLY
Should I?

                    DOC
Go for it!

(EXT. BY BARN)

                    DOC
                    (O.C.)
Say Bat, your shoe's untied.

                    BAT
You can't fool me. I'm not falling for that.

DOC
I was just trying to help.

BAT
Well I've had it. I want you both out of town.
(O.C.)
Aaaagh.

(SFX: FALLING DOWN)

DOC
Gee, I tried to tell him his shoe was untied.

(EXT. AMONGST THE ROCKS)

BILLY
I feel terrible.

DOC
Why's that?

BILLY
We've been kicked out of town and you've got the last sucker.

DOC
It's grape, my favorite flavor. I'll tell you what, Billy, you can have all the tang.

BILLY
Blech.

DOC
What's the matter?

BILLY
Ptui. Look!

DOC
Didn't you read the instructions? You have to mix it with water.

BILLY
Ptui!

(EXT.)

DOC
SONG
Oh bury me not, on the lone prairie.

BILLY
You're a drunken sot and your face is hairy.

DOC
Hey!

BILLY

Well it's true. Give me some gummy bears.

                    DOC
Save me the red ones.

                    BILLY
Forget it. I'm eating 'em all myself.

                    DOC
Well there's no sense in being such a pig about it.

                    BILLY
Oink. Oink.

                    DOC
Don't you enjoy sleeping out in the open under the stars and under the birds?

                    BILLY
No!

                    DOC
Is it because they ruined your hat?

                    BILLY
No, it's not.

                    DOC
Well, maybe you're afraid an Indian might sneak up and goose you.

                    BILLY
No, my back hurts from sleeping on rocks.

(INT. BEDROOM)

                    BILLY
My back is killing me.

                    SUBPOENA
You should sleep on something soft.

                    BILLY
Sounds good to me.

                    SUBPOENA
Billy, you mustn't. I get sick on seesaws.

                    BILLY
I want to teeter with your totters.

                    SUBPOENA
But I want you to respect me and uh, oh,
                    (O.C.)
forget it, let's neck 'til the cows come home.

BILLY
(O.C.)

Alright but I have a large herd of cows. Hey watch out! Ow, my eye!

(INT. SALOON)

BAT

Why'd you come back?

DOC

We had to, Bat.

BAT

I warned you what would happen.

DOC
(O.C.)

We ran out of food.

BILLY

I kept thinking about donuts.

BAT

Well now you're gonna pay the price.

BILLY

I'm ready, Bat. They're about a dollar twenty-five a dozen, right?

BAT
(O.C.)

It's about time we found out who's got the fastest gun, you or me, Billy. You just stand there and I'll hide behind these two guys.

DOC

You're not going to have a shootout with your pants falling down, are ya, Bat?

BAT

Leave my pants alone, Doc. I've been aerobicizing lately and I've lost some weight.

DOC

We're ready.

COWPOKE
(O.C.)

Where's the bathroom?

(SFX: GUN SHOT)

(B.T.C.)

I can wait.

DOC

You okay, Billy?

BILLY
Yeah, he missed me. I just got a bad case of gas.

BAT
How could I have missed from only this far away?

(INT. HOUSE)

DOC
Subpoena, you're too much of a woman for Billy.

SUBPOENA
Don't say that, Doc.

DOC
You need a man like me.

SUBPOENA
No.

DOC
What do you mean, no?

SADIE
Come eat your matzah balls.

SUBPOENA
You don't do anything for me but Billy makes me hot.

SADIE
The lentil soup was hot and now it's gotten cold.

SUBPOENA
I just ache for him.

SADIE
It's probably hunger. At least have a knish!

SUBPOENA
(B.T.C.)
You just don't excite me, Doc.

DOC
I don't know why not. I got class.
(Belch)
Is dinner ready yet?

SADIE
(O.C.)
Oy vey! I work all day over a hot stove and for what?

DOC
Someday I think you'll like me.

SUBPOENA

(O.C.)
Not if you eat those beans. Besides, you have fleas.

DOC
Is that what those are? I was going to say something 'cause they were on my plate, but I was too polite.

(EXT.)

BAT
What are you doing?

BILLY
I'm looking at that.

BAT
Oh yeah…what the heck is that?

BILLY
Don't start that again.
(O.C.)
They're smoke signals.

BAT
(O.C.)
What do they say?

BILLY
(O.C.)
I don't know, I don't smoke.

BAT
Hey, Doc!

DOC
(O.C.)
Just a minute…I think I sprained my wrist killing fleas.
(ON C.)
Oh smoke signals, I'm an expert on those.

BAT
Well Doc, what do they say?

DOC
Help, help, someone call the fire department.

(EXT.)

BILLY
(O.C.)
I guess their smoke signals got out of hand.

BAT
Look at that bed. I guess the fire must have started from body friction.

DOC
Go get us some marshmallows.

(EXT.)

BAT
I'm Bat Masterson, I have reservations for four.

JUAN
No problem. We can seat you right away. Barry Manilow come on at eight. Let me stamp your hands.

(INT.)

BILLY
(B.T.C.)
We've been standing here for twenty minutes. Why haven't we been seated?

BAT
I know why. Doc's zipper is down. Look!

DOC
Ha! You can't fool me! Oh wow. Well, I'm not going to zip it up with you staring at me.

BILLY
I don't think that's the only reason why we haven't been seated.

DOC
Oh and what's the other reason, mister book of etiquette?

BILLY
I'll tell you.
(O.C.)
It's your clothes.

DOC
Yeah, what's wrong with 'em?

BILLY
Those checkered pants you're wearing are out of style. They have been for years.
(O.C.)
Most cowboys are wearing scarves these days and if you're going to wear a coat you should wear it buttoned up.

DOC
How's this?

BILLY
Well now you look dapper.

DOC
That does it. I've had enough of your insults. We're having it out.

CHYRON…NEXT…THE BIG SHOWDOWN

COMMERCIAL #3

(INT. ROOM)

        DOC
We're having it out.

        BAT
Huh?

        DOC
Hmmmm.

        SUBPOENA
Huh!

        BILLY
Huh!

        DOC
Mmm!

        CLOCK
Cuckoo!

        BAT
Huh?

        DOC
Mmm!

        SUBPOENA
Huh?

        BILLY
Huh?

        DOC
Hmm.

        CLOCK
Cuckoo!

        SUBPOENA
I've had enough. Somebody shoot.

        BILLY
        (B.T.C.)
I put taffy in your holsters.

        DOC
For that, I'm shooting your nose off.

(SFX: SUCKING-POP)

                                BILLY

Make my day.

(SFX: GUNSHOT)

                            SUBPOENA

Doc! That's not his nose.

(SFX: GUNSHOT)

                                 DOC

Ooops!

                            SUBPOENA

(SFX: GUNSHOT)
                              (O.C.)

That's not his nose either.

                                 DOC

How could I have missed standing this close? You're supposed to stand still.

                              BILLY

What did you say, Doc? I couldn't hear you. I'm out of ear shot.

                                 DOC

Sorry Billy, I'll move closer.
                              (O.C.)

I said stand still.

                              BILLY

You know, we could use some practice.

                                 DOC

You're right, Billy. Why don't we go off and practice together. Can I have that sucker?

                              BILLY
                              (B.T.C.)

It's my last one.

                                 BAT

Wait, I need some practice, too.

                                 DOC

Sorry, Bat, practice on your own.

                               BAT

Huh? Alright.

(SFX: CLICK)

(SFX: GUNSHOT)

                              BILLY

Say...

                DOC

What happened to the rest of my bullets?

              SUBPOENA
                (O.C.)

I put 'em on the bulletin board.

                DOC

Thanks, I owe you one.

                BAT
             (Starts O.C.)

Look at that. I finally shot someone. But it was my friend. I killed Doc.

                DOC

No you didn't, you missed.

(EXT. RANCH)

                HOST

Well, that was our version of "The Outlaw." But that's not the only thing we've revoiced. Geoffry Smith of Anchorage, Alaska sent us his home movie. And as always, we edit them and add dialogue. It's tonight's home movie, entitled, "Unelectric Cowboy."

(SFX: GUNSHOTS)

Oh-Oh. Sounds like I better get ready for my showdown.

FOUR SECOND CHYRON...UN-ELECTRIC COWBOY...

The un-electric cowboy was determined to make a comeback. But he was lousy. When townsfolk heard the old man was riding again, they came from miles around, just to laugh at him.
               (LAUGH)
The cowboy got scared and tried to back out of his commitment, but the town wouldn't let him do it. So he went out and got falling-down drunk
               (HIC!)
...three times. And then he tried to ride. But—as well all know—whiskey and ponies don't mix.
             (HIC; BURP)
Thoroughly frustrated, he decided to beat everybody's brains in with a baseball bat. But a big old cowpoke got hold of him and threw him into the calf wrestling event.
               (MOOO!)
His Indian sidekick tried to do a good luck dance for him, but he forgot his moccasins.
            (OWW, OOH, OWW)
Screaming wild fans packed the stands on the day of the big rodeo. And when that buzzer rang, he surprised everyone. He'd never ridden any better—but he was still lousy.

(EXT. BARN)

> HOST
> If you'd like your home movies made into Mad Movies, send them to

(OVER ADDRESS)

> the L.A. Connection, 6464 Sunset Blvd, Suite 820, Hollywood, California, 90028.

(EXT.)

SHOT OF FOOTSTEPS PREPARING FOR SHOWDOWN, SHOT OF HAND ON GUN, FOOTSTEPS, HOST'S FACE, FOOTSTEPS, PUSH TO REVEAL OPPONENT IS A TEN YEAR OLD YOUNGSTER.

> KID
> Okay, partner. Reach for your guns.

BLOWS HOST'S HOLSTER OFF.

> HOST
> Well, you beat me fair and square.

> KID
> That's okay, I'll buy you a root beer.

> HOST
> Root beer? How about a Perrier?

> KID
> Sure.

> HOST
> Great. Hey, you think you can teach me how to shoot those guns?

> KID
> If you teach me how to play pool.

> HOST
> Alright, let's go to my place.

(EXT. STREET)

> DOC
> So what did you think of Mad Movies?

> BILLY
> It was funny.

                              DOC
        One more thing.

                              BILLY
        Yeah, what is it?

CREDITS

                              DOC
        You're in the non-smoking section.

                              BILLY
        Sorry.
                              (ptui)

HOST V.O. OVER CREDITS…ADDITIONAL VOICES BY ROZ TUREK

OPENING CRAWL*

SHOW #<u>121</u>

SHOW NAME   <u>The Outlaw</u>

*Each numbered item as a single page…
Items #1-5 Centerframe
Items #6-10 Lower third of page

1   FOUR STAR
         in association with
          KENT SKOV

2   Presents
       as L.A. Connection
        production of

3   MAD MOVIES WITH THE L.A. CONNECTION

4   Tonight's Feature   The Outlaw

5   Starring
          the
         Voices
          of

6   Bob Buchholz

7   Connie Sue Cook

8   Stephen L. Rollman

9   Steve Pinto

10   Kent Skov

GENERIC BUMPERS*

SHOW #<u>121</u>

SHOW NAME   <u>THE OUTLAW</u>

*Each numbered item as a single page…

1   We'll be right back…

2   Coming Up
    More Mad Movies

3   Stay Tuned for
    "Your Home Movies"

4   Send Your Home Movies to…
    L.A. Connection Productions
    6464 Sunset Blvd., #820
    Hollywood, CA 90028
    (Include a self-addressed, stamped envelope for return of films)

5   Next…
    The Big Showdown

CLOSING CRAWL*

SHOW #<u>121</u>

SHOW NAME   <u>The Outlaw</u>

*Each numbered item as a single page...

1   Directed by
    Kent Skov

2   Written by
    Bob Buchholz
    Stephen L. Rollman

3   Produced by
    Randal W Ridges

4   Featuring
    Bob Buchholz
    Connie Sue Cook
    Steve Pinto
    Stephen L. Rollman
    Kent Skov

5   Associate Producers (each name single page)
    Martha Whitney

6   Kent Weishaus (single page)

7   Music Composed and arranged by
    Richard Baker
    Mary Newland
    For Panda Productions

8   Music recorded by
    Richard Baker

9   Theme performed by
    Mary Newland

CLOSING CREDIT CRAWL (CONT'D)

10	Research by	Bob Petrella
		Ken Segall
		April Winchell
		Ted Hardwick
11	Talent Coordinator	Martha Whitney
12	Associate Director/Stage Manager	Randal W Ridges
13	Assistants to the Producers:	Bob Buchholz
		Connie Sue Cook
		Steve Pinto
		Stephen L. Rollman
14	Facilities Provided by	Hy-Tone Video
15	Lighting and Camera	Bill Sheehy
16	Production Sound	Eric Zeehandelaar
17	Gaffer	Jim Drewry
18	Production Assistants	Lisa Gougas
		Ted Hardwick
19	Make-Up	Lora Sanders
20	Wardrobe	Annie Viccari
21	Production Secretary	Eloise Gonzalez
22	Post-Production Coordinated by	Monti Santilli Rainbolt
23	Post-Production Facilities	Complete Post, Inc.
23a	Editor	Brent Carpenter
24	Post-Production Audio by	Michael Perricone
		Michaele Hogan
		For Interloc Prod. Studios

CLOSING CREDIT CRAWL (CONT'D)

25	"Your Home Movies" submitted by Geoffrey Smith Anchorage, AK
26	Location provided by
27	Executive in Charge of Production for Four Star Television Bob Bosen
28	Special Thanks to: Susan Lenti Dennis Condon Budget Films Snagglepuss Richard Holiday
29	Promotion by Dan Acree
30	Opening Title Montage by Homer & Associates
31	Opening Title Photography by Abe Perlstein
32	Post-Production Supervised by Randal W Ridges
33	Executive Producer Kent Skov
34	"Celebrity Voices and Appearances Impersonated"
35	Copyright 1985 Four Star International, Inc. All Rights Reserved

OUTPOST IN MOROCCO

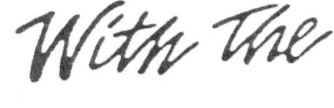

SHORT RUNDOWN FOR SHOW #112 OUTPOST IN MOROCCO

Description	In	Out	Seg Time
Show Open	00:00	01:10	01:10
Commercial Break #1	01:10	03:13	02:02
Act I	03:13	09:48	06:35
Commercial Break #2	09:48	11:50	02:03
Act II	11:50	21:26	09:36
Commercial Break #3	21:26	23:28	02:02
Act III/Show Close	23:28	28:00	04:32

MAD MOVIES WITH THE L.A. CONNECTION

RUNDOWN SHOW #112 OUTPOST IN MOROCCO

All times are in minutes and seconds	IN	OUT	DURATION
Four Star Logo (slug Black)	00:00	00:05	00:05
Show Open: Clip Tease.	00:05	00:20	00:15
Opening Montage.	00:20	01:10	00:50
Commercial Black #1	01:10	03:13	02:03
Bumper #1	03:13	03:16	00:03
Wrap #1	03:16	03:50	00:35
Movie Segment #1	03:50	09:45	05:55
Bumper #2 (Next…Your Home Movie)	09:45	09:48	00:03
Commercial Black #2	09:48	11:50	02:02
Bumper #3	11:50	11:53	00:03
Man On The Street Intro. (as needed)	11:53	12:01	00:08
Man On The Street or Interview Segment.	12:01	13:45	01:44
Movie Segment #2	13:45	16:48	03:03
Home Movie Intro.	16:48	17:37	00:49
Home Movie	17:37	18:41	01:05
Movie Segment #3	18:41	21:23	02:42

MAD MOVIES WITH THE L.A. CONNECTION

RUNDOWN SHOW #112 OUTPOST IN MOROCCO

All times are in minutes and seconds	IN	OUT	DURATION
Bumper #4	21:23	21:26	00:03
Commercial Black #3	21:26	23:28	02:02
Bumper #5	23:28	23:31	00:03
Movie Segment #4	23:31	26:58	03:27
Toss to Preview			
Preview			
Final Close	26:58	27:24	00:26
Closing Montage	27:24	27:50	00:26
L.A. Connection Logo	27:50	27:55	00:05
Four Star Logo (slug black)	27:55	28:00	00:05

OUTPOST IN MOROCCO #112

CLIP TEASE

MAN #1

I hear Mad Movies is coming on.

MAN #2

Yeah, but I can't see the T.V. from here.

MAN#1

Maybe you need glasses, what's your eyesight anyway?

MAN #2

I got 20/20 vision.

MAN #1

Yeah, that's what you think.

MAN #2

What do you mean, sailor?

MAN #1

T.V.'s over there. Ga, ga, ga…

MUSIC THEME

COMMERCIAL #1

ACT I

(INT.—LIVING ROOM)

SHOW INTRO

HOST

Hi! I'm Kent Skov and welcome to Mad Movies with the L.A. Connection. Tonight's feature is Outpost in Morocco, starring our guest, Marie Windsor. Marie's career has spanned over 4½ decades that includes 75 feature films and a long list of famous co-stars. Originally, Outpost in Morocco was about the French Foreign Legion…But, well, we've changed that…

(MARIE INTERUPTS BY LAUGHING)

What's so funny?

MARIE

I'm just thinking and a little afraid of what you're going to do to this.

HOST

Our's is a super sup thriller. So why don't you guys watch the movie and we'll be back shortly to chat with Marie Windsor.

(EXT.—FORT)

> MEN PULLING DONKEYS
> Wouldn't it be easier if we rode these mules?

(INT.—M's OFFICE)

> TED
> M, I told the chef you wanted water with dinner and he got angry and hit me on the head with this angel food cake.

> CAPTAIN
> Well, this really shoots my birthday party all to hell. Let's ask Jacque what the forecast is for today.

> TROUSEAU
> Thanks M, according to the weather map, it'll be fair to partly cloudy…clearing by noon with a strong chance of moisture around my stomach.

> TED
> You could drink his shirt with dinner.

> CAPTAIN
> We need help.

> MAN
> Hello, M.

> BOND
> The name is Bond, Ward Bond.

> MAN
> Don't you ever knock, who the heck are you?

> CAPTAIN
> If you're a true agent, you'll know the secret handshake very good. Say "hi" to Jacque.

> BOND
> Hi!

> TROUSEAU
> Hello.

> CAPTAIN
> We must recover our water from the Sultan. He's given it to his daughter Kitty. You'll be working with Jacque.

> BOND
> I feel safer with a Jacque. Here's a birthday card, it's not much.

> CAPTAIN
> You bet it's not much. The least you could have done was buy me a nice cape like yours.

> BOND

I couldn't go shopping cause my camel's hump had a blowout.

CAPTAIN
Jacque gave me this, an empty bottle.

BOND
Very nice.

JACQUE
I picked it out myself.

(INT.—DINING AREA)

KITTY LUSTER
(O.C.)
It's about an hour I guess, I should move. Doubles, I get to roll again. O, I'll have to go to jail.

DAD LUSTER
(thought)
Do not go pass go, do not collect 200 sheckels.

KITTY
I don't want to play, you're the one who should go to jail. You took all water in the, all I wanted was a wading pool, a wading pool.

DAD
I only did it to make you happy, Kitty.

KITTY
So?

DAD
You remind me so much of your Mother.

KITTY
You know mother had a beard. Do you know how hard it was to tell you two apart, particularly at the breakfast table?

DAD
But I was the one wearing the bra.

KITTY
Go kiss a camel.

DAD
(thought)
I didn't think anyone saw me.

(INT.—DANCE HALL)

WOMAN DANCING
Ow! My foot.

BOND
Sorry.

TED
Sit down, excuse me please tell everyone to sit down. I'm gonna sing.

HEAD WAITER
Ted's gonna sing. Do you have any requests?

BOND
Tell him not to.

TED
Maestro! She'll be comin' around the mountain when she comes… Get out of my way…

SHRINER
Excuse me, I'm lost, I'm looking for the Shriner's convention.

BOND
Sorry, I'm an Elk.

TED
She'll be drinkin' lots of moonshine when she comes…

CROWD
Shut up!

BOND
You should take some lessons?

TED
I did, but not for singing.

BOND
Were you able to find the water?

TED
No, but I found car keys.

MARIA
Here's a quarter. Keep him quite.

TED
Hey, there's a pac-man in the hallway.

BOND
Forget it. You have to find the Sultan's daughter, Kitty.

(INT.—WINDOWSIL)

TED
Pardon me, are you Kitty Lustworth?

GIRL
No, but I'll have a "Papa" burger and an order of fries.

TED
Alright.

(EXT.—DOORWAY)

(SFX: DOORBELL)

        TED
Are you -?

        GIRL #2
No.

        TED
Didn't think so—
         (mumbles fast)
Speed reading class paid off.

(EXT.—DOOR)

        TED
Excuse me, Mr. Bush. Here, Kitty, Kitty.
         (Affected)
Kitty, Kitty.

        TALL DUDE
I hate nosey people.

(SFX: VELCRO)

(EXT.—FIELD)

        TED
        (O.C.)
Mr. Bond—I couldn't find Kitty because I had to stop at "Noses 'r Us". Here's the bill.

        BOND
Mount the troops.

        TED
Woooooo… men, let's mount.

        CROWD
Alright, yeah.

        BOND
        (thought)
Eighty bucks for a nose, he blew it.

(EXT.—DESERT)

        WALLY
Hey, hey, Beav! Come look at this, Beaver.

        BEAVER
What is it, Wally?

WALLY
Take a look at this, Beav.

BEAVER
Man oh man, ain't she something. Boy oh boy, look at those things. I gotta go.

WALLY
Where are you going, you little goof?

BEAVER
I better go signal Mr. Bond.

(SFX: HORN-OOGA)

BOND
Hey, that's the Beaver's signal.

TROUSEAU
Give me your binoculars.

BOND
Use your own.

TROUSEAU
Oh yeah, man oh man, ain't she something.

BOND
Boy oh boy, look at those things. I'd like to take a dip in that water hole. Last one in is the African Queen.

(EXT.—HORSE TRAIL)

BOND
What happened to the troops? There's just a movie screen behind us.

TROUSEAU
Oh, my butt fell asleep.

COMMERCIAL #2

BUMPER—Next…Marie Windsor

ACT II

WRAP AROUND—INTERVIEW

(MONTAGE OF MARIE WINSOR CLIPS)

(INT.—LIVING ROOM)

KENT
(V.O.)
For most of her career Marie Windsor portrayed an aggressive domineering lady. However, for her role in "Outpost in Morocco" she played a different kind of character.

MARIE

I played a Princess. And that was very nice to have a role like that where I wasn't a heavy. And I didn't get the man either, I guess, either in a lot of pictures. I didn't get the man. If they didn't shoot me first I didn't get the man.

(KENT IS LAUGHING)

It was very sad.

KENT

Are there any co-stars you particularly liked to work with?

MARIE

I guess I could say I'm grateful to people like Wild Bill Elliott, George Raft, and Julie Garfield, for allowing me to play in their pictures. Particularly, since I was taller than two of those.

KENT

Did they have to stand on anything to …

MARIE

Sometimes they did. We manipulated things around the set. In "Outpost in Morocco" a special dress was designed for me in the Tango.

(CLIP OF M. WINDSOR'S DRESS)

I don't know if you're using that in your show. It was a very full dress, so that as I walked towards him, I practiced and my knees would bend a little more and a little more so by the time we got together I was a little shorter and I danced with great bended knee.

KENT

Now, how would this movie compare, say, to some of the other movies you've done?

MARIE

Well, that was considered an 'A' picture which I haven't done a lot of. At least it was on the verge of being an 'A' picture.

KENT

You've been called the Queen of 'B' movies. How do you feel about that?

MARIE

Yes, I don't know whether if I, well, I never made up my mind if I liked that or not. 'Course, it's always nice to be the Queen of something.

(EXT.—POOL SIDE)

MARIA
(thought)
If this axe were sharper, I could lop off her head.

BOND

Hey! What are you…

MARIA
Shh! I'm blow drying her hair.

BOND
If I didn't have chapped lips, I'd do it myself. Think she would let us use her pool?

KITTY
Who are you?

BOND
Good afternoon, Kitty. The name is Bond, Ward Bond.

KITTY
You want to go swimming? You'll have to talk to my father. Excuse me, I have a guppy in my ear. I hear you're quite a ladies man, Mr. Bond.

BOND
I'll take you to the disco but I won't dress like a monk.

(INT.—HALL)

BOND
(thought)
I knew this would happen.

CROWD
Hey, no cuts. No butting in. What's going on, Bud!

ABDUL
Tickets, next, tickets, tickets, please keep the line moving. Look at that outfit.

CROWD
Here's your tickets.

BOND
Excuse me, pardon me, sorry, excuse me. This place is really nice.

CROWD
Hey, the music started.

BOND

(INT.—LADIES ROOM)

Let's see. Kitty said she'd meet me outside the ladies room. Care to dance?

KITTY
Bond!

BOND
Kitty!

KITTY
(O.C.)

>   Is that a gun or are you just glad to see me? What did you do to
>   your head?

(SFX: KISS)

>   BOND
>   I got a bad haircut.

>   KITTY
>   It can't be that bad. Let me see it.

>   BOND
>   No, I'm not going to expose my head in public.

>   KITTY
>   Let's go in the ladies room.

(INT. BEDROOM)

>   KITTY
>   You were wonderful, Ward.

>   BOND
>   I know.

>   KITTY
>   Thanks.

>   BOND
>   Oh great, she took my last cigarette. What am I going to smoke? I
>   wonder if she'll think I'm strange if I smoke this piece of paper?

>   KITTY
>   What are you doing?

>   BOND
>   I'm smoking this piece of paper. But you know, it's not quite the
>   same if you don't put it in your mouth.

>   KITTY
>   I know exactly what you mean.

(SFX: KISS)

>   BOND
>   Should I?

>   KITTY
>   Will he?

>   BOND
>   Should I?

>   KITTY
>   Will he?

(SFX: KISS)

(INT.—DINING AREA)

SULTAN
Mr. Bond, let's take the cola challenge. I prefer the new cola, I love those bubbles.

BOND
I like the classic, but that's not why I'm here.

SULTAN
Ah yes, Mr. Bond, the water. What would you do with it if you had it?

BOND
Well for one thing, I'd take a bath.

SULTAN
Yeah, you need one. Should we give back the water, Sultan Pepper?

SULTAN PEPPER
No way. Never! Absolutely not. Maybe?

SULTAN
Well Mr. Bond, until we meet again.

BOND
Wait. What the hell did we resolve?

SULTAN
Nothing. That's how negotiations work.
(BURP)

BOND
That cola gave us gas. Oh, I wish I could do that.

WRAP AROUND

(INT.—BAR)

HOST
Well Marie, you certainly have done a lot of feature films, look at all the pictures on the wall. What about that one there?

MARIE
Oh, that's Bill Powell, that was from the "The Song of the Thin Man". I did that at Metro when I was under contract.

HOST
Uh, and, uh, what about this one right here?

MARIE
Oh, that's David Niven and me in a picture called "Bedtime Story". And Marlon Brandon and Shirley Jones were in that one.

HOST

Ah, and what about that one with John Wayne, up there?

MARIE

Oh, that one's from "Cahill U.S. Marshall". We did that one in Durango, Mexico.

HOST

Um, and how about that one right there?

MARIE
(LAUGHING)

Oh, uh, that's Young Olga, isn't it? I mean, you oughta know, you brought the picture.

HOST

I forgot. I always believe when you go to a guest's house you should bring them something. So I brought you "Young Olga". She's a Russian gymnast and she sent us a wonderful home movie. So, you want to watch it?

MARIE

Sure!

HOST

Ok.

HOME MOVIE

NARRATOR

Little 17 year old Olga Komeneski, after her Olympic triumph, was given a hero's parade down the streets of Moscow. A grateful nation gave her the hottest sportscar available. Then the plucky gymnast was given her own mountain, to do with as she pleased. It was here where she opened Little Olga's Snow World, where athletes were taught to plunge down treacherous slopes at breakneck speeds. Little Olga's Mountain Spice Ranch brought new flavor to the tables of her countrymen. But she looked around, and saw a bigger problem still. For years, her nation's only transportation was running and jumping. Little Olga, in an act of generosity, donated one car. It had no engine, but the people still rejoiced. With the establishment of Little Olga's House of Water, a landlocked nation began swimming like fish. Reactionary groups protested Olga's growing sphere of influence, but Olga continued to perfect her flawless Olympic technique on a balance beam of her own design.

(EXT.—FORT)

SOLDIERS

Left, left, left my wife and fourty-six children in starving condition without any credit cards. Did I do right, right, right by my country. But jingo I had an affair but she left, left, left...etc.

GUARD

What's the password?

ANNOUNCER

                    (PSEUDO WHISPER)
The password is Betty White.

(INT.—OFFICE)

                    TROUSEAU
Well Mr. Bond, tell me, have you had any progress in retrieving the world's water from the Sultan?

                    BOND
No, but I think I can get to the Sultan through Kitty.

                    TROUSEAU
Kitty, huh?

                    BOND
I think she likes me. She showed me her cannon balls off the high dive.

                    TROUSEAU
Huh? You let her splash out the water? You should be shot! Bang, bang, bang, bang, bang.

                    BOND
You missed me, you missed me.

                    GENERAL
Knock it off. M wants a report.

                    BOND
Bring your clarinet.

(EXT.—FORT)

                    GUIGI
Mama mia…ain't she something. Boy, oh boy, look at those meatballs. Okay, everybody go home, get out of my face, Arrivie derci! Ciao, bambini.

                    CROWD
Race you to the rock. Which rock?

(INT.—BEDROOM)

                    TROUSEAU
Ted, Bond has to get our water back. I can't shave. A handsome guy like me has a responsibility to keep my good looks.

                    TED
That's right, keep 'um to yourself.

                    TROUSEAU
Yeah, I will. Hey you! Come back here!

(EXT.—FORT)

                    BOND
                  (thought)

                    Let's see, where am I? The sun rises in the east, it's moving to the left, so north is front. Ah, these compasses never work.

(EXT.—DESERT)

(SFX. TRUMPET)

                              TROUSEAU
                    Oh no, the trumpet is skipping. Thank goodness I'm shielding my ear.

(EXT. FORT)

                              CROWD
                    Come on, bring it in. You almost got it pal, pull, pull. Go, go, go, go, go.

(PULLS IN ROPE)

                    Ahw, phooey. Darn fish took your bait. Ah, shoot.

                              BOND
                    Not a very good year for sand fishing.

                              TROUSEAU
                    That's true.

                              PEEING SOLDIER
                    It's so hot, I wonder if I still have a forehead. Oh, there it is. Thank goodness I was so worried there for a minute.

                              BOND
                    Take a look.

                              TROUSEAU
                    Man oh man, ain't she…

                              BOND
                    Enough already.
                              (O.C.)
                    One of us should volunteer to be lifeguard.

                              TROUSEAU
                    Me!

COMMERCIAL BUMPER—"BOND TAKES A PLUNGE"

(INT.—ROOM)

ACT II

                              BOND
                    Kitty, it's been months and you're still retaining the water. Aren't you ashamed?

                              KITTY
                    It's just that my father always wanted me to be an Olympic swimmer.

BOND
Well, if you marry me and give back the water, I'll be your partner in synchronized swimming.

KITTY
Oh Ward, we'll wear matching goggles and smell like chlorine.

(SFX: KISS-A-ROO)

(INT.—SULTAN'S ROOM)

SULTAN
So, you're gonna marry Bond.

KITTY
Yes, Father.

SULTAN
Are you sure? You're happy about this? Why are your eyes watering?

KITTY
I'm allergic to my hanky.

SULTAN
So you want a wedding gift. I'm sure Kitty, what? I'll give you anything, can I get you?

KITTY
I want you to give me the water.

SULTAN
Anything else you want my little darling.

KITTY
Yes, I'd like a new camel.

SULTAN
That's no problem. One hump or two?

KITTY
I'll pick my own humps—if you don't mind.

(INT.—BOND'S ROOM)

BOND
Gotta pack for my honeymoon. I'll take a nice dinner jacket. Hey, somebody bent the sleeve, well it'll be easier to pack. Say, now that we're getting the water back, I'll have a chance to use my pocket fisherman.

(INT.—BOND'S OFFICE)

TROUSEAU
I hear you're getting married, Mr. Bond.

BOND
Yeah, that's right, Jacque.

TROUSEAU
Gee, I was kind of hoping that uh, maybe I could be in a…

(SFX: WOOD CRACKING)

What was that? I hear that noise every time I sit down.

BOND
Here's your invitation. I ran out of stamps, sorry. Oh, and you will pick me out a nice wedding gift, won't you, Jacque?

MUSIC-BAD BUGLER

(EXT.—OUTSIDE FORT)

MAN
Who wants to be the first to kiss the bride? How about the grocery

GUARD
I do.

V.O.
Friends, Romans, countrymen, of the groom on the left…friends of the bride on the right.

(INT.—BOND'S OFFICE)

TROUSEAU
How do you like my wedding gift? It's a puzzle…move it 'till the beads go on the clown's eyes.

BOND
Oh!

(EXT.—OFFICE)

SULTAN LUSTER
I'm not waiting for the parking valet any longer. I've got to go give this message to Bond. Mr. Bond, I have this message for you from my daughter Kitty. "Kiss off, I'm heading out. You make me sick." During the night she filled her bags and ran off with Greg Louganis and all the water.

BOND
I'm not returning any of the wedding gifts. And if I'm not mistaken, those are my monogrammed towels.

DUO (SULTAN & PAL)
"Kiss off, we're heading out. You make us sick, also."

BOND
(thought)
That was a close one, but I wish I'd had one more chance to touch Kitty's -

(O.C.)
Oh look, the band left their clarinets.

THE END

COMMERCIAL #3

WRAP AROUND

ACT III

> HOST
> Thanks for joining us and I would especially like to thank our guest, Marie Windsor. It's been a real pleasure.

> MARIE
> It has been for me too, Kent.

> HOST
> Good.

> MARIE
> Very good interviewer. It's been a lot of fun and a great crew.

> HOST
> Well thank you. We'll see you soon. Maybe next time on Mad Movies.

ENDING CRAWL

(OVER CRAWL)

> HOST
> So, Marie, in that swimming scene, were you wearing a swimming suit or what…?

> MARIE
> It was a body suit.

> HOST
> It was a body suit.

> MARIE
> I kept it for a long time, but it stretched out.

> HOST
> Do you still have it?

PANDA PRODUCTIONS

MAD MOVIES

TITLE: OUTPOST IN MOROCCO

SHOW # 112 DATE: 11/30/85

PAGE 1 of 2

CUE	TITLE	COMPOSER	SOC	PUBLISHER	USEAGE	TIME
T 1	MAD MOVIES THEME	RICHARD BAKER AND MARY NEWLAND	ASCAP	SONGSYNC MUSIC	SHOW OPEN VOCAL/INST	:50
B A	MAD MOVIES BUMPER				COMM/BUMPER VOCAL/INST	:03
BG1	KENT'S THEME				B.G. INST	:34
M 1	OUTPOST IN MOROCCO: THEME					:15
M 2	WEATHER FORECAST					:11
M 3	I'M BOND					:04
M 4	AN EMPTY BOTTLE					:08
M 5	ALL THE WATER					:07
M 6	MOTHER HAD A BREAD					:09
M 7	GO KISS A CAMEL					:04
M 8	DANCING CLUB					:08
F 1	SHE'LL BE COMIN ROUND THE MOUNTAIN	TRADITIONAL FOLK SONG: P.D. ADAPTED BY R. BAKER/M. NEWLAND			FEATURED SONG	:46
M 9	LOOKING FOR KITTY	R. BAKER/M. NEWLAND			B.G. INST	:49
M10	MOUNT THE TROOPS					:18
M11	KITTY'S WATER MUSIC					:12
M12	BEAVER SIGNAL					:09
M11a	KITTY'S WATER MUSIC					:04
M13	TAKE A DIP/WHAT HAPPENED TO THE TROOPS					:16
B B	MAD MOVIES BUMPER				COMMERCIAL BUMPER VOCAL/INST	:04
B A	MAD MOVIES BUMPER					:03
M14	I'M BLOW DRYING HER HAIR					:04
M 3	I'M BOND					:04
M15	DISCO MONK				B.G. INST	:39
M16	IS THAT A GUN/CIGARETTE					1:04
01-M7	COLA CHALLENGE					:39
HM1	"LITTLE OLGA"				B.G. INST	1:03

PANDA PRODUCTIONS

MAD MOVIES

TITLE: OUTPOST IN MOROCCO

SHOW # 112   DATE: 11/30/85

PAGE 2 of 2

CUE	TITLE	COMPOSER	SOC	PUBLISHER	USEAGE	TIME
M 3	WELL MR. BOND	R. BAKER/M. NEWLAND	ASCAP	SONGSYNC MUSIC	B.G. INST	:04
M 4	"M" WANTS A REPORT					:08
M11	KITTY'S WATER MUSIC					:12
M 5	I NEED TO SHAVE					:07
M 6	KEEP THEM TO YOURSELF					:09
M10	SAND FISHING					:15
M11b	KITTY'S WATER MUSIC				COMM/BUMPER	:10
B B	MAD MOVIES BUMPER				VOCAL/INST	:04
B A	MAD MOVIES BUMPER					:03
M16	IT'S BEEN MONTHS					1:04
M 4	POCKET FISHERMAN					:08
M17	I HEAR YOU ARE GETTING MARRIED					:23
M18	KISS THE BRIDE	TRADITIONAL WEDDING MARCH: P.D. ADAPTED BY R. BAKER AND M. NEWLAND R. BAKER/M. NEWLAND				:18
M19	WEDDING GIFT					:18
M 6	MESSAGE TO MR. BOND					:09
M 6	ALL THE WATER					:09
M15a	KISS OFF/THE END/CLOSE					:14
T 2	MAD MOVIES THEME					:50

OPENING CRAWL*

SHOW #<u>112</u>

SHOW NAME <u>OUTPOST IN MOROCCO</u>

*Each numbered item as a single page…
Items #1-4: Center frame
Items #5-9: Lower third of page

1   FOUR STAR
   in association with
   KENT SKOV

2   Presents
   an L.A. Connection
   production of

3   Tonight's Feature

4   Starring

5   Bob Buchholz

6   Connie Sue Cook

7   Stephen L. Rollman

8   Steve Pinto

9   Kent Skov

GENERIC BUMPERS*

SHOW #<u>112</u>

SHOW NAME   <u>OUTPOST IN MOROCCO</u>

*Each numbered item as a single page…

1   We'll be right back…

2   Don't Go Away

3   More Mad Movies
                Coming Up

4   Coming Up…
                More Mad Movies

5   Stay Tuned for
                "Your Home Movies"

6   Next…
                "Your Home Movies"

7   Write Us…
                L.A. Connection Productions
                6464 Sunset Blvd., #820
                Hollywood, CA 90028

8   Send Your Home Movies to…
                L.A. Connection Productions
                6464 Sunset Blvd., #820
                Hollywood, CA 90028
                (Include a self-addressed, stamped envelope for return of films)

9   Next…
                Mad Movies takes it to the streets

10   Next…
                Marie Windsor

11   Next…
                Bond takes a plunge

CLOSING CRAWL*

SHOW #112

SHOW NAME   OUTPOST IN MOROCCO

*Each numbered item as a single page…

1   Directed by
         Kent Skov

2   Written by
         Connie Sue Cook
         Steve Pinto
         Kent Skov

3   Produced by
         Randal W Ridges

4   Featuring
         Bob Buchholz
         Connie Sue Cook
         Steve Pinto
         Stephan L. Rollman
         Kent Skov

4a   Special Guest
         Marie Windsor

5   Associate Producers (each name single page)
         Martha Whitney

6   Kent Weishaus

7   Music Composed and arranged by
         Richard Baker
         Mary Newland
         For Panda Productions

8   Music recorded by
         Richard Baker

9   Theme performed by
         Mary Newland

CLOSING CREDIT CRAWL (CONT'D)

10   Research by
Bob Petrella
Ken Segall
April Winchell
Ted Hardwick

11   Talent Coordinator
Martha Whitney

12   Associate Director/Stage Manager
Randal W Ridges

13   Assistants to the Producers:
Bob Buchholz
Connie Sue Cook
Steve Pinto
Stephan L. Rollman

14   Facilities Provided by
Hy-Tone Video

15   Lighting and Camera
Bill Sheehy

16   Production Sound
Stu Fox

17   Gaffer
Jim Drewry

18   Production Assistants
Lisa Gougas
Ted Hardwick

19   Make-Up
Lora Sanders

20   Wardrobe
Annie Vicari

21   Production Secretary
Eloise Gonzalez

22   Post-Production Coordinated by
Monti Santilli Rainbolt

23   Post-Production Facilities
Complet Post, Inc.

24   Post-Production Audio by
Michael Pericone
Michaele Hogan
For Interlok Productions

CLOSING CREDIT CRAWL (CONT'D)

25   "Your Home Movies" submitted by
Maria Vella
Fresno, CA

26   Executive in Charge of Production for Four Star Television
Bob Bosen

27   Special Thanks to:
Susan Lenti
Budget Films, Inc.
Richard Holiday
Dennis Condon
Snagglepuss

28   Opening Title Montage by
Homer & Associates

29   Opening Title Photography by
Abe Perlstein

30   Post-Production Supervised by
Randal W Ridges

31   Executive Producer
Kent Skov

32   "Celebrity Voices and Appearances Impersonated"

33   Copyright 1985 Four Star International, Inc.
All Rights Reserved

PERILS OF PAULINE

With the

SHORT RUNDOWN FOR SHOW #118 PERILS OF PAULINE

DESCRIPTION	IN	OUT	SEGMENT TIME
SHOW OPEN	00:00	01:45	01:45
COMMERCIAL BREAK #1	01:45	03:49	02:04
ACT I	03:49	12:23	08:12
COMMERCIAL BREAK #2	12:23	14:26	02:03
ACT II	14:26	21:46	07:20
COMMERCIAL BREAK #3	21:46	23:49	02:03
ACT III/SHOW CLOSE	23:49	28:00	04:11

MAD MOVIES WITH THE L.A. CONNECTION

RUNDOWN SHOW #<u>118 PERILS OF PAULINE</u>

TIMES IN MINUTES AND SECONDS	IN	OUT	DURATION
FOUR STAR LOGO	00:00	00:05	00:05
OPENING CLIP TEASE	00:05	00:27	00:22
OPENING MONTAGE	00:27	00:54	00:27
OPENING WRAP	00:54	01:14	00:20
CLIP #2	01:14	01:29	00:15
TOSS TO COMMERCIAL	01:29	01:46	00:17
COMMERCIAL #1	01:46	03:49	02:03
BUMPER #1	03:49	03:52	00:03
TOSS TO FEATURE	03:52	03:58	00:06
FEATURE SEGMENT #1	03:58	11:44	07:46
TOSS TO CLIP #3	11:44	12:13	00:29
CLIP #3	12:13	12:23	00:10
COMMERCIAL #2	12:23	14:26	02:03
BUMPER #2	14:26	14:30	00:04
FEATURE SEGMENT #2	14:30	21:42	07:12
BUMPER #3	21:42	21:46	00:04

MAD MOVIES WITH THE L.A. CONNECTION

RUNDOWN SHOW #<u>118 PERILS OF PAULINE</u>

TIMES IN MINUTES AND SECONDS	IN	OUT	DURATION
COMMERCIAL #3	21:46	23:49	02:03
BUMPER #4	23:49	23:52	00:03
FEATURE SEGMENT #3	23:52	25:07	01:15
HOME MOVIE INTRO	25:07	25:24	00:17
HOME MOVIE	25:24	26:40	01:16
CLOSING WRAP	26:40	27:10	00:30
CLOSING CLIP	27:10	27:22	00:22
CLOSING MONTAGE	27:22	27:50	00:28
L.A. CONNECTION LOGO	27:50	27:55	00:05
FOUR STAR LOGO	27:55	28:00	00:05

PERILS OF PAULINE SHOW #118

CLIP TEASE

(INT. DRESSING ROOM)

> OLD WOMAN
> I want you to watch Mad Movies with my daughter.

> MAN
> I wanna watch Mad Movies with you, not her.

> OLD WOMAN
> Watch it with her and um…

> MAN
> And what?!

> OLD WOMAN
> And I let you have what's inside that box.

> GIRL
> It's a hat just like my mom's.

> MAN
> That ugly thing?

> OLD WOMAN
> Yes.

> MAN
> Good, it'll go great with my ugly dress.

MUSIC THEME

(INT. CAMPAIGN HEADQUARTERS)

> HOST
> Hi, I'm Kent Skov and welcome to Mad Movies with the L.A. Connection. The clip you've seen is from our version of "Perils of Pauline." It was originally a musical comedy about silent screen star Pearl White. However we've redubbed all the dialogue and in keeping with the trend of today's career oriented women, we've made our heroine a candidate for mayor.

(INT. THEATRE)

> PAULINE
> Hi, I'm Pauline. I'm running for mayor. I'm here to talk about Women's Rights. We don't like being referred to as chicks, babes or tomatoes.

> MAN IN CROWD
> Ah, here's your tomato!

(THROW TOMATO)

(INT. CAMP. HQS)

> **HOST**
> Of course, everyone remembers Jane Bryne was elected mayor of Chicago. And Diane Feinstein was successful in San Francisco. In a minute, we'll be right back with our star's campaign for mayor. Everyone knows there's a lot of hot air in politics, and we're going to let some of it out right now.

(POPS BALLOON).

COMMERCIAL #1

(INT. CAMP. HQS.)

> **HOST**
> Now with all new dialogue, here's the L.A. Connection's version of "Perils of Pauline."

TITLE

(INT. DRESS FACTORY)

> **GILLIS**
> Kiss me, Pauline.

> **PAULINE**
> Not with that toothpick in your mouth.

> **GILLIS**
> (spits out toothpick)

> **PAULINE**
> No, no one's unwrapping me 'til Christmas.

(SFX: FIGHT 2 PUNCHES)

> **GILLIS**
> Happy holidays.

> **MOM**
> Pauline, I brought you a carrot for lunch.

> **PAULINE**
> (O.C.)
> Mom!

> **MOM**
> But I see you're serving knuckle sandwiches.

> **PAULINE**
> Yes, I gave him a full helping. If he wants seconds, I'm ready.

> **MOM**
> He should have something to wash it down.

(SFX: WATER)

PAULINE
(O.C.)

I just gave him some punch.

GILLIS

Hey, there's no lifeguard on duty. I should have never put that faucet on the file cabinet.

MOM

That's right! Wipe that silly look off your face. I'll stay and bop him too.

(INT. DRESS FACTORY)

PAULINE
(Whistles)

Hey, here's something for the baboon!

HURDY GURDYMAN

Thanks, how 'bout a treat for my monkey?

PAULINE

Here, I'll get him an odor eater.

FEMALE V.O.

Hey boss, nice shells, been to the beach?

GILLIS

Yeah...hey Pauline, nice view.
(O.C.)
Next time look out the window.

GILLIS

You don't do anything I hired you to do. You won't kiss me, or sit on my lap or do your Elvis impression. I don't want you lookin' out the window. I hired you to sew. I hired my brother-in-law to look out the window.

PAULINE

Well, where is he?

GILLIS

Well, we had a kind of a falling out, but the police can't prove a thing.

PAULINE

My talents are wasted here sewing. I'm not a material girl. You know, there's an election coming up. Maybe I ought to run for mayor. I'd get rid of high taxes, hyenas and best of all, these black sleeves on our shirts.

(INT. CAMPAIGN HEADQUARTERS) CHARLIE

Listen everyone, I've got a flash for ya.

(SFX: FLASH POWDER)

Well, that was it.

PETE
(Thought)
He's runnin' my wife's campaign!?
(Pause)
My shorts are creepin' up.

JACK
Is your husband upset about you running for Mayor?

PAULINE
Oh, he feels his masculinity is constricted.

MOM
The guy's shorts are creepin' up.

PETE
(Thought)
Great, why don't they put it in the paper!?

REPORTER
I'm from the Inquirer, can I put that in the paper?

PAULINE
Okay, where's Pete?

CHARLIE
Pete, Pete!

PETE
(O.C.)
Over here.

CHARLIE
You're over there.

PETE
(O.C.)
I'm over here.

CHARLIE
This guy on my left will give you some string cheese if you take a picture with your wife.

PETE
(Grumbles)
I didn't want her to do this. I hate string cheese.

PAULINE
Straighten your toupee.

CHARLIE
Yeah, just stand in front of these flowers we stole from Pearl and Mike's Bar Mitzvah. Oh, let me out of the way. This stuff's dangerous. It makes you wanna buy Slim Whitman records. Come on everybody, I got some cow pot pies in the back.

CROWD V.O.

Cow pot pies!?

PAULINE
Come on honey, they're your favorite.

CHARLIE
He won't like 'um. They don't have crust on the bottom.

CROWD V.O.
Cow pot pies! I can't wait.

(INT. CAMPAIGN OFFICE)

CHARLIE
Okay, fellas. Any of you reporters have any questions? Just go ahead. Alright.

(SFX: PHONE RINGS)

What? Hey, quiet down, I'm on the phone. Jim, it's for you. Alright, everybody, let's line up one more time here, we'll get a picture of…

JIM
What? Hey quiet down. I'm on the phone.

CHARLIE
That's no way to talk to people.

JIM
What's that? We'll be right there.

VARIOUS REPORTER V.O.'S
What's up? Where ya going? What's the deal?

JIM
Seems Pearl and Mike were having a Bar Mitzvah downstairs, and their flowers were stolen.

CHARLIE
Hey, hey, you guys. Where you going? I stole those flowers. You should be interviewing me. How do you like that? I'm always getting passed over. I helped raise three sons on a tv sitcom and what did I get for it? Nothing.

PAULINE
With Fred MacMurray?

CHARLIE
Yeah, everyone remembers his name, but no one remembers mine. Hey! Hey!

PAULINE
Pete. I forgot about him.

CHARLIE
I want you guys to start working on some campaign slogans.

GUY
I'll fix em' up, Chuck.

CHARLIE
And get me some more beef jerky, this one's almost gone.

(INT. CAMPAIGN HEADQUARTERS)

PETE
I don't want you to be my mayor, I want you to be my wife. I want you to stay at home, plant a garden, vacuum the dog, make hamburgers, and darn my socks and raise our children.

PAULINE
What are you saying? You know we don't have any children to raise. And you know why we don't, it's cause you can't raise your…Oh, oh, I'm sorry. I didn't mean to bring that up. Oh, oh, I'm sorry. I just meant that I wanted something solid between us. Oh, oh, I'm sorry.

PETE
I'm not going to vote for you.

PAULINE
Wait a minute, Pete, I want you to come with me. We'll be together. I give the speeches. You can be the helper. You can. You can make hamburgers.

PETE
So what you're saying is I can be your little hamburger helper. Thanks a lot!

(SFX: MAN BLOWING UP BALLOON)

(EXT. FIELD/BALLOON)

PAULINE
This oughta show the voters how I'll deal with inflation. Thanks for coming with me, honey.

PETE
Ohh, you've gained some weight.

V.O.
Remember…keep your arms and legs inside the balloon at all times.

PETE
How we gonna pay for this?

PAULINE
Oh, we'll make balloon payments.

PETE
You know, I might have considered doing this again if we'd have been turned around the other way. When I said, "Tie one on," this isn't what I had in mind.

CHARLIE

Get ready to shoot 'im.

MOM

Don't shoot her, that's my daughter. But you can leave Pete in the balloon. And when it goes up, poke a hole in it with this umbrella.

CHARLIE

I know you don't like your son-in-law, but Pauline does.

MOM

So what!

CHARLIE

We've got to get these campaign films done. The election is just around the corner. Go find a house to haunt! Alright everybody, smile pretty for the camera. Good, cut.

(SFX: ROPE CUT W/HATCHET)

(O.C.)

Wait! I gotta get that back to the Wizard of Oz by 8 o'clock.

(ON C.)

Darn it! What am I gonna tell the reporters?

(To reporters)

So you see fellas, that's how she plans to deal with run-away inflation. She takes it into the sunset with a democrat on the rope. Now print that in the paper.

(SFX: GOLF CLUB SOUND)

MOM

You dirt bag. Pauline borrowed my best dress for this thing and now it's going to be ruined.

CHARLIE

Calm down, calm down. The balloon will float to safety in a field and the dress will be okay. Don't worry.

BALLOON PILOT

Excuse me, the balloon landed in a nudist colony. They ripped the dress to shreds. Pauline's fine.

MOM

You're dead meat, Charlie.

CHARLIE

Ow! Ow! Ow!

(INT. TRAIN CAR—NIGHT)

MOM

So Pete couldn't come. Well, wishes do come true.

PAULINE

Oh Mom, if I can get through those speeches, my wish will come true and I'll be Mayor.

WOLFIE

> Pauline, I'm Wolfie. Charlie hired me to help you with your speeches.

PAULINE
Well my speech on organized boxing could use a little punching up. And I'm addressing a woman's group on protective clothing, the safety bra part's a little flat.

WOLFIE
Well, we could start now, as long as I'm not interrupted.

MOM
(Burps)

WOLFIE
Like that. Remember, what you say goes. Like from the horse's mouth not the pigs or the chickens or the ducks or the dogs.
(O.C.)
And politicians always tell the truth. The truth.

PAULINE
Truth.

WOLFIE
The truth, very good. Now repeat after me. You are the mayor to be…

PAULINE
I am the mayor to be a-lected.

WOLFIE
Not a-lected…e-lected, e-lected, e-lected.

PAULINE
E-lected, e-lected, e-lected.

(INT. STAGE/AUDITORIUM)

PAULINE
Hi I'm Pauline, I'm running for mayor. I'm here today, to talk about women's rights. We don't like being referred to as chicks, babes, or tomatoes.

AUD. DUDE
Here's your tomato.

(SFX. "BOINK, SPLAT"—AS P. DUCKS AND TOMATOES HIT BACKDROP)

PAULINE
Hey, oof, whoa. (picks up tomato) Give me that tomato, I used to pitch for a farm team.

AUD. DUDE
(Crying)

PAULINE
Where's George Steinbrenner when you need him?

GEORGE

I'm up here. You got my vote.

(INT. BACKSTAGE)

PAULINE

Pete, when I went out there, they came unglued.

PETE

So did my wig.

PAULINE

Oh...wow!

(INT. CAMP. HQS)

HOST

Well, things seem to be coming together for our star.

(PHONE RINGS)

Oh, excuse me one second. Hello.

V.O.

Is Pauline there?

HOST

Uh, no she's not. You see, she's not really running for mayor. This is just a tv show and what've done is revoiced all the dialogue and made our story into a...

V.O.

You mean I can't vote for her?

HOST

Well, no.

V.O.

Well, can I vote for you?

HOST

No, but thank you anyway.

(HANGS UP PHONE)

V.O.

What!?

HOST

You can't vote, but if you elect to, you can stay through the commercial and see what happens next.

CLIP

(EXT. TRAIN)

WOLFIE

Keep it down, I'm on the phone.

        PAULINE
Wolfie, coming to the dance tomorrow.

CHYRON OVER PIX—"WE'LL BE RIGHT BACK."

        WOLFIE
Oh honey, let's go. I'll get you that leather skirt you wanted. We'll double date.

(INT. THEATRE)

        MOM
That's the Gallup Poll Brothers.

        GALL BRO #1
       (Mumbles—whispering)

        GALL BRO #2
       (Mumbles—whispering)

        GALL BRO #1
       (Mumbles—whispering)

        MOM
Well? The Poll results?

        GALL BRO #1 & 2
        (Low)
Oh, uh, oh.

        MOM
Excuse me? Speak up!

        GALL BRO #1
       (Mumbles louder)

        GALL BRO #2
       (Mumbles louder)

        MOM
What the heck are you sayin'?

        GALL BRO #2
       (Mumbles louder)

        GALL BRO #1
       (Mumbles louder)

(SFX: PHONE RINGS)

      (Mumbles "Hello" on the phone)

        MOM
C'mon, Pauline. We've got to get this couch back to the psychiatrist by 8 o'clock.

(INT. CAMPAIGN OFFICE)

> CHARLIE
>
> Don't count on kick-backs, fellas. This dame just ain't crooked.

> CHIEF OF POLICE
>
> She's a politician, isn't she?

> CHARLIE
>
> Yeah, but I ain't seen nothing like it. She's got her feet on the ground and her head up her hat.

> UNION HEAD
>
> Her Mom with the wig could get to her.

> BLDG. CONTRACTOR
>
> Or her husband with the big toupee. Have you tried him?

> CHARLIE
>
> Sure I have. Ya think I'm an idiot?

> V.O. THREE MEN
> (O.C.)
>
> Yeah!

> CHARLIE
>
> That's not the point. I think that lousy husband of hers is influencing her to be honest.

> CHIEF OF POLICE
>
> Yeah?

> SECRETARY
>
> He typed this letter to Dear Abby. I forged her name.

> CHARLIE
>
> Wait 'til her husband Pete see's this letter. He'll think it's from Pauline. I'll show it to him. His influence over her will run out of gas.
> (Burp)

> BLDG. CONTRACTOR
>
> My glasses are fogging up.

> UNION HEAD
>
> Oh gee, let's get out of here.

> CHIEF OF POLICE
>
> Whew!

(INT. BACKSTAGE)

> PAULINE
>
> Tired of ironing, while he goes out nights? Vote for Pauline, and stand up for yourself.

> WOLFIE

No, no, no, Pauline. It's "stand up for your rights!"

        PAULINE
Stand up for your rights. Oh, I'll never be ready for this commercial.

        MOM
Pauline, we have to get that iron back to Arnold Palmer by 8 o'clock.

(INT. CAMPAIGN OFFICE)

        PETE
You wanted to see me, Mr. O'Stacey.

        CHARLIE
Call me Chuck, Pete.

        PETE
Alright Chuck—Pete.

        CHARLIE
Better yet, call me Chuckie-Wuckie. All my friends do. I consider you my friend.

        PETE
What's this you were telling me on the phone, about a letter from Pauline to Dear Abby?

        CHARLIE
Why don't you have a seat?

        PETE
Yeah, I want yours.

        CHARLIE
Hold on, Pete. There's more than one chair in the room.

        PETE
Where's the letter?

        CHARLIE
Well, here.

        PETE
       (Thought-Reading)
"Dear Abby, I want to be mayor but I don't want to be married. Use my real name, Pauline."

        CHARLIE
So, I guess this means you'll be breaking up with Pauline.

        PETE
I don't know.

        CHARLIE

This mayor thing means a lot to her. You know, if I loved her as much as you do, I'd do what I could to make her happy. I'd dump her and then I'd lay low for a while.

                    PETE
                    (O.C.)
Thanks for showing me the letter, Chuckie-Wuckie.

(SFX: DOOR SLAMS)

                    CHARLIE
That guy's a log brain.

(EXT—DAY, FIELD, TRAIN TRACKS)

(SFX: TRAIN WHISTLE)

                    CHARLIE
                    (O.C. Long shot)
We got one campaign commercial left to shoot. Come on.
                    (Med shot)
Pauline, the train will roll at 3:14, you jump at 3:16. Timing must be perfect or you'll be caught in the wheels and be squashed. Smashed like a grape.

                    PAULINE
Wha'd ya say?

                    CHARLIE
That's not important. But what is important, is next time. I say I want a director's chair. Don't bring me one of these. Okay, let's roll.

(SFX: CAR, HORSES, TRAIN, TUG BOAT WHISTLE)

Hey, hey, drive this car straight. Ok, look at the tax bandits. They're behind you. Turn around, pretend you're shooting 'em. Wait, they used too much saddle

(SFX: SHOTS)

soap again. They'll have saddle sores this big.

                    STUNTMAN V.O.
Hey Pauline, nice caboose.

                    PAULINE
                    (Thought)
I hate that talk. I'm usin' real bullets now.

                    STUNTMAN V.O.
                    (O.C.)
You missed me, you missed me. You aaaaaaaagh!

(SFX: SHOTS)

                    WOLFIE
Keep it down, I'm on the phone.

PAULINE
Wolfie, comin' to the dance tomorrow?

WOLFIE
Honey, let's go. I'll get you that leather skirt you wanted.
(O.C.)
We can double date.

PAULINE
That's perfect.

WOLFIE
Thanks, it was Elsie's idea.

PAULINE
Oh, after the fund-raiser, we'll all go to McDonald's and we'll all have hamburgers.

WOLFIE
Don't ever say that in front of Elsie.

(INT. CAMPAIGN HEADQUARTERS)

MOM
Take these pills, dear, and don't drive any heavy equipment.

PETE
So long everyone. Pauline, I'm going to Tahiti.

MOM
Oh, too bad, Pete, can I help you pack your luggage?

PETE
I'm leaving my suitcase behind, especially you, you old bag. I'm going where the women are beautiful and have great big papayas.

WOLFIE
Tahiti's great this time of year. While you're down there tell Bali, "hi".

PETE
My leaving should make Pauline happy.

PAULINE
(Cries)

WOLFIE
Cry-baby.

PETE
(O.C.)
This mayor thing means a lot to you but I can't take any more.

PAULINE
Oh Pete, I'm sorry, but we're all making sacrifices. I gotta wear a wok pan on my head.

PETE
Oh yeah, well I've got a skillet down my pants. Doesn't that make us a couple of fry cooks. I'm going to Tahiti and live off the fat of the land.

PAULINE
Why don't you start with your head?

(INT. CAMPAIGN HEADQUARTERS)

WOLFIE
Okay, everyone enjoy Pauline's victory celebration. As you know our new mayor only got 10 votes, but that was enough to win, since the other candidate was trampled by belly-dancers. Unfortunately, Pauline's missing, so we hope to find her before all the clam dip is gone.

(INT. RADIO STATION)

ANNOUNCER
Mayor Pauline Missing!

(INT. PHONE CO.)

OPERATOR V.O.'S
The mayor's still missing. No sight of Pauline. Mayor gone.

(INT. POLICE STATION)

COP DISPATCHER
My shadow has a hat?

(EXT—DAY TAHITIAN HUT)

PETE
Oh Pauline, why did you have to run for Mayor. I miss you Pauline, Pauline.
(Snores)

(EXT—BURNING STAKE B&W FOOTAGE)

PAULINE
Pete, Pete.

(INT. TORTURE CHAMBER)

PAULINE
When I said I wanted steak, this isn't what I meant.

PETE
Pauline always was a cry baby.

(B/W PLACARD)

PAULINE
Will Lady with crying baby, please take it outside.

(INT. SAW MILL B/W)

                PAULINE
Pete, we had so much fun, you were such a cut up.

(EXT. TRAIN TRACK)

                PAULINE
I was crazy for you. We were on the right track, and I was loco for you.

                MOM V.O.

(AS VOICE OF TRAIN WHISTLE)

You, you, you, you.

(EXT. TAHITIAN HUT)

                MOM
You, you, you wake up. My daughter's missing and it's all your fault.

                PETE
Get out of here, you second rate Mary Poppins!

                MOM
I'm going hang gliding.

(EXT. TAHITI BEACH)

                PAULINE
                (Thought)
Wait 'til Pete sees me here. Hi, Pete.

                PETE
You sacred the bee-geebies out of me. You can't just sneak up on someone in Tahiti. It's a federal offense down here. And what's that thing on your head?

                PAULINE
I don't know, Pete.

                PETE
You'd better get rid of it. It looks like it's ready to multiply.

                PAULINE
I know.

                PETE
I hope it's not contagious.

                PAULINE
I didn't come down here to talk about this.

PETE
I didn't either. Funny how these things work out. I suppose you're here to ask me to come home. Alright, I will. You dragged it out of me. There, satisfied?

(INT. DRESSING ROOM)

PAULINE
Why didn't you tell me Chuck made up that letter to Dear Abby and signed my name?

MOM
I got this coupon to have stuffed mushrooms glued to my neck. Otherwise I would have told you sooner about the letter. But then I was hoping Pete would stay in Tahiti. I mean, the guy's a bum, a loser, a jerk, an idiot, an amateur, a moron, a weasel. But if that's what you want.

PAULINE
What do you mean an amateur? He tries real hard and I love him.

MOM
(O.C.)
Well, I love mangos but I don't go to Tahiti for them.

PAULINE
Well I do.

MOM
Next time pick up the phone and have them delivered.

PAULINE
I'm not talking about food. I'm talking about Pete. I'm the new mayor and tonight's my inauguration and I'm gonna find him if it kills me. Even if the hair dresser did dye my hair blue.

MOM
Oh, it's punk.

CHYRON—"NEXT…PAULINE TO THE OCCASION."

COMMERCIAL #3

(INT. STAGE SHOW)

THREE WOMEN
Help, get us down. Help us.

ANNOUNCER
Ladies and gentlemen, I would like to present our new mayor, Pauline, and will the owner of a blue Ford, license 777 LAC, please return to your car, your lights are gone.

(MUSIC FANFARE, APPLAUSE)

PAULINE
The first thing I'm going to do as mayor is to elevate my mother to council person at large and men, if you don't like it, too bad.

PAULINE
I'm so glad you came home, Pete. I missed chewing on your eyebrows, and feeling your scraggly face and touching your toupee glue.

PETE
Did you miss smelling my breath? Huh?

PAULINE
Hm-hmm.

MONKEY KISS.

(Thought)
When's the next boat to Tahiti?

(INT. CAMP. HQS.)

HOST
Well, another successful campaign.

(WALKING TOWARDS WALL)

You know several political campaigns were remembered by their bumper stickers. Uh, I Like Ike…

(HOLDING UP RESPECTIVE BUMPER STICKERS)

Nixon's the One, and of course, our current president, Reagan, One More Time. And here's kind of a different bumper sticker…It's the title of our home movie. It was sent in by Dr. and Mrs. Howard Cremin of Los Angeles, California. It's called Home Entertainment.

FOUR SECOND CHYRON OVER MAN DANCING—"HOME ENTERTAINMENT".

Make this yuletide season the most exciting one ever by bringing home the only do it yourself kit that teaches you how to imitate your favorite superstar performers. Learn to be the kind of comedian whose every move knocks 'em dead. Before you know it you'll be able to belt out a song better than any two of the Supremes, or the Mandrell Sisters. For guy and girl acts, you can start by doing a perfect impersonation of Sonny and Cher and work your way up to the original dance routines of Fred Astaire and Ginger Rogers. Now you're ready for your own man show. You can do it all. Move over, Sammy Davis Jr. Watch out, John Travolta. Or how about a magic act? Make a glass appear from out of nowhere. Then just by laughing, fill it full of wine. Doug Henning never had it so good.

WOMAN: Ah-choo.

The secrets of escaping from a straightjacket are yours and you're suddenly a modern-day Houdini. Before you know it, the evening of fun is almost over, but not before you master an illusion worthy of David Copperfield. Believe or not, any two people can learn how to press their heads together and become…Me…Ah…ha, it works.

(INT. CAMP. HQS.)

HOST

(WITH BALLOONS)

If you'd like your home movies made into Mad Movies, send them to the L.A. Connection,

(OVER ADDRESS)

6464 Sunset Blvd., Suite 820, Hollywood, California, 90028.

(INT. CAMP. HQS.)

HOST

Well, thanks for joining us. I'm just going to grab a few souvenirs from the campaign. You never know, they might be valuable someday.

(PICKING UP SOUVENIRS)

(STRUGGLING TO GET OUT DOOR AS BALLOONS BEGIN POPPING)

Ah, well, whoever heard of saving balloons anyway. See you next time with more Mad Movies.

CLOSING CREDIT ROLL

CLIP TEASE

(INT. BACKSTAGE DRESSING ROOM)

PAULINE

I was on Mad Movies, I was on Mad Movies. Did you…did you see me on Mad Movies?

PETE

Ah, yeah, yeah, yeah.

PAULINE

Oh, woo, oh,…yahoo…wow! AH, Excuse me, howww did I sound.

PETE

Great, considering it wasn't your voice.

PAULINE

GREAT, considering it wasn't…my…uh…

HOST (V.O.)

Additional voices by April Winchell.

OPENING CRAWL*

SHOW #<u>118</u>

SHOW NAME   <u>Perils Of Pauline</u>

*Each numbered item as a single page…
Items #1-5 Centerframe
Items #6-10 Lower third of page

1	FOUR STAR in association with KENT SKOV	
2	Presents as L.A. Connection production of	
3	MAD MOVIES WITH THE L.A. CONNECTION	
4	Tonight's Feature	PERILS OF PAULINE
5	Starring the Voices of	
6	Bob Buchholz	
7	Connie Sue Cook	
8	Stephen L. Rollman	
9	Steve Pinto	
10	Kent Skov	

6464 Sunset Blvd., Suite 820 Hollywood CA 90028 (213) 465-2449

Mad Movies with the L.A. Connection

GENERIC BUMPERS*

SHOW #118

SHOW NAME   Perils Of Pauline

*Each numbered item as a single page…

1   We'll be right back…

2   Coming Up
         More Mad Movies

3   ~~Stay Tuned for~~
         ~~"Your Home Movies"~~

4   Send Your Home Movies to…
         L.A. Connection Productions
         6464 Sunset Blvd., #820
         Hollywood, CA 90028
         (Include a self-addressed, stamped envelope for return of films)

5   ~~BABY-ROBICS~~ [HOME ENTERTAINMENT]

[6   TEASE]

CLOSING CRAWL*

SHOW #118

SHOW NAME   Perils Of Pauline

*Each numbered item as a single page…

1   Directed by
         Kent Skov

2   Written by
         Bob Buchholz
         Stephen L. Rollman

3   Produced by
         Randal W Ridges

4   Featuring
         Bob Buchholz
         Connie Sue Cook

	Steve Pinto
	Stephen L. Rollman
	Kent Skov
5	Associate Producers (each name single page)
	Martha Whitney
6	Kent Weishaus
7	Music Composed and arranged by
	Richard Baker
	Mary Newland
	For Panda Productions
8	Music recorded by
	Richard Baker
9	Theme performed by
	Mary Newland

CLOSING CREDIT CRAWL (CONT'D)

10   Research by
            Bob Petrella
            Ken Segall
            April Winchell
            Ted Hardwick

11   Talent Coordinator
            Martha Whitney

12   Associate Director/Stage Manager
            Randal W Ridges

13   Assistants to the Producers:
            Bob Buchholz
            Connie Sue Cook
            Steve Pinto
            Stephen L. Rollman

14   Facilities Provided by
            Hy-Tone Video

15   Lighting and Camera
            Bill Sheehy

16   Production Sound
            Mark Hanes

17   Gaffer
            Jim Drewry

18   Production Assistants
            Lisa Gougas
            Ted Hardwick

19   Make-Up
            Lora Sanders

20   Wardrobe
            Annie Vicari

21   Production Secretary
            Eloise Gonzalez

22   Post-Production Coordinated by
            Monti Santilli Rainbolt

23   Post-Production Facilities
            Complete Post, Inc.

24   Post-Production Audio by
            Michael Perricone
            Michaele Hogan
            For Interloc Prod. Studios

CLOSING CREDIT CRAWL (CONT'D)

25   "Your Home Movies" submitted by
Dr. and Mrs. Howard Cremin
Los Angeles, CA

26   Location provided by
Burt Goodman and the Bay View Plaza Hotel, Santa Monica, CA

27   Executive in Charge of Production for Four Star Television
Bob Bosen

28   Special Thanks to:
Susan Lenti   Dennis Condon
Budget Films   Snagglepuss
Ridhard Holiday

29   Promotion by
Dan Acree

30   Opening Title Montage by
Homer & Associates

31   Opening Title Photography by
Abe Perlstein

32   Post-Production Supervised by
Randal W Ridges

33   Executive Producer
Kent Skov

34   "Celebrity Voices and Appearances Impersonated"

35   Copyright 1985 Four Star International, Inc.
All Rights Reserved

SANTE FE TRAIL

SHORT RUNDOWN FOR SHOW #101 "SANTA FE TRAIL"

Description	In	Out	Seg Time
Show Open	01:00	1:10	1:10
Commercial Break #1	1:10	3:13	2:03
Act I	3:13	9:45	6:32
Commercial Break #2	9:45	11:48	2:03
Act II	11:48	22:14	10:26
Commercial Break #3	22:14	24:17	2:03
Act III/Show Close	24:17	28:00	3:43

MAD MOVIES WITH THE L.A. CONNECTION

RUNDOWN   SHOW #<u>101</u> Page 1 of 2

ALL TIMES ARE IN MINUTES AND SECONDS	IN	OUT	DURATION
Four Star Logo (slug black)	00:00	00:05	00:05
Show Open: Clip Tease.	00:05	00:20	00:15
Opening Montage.	00:20	01:10	00:50
Commercial Black #1	01:10	03:13	02:03
Bumper #1	03:13	03:16	00:03
Wrap #1	03:16	04:08	00:22
Movie Segment #1	04:08	09:42	05:34
Bumper #2	09:42	09:45	00:03
Commercial Black #2	09:45	11:48	02:03
Bumper #3	11:48	11:51	00:03
Man On The Street Intro	11:51	12:01	00:10
Man On The Street	12:01	12:57	00:56
Movie Segment #2	12:57	16:47	03:50
Home Movie Intro	16:47	17:14	00:27
Home Movie	17:14	18:21	01:07
Movie Segment #3	18:21	22:11	03:50

MAD MOVIES WITH THE L.A. CONNECTION

RUNDOWN   SHOW #<u>101</u> Page 2 of 2

Bumper #4	22:11	22:14	00:03
Commercial Black #3	22:14	24:17	02:03
Bumper #5	24:17	24:19	00:02
Movie Segment #4	24:19	25:16	00:57
Close Wrap	25:16	25:30	14:00
Slug Black—"L.A."	25:30	26:06	00:36
Final Wrap	26:06	26:18	00:12
Closing Montage	26:18	27:50	01:32
L.A. Connection Logo	27:50	27:55	00:05
Four Star Logo	27:55	28:00	00:05

SANTA FE TRAIL SHOW NUMBER 101

CLIP TEASE

INT. BARN

COWBOY
Say everybody, I found the T.V. listing. Trigger was sitting on it.

VOICES
Mad Movies is on. Come on everybody, let's go. Don't let Trigger sit on the couch.

MUSICAL THEME

COMMERCIAL #1

SHOW INTRO

INT. MOVIE THEATRE

HOST
Hi, I'm Kent Skov and welcome to Mad Movies with the L.A. Connection. Tonight's feature stars a man whose hairstyle hasn't changed in over forty years. Recognize him? I do. It's President Ronnie Reagan in tonight's feature, "Santa Fe Trail", made in 1940. Now let's take the Reagan challenge. Has his hair changed? Not to me. You're probably asking yourself, what's the point to all this… nothing! The movie's been changed a little bit. The picture's the same, but the words are different. You see, in our version the President's toe tapping son, Ron Jr., dreams his father is running for President against Abraham Lincoln. I don't want to miss it. Come on everybody, let's go watch the "Santa Fe Trail".

CROWD
Five, four, three, two, one!

ACT I

INT. HOUSE

OLIVIA
Oh Ron Jr, you were whining a lot in your sleep. Were you having a bad dream?

RON JR.
Yeah. It was about Dad. It was horrible, he was running for the Presidency.

OLIVIA
But he *is* the President and it is HORRIBLE.

RON JR.
NO, NO, this was back in the 1800's. It all started in a bunkhouse with a bunch of guys in pajama tops all sitting around trying to decide who was going to run against Abraham Lincoln.

                    FLYNN
I think it should be Ronald Reagan.

                    CROWD
                    (Mumbling)
Ronald Reagan, Ronald Reagan.

                    FLYNN
He is the perfect choice.

                    HEFLIN
Why, because he knows all the words to Louie Louie?

                    FLYNN
Well, that's one.

                    HEFLIN
Go ahead, sing that tune.

                    RON
Please Errol, don't make me sing. I only know the first three lines to "Happy Birthday".

                    FLYNN
The first three lines are all the same.

                    HEFLIN
Our candidate should have courage and stamina.

                    FLYNN
He should also have hair that doesn't move.

EXT. WALKING HORSES—DAY

                    FLYNN
You know Ron, you're going to need a wife.

                    RON
We've asked everyone. Nancy is the last girl available.

                    FLYNN
Hey, I've got an idea. Give her some flowers.

                    RON
Sounds good.

                    FLYNN
Here. Sure.

                    RON
She'll like these.

                    FLYNN
Hey wait a minute, don't you know anything about flowers? You have to put them in water first.

OLIVIA

I can't marry Ron today, because I'm sitting on some eggs that I am trying to hatch.

MAN

Put another quarter in and take my picture. Is anybody listening?

RON

Excuse me Errol, do you mind holding my gum for me? I'll take over from here.

FLYNN

He's alright but keep him away from your eggs. Don't blow it.

RON

I'll pay you anything to be my wife. Just name it and it's yours.

OLIVIA

What kind of girl do you take me for?

FLYNN

There you go again. He misspoke himself. What he means to say is that you are worth your weight in gold.

OLIVIA

How much do you think I weigh?
(Bleep)
you!

(SONG)

THE CAMPAIGN WAS GOING WELL
A LOT OF MONEY WAS SPENT
IN THE SEARCH FOR A MAN
TO BE OUR PRESIDENT
RONNIE REAGAN IS THE CANDIDATE WHO'LL BE THE BEST LOT'S OF PEOPLE LIKE HIM AND HE'LL FOOL THE REST.
SAY, GO, GO, GO, GO RONNIE, GO, GO.

PAPPY

There is a chicken stuck to your butt.

OLIVIA

Yes, I know.

PAPPY

Well now that you are going to be First Lady, I hope you don't forget your old Dad.

OLIVIA

I won't forget you…say, what's marriage like?

PAPPY
(Whisper…spit…mumble)

OLIVIA

I'm gonna like that.

INT. BEDROOM

                    RON JR.
But then the dream got worse, you and dad got married. Then you were kissing Errol Flynn. Then Dad came in. And then you… then…he…then we…and they.

EXT. DAY

                    FLYNN
Let me congratulate you.

                    OLIVIA
No. Okay.

                    RON
You've been congratulated by the whole Army. Can I get in on this?

                    OLIVIA & FLYNN
Sure.

                    FLYNN
I'm not going to kiss you.

                    RON
I wasn't talking to you, I was talking to Nancy. We had a wonderful honeymoon. We went to Death Valley. Didn't we? Missed again.

(SFX. BELLS)

Hey, the ice cream truck is here. Want anything?

                    FLYNN
Snow cone.

EXT. BANDSTAND DAY

(SFX RIMSHOT)

                    GRANT
Hello, ladies and germs.

(SFX RIMSHOT)

I'd like to give you a man who is running for his second term in office—I'd also like to give you a hickey.

(SFX RIMSHOT)

Let's have a big log cabin welcome for Abe Lincoln.

                    LINCOLN
I was going to start with "Four score and seven years ago", but a funny thing happened to me on the way to Gettysburg. A woman walks into a bar with a duck on her shoulder, and bartender says, "Hey, you can't come in here with a pig…"

OLIVIA
(BURP)

Ooops.

FLYNN

Nice timing.

OLIVIA

Thanks.

LINCOLN

Well, are you done? Are you?

OLIVIA

Yes.

LINCOLN

Fine. Well there's one in every crowd. Now that you've gone and ruined my joke, I'm going back to four score and seven years ago.

(VOICE OVER—RON JR.
The campaign started to get ugly and so did the men.)

INT. GRANT'S OFFICE

GRANT

Mr. Lincoln doesn't appreciate you spreading rumors that he plays poker with the Ayatollah Komeini and two pelicans. So we'll publish this letter that Ron wrote to his fiancée.
Dear Nancy Wancy: You look good in skin tight jeans, so let me touch your jelly beans.
What do you think of it?

MEN

No way, etc.

ADJUTANT

Wait, I'd like to hear the rest.

GRANT

What do you want, a kiss or a medal?

MAN #1

I can't believe how scootily that letter was.

MAN #2

"Let me touch your Jelly beans?"

FLYNN

It is a good thing Ron doesn't write his own speeches.

RON

Make fun of me if you want, but Nancy married me.

HOLIDAY

Marriage stinks, I'd rather play spin the bottle.

                                      FLYNN
That's an idea!

                                    HOLIDAY
We can all play. Flynn here can go first.

                                      FLYNN
Then you be the bottle.

BUMPER #1 NEXT: YOUR HOME MOVIES

COMMERCIAL #2

MAN ON THE STREET

                                      KENT
We've decided to ask some actual Americans who they'd vote for if Ronald Reagan were running for President against Abraham Lincoln. Let's find out.

                                  RESPONSES
"If Reagan could grow a beard like that, it be Reagan. But a…it's Lincoln."
"I hate men with facial hair."
"Well, Reagan for a couple of reasons. Like he's from California, the karma's there, right? And Lincoln never took his hat off. That bothered me. You never knew if the guy was bald or not."
"Abe Lincoln, you trust a guy with a beard."
"I'd probably vote for Reagan. Lincoln's a little behind the times."
"Lincoln…strong domestic policy."
"Oh please. This is a tough question. I wouldn't vote."
"I think if, if Abraham Lincoln were a real person, if I knew them both then it would depend like which one I liked, but probably I'd back Reagan."
"Abraham Lincoln…he's a man of few words and much action."

                                      KENT
Did you know him personally?
"No I did not."
"Ronald Reagan."

                                      KENT
Why?
"He's alive."

INT. OFFICE

ACT II

                                      PAPPY
As Secretary of the Interior, you ought to know about decorating. Your desk would look better in the corner.

                                    COLONEL
I like my desk where it is. Besides, my chair and a lamp were already here. Not to mention the fact that I can see who comes in through the door from here.

PAPPY

Nobody comes through that door. If I weren't your brother, I wouldn't come through that door.

COLONEL

That's it. I'm gonna write mom, and tell her what you said.

PAPPY

Mom.

COLONEL

Yeah, and I'm gonna tell her you stole two of my hats last week.

PAPPY

Well, if that's the way you're gonna be, I'm gonna tell her what you did. You used to wet the bed and blame it on me. And that was when you were 16. And that's not all. I'm gonna take this hat too. I can steal 'em as fast as you can buy them, buster.

COLONEL

Why you...

FLYNN

Yes sir.

COLONEL

What do you want?

FLYNN

Well I...don't you know? You sent for me.

COLONEL

Touch your hat and get out of here.

FLYNN

Yes sir.

COLONEL

This is my last hat.

PAPPY

Then you better nail it to your head, tattle-tale.

EXT. GROUP OF MEN DAY

KID

Ayatollah, Ayatollah.

AYATOLLAH

What news do you have about the campaign?

MESSENGER

It doesn't look good, Ayatollah. The latest polls show that Reagan is ahead.

AYATOLLAH

We can't let Reagan win. He thinks ketchup is a vegetable.

MESSENGER
I thought it was a beverage.

AYATOLLAH
There is a fly on your face...I'm sorry, it was a mole. We're gonna ride. Who's gotta use the bathroom?

EXT. DAY

RON
Hey everybody, look! Errol's wearing a skirt!

FLYNN
(THOUGHT)
There he goes again.

HEFLIN
So you're wearing a skirt.

FLYNN
Yeah, it keeps me cooler.

AYATOLLAH
It looks good on you.

HEFLIN
But isn't that uncomfortable? How do you keep the leather saddle from chaffing your thighs, or maybe you just ride bareback, huh Errol?

RON
No, he wears panty-hose.

SOLDIER
Panty hose.

ALAN HALE
Panty hose.

AYATOLLAH
Panty hose. This is ridiculous. I'm going back to Iran.

(V.O. RON JR.
And I was in the dream too, Mom. I was on the campaign trail.)

EXT. BY WAGON DAY

RON JR.
Oh boy, Errol, am I glad to see you.

FLYNN
What happened, Ron Jr., what happened?

RON JR.
Well, I was dancing on the wagon and pirouetted off the back and screwed myself into the ground. Just like Wile E. Coyote.

FLYNN
Give me hand. He weighs a ton.

EXT. RIDING HORSES DAY

FLYNN
It is shame about Ron Jr. The way he pirouetted off the back of the wagon and screwed himself right into the ground.

VO: RON JR.
And then mom, you, dad, and the rest of guys went to get your fortunes told.

EXT. CAMPFIRE NIGHT

FLYNN
Nancy, ask the woman who is going to win the election.

RON
Yeah, is it gonna be me?

OLIVIA
Tell us, Squawking Beaver.

SADIE
Well it says that if you have children, they'll never xxx you. If you take sick, take chicken soup. And never pay full price for anything.

FLYNN
Well, what did she say? What does it mean?

OLIVIA
She said one of you will be President, and one of you is wearing pantyhose.

SOLDIER
It was Errol.
(ALL LAUGH)

SADIE
Next time curb your dog.

EXT. CAMPFIRE NIGHT

FLYNN
It's been a long hard tough campaign. Ron, there's been a lot of mudslinging.

RON
Yeah. I seem to have taken most of it…on my face.

FLYNN
There you go again. What a scum-blossom.

HOME MOVIE

KENT
Well...I'd like to show this week's home movie, sent in by Lee and Sylvia Smith of Palo Alto, California. And remember, if you'd like to see your home movies on the air, just send them to this address.

ANNOUNCER
The pine cone mold had grown to unbelievable proportions. Cautiously, young Doctor Volmer proceeded to follow standard laboratory procedures. Everything seemed to be in order, but then strange effects began to take hold. First, Volmer's pants became uncomfortably tight. / Then they disappeared altogether. / He left the world of science and moved to Arizona… / but he could not escape the force growing within him. / First, he built a swimming pool, which took enormous strength and pleased his friends. / Then, overnight, he enlarged it to a lake the size of Ohio / and went on to hand-craft a little something to ride around it in. / Volmer was sought out by the finest scientific minds of his time. He showed them all how to transform a toy train… / into the real thing. / He went on to develop a way to straighten peoples' teeth without using braces. / Then Dr. Volmer set out alone on a cross-country goodwill mission. When he came to a stop / he paused to build a tasteful monument and research center, dedicated to the spirit of scientific knowledge. When his work was done, he turned himself into an old man and retired.

INT. BARBERSHOP

CB 1
I never did like windows, no how!

CB 2
We heard a rumor you're gonna style Abraham Lincoln's hair like Reagan's, you weasel.

BARBER
Har ni Volvo smorgasbord.

CB 1
What'd he say?

BARBER
Myorkin Bjorn fjord by jiminy.

CB 2
How'd you like me to take this razor and shave off your moustache, then strap it on your liver and BBQ your carcass? C'mon, little buddy.

BARBER
I'm not even the barber.

INT. DISPATCHER'S OFFICE

DISPATCHER
Please be informed that the polls have closed. Reagan's been declared the winner. Lincoln is to concede. Pass it on.

CONGRESSMAN
Please be informed that the rolls have mold. Reagan is coming to dinner. Lincoln is not to be seated.

INT. LINCOLN'S OFFICE

LINCOLN
Please be informed that your nose is cold. Reagan's hair is thinner. And Lincoln is too conceited.

EXT. DAY

RON
I won! Congratulate me!

OLIVIA
Not yet, Ron.

RON
Well, why not?

FLYNN
Because she has to congratulate me first, don't you, Nancy?

OLIVIA
Well, okay.

(SFX: KISS)

RON
Wait a minute, I thought I was the winner.

FLYNN
I'm not going to kiss you. At least not yet.

VO: RON JR.
My father's inaugural was the best since Eisenhower.

EXT. STEPS TO BALL NIGHT NAPOLEON

Simon says touch your hat. Very nice.

BALD OFFICER
Touch your hat. Very nice.

BALD OFFICER
Touch your hat.

SOLDIER #1
Uh-oh.

ALAN HALE
What?

SOLDIER #1

He didn't say Simon says, so I guess we're out, huh?

ALAN HALE

Well Dagnabit, I was just following you. Now we have to turn in our hats.

BUTLER

Excuse me, did you two have your hands stamped?

SOLDIER #1

Hand stamped.

ALAN HALE

I've got an idea. We washed our hands. Can we get in on our looks alone?

BUTLER

No sir. In that case you two would have a long wait.

INT. BALL NIGHT

RON

Tell me something, Harold, why did the chicken cross the road?

FLYNN

TO GET TO THE OTHER SIDE! Everyone knows that!

RON

Gee, I thought I just made that up.

FLYNN

Oh hell.

OLIVIA

This girl is interested in politics. I'm sure there is some place that she can fit on your staff.

FLYNN

Hello, Bubbles.

RON

Do you have any experience?

PENNY

I'd like to get down and boogie with you.

RON

Well that is just the kind of experience I'm looking for. Do you take dictation? I've got a lot to say.

(RAMBLES IN BACKGROUND)

OLIVIA

Well, there he goes again. Harold, why don't you congratulate me again.

INT. BALL NIGHT

ALAN HALE
Hold it! Simon says take a drink.

(SFX: HORRIBLE SLURPING NOISE)

GUY
That's the dishwater.

ALAN HALE
I know. It's good. Needs more salt.

INT. BALL NIGHT

PENNY
Ron, I'd like you to meet Abraham Lincoln, and this is Ulysses Grant.

LINCOLN
So you're Mr. Reagan. Congratulations.

RON
Thank you.

GRANT
I didn't vote for you.

RON
That's OK. I didn't vote for myself.

GRANT
Nice going.

PENNY
Mr. Lincoln freed the slaves during his first term as President, that's quite an accomplishment.

LINCOLN
That's right, Mr. Reagan, I did. Say, what do you plan to accomplish?

RON
Well I…I hope to…I mean I'd like to. I better go ask Nancy.

BUMPER #2

COMMERCIAL #3

ACT III

INT. TRAIN DAY

RON
I have a lot of power for a President. The first thing I did was move the White House to Santa Barbara.

OLIVIA

Yes, I know.

FLYNN
His second act was to make Tip O'Neil the conductor on this train.

TIP
Attention, tickets please.

INT. TRAIN DAY

OLIVIA
(BURPS)

FLYNN
You should have something done about that.

OLIVIA
I tried, nothing seemed to work. Now I just use it as a flirtatious gesture.

FLYNN
Oh, I see, well it got my attention.

RON
Me, too.

FLYNN
Me, too.

OLIVIA
Me, too.

RON JR.
Don't leave, mom. Where are you going? I'm not through with my dreams.

DOCTOR
I can't take any more of this…
(mumbling)

OLIVIA
(Thought)
I wish I hadn't turned down that role on "Falcon Crest". Someone stop him, please.

SHOW CLOSING

KENT
Boy, what a nightmare. Just think, we could've had Reaganomics instead of the Gettysburg Address.

KENT
Here's a sneak preview for next week's feature…

PREVIEW BREAK

KENT

Thanks for joining us, and remember don't forget to send in your home movies.

PANDA PRODUCTIONS

MAD MOVIES

TITLE: SANTA FE TRAIL

PAGE 1 of 2   SHOW # 101   DATE: 10/5/85

CUE	TITLE	COMPOSER	SOC	PUBLISHER	USEAGE	TIME
T 1	MAD MOVIES THEME	RICHARD BAKER AND MARY NEWLAND	ASCAP	SONGSYNC MUSIC	SHOW OPEN VOCAL/INST	:50
B B	MAD MOVIES BUMPER					:04
BG1	KENT'S THEME				B.G. INST	:48
M 1	SANTA FE TRAIL: THEME					:31
M 2	NEED A WIFE					1:01
F 1	CAMPAIGN SONG	COMPOSERS: R. BAKER/M. NEWLAND AUTHORS: STEVE PINTO CONNIE COOK STEVE ROLLMAN BOB BUCHHOLZ KENT SKOV	ASCAP	SONGSYNC MUSIC	FEATURED SONG	:15
M 3	CHICKEN ON YOUR BUTT	R. BAKER/M. NEWLAND			B.G. INST	:21
M 4	RON'S DREAM					:13
M 5	ABE LINCOLN INTRO					:03
M 6	RUMORS ABOUT THE PRESIDENT					1:04
B A	MAD MOVIES BUMPER				COMM/BUMP VOCAL/INST	:03
B A	IYATOLA	R. BAKER/M. NEWLAND	ASCAP	SONGSYNC MUSIC	B.G./INST	:03
M 7	ERROL WEARS A SKIRT					:28
M 8	RON'S DREAM CONTINUES					:28
M 9	SHAME ABOUT RON JR.					:03
M10	RON'S DREAM CONTINUES					:06
M11	SQUAKING BEAVER					:06
M12	LONG HARD CAMPAIGN					:43
M13	HOME MOVIE: WRAP					:13
M 6	"YOUNG DOCTOR VOMER"					:23
HM1	SWEDISH BARBER					1:06
M14	THE POLES HAVE CLOSED					:33
M15						:30

PANDA PRODUCTIONS MAD MOVIES

TITLE: SANTA FE TRAIL

PAGE 2 of 2 SHOW # 101 DATE: 10/5/85

CUE	TITLE	COMPOSER	SOC	PUBLISHER	USEAGE	TIME
M16	RON REMEMBERS	R. BAKER/M. NEWLAND	ASCAP	SONGSYNC MUSIC	B.G INST	:03
M17	WASHINGTON D.C. PARTY					2:16
B A	MAD MOVIES BUMPER				COMM/BUMPER VOCAL/INST	:03
B A	MAD MOVIES BUMPER					:03
M18	MOVE TO SANTA BARBARA				B.G. INST	:33
M19	SANTA FE TRAIL: CLOSE					:21
M19a	CLOSING WRAP					:12
T 2	MAD MOVIES THEME				SHOW CLOSE VOCAL/INST	1:46

Generic Bumpers　　　　Show #<u>101</u>　　　<u>Santa Fe Trail</u>

Each numbered item as a single page…center characters

1　　　　We'll be right back

2　　　　Don't Go Away

3　　　　More Mad Movies
　　　　　Coming Up

4　　　　Next…"Your Home Movies"

5　　　　Stay Tuned for
　　　　　"Your Home Movies"

6　　　　Next…Mad Movies
　　　　　takes it to the Streets

7　　　　Write Us…L.A. Connection
　　　　　　　　6464 Sunset Blvd., #820
　　　　　　　　Hollywood, CA 90028

　　　　　Disclaimers…

8　　　　Send Your Home Movies to…
　　　　　L.A. Connection Productions
　　　　　6464 Sunset Blvd., #820
　　　　　Hollywood, CA 90028

9　　　　L.A. Connection Productions
　　　　　6464 Sunset Blvd., #820
　　　　　Hollywood, CA 90028

10　　　 Next…
　　　　　Reagan Moves the White House

11　　　 Next…

12　　　 Next…
　　　　　The Western White House?

1　　　　"Celebrity Voice and Appearance Impersonated"

Opening Crawl   Show #101   Santa Fe Trail

Each numbered item as a single page…center characters.

1   FOUR STAR
    in association with
    KENT SKOV

2   Presents
    an L.A. Connection
    production of

3   Tonight's Feature
    "Santa Fe Trail"

4   Starring

5   Bob Buchholz

6   Connie Sue Cook

7   Stephen L. Rollman

8   Steve Pinto

9   Kent Skov

Closing Crawl   Show #101   "Santa Fe Trail"

(Please prepare each line as a single page. Corrections and/or additions-deletions may be necessary)

1. Directed by
   Kent Skov

2. Written by
   Connie Sue Cook
   Steve Pinto
   Kent Skov

3. Produced by
   Randal W Ridges

4. Featuring
   Bob Buchholz
   Connie Sue Cook
   Steve Pinto
   Stephen L. Rollman
   Kent Skov

5. Associate Producers
   Martha Whitney (single page)

6. Kent Weishaus (single page)

7. Music Composed and Arranged by
   Richard Baker
   Mary Newland

8. Theme performed by
   Mary Newland

9. Research by
   Ken Segall
   Bob Petrella

10. Talent Coordinator
    Martha Whitney

11. Associate Director/Stage Manager
    Randal W Ridges

12. Facilities provided by
    Mike Craven Productions

13. Lighting and Camera
    Mike Craven

Page 2   show 101

14	Grip Lloyd Nyburg
15	Production Assistants Lisa Gougas Ted Hardwick Monti Rainbolt
16	Make Up Lora Sanders
17	Wardrobe Annie Vicari
18	Production Secretary Eloise Gonzales
19	Post-Production Facilities Compact Video Systems, Inc.
20	Post-Production Audio by Airetight Productions, Michael Perricone and Michaele Hogan
21	"Your Home Movie" submitted by Lee and Slvia Smith Palo Alto, CA
22	Executive in Charge of Production for Four Star Television Bob Bosen
23	Special Thanks to: Susan Lenti, Robert E. Evans, [Richard Hollony, Dennis Conoon,] Sonja Bracy, Tom Fortuin, Molly De Hetre, Budget Films, Inc., Snagglepuss
24	Taped on Location at the NUART THEATER in West Los Angeles, CA
24a	Automobile Provided by David Rego of Pace Development
25	Post-Production Supervised by Randal W Ridges
26	Executive Producer Kent Skov
27	Copyright 1985 Four Star International, Inc. ~~L.A. Connection Productions.~~ All Rights Reserved

SHERLOCK HOLMES

With the

MAD MOVIES WITH THE L.A. CONNECTION

RUNDOWN   SHOW# 108 "SHERLOCK HOLMES"

All times are in minutes and seconds	IN	OUT	DURATION
Four Star Logo (slug Black)	00:00	00:05	00:05
Show Open: Clip Tease.	00:05	00:20	00:15
Opening Montage.	00:20	01:10	00:50
Commercial Black #1	01:10	03:13	02:03
Bumper #1	03:13	03:16	00:03
Wrap #1	03:16	04:07	00:51
Movie Segment #1	04:07	09:33	05:26
Bumper #2 (Next…Your Home Movie)	09:33	09:36	00:04
Commercial Black #2	09:36	11:40	02:03
Bumper #3	11:40	11:43	00:03
Man On The Street Intro. (as needed)	11:43	11:49	00:06
Man On The Street or Interview Segment.	11:49	12:22	00:33
Movie Segment #2	12:22	15:22	03:00
Home Movie Intro.	15:22	15:30	00:08
Home Movie	15:30	16:42	01:12
Movie Segment #3	16:42	21:04	04:22

MAD MOVIES WITH THE L.A. CONNECTION

RUNDOWN   SHOW #<u>108</u> "SHERLOCK HOLMES"

Bumper #4	21:04	21:08	00:04
Commercial Black #3	21:08	23:11	02:03
Bumper #5	23:11	23:14	00:04
Movie Segment #4	23:14	26:25	03:14
Toss to Preview	26:25	26:30	00:05
Preview			
Final Close	26:30	26:51	00:21
Closing Montage	26:51	27:45	00:54
L.A. Connection Logo	27:45	27:50	00:05
Four Star Logo (slug black)	27:50	27:55	00:05

SHERLOCK HOLMES AND THE SECRET WEAPON #108

CLIP TEASE

MARCH
Let's go, honey.

LOMBARD
Wait a minute! Mad Movies is on!

MARCH
Mad Movies!

LOMBARD
Yeah, Mad Movies with the L.A. Connection! Don't you want to watch?

MARCH
We're getting married today.

LOMBARD
We can do that some other time.

MARCH
Well, ok.

LOMBARD

(RUNNING DOWN THE STREET)

Hooray! Mad Movies is on! Yeah! Come on, Checkers! Neener, neener!

(DOG BARKS)

MARCH
Oh wow! That was a close one.

LOMBARD
Yeah! Mad Movies!

MUSIC INTRO

COMMERCIAL #1

(INT.—LIBRARY)

SHOW OPEN

HOST
Hi, I'm Kent Skov and welcome to Mad Movies with the L.A. Connection. I'm here at the library looking through several Sherlock Holmes books…Ah, let's see, "Hound of the Baskervilles", "The Last Adventure of Sherlock Holmes", "Sherlock Holmes Meets Larry Holmes"…and ah, tonight's movie "Sherlock Holmes And The Secret Weapon". But, as always we've changed the plot of the original movie to our own. So, uh, we, won't need these…Ours is about The Library Police. See, people

are keeping library books past the due date and the Library Police are called in to restore justice. So in our Mad Movie the library can be a pretty scary place.

(O.C.)

Shhh! Here's the movie.

(INT.—LIVING ROOM)

SHERLOCK HOLMES

So Daphne, you say books aren't being returned to the library and you want me to find them?

DAPHNE

Yes, Sherlock!

SHERLOCK HOLMES

Because I'm a better detective than Magnum P.I. and cheaper than wine.

(SFX: SUCKING NOISE)

Wanna light?

DAPHNE

I don't smoke.

(SFX: PHONE RINGING)

Hello…yes. Try a cucumber. What! The doctor says it's perfectly alright.

SHERLOCK HOLMES

That was the phone, wasn't it?

DAPHNE

Yes, that was my assistant librarian. *The Joy of Sex* is overdue.

SHERLOCK HOLMES

Did he learn anything from it?

DAPHNE

Not that I could tell. I know you want to get started so I'll pay you in advance. Here's three dollars.

(EXT.—FRONT PORCH-NIGHT)

DR. F. TOBEL

Granpa Holmes, how long have you been standing out here?

GRANPA HOLMES

About an hour and a half. I knew I should have knocked. I got some more books for you. One of them's *One Hundred and One Decorating Ideas With Toenail Clippings*.

DR. F. TOBEL

We've had a lot of requests for that.

GRANPA HOLMES
I think the Library Police have been following me.

(INT.—LIVING ROOM-NIGHT)

GRANPA HOLMES
I need a better look.

LIBRARY COP #1
He's gonna get naked.

DR. F. TOBEL
I don't want you getting undressed in front of the window anymore. I got nineteen complaint letters here.

GRANPA HOLMES
So what! You're the only one who knows I'm not wearing any clothes under this coat.

DR. TOBEL
Your grandson Sherlock would know, isn't he the best detective in the world?

GRANPA HOLMES
No, he just works cheap. Listen Tobel, I made some alterations in *The Joy of Sex* book. I hope you don't mind.

DR. TOBEL
Alterations like what?

GRANPA HOLMES
I cut out all the pictures. It makes a handy, dandy lunch box. I put my sandwich and a box of raisins in here. Goes anywhere.

(EXT.—STREET)

GRANPA HOLMES
The library cops are leaving.

LIBRARY COP #2
Our car's getting towed away, come back.

GRANPA HOLMES
They should've known not to double park.

DR. TOBEL
Now's our chance to get away.

GRANPA HOLMES
Not yet…I want to watch those ninnies chase the tow truck.

DR. TOBEL
We've got to meet the black market book buyers.

GRANPA HOLMES
When you're my age, this is more fun. Hey wait a minute, the time's run out on our parking meter. Race you to the car.

> DR. TOBEL
> Don't you think I should drive, Granpa Holmes?

> GRANPA HOLMES
> No. Who put the steering wheel over here?

> DR. TOBEL
> Put it in 'R' for really fast, put it in drive! Put it in drive!

> GRANPA HOLMES
> Don't tell me how to drive, you little snot!

(SFX: CAR SMASHING INTO TRASH CANS)

> DR. TOBEL
> You sure you don't want me to drive?

> GRANPA HOLMES
> No! I'm fine!

(INT.—BAR)

> PIRATE DINO
> Aaar Aaar Aaar.

> FAT PIRATE
> Aar Burp Aar.

> PIRATE DINO
> Aaaar Aaar.

(SFX: GLASS BREAKING)

> FAT PIRATE
> Aaar.

(SFX: WOODEN LEG CLUMPING)

(EXT. STREET)

> PEG LEG
> Say buddy, could you spare a quarter? I need to buy another leg.

> PIRATE DINO
> What happened to yours?

> PEG LEG
> I traded it for this lovely pirate outfit. But yours is even nicer.

> PIRATE DINO
> What of it?

> PEG LEG
> I'd like to trade for it. I'll give you my other leg for it. I'll even throw in an eyeball or what's under my hat. Is it a deal?

                    PIRATE DINO
You're nuts.

                    PEG LEG
                    (O.C.)
I draw the line somewhere.

                    PIRATE DINO
Listen you, I be looking for books.

                    PEG LEG
Don't get your dander up, I know where there are more books than you could check out with a library card…walk this way.

(INT.—RESTAURANT)

                    NICK
You're late.

                    GRANPA HOLMES
Do either of you two own a white, two-door Sedan with a scratch in the side, a bumper hanging loose and a broken taillight?

                    SONNY
No, why?

                    GRANPA HOLMES
No reason.

                    BARTENDER
I can see your ugly face from the bar.

                    SONNY
You want me to change seats?

                    BARTENDER
Yeah.

                    SONNY
You're not so pretty yourself.

                    GRANPA HOLMES
How much would you pay for this fine collection of stolen library books? Don't answer yet, because you'll also get this free cookbook "Fear of Frying". But wait, because you'll also get a free set of knives. Now how much would you pay?

                    SONNY
Twenty-nine, ninety-five.

                    BARTENDER
Hey old man, I just saw my car in the parking lot. Did you win your driver's license in a raffle? You're gonna pay for that bumper and I'm gonna call your parents. Now get your stuff and get out of here.

                    GRANPA HOLMES

Aw—pack it in your shorts.

(EXT. STREET)

DR. TOBEL
We gotta get this pile of stolen books ready for the pirates to ship. So, a…

GRANPA HOLMES
(On Tobel's trip)
Hey, been walkin' long?

DR. TOBEL
Oh I tripped over *Moby Dick*.

GRANPA HOLMES
Damn that whale.

DR. TOBEL
I see you're stocking up on fertilizer for the spring.

BLACK

(INT. OFFICE)

DR. TOBEL
These are all overdue books?

GRANPA HOLMES
I have every book ever written, from every library ever built. I owe fifty-thousand dollars in fines, and I'm proud of it.

DR. TOBEL
But won't my girlfriend Daphne lose her librarian job?

G. HOLMES
So what. I've been shushed by so many librarians like her, I caught pneumonia from the draft. Listen Franz, excuse the appearance of the house, I still have to dust there!

COMMERCIAL #2 BUMPER   Next…Your Home Movie

MAN ON THE STREET

ACT II

KENT VOICE OVER
We were wondering what the punishment should be for people who keep library books past the due date.
—Cut off their eyes so they couldn't read anymore.
—Public Flogging.
—I guess you could make them wear gum on their nose or something crazy.
—They have to abolish reading, altogether.
—I think I'd hit 'em with the book they checked out.
—Set off a bomb and have it go off at a zoo or something.

                        KENT
In the book?
—Yeah.
—I think death…by hanging, preferably in front of the library. Could be good.
—Oh, I think that's great because that means they're really reading them.
—Cut off their hands.
—Ha, ha, I have one that's overdue, today!

(INT.—ROOM)

                        TOBEL
Here's a sympathy card. I'm sorry you lost your job at the library.

                        DAPHNE
You hand-delivered it, too.

                        TOBEL
In an envelope.

                        DAPHNE
Then let me deliver this.

(SFX: MONKEY KISS)

(EXT.—STREET)

                        TOBEL
                        (Thought)
A kiss for a card—wonder what I would have gotten if I'd given her a toaster-oven.
                        (Hums)
Officer. Oh, that shark bites, oh, that shark bites.

                        MUGGER
Those aren't the words to the song. Get it right.

(SFX: MUGGING SOUNDS)

                        TOBEL
Officer, help me, help me.

                        OFFICER
To heck with you, he's stealin' my car…come back here.

(INT.—RESTAURANT)

(INTERMISSION—GENERATE TITLE)

(INT.—ROOM)

                        SHERLOCK
Watson! Watson, wake up! The back room is missing.

                        WATSON
You mean the one back there?

SHERLOCK
Yes, where is it?

WATSON
Well, it was there a minute ago. I just stepped out here to sit with the cat…

SHERLOCK
Why are you still in pajamas?
     (Tobel enters)
Hello there! I'm Sherlock Holmes.

TOBEL
Hip! Hip! Hooray!

HOLMES
I think so.

WATSON
Oh my goodness! Let me look at your head. What happened to your head?

TOBEL
I had my appendix removed.

WATSON
I hope you know a good lawyer. I recognize him from somewhere.

SHERLOCK
I know who he is, I know it all. I can tell from the flapjack batter on your lapel, you're Long John Silverman, international spy and pancake salesman. He's wanted in 32 countries and 18 delicatessens.

TOBEL
That's not true at all.

SHERLOCK
Alright then, I can tell from the soap on your sleeve that you've just returned from robbing an Amway meeting.

WATSON
I must say…

SHERLOCK
Trust me on this, Watson.

WATSON
I think he's Franz Tobel, suspected of stealing library books.

SHERLOCK
Don't be absurd, Watson, I'm the expert here. I've had years of experience and I never miss a thing. He's a mass murderer.

WATSON
But Holmes, I really…

HOLMES
Oh chill out, Watson—I can tell just by looking at his eyes. And this handkerchief has blood all over it. Tell me now he's not a mass murderer, eh!

WATSON
That's lipstick. It's nothing.

TOBEL
Watson's right, I am Franz Tobel.

SHERLOCK
Damn!

(INT.—OFFICE)

TOBEL
I helped steal the books, I'm turning myself in.

ARMY OFFICER
We all knew it was you.

WATSON
Not everyone here. Holmes thought he was a pancake salesman.

(SFX: SLAP)

WATSON
(O.C.)
Ow! Holmes!

INSPECTOR
So, you're turning states evidence because you're a changed man?

TOBEL
No, because since my girlfriend lost her job, she won't sleep with me.

INSPECTOR
What's she look like?

TOBEL
She's a little big in the hips but if she can have her job back…I'll help you round up the rest of the gang.

INSPECTOR
What do you think, Holmes, should we let him help us?

HOLMES
Why ask me? I thought he was a pancake salesman. Ask smarty pants, Watson.

WATSON
Childish.

HOLMES
Oh shut up.

HOST
You know books aren't the only thing you can check out from a library. You can also check out some of your favorite films…Could I see this?

HOME MOVIE

NARRATOR
They knew this baby was super by the horse he rode. Across the cosmos. Signals were sent to worlds in need of help. He got a super haircut, and was taught the basics of super flying. Then our hero bid farewell to his home planet and boarded the capsule which took him to earth where he became, "Superbaby", with incredible powers— as well as an indestructible designer uniform. Then his super strength was magnified tenfold by a freak meteor shower. Setting out on his first patrol, Superbaby was faced with the evil Dr. Fido, a villain who drooled on innocent old men. Without hesitation Superbaby sped to the rescue and justice was done.
But Fido lived…to harass a young woman pole vaulter. And then, arming himself with a five-ton boulder, Superbaby sent Fido packing with a massive show of strength. And the world was safe…for now. People could sleep in peace, because in the face of danger…here was one baby who would always stand tall.

(INT.—OFFICE)

WATSON
Here, Mr. Tobel, do a duck call.

TOBEL
Certainly.

WATSON
Then take a drink of water. I'm easily amused. Now talk at the same time. No! Didn't think you could do it. Well I'm in my jammies, got my pipe and six-shooter.

TOBEL
All set for the evening, huh?

WATSON
Right! Gonna sit with the cat and watch "The Brady Bunch".

TOBEL
You are easily amused.

(SFX: CAT CRY)

WATSON
Who let the cat out of the bag?
(O.C.)
"It's the story…"

(SFX: SHOT/TV EXPLODING)

TOBEL
(thought)

Now's my chance to call my cousin in Taiwan and charge it to Watson's phone.
(on phone)
Chow Pang…this is cousin Franz. Did you get that fruit cake I sent you for Passover?
(Oriental Gibberish)
Yeah, what? I forgot it's 3:00 am—It's afternoon here. Hold on.
(THOUGHT)

xxx
Snores.
(Thought)
Darn cat fleas.

(INT.—BEDROOM)

PIRATE DINO
Do you be a black marketer?

ANNETTE
Yeah, my name be Annette.
(ARGH)

PEG LEG
Ha, ha, ha, ha.

PIRATE DINO
No, I said *MARKETEER*…what the ye laughing at?

PEG LEG
Me?

PIRATE DINO
Yeah, you. Gimme a dollar.
(AARRRGH)

ANNETTE
Now dance for him. He's a pirate dancer, he dances for money, any old dollar will do. He's a pirate dancer, his dancin' is funny, 'cause he's only wearing one shoe. AAAAAAAARRR!

PIRATE DINO
Teach me how to sing.

ANNETTE
Your breath smells like a barrel of fish. AAAAAAAARRRRRRR!

PIRATE DINO
Why you…

ANNETTE
Stick of gum. Lloyd?

MORIARITY
Everybody loves somebody sometime.

PIRATE DINO
Do you think I look like Dean Martin?

MORIARITY

A little bit, but he wears a tuxedo. You should lose that outfit. I'm sure Peg Leg would give you an arm and another arm for it, but it's a good book smuggling outfit. Get ready to sail, Annette. You've got a job.

PIRATE DINO

Shiver me timber…I'll go get my parrot and my eye patch.

(INT.—BATHROOM)

WATSON

You know, Holmes, I thought your mother told you not to play with her make-up. It's not your color.

HOLMES

Mom wouldn't be home 'til eleven. She went to a "Star Trek" convention. Besides, don't you have anything better to do than stand around picking on me?

WATSON

I thought we were going to work on the book case.

HOLMES
(O.C.)

I hired a carpenter for that. We must concentrate on the library mystery as soon as I finish with my eye shadow.

(EXT.—DOORWAY)

TOBEL
(Thought)

I've got to see Holmes and tell him there's a pirate ship full of books leaving tonight. Sandra Dee, Aunt Bee and Mr. Tee. I've got to get something for my hand—maybe butter.

O.C. VOICE

Parkey.

THUG #1

Ah, huh! Unbelievable.

O.C. VOICE

What did you find out?

THUG #1

Well, well, I'm a…what was I supposed to do again?

O.C. VOICE

Twit!

(EXT.—STREET)

WATSON

I'm hungry.

LE STRAD

We just ate six months ago. Hey, you quit messing around with the trunk of my car. I'm library police.

ANNETTE
Let's get out of here. If we get caught the boss will bust our butts.

LA STRAD
Come back here!
Can't catch 'em. They got a one foot lead and he's limpin' too fast. Let's see if they got away with anything. Here's my tools, my square tire, my neru jacket…here's my book pirate. Wait a minute.

PIRATE DINO
Aaaaaaargh.

WATSON
Well, what's your story?

PIRATE DINO
My friends turned on me because of my parrot. It kept biting them on the back of the neck. It bit me too.

LA STRAD
Do I know you? You look kind of familiar.

PIRATE DINO
A lot of people have said I bear a resemblance to Dean Martin.

COMMERCIAL #3

BUMPER
Next…Holmes Shot?

(INT.—DARK ROOM)

(SFX: SLIDE WHISTLE)

MORIARITY
You turned state's evidence, Tobel. Now I'm gonna steal your pants.

TOBEL
No, they won't fit you. At least undo my suspenders first.

BLACK

(INT. OFFICE)

DAPHNE
Why don't you use a pencil to write with?

HOLMES
A pencil? You mean this?

DAPHNE
No, no. This is a pencil.

HOLMES
Hmmm, ingenious. It's sharp and what's this?

DAPHNE
Paper.

HOLMES
This is paper?

DAPHNE
Of course.

HOLMES
It's so thin. How does it work?

DAPHNE
You write on it.

HOLMES
With the pencil? Why, the people who invent these kinds of things simply amaze me.

(INT.—MORIARITY'S OFFICE)

THUG #2
Which one's me?

MORIARITY
The one with the tie. It's taken me over 30 years to complete this master plan for stealing books. Oops!

THUG #2
(O.C.)
Hey! Boss, you just spilled your specimen over that plan.

MORIARITY
Well, that plan's ruined and postpone my doctor's appointment for 30 minutes.

(INT.—OFFICE)

SCIENTIST/HOLMES INCOGNITO
(Thought)
It'd be a lot easier to fix this vegamatic if I didn't have this champagne cork in my eye.

(SFX: GUN CLICKING)

THUG #1
Say, will you fix my gun?

(INT.—LIVING ROOM)

MORIARITY
Send two dollars to names on the bottom.
(thought)

I hate chain letters—that's a lousy disguise, if you'd worn that bandana on your forehead, I might have believed that you were Willy Nelson.

(SFX: VELCRO)

SHERLOCK
This hurts like hell, got any baby oil?

MORIARITY
You're through. Any last requests?

SHERLOCK
Led Zeppelin—I've always loved "Stairway to Heaven".

(EXT.—STREET)

(SFX: CAR CHUGGING)

LE STRAD
You fool, we've run out of gas. I told you to fill the car up at the car wash.

(INT.—DENTIST OFFICE)

E.T. DRIVER
There's a gas station down there. We can phone home.

MORIARITY
My work is through.

HOLMES
I didn't know you were a dentist, professor.

MORIARITY
I'm not. But I -

(EXT. STREET)

WATSON
We're here, let's park in the garage. Stop! Stop!

(SFX: CAR CRASHING THRU BACK OF GARAGE)

You should have your brakes fixed.

(INT.—DR.'S OFFICE)

HOLMES
(O.C.)
Weren't you supposed to give me a shot so I wouldn't feel any pain?

MORIARITY
Oh yes, Holmes, thank you for reminding me.

HOLMES
When can I chew on my left-side?

MORIARITY

(SFX: GUN CLICK)

You can now, I worked on your right.

LA STRAD

There's the man responsible for stealing all the library cards.

WATSON

Holmes!

MORIARITY

I suppose you're going to revoke my library card.

BLACK

(EXT.—OUTDOORS)

INSPECTOR

Well, the case is solved. No thanks to Sherlock Holmes.

TOBEL

Daphne's got her job back…all the books are being returned, including *The Joy of Sex*.

DAPHNE

He didn't understand a word of it.

LA STRAD

I liked the pictures.

V.O. PILOT

(SFX: HUMAN PLANE NOISE)

Hey captain, can I make the airplane noises for a while?

V.O. CAPTAIN

Sure.

(SFX: HUMAN PLANE NOISE)

(EXT.—OUTDOORS)

WATSON

You've blown another case, Holmes. Are you going back to school?

HOLMES

Yes, elementary, my dear Watson.

(SFX: XYLOPHONE)

THE END

(INT.—LIBRARY CHECK OUT)

WRAP AROUND

                        HOST
Well, that's our Mad Movie for tonight. I'd like to check out some
books though, uh, this is "First Blood, Part VII", "Rambo Meets
Gidget". Uh… while I'm checking out these books, though, why
don't you guys watch these previews.
Well, thanks for joining us. I've got some reading to catch up on.

(EXT.—LIBRARY)

(SFX: SIREN)

                        VOICE O.C.
All right, this is the Library Police. Stop what you're doing! Drop
those books! You have the right to remain silent.

                        HOST
See you next time.

                        VOICE O.C.
Anything you say above a whisper may be used against you.

ENDING CRAWL

PANDA PRODUCTIONS   MAD MOVIES

TITLE: SHERLOCK HOLMES

PAGE 1 of 2   SHOW # 108   DATE: 10/19/85

CUE	TITLE	COMPOSER	SOC	PUBLISHER	USEAGE	TIME
T 1	MAD MOVIES THEME	RICHARD BAKER AND MARY NEWLAND	ASCAP	SONGSYNC MUSIC	SHOW OPEN	:50
B A	MAD MOVIES BUMPER				VOCAL/INST	
BG 1	KENT'S THEME	RICHARD BAKER AND MARY NEWLAND			COMM. BUMP VOC/INST	:03
M 1	SHERLOCK HOMES: THEME				B.G. INST	:51
M 2	GRANDPA HOLMES					:09
M 2	COMPLAINT LETTERS					:23
M 3	LIBRARY COPS					:23
M 4	SAY BUDDY					:49
M 5	HOW MUCH WOULD YOU PAY					:40
M 6	PILE OF STOLEN BOOKS					:29
B B	MAD MOVIES BUMPER				COMM/BUMPER	:23
B A	MAD MOVIES BUMPER					:04
M 7	SYMPATHY CARD				B.G. INST	:03
M 8	SHARK FIGHTS					:10
M 9	INTERMISSION					:16
M10	THE BACK ROOM IS MISSING					:08
M11	I KNOW WHO HE IS					:22
M14	I HELPED TO STEAL BOOKS					:54
HMI	"SUPER BABY"					:36
M11	DO A DUCK CALL					1:10
M12	DARN CAT FLEAS					:54
M13	BLACK MARKATEER					:04
M13a	REPRISE					:39
M10	PLAY WITH MAKE-UP					:03
M14	GO TO SEE HOLMES					:22
M15	IM HUNGRY					:36
B B	MAD MOVIES BUMPER				COMM/BUMPER	:40
B A	MAD MOVIES BUMPER					:04
M 5	PENCIL AND PAPER					:03
M 16	VEGAMATIC					:29
M10	CHAIN LETTERS					:18
						:22

PANDA PRODUCTIONS

MAD MOVIES

TITLE: SHERLOCK HOLMES

PAGE 2 of 2 SHOW # 108 DATE: 10/19/85

CUE	TITLE	COMPOSER	SOC	PUBLISHER	USEAGE	TIME
M 17	PHONE HOLMES	R. BAKER/ M. NEWLAND	ASCAP	SONGSYNC MUSIC	B.G. INST	:12
M 18	MY WORK IS COMPLETE					:48
M 19	THE CASE IS SOLVED					:27
M 20	THE END/LIBRARY WRAP				SHOW CLOSE	:13
T 2	MAD MOVIES THEME				VOCAL/INST	1:19

OPENING CRAWL*

SHOW #<u>108</u>

SHOW NAME   <u>Sherlock Holmes And The Secret Weapon</u>

*Each numbered item as a single page...
Items #1-4: Centerframe
Items #5-9: Lower third of page

1   FOUR STAR
          in association with
          KENT SKOV

2   Presents
        an L.A. Connection
          production of

3   Tonight's Feature

4   Starring

5   Bob Buchholz

6   Connie Sue Cook

7   Stephen L. Rollman

8   Steve Pinto

9   Kent Skov

Mad Movies with the L.A. Connection

GENERIC BUMPERS*

SHOW #<u>108</u>

SHOW NAME <u>Sherlock Holmes And The Secret Weapon</u>

*Each numbered item as a single page…

1. We'll be right back…

2. Don't Go Away

3. More Mad Movies
Coming Up

4. Coming Up…
More Mad Movies

5. Stay Tuned for
"Your Home Movies"

6. Next…
"Your Home Movies"

7. Write Us…
L.A. Connection Productions
6464 Sunset Blvd., #820
Hollywood, CA 90028

8. Send Your Home Movies to…
L.A. Connection Productions
6464 Sunset Blvd., #820
Hollywood, CA 90028
(Include a self-addressed, stamped envelope for return of films)

9. Next…
Mad Movies takes it to the streets

CLOSING CRAWL*

SHOW #<u>108</u>

SHOW NAME   Sherlock Holmes And The Secret Weapon

*Each numbered item as a single page…

1	Directed by Kent Skov
2	Written by Connie Sue Cook Steve Pinto Kent Skov
3	Produced by Randal W Ridges
4	Featuring Bob Buchholz Connie Sue Cook Anthony R. Lovett Steve Pinto Stephen L. Rollman Kent Skov
5	Associate Producers (each name single page) Martha Whitney
6	Kent Weishaus (single page)
7	Music Composed and arranged by Richard Baker Mary Newland For Panda Productions
7a	Music Recorded by Richard Baker
8	Theme performed by Mary Newland

CLOSING CREDIT CRAWL (con't)

9	Research by Bob Petrella Ken Segall April Winchell Ted Hardwick
10	Talent Coordinator Martha Whitney
11	Associate Director/Stage Manager Randal W Ridges
11a	Assistants to the Producers: Bob Buchholz Connie Sue Cook Steve Pinto Stephen L. Rollman
12	Facilities provided by Hy-Tone Video
13	Lighting and Camera Bill Sheehy
14	Gaffer Jim Drewry
14a	Production Sound Stu Fox
15	Production Assistants Lisa Gougas Ted Hardwick
16	Make Up Lora Sanders
17	Wardrobe Annie Vicari
18	Production Secretary Eloise Gonzalez
18a	Post-Production Coordinated by Monti Santilli rainbolt
19	Post-Production Facilities Comple Post, Inc.
20	Post-Production Audio by Michael Pericone Michaele Hogan For Interlok Productions

CLOSING CREDIT CRAWL (con't)

21	"Your Home Movie" submitted by Todd Smith Palo Alto, CA.
21a	Special Thanks to (single page) Ronald Thronson and President G.T. Smith of Chapman College, Orange California
22	Executive in Charge of Production Bob Bosen
23	Special Thanks to: Carole Fisher Susan Lenti Budget Films, Inc. Richard Holiday Dennis Condon Snagglepuss
23a	Opening Title Montage by Homer & Associates
23b	Opening Title Photography by Abe Perlstein
24	Post-Production supervised by Randal W Ridges
25	Executive Producer Kent Skov
26	"Celebrity Voices and Appearances Impersonated"
27	Copyright 1985 Four Star International, Inc. All Rights Reserved

SHOCK Pt. 1

With the

SHORT RUNDOWN FOR SHOW #104 Shock Pt. 1

Description	In	Out	Seg Time
Show Open	00:00	01:10	01:10
Commercial Break #1	01:10	03:13	02:03
Act I	03:13	09:48	06:35
Commercial Break #2	09:48	11:50	02:03
Act II	11:50	20:33	08:43
Commercial Break #3	20:33	22:37	02:03
Act III/Show Close	22:37	28:00	05:23

MAD MOVIES WITH THE L.A. CONNECTION

RUNDOWN   SHOW #<u>104 SHOCK Pt. 1</u>

All times are in minutes and seconds	IN	OUT	DURATION
Four Star Logo (slug Black)	00:00	00:05	00:05
Show Open: Clip Tease.	00:05	00:20	00:15
Opening Montage.	00:20	01:10	00:50
Commercial Black #1	01:10	03:13	02:03
Bumper #1	03:13	03:16	00:03
Wrap #1	03:16	03:47	00:31
Movie Segment #1	03:47	09:44	05:56
Bumper #2 (Next…Your Home Movie)	09:44	09:48	00:04
Commercial Black #2	09:48	11:50	02:03
Bumper #3	11:50	11:54	00:04
Man On The Street Intro. (as needed)	11:54	12:59	01:05
Man On The Street or Interview Segment.	12:59	13:53	00:59
Movie Segment #2	13:53	17:20	03:27
Home Movie Intro.	17:20	17:39	00:19
Home Movie	17:39	18:45	01:06
Movie Segment #3	18:45	20:29	01:44

MAD MOVIES WITH THE L.A. CONNECTION

RUNDOWN SHOW #<u>104 SHOCK PART I</u>

Bumper #4	20:29	20:33	00:40
Commercial Black #3	20:33	22:37	02:03
Bumper #5	22:37	22:40	00:03
Movie Segment #4	22:40	26:49	04:09
Toss to Preview			
Preview			
Final Close	26:49	27:13	00:24
Closing Montage	27:13	27:50	00:37
L.A. Connection Logo	27:50	27:55	00:05
Four Star Logo (slug black)	27:55	28:00	00:05

SHOCK PART I SHOW NUMBER 104

CLIP TEASE

INSPECTOR GENERAL

You know Mad Movies is on? How about you…do you know Mad Movies is on?

MAN

Sad movies?

I.G.

No, Mad Movies!

MAN

Bad movies?

I.G.

Mad Movies with the L.A. Connection!

MAN

Mad Movies! Why didn't you say so?

MUSIC INTRO

COMMERCIAL #1

KENT

Hi, I'm Kent Skov and welcome to Mad Movies with the L.A. Connection. I've got an emergency here!

MANNEQUIN
(Groans)

KENT

I'll be right with you. Tonight's feature is entitled "Shock" and it stars one of Hollywood's most shocking actors. In our version, he plays a doctor who gets involved in activities unbecoming a man of medicine. You see, he's very interested in how his nurse's body works. And he's more than willing to make house calls…free of charge to every woman in the movie.

MANNEQUIN
(Groans again)

KENT

I'm finished. So drink lots of fluids and enjoy the movie.

ACT I

(V.O.)

Meanwhile in San Francisco.

(SFX: DOORBELL) (V.P. THROWS CIGARETTE, CAT CRIES)

V.P.
(Thought)
I've got to get an ashtray. Oh, collecting for the paper again. Here's my payment.

(HISS)

LATRINE
I wish I delivered your milk.

V.P.
So do I.

(V.O.)
Meanwhile in San Francisco.

BUDDY
This is fine, Cabbie, thank you.

CABBIE
Hey, hey, hey Buddy, don't you ever close the door? Were you born in a barn? I found this in the back seat. It's a picture of you naked.

BUDDY
Here's $900.00—pass that photo among your friends.

CABBIE
Thanks, close the door. Hey, Buddy, hey.

D.C.
Hello.

BUDDY
Good evening, do you have a recipe for muffins?

DESK CLERK
Let me check my file.

BUDDY
You see, I'm here to have an affair with Dr. Forapain. We were hoping to have them for breakfast.

DESK CLERK
Well, what's your name, Buddy?

BUDDY
That's right, Buddy.

DESK CLERK
There's no Buddy on the list, in fact, there is no list.

BUDDY
There must be a mistake.

DESK CLERK
I don't make mistakes, the cook does that.

BUDDY
Are you sure?

DESK CLERK
Dr. Forapain is still having an affair with his nurse.

BUDDY
That can't be. He said he was going to have an affair with me. I've been on the waiting list since June and I've come all the way from Boise.

OLD DESK CLERK
There's no need to cry, ma'am. I'm sure we can find a sailor for you or, wait…isn't there an army base nearby?

DESK CLERK
By golly, I think you're right.

OLD DESK CLERK
Sure, we'll find a nice soldier for you. How would that be, Buddy?

BUDDY
That'll be just fine. Thank you very much.

OLD DESK CLERK
We aim to please.

V.P.
My reputation is shot. I was supposed to have an affair with Buddy Gotrocks, at this hotel at 6:00 and I missed it. I was even going to take her shopping. Ya know, Latrine, I've never missed an affair in my life.

LATRINE
You never took me shopping. I'm wearing a shirt so tight that I can't sit down.

V.P.
I don't want to hear it.

LATRINE
Listen, mister, and listen good.

BUDDY

(SFX: BELL RINGS)

Who is it?

(SFX: BELL RINGS)

Hello, are you trying to play a trick on me? What's the deal here?

(PICKS UP CLOCK)
(Thought)
I'm such a genius.

MAN EXITING

I meant to tell you, honey—how much I love your hat.

WOMAN EXITING

It's not a hat.

MAN EXITING

Oh dear!

SOLDIER

Good morning.

DESK CLERK

Good morning.

SOLDIER

I'm here for the affair.

DESK CLERK

Oh yes, Lieutenant, we've been expecting you. Miss Gotrocks is going to be happy to see you, Mr. Ramada. This is the soldier we've sent for from the fort.

OLD DESK CLERK

She's waiting for you. She's in room 816-C.

SOLDIER

I'm eager to serve my country. I've been in basic training for a long time.

OLD DESK CLERK

You're in for a real surprise.

DESK CLERK

Grab that Valise.

SOLDIER

No man named Valise is carrying my bag.

BAGGAGE BOY

Drop dead, creep.

SOLDIER

Thanks.
(LAUGHING)

(SOLDIER WALKS DOWN HALL WHISTLING—HEARING SPLASHING)

(CUT TO INSERT SHOT FROM INSPECTOR GENERAL)

(V.O.)

Meanwhile in San Francisco.

LATRINE

Why don't you kiss me, Latrine? Is it because of my breath? Is it because I'm a woman? Or is it something else?

V.P.
It's because of the kink in my neck.
(NECK CRANKS)
That did it.
(V.O.)
Meanwhile in San Francisco.

SOLDIER
Hello, is this Private Parts in 816-C? Are you sure you gave me the right room? Oh, 816-C on the fifth floor.

DR.
(Thoughts)
Is he gonna stand there and stare over my shoulder all day? I hope he doesn't ask me any questions.

SOLDIER
Well.

DR.
(Thoughts)
Oh fine. Now I gotta think fast. I'll make up something and charge him $21,000. How come her eyes are closed that way?

SOLDIER
What's wrong with her doctor?

DR.
Yuh! Well, I'll have to examine her to be sure. But this girl's head is steaming. I'd say she's having an affair.

SOLDIER
An affair. Are you sure?

DR.
Either that or she's been hit by a truck.

SOLDIER
Was it a big one?

DR.
It was either a big affair or a small truck. I'm calling a specialist. Operator, get me Dr. Ruth.

V.P.
Ruth sent me.

DR.
What took you so long?

V.P.
I had to come from San Francisco. Thanks for calling me, I need the money.

COMMERCIAL #2/BUMPER #1

HOST IS SEATED, FACING CAMERA
We're very fortunate to have Vincent Price with us for a brief interview. But before we talk to him, I think I should make a little adjustment.

HOST CLOSES HIS EYES…SHOT TURNS TO BLACK AND WHITE.

HOST:		That's better. Mr. Price, I understand you were on vacation. Was it tough to tear yourself away to do this interview?
PRICE:	(1:20:26:)	I told the hotel manager I was joining my wife in Carmel for a few days.
HOST:		Good thinking. Was "Shock" a fun movie to make?
PRICE:	(1:20:19:)	It was horrible, Elaine.
HOST:		Elaine?! Please, Mr. Price, it bothers me when people call me Elaine.
PRICE:	(1:24:16:)	That's perfectly understandable.
HOST:		Thank you. You seem to be wearing different clothing for every question I ask. How do you change so fast?
PRICE:	81:13:05: - 1:13:09:15)	That's difficult to say…
HOST:		Well, we're out of time. By the way, your agent told us you'd be doing this interview for free.
PRICE:	(1:38:36: - END OF CUT)	I see…
HOST:		Hey, don't take it so hard. Stick around and watch the rest of the show.

KENT
Ah, back to normal. You know the whole evening is turning out to be a shock. What shocks you?

RESPONSES
"Driving along route 1 on the California coast."
"Waking up in the morning and seeing myself without make up on. That's bad."
"Freeway traffic in L.A."
"Nothing."
"Electricity."
"To be stood up."
"Reagan shocks me, Madonna shocks me."
"Getting caught in a major lie by a boyfriend."
"Naked women."
"Dentists charging $500 to give you pain and be rude to you shocks me."
"You know what shocks me…being in the sun shocks me."
"Waking up in a strange city, naked, with a dollar taped to my chest. It happened to me in Philadelphia."
"The boogie man shocks me."

SOLDIER
Is there anything you can do for her? You're the expert. Please tell me. I'm in the army. I can take it.

V.P.
Looks like she's gotta dislocated "hooter". Wonder why her eyes are closed like that?

SOLDIER
Well, Dr., tell me, please…no. Go ahead, tell me, give it to me straight.

                              V.P.
Alright. You're obnoxious.

                              SOLDIER
It's not my fault, it's all the white sugar. I'm worried about her. The other doctor said she was hit by a truck.

                              V.P.
These kinds of things happen every day.

(SFX: CRASH)

See what I mean?

                              SOLDIER
Was it a big truck?

                              V.P.
No, it was an import. But you get the idea.

(SFX: PHONE RINGING)

                              V.P.
Hello, yes this is her room.

                              PVT.
Who's that on the phone, doctor?

                              V.P.
Room service. Buddy ordered a three-bean salad and they can only find two beans. She can't eat in her condition. I'll tell them not to bother.

                              PVT.
Don't do that! I like two-bean salad.

                              V.P.
You're right, Buddy. Wouldn't want us to starve. Send up that salad, along with a rack of lamb, six steaks, some lobster thermadore, a pheasant under glass, oysters Rockefeller, some champagne and a corn dog. Young man, are your hands for dinner?

                              PVT.
Well, one of 'um.

                              V.O.
Meanwhile in San Francisco.

                              ORDERLY
Hi, Latrine. You know it's funny. It always rains on this side of the hospital.
                              (PAUSE)
I love a woman in uniform—take it off! Can I have some of that? You know we have to stop making our coffee here in the linen supply room. It tastes like fabric softener.

LATRINE
It is.

ORDERLY
Great. You know, it was fun in front of the fire last night. It's amazing how a burning house can attract such a large crowd.

NURSE
You can get the kind with rechargeable batteries.

LATRINE
Leonard, my love, my love.
(LIGHTS)

ORDERLY
Leonard, what are you doing?

LEONARD
Nothing.

ORDERLY
Leave Latrine alone. She's not your girl. Leonard, she's my girl, on Tuesdays. Now you go to your room and think about it.

LEONARD
My girl, his girl, my girl, his girl.

KENT
Inside this bag are several vital and important instruments necessary to the medical profession. A stethoscope, ahh tongue depressor and of course tonight's home movie, sent in by Todd Lee of Boston, Mass.

ANNOUNCER
From around the world to you…these are Nature's Oddities! Here's a baby who does a perfect imitation of a chicken. Bock, bock, bock, begock! *This* baby is a musical instrument. It plays different kinds of tunes, depending on where you touch it. Instead of hair, this youngster has a head of toilet paper, so convincing that just the sight of him gives people the runs. Here's the disappearing girl of Denver. And believe it or not, these women are playing ping-pong with a grizzly bear's eyeball.

The Purple People of the North Country actually worship deflated volleyballs. Here their queen prepares to perform an annual ritual dance, a dance that will conclude with her stomping her subjects into grape juice. These folks live in a valley where it snows duck feathers. Each year they handcraft enough pillows for the annual Rose Bowl Pillow Fight. But even a woman who can ski sitting down is nothing compared to the amazing water skiing head of Boise, Idaho.

CABBIE
Hey lady, come back and close the door.

LATRINE
Where's your produce department?

DESK CLERK

Next to the frozen meats.

                        LATRINE
Thank you Dr. Da-For a-Pain.

                        V.P.
Oh Latrine, you see I was called here for…uh…and there was an accident. You see, there was a dislocated "hooter".

                        LATRINE
Oh I see. You mean you're having an affair with her? Jerk!
                        (Thought)
I'll roll her in front of a trolley.

                        SOLDIER
You handled that pretty well.

                        V.P.
Shut up! Nobody asked you.

(SFX: CAR SCREECHING/GEARS GRINDING)

                        V.P.
I wish she gets carsick—I'd have had her sit next to the window. I'm gonna get some paper towels.

                        LATRINE
Hurry!

(SFX: CAR SCREECHING AWAY ON GRAVEL)

                        V.P.
Oh, Miss Rachet.

                        NURSE W/GLASSES
Yes, doctor.

                        V.P.
When you're through with your patients, will you hose out the inside of my car?

                        NURSE W/GLASSES
Did you have Mexican food again, doctor?

                        V.P.
Yes.

                        OLDMAN
Say, what are we having for lunch? Hot dogs, I love hot dogs.

                        V.P.
They taste better smoked.

                        OLDMAN
Hot dogs. They remind me of when I was a kid. You know, family.

                    V.P.

Yeah, baseball! Fourth of July.

                    OLDMAN

Yeah, say I was wondering if you were having an affair with your nurse?

                    V.P.

Well. I Homina, Homina, Homina.

                    OLDMAN

So am I.

                    V.P.

She can do wonders with a thermometer.

                    OLDMAN

First time I saw her take a bedpan out of the freezer I knew she was the girl for me.

COMMERCIAL #3/BUMPER #2

                    V.P.

Hold ice cream cone firmly in hand, uh, place tongue on ice cream and with sweeping motion, ah, forget it.

                    LATRINE

Well, she's ready for you.

                    V.P.

I've got to tell her that the affair is off.

                    LATRINE

She won't listen.

                    V.P.

I'll pound it into her.

                    V.P.

You've got to go back to the pig farm in Boise.

                    BUDDY

No, I can't, oink, oink.

                    V.P.

You must go back, oink, oink.

                    BUDDY

No, no, oink.

                    V.P.
                    (SLOWLY)

Oink, oink.

                    V.O.

Meanwhile in San Francisco.

SOLDIER

Listen doctor, I have to talk to you about, oops, you're not the doctor.

(WALKS IN)

NURSE

Just because I'm a woman.

SOLDIER

Listen doctor, I've got to talk…

DR.

Just a minute. The city is grateful for your help, Batman.

SOLDIER

I had to see you. It's about Buddy. I've fallen in love with her.

DR.

Fallen in love with her, you hardly know her. You were sent in there to have a tawdry love affair.

SOLDIER

But things have changed. I'm concerned about her. I don't trust her, doctor.

DR.

Which doctor?

SOLDIER

No, a regular doctor.

DR.

Dr. Forapain is right. You are obnoxious.

SOLDIER

I don't trust Dr. Forapain. All doctors are creeps.

DR.

Get your hand off my desk, punk.

SOLDIER

What are going to do about it?

DR.

Do you know karate?

SOLDIER

Yes I do.

DR.

Oh.

ORDERLY

Buddy—what are you doing out here in that ugly robe?

BUDDY

Please, Skip, will you help me? Please, Skip, help me. Please, Skip, help me.

> ORDERLY

Oh come on now. Let's go back into your room.

> BUDDY

You don't understand. They're painting in there. It stinks and they used my bedsheet as a drop cloth.

> ORDERLY

Come on, they finished that two days ago.

> BUDDY

No, no, they came back to do the trim.

> ORDERLY

You'll have to clear the hall. We're having wheelchair races. Come on.

> BUDDY

They make me shake the paint. They strap it to my waist and make me break-dance.

> ORDERLY

Hold ice cream cone firmly in hand. Place tongue on ice cream and with sweeping motion, turn cone counter clockwise.
> (KNOCK)

Come in. Who are you?

> SOLDIER

I'm Private Parts, United States Army.

> ORDERLY

Gee Private, that's a swell uniform.

> SOLDIER

Yup, why don't you join? Army, Navy, Air Force, Marines…be all that you can be.

> ORDERLY

You're really buffed out.

> SOLDIER

Nautilus, Aerobics, Jane Fonda Workout…do you want to enlist?

> ORDERLY

Nah! I'm kinda shy. I can't shower with more than 6 men in a room.

(CUT OUT SAN FRANCISCO)

> V.P.

Next time you want to make a long distance call, wait till the weekend. You want to use the phone, you say please.

                        BUDDY
                       (Thought)
Yeah, rates are cheaper then.

                         V.P.
Sorry.

                        BUDDY
Oink.

                         V.P.
These would make a great dress.

                         V.O.
Who died by the candlestick? Was it Latrine, who cheated on all
her men? Was it AWOL Private Parts, who didn't trust Dr.
Forapain? Was it Leonard, who played King Lear on Broadway
once? Was it Skip, who combed his hair like Ronald Reagan? Or
was it this lady? Who is this lady? Or did he kill himself? Tune in
next time for the electrifying conclusion of "Shock".

                         KENT
Tune in next time to see who the doctor's victim is and also for an
interview with Anabel Shaw, the small town girl who got to know
our doctor…up close and personal.

                      MANNEQUIN
Gotta go, see you next time.

CLOSING CREDITS

PANDA PRODUCTIONS   MAD MOVIES

TITLE: SHOCK PART I

PAGE 1 of 2   SHOW # 104   DATE: 11/9/85

CUE	TITLE	COMPOSER	SOC	PUBLISHER	USEAGE	TIME
T1	MAD MOVIES THEME	BAKER/NEWLAND	ASCAP	SONGSYNE MUSIC	MAD MOVIES SHOW OPENER (VOCAL INST)	:50
Ba	MAD MOVIES BUMPER				COM BUMPER	:03
BG1	KENT'S THEME					:30
M1	SHOCK: THEME				B.G. INST.	:15
M2	KISS				B.G. INST.	:05
M3	MEANWHILE					:05
M4	BUDDY'S THEME	BAKER/NEWLAND	ASCAP	SONGSYNE MUSIC		:20
M5	SOME MISTAKE					:38
M6	MY REPUTATION IS SHOT					:18
M7	TRANSITIONAL PIECE					:07
M4	PRIVATE PARTS					:20
M3	MEANWHILE	BAKER/NEWLAND	ASCAP	SONGSYNE MUSIC	B.G. INST.	:05
M8	WHY DON'T YOU KISS ME					:12
M3	MEANWHILE					:05
M7	TRANSITIONAL PIECE					:07
M5	WHAT'S WRONG WITH HER					:38
BB	MAD MOVIES BUMPER	BAKER/NEWLAND	ASCAP	SONGSYNE MUSIC	B.G. INST.	:03
M9	ANYTHING YOU CAN DO					:49
M3	MEANWHILE					:05
M10	IT ALWAYS RAINS ON THIS SIDE	BAKER/NEWLAND	ASCAP	SONGSYNE MUSIC	B.G. INST.	:30
M1	HALLWAY LEONARD					:05
M1	HALLWAY NURSE					:06
M1	LEONARD, NURSE, ORDERLY					:11

PANDA PRODUCTIONS MAD MOVIES

TITLE: SHOCK PART I

PAGE 2 of 2　　SHOW # 104　　DATE: 11/9/85

CUE	TITLE	COMPOSER	SOC	PUBLISHER	USEAGE	TIME
M11	THINK ABOUT IT	BAKER/NEWLAND	ASCAP	SONGSYNE MUSIC	B.G. INST.	:24
HM1	NATURE'S ODDITIES					1:04
M3	MEANWHILE					:05
M4	PRODUCE DEPT.					:20
M7	TRANSITION PIECE					:07
M5	HOT DOGS	BAKER/NEWLAND	ASCAP	SONGSYNE MUSIC	B.G. INST.	:38
BB	MAD MOVIE BUMPER				COMMERCIAL BUMPER	:03
BA	MAD MOVIE BUMPER					:03
M12	THE AFFAIR IS OVER				B.G. INST.	:18
M13	BACK TO BOISE					:30
M3	MEANWHILE	BAKER/NEWLAND	ASCAP	SONGSYNE MUSIC	B.G. INST.	:05
M14	GOT TO SEE THE DOC					:05
M14a	FALLEN IN LOVE					:31
M15	ICE CREAM CONE					:16
M16	ARMY, NAVY, AIR FORCE, MARINES					:26
M13	LONG DISTANCE CALL	BAKER/NEWLAND	ASCAP	SONGSYNE MUSIC	B.G. INST.	:28
M17	CLOSING SHOCK I MONTAGE					:14
M18	CLOSING SHOCK THEME					:08
T2	MAD MOVIES THEME	BAKER/NEWLAND	ASCAP	SONGSYNE MUSIC	MAD MOVIES SHOW CREDITS VOL/INST.	1:03

OPENING CRAWL*

SHOW #<u>104</u>

SHOW NAME   <u>SHOCK PT. 1</u>

*Each numbered item as a single page…
Items #1-4: Centerframe
Items #5-9: Lower third of page

1   FOUR STAR
         in association with
          KENT SKOV

2   Presents
      an L.A. Connection
        production of

3   Tonight's Feature

4   Starring

5   Bob Buchholz

6   Connie Sue Cook

7   Stephen L. Rollman

8   Steve Pinto

9   Kent Skov

GENERIC BUMPERS*

SHOW #<u>104</u>

SHOW NAME   <u>SHOCK PT. 1</u>

*Each numbered item as a single page…

1   We'll be right back…

2   Don't Go Away

3   More Mad Movies
            Coming Up

4   Coming Up…
            More Mad Movies

5   Stay Tuned for
            "Your Home Movies"

6   Next…
            "Your Home Movies"

7   Write Us…
            L.A. Connection Productions
            6464 Sunset Blvd., #820
            Hollywood, CA 90028

8   Send Your Home Movies to…
            L.A. Connection Productions
            6464 Sunset Blvd., #820
            Hollywood, CA 90028
            (Include a self-addressed, stamped envelope for return of films)

9   Next…
            Mad Movies takes it to the streets

CLOSING CRAWL*

SHOW #104

SHOW NAME   SHOCK PT. 1

*Each numbered item as a single page…

1   Directed by
       Kent Skov

2   Written by
       Connie Sue Cook
       Steve Pinto
       Kent Skov

3   Produced by
       Randal W Ridges

4   Featuring
       Bob Buchholz
       Connie Sue Cook
       Steve Pinto
       Stephan L. Rollman
       Kent Skov
       April Winchell

5   Associate Producers (each name single page)
       Martha Whitney

6   Kent Weishaus (single page)

7   Music Composed and arranged by
       Richard Baker
       Mary Newland
       For Panda Productions

8   Music recorded by
       Richard Baker

9   Theme performed by
       Mary Newland

CLOSING CREDIT CRAWL (CONT'D)

10   Research by
         Bob Petrella
         Ken Segall
         April Winchell
         Ted Hardwick

11   Talent Coordinator
         Martha Whitney

12   Associate Director/Stage Manager
         Randal W Ridges

13   Assistants to the Producers:
         Bob Buchholz
         Connie Sue Cook
         Steve Pinto
         Stephan L. Rollman

14   Facilities Provided by
         Hy-Tone Video

15   Lighting and Camera
         Bill Sheehy

16   Production Sound
         Walt Hoylman

17   Gaffer
         Jim Drewry

18   Production Assistants
         Lisa Gougas
         Ted Hardwick

19   Make-Up
         Lora Sanders

20   Wardrobe
         Annie Vicari

21   Production Secretary
         Eloise Gonzalez

22   Post-Production Coordinated by
         Monti Santilli Rainbolt

23   Post-Production Facilities
         Complete Post, Inc.

24   Post-Production Audio by
         Michael Perricone
         Michaele Hogan
         For Interlok Productions

CLOSING CREDIT CRAWL (CONT'D)

25   "Your Home Movies" submitted by
Todd Lee

25   Boston, Massachusetts
Location Courtesy of
Bill & Patti Teague
Studio City, CA

26   Executive in Charge of Production for Four Star Television
Bob Bosen

27   Special Thanks to:
Susan Lenti
Budget Films, Inc.
Richard Holiday
Dennis Condon
Snagglepuss

28   Opening Title Montage by
Homer & Associates

29   Opening Title Photography by
Abe Perlstein

30   Post-Production Supervised by
Randal W Ridges

31   Executive Producer
Kent Skov
"Celebrity Voices and Appearances Impersonated"

33   Copyright 1985 Four Star International, Inc.
All Rights Reserved

SHOCK Pt. 2

With the

SHORT RUNDOWN FOR SHOW #105 Shock Pt. 2

Description	In	Out	Seg Time
Show Open	00:00	01:10	01:10
Commercial Break #1	01:10	03:13	02:03
Act I	03:13	10:10	06:57
Commercial Break #2	10:10	12:13	02:03
Act II	12:13	21:44	09:31
Commercial Break #3	21:44	23:47	02:03
Act III/Show Close	23:47	28:00	04:13

MAD MOVIES WITH THE L.A. CONNECTION

RUNDOWN   SHOW #105 "SHOCK" Pt. 2

All times are in minutes and seconds	IN	OUT	DURATION
Four Star Logo (slug Black)	00:00	00:05	00:05
Show Open: Clip Tease.	00:05	00:20	00:15
Opening Montage.	00:20	01:10	00:50
Commercial Black #1	01:10	03:13	02:03
Bumper #1	03:13	03:16	00:03
Wrap #1	03:16	03:42	00:26
Movie Segment #1	03:42	10:06	00:24
Bumper #2 (Next…Your Home Movie)	10:06	10:10	00:04
Commercial Black #2	10:10	12:13	02:03
Bumper #3	12:13	12:16	00:03
Man On The Street Intro. (as needed)	N.A.	N.A.	N.A.
Man On The Street or Interview Segment.	12:16	14:20	02:03
Movie Segment #2	14:20	17:35	03:15
Home Movie Intro.	17:35	17:47	00:12
Home Movie	17:47	18:49	01:01
Movie Segment #3	18:49	21:40	02:51

MAD MOVIES WITH THE L.A. CONNECTION

RUNDOWN   SHOW #105 "SHOCK" Pt. 2

All times are in minutes and seconds	IN	OUT	DURATION
Bumper #4	21:40	21:44	00:04
Commercial Black #3	21:44	23:47	02:03
Bumper #5	23:47	23:50	00:03
Movie Segment #4	23:50	25:41	01:51
Toss to Preview	25:41	25:46	00:05
Preview	25:46	26:16	00:30
Final Close	26:16	26:33	00:17
Closing Montage	26:33	27:50	01:17
L.A. Connection Logo	27:50	27:55	00:05
Four Star Logo (slug black)	27:55	28:00	00:05

SHOCK PART II SHOW NUMBER 105

CLIP TEASE

DOLL FACE
Hi mom, look, I just wanted to let you know that Mad Movies with the L.A. Connection is coming on. What do you mean, "Who is this?" I called you mom, didn't I? That's right, it's your son. Bye. Must be the dress.

MUSIC INTRO

COMMERCIAL #1

KENT
Hi, I'm Kent Skov and welcome to Mad Movies with the L.A. Connection. Tonight's feature is the conclusion of our two part story: "Shock". In our Mad Movie the star is a doctor with a hyperactive bedside manner. Also starring in "Shock" is Anabel Shaw, the small town girl who goes to the big city to find romance. We'll be talking to Anabel about the movie later in the show. First, let's take a look at what happened in Part I, and then it's time for "Shock" part II.

ACT I

V.O.
As you remember, in the last episode, Dr. Forapain and his nurse, Latrine, were doing this together.

(SFX: LOUD KISS)

But we also saw Skip, the orderly, asking Latrine to serve up more than just a cup of bad coffee…much more. And she served it.
Latrine didn't stop there. She went on to do some fast dancin' with Leonard.
But Leonard wanted Buddy in the worst way.
Yet, Buddy didn't know what she wanted and couldn't ask for it anyway.
(BUDDY MUMBLES)
And then there was Private Parts, who loved Buddy. "I love you, Buddy".
Which brings us back to Dr. Forepain who promised Buddy romance if she left her pig farm in Boise.
(BUDDY OINKS)
But, he didn't come through.
He was a quick tempered man who didn't like anyone to use his phone without his permission.

PRICE
I said, "Say PLEASE".

BUDDY
Oink.

PRICE
Sorry.

                    V.O.
Now for the electrifying conclusion of "Shock". Meanwhile in San Francisco.

                    SKIP
                (Reading Paper)
Listen to Virgo—"Romance intensifies, also be aware of possible candlestick injuries".

                    LATRINE
                  (Thought)
Oh I'm a Virgo.

                NURSE W/GLASSES
                (To Dr. Forapain)
Doctor, can you keep a secret?

                    PRICE
You bet.

                    LATRINE
Take a letter, Maria…can I have a word with you?

                    PRICE
Perhaps. What word is it?

                    LATRINE
Candlestick. Have you killed anyone lately, doctor?

                    PRICE
Maybe.

                    LATRINE
Leonard's missing.

                    PRICE
Oh, they found Leonard with a candlestick stuck in his head. The police think it was an accident. Does that turn you on?

                    LATRINE
Oh yes.
                  (THEY KISS)
Do you hear a funny noise when we kiss?

                    PRICE
Yes Latrine, why do you do that?

                    LATRINE
I didn't do anything. I thought it was you.

                    PRICE
Not me.

                    V.O.
Meanwhile in San Francisco.

BUDDY
Won't you help me get out of here? The hospital food is terrible. Yuk, oh no, it's them again. They made me eat the fruit medley with ham.

LATRINE
Private Parts. Care to dance, big boy?

BUDDY
No, don't dance with her. She's the one that brought me those mashed potatoes. The ones they used to spackle the walls when the painters were here. And Dr. Forapain, he promised to have an affair with me if I left the pig farm, but he lied to me. He never showed up.

PRICE
She doesn't know what she's talking about. I left a message with the pigs…get her a lollipop.

BUDDY
I want a balloon…a big red one.

LATRINE
(Over Buddy's whines)
Calm down, or we'll paint your room again.

PARTS
Something doesn't wash. I think it's you.

PRICE
That's not true. I'm a doctor. I have to wash after most operations. I know you think I killed Leonard, but it was an accident. We get two or three cases a day of people with candlesticks imbedded in their heads. It's very common.

PARTS
Liar!

PRICE
Well, correct me if I'm wrong, but I suspect you don't believe me. I'll have to prove my innocence. Follow me.

MOM
(Singing)

PRICE
Hello, Mom.

MOM
Oh hello, dear.

DR. F.
Where was I last Thursday?

MOM
Which alibi this time?

DR. F.
Hang gliding with Grandpa.

MOM
Oh yes, now I remember.

MOM
You know, dear, my memory would be a lot more reliable if you got your payments to me on time. I'm saving up to get concert tickets for Springsteen.

DR. F.
You made your point, Mom. I'll give the rest of it as soon as I get it.

MOM
Good, now, away you murderous sniveling twit or I'll call the cops.

V.P.
She's old.

V.P.
I'm sure Mom put your mind at ease. You can trust me now. Besides, we have so much in common.

PRIVATE PARTS
What do you mean? I'm a soldier and you're a doctor.

V.P.
We both face life and death every day. You go to war, I have to eat hospital food. We both wear uniforms and we both have noses. So Private Parts, are things clearer now?

PVT.
Yes, but one thing. Tell me again about the noses.

V.P.
Get your hand off my arm right now!
(Thought)
I wonder of he'd like...no.

NURSE x1
Get more batteries.

NURSE W/GLASSES
Dr. Forapain.

DR. F.
Yes.

NURSE W/GLASSES
You got a phone call from your Mother.

DR. F.
What did she say?

NURSE W/GLASSES
Your check bounced, sucker, you're dead meat. Remember to sit up straight in the electric chair. Love, Mom.

DR. F.
Oh yes, thank you.
(MUMBLES DOWN HALL)

(OVERHEARS D.A. PRACTICING STAND-UP ROUTINE)

(FROM DOOR)

[D.A.]
Oh baby, you're the greatest. I'd like to line you up with the sun and watch it set between the twin peaks, with the hallelujah chorus playing in the background. Your skin is as soft and smooth as pudding on a hot day.

D.A.
The day I met you was the luckiest day of my life.

DR. F
Hey! What's going on here?

JACK
Nothin'.

DR. F.
Who the hell are you?

JACK
The name's Jack Bumps, and I'm a plain clothes detective.

DR. F.
Yup, I can tell by your suit.

JACK
I paid $18.95 for this suit.

DR. F.
Wow…you got ripped off.

SKIP
Break's over. Thanks for breakfast, the waffles were great.

LATRINE
I didn't make waffles.

SKIP
Yeah, then what were those things I ate?

LATRINE
I don't know, but some of the mattress pads are missing.

SKIP
Well…they were great with syrup.

LATRINE
What syrup?

SKIP
Oh…I gotta get my stomach pumped!

COMMERCIAL #2/BUMPER #1

KENT
We're back and as promised, we're here with Anabel to talk about the movie. What was it like to work with Vincent Price?

ANABEL
Marvelous. I think he set an atmosphere that was congenial and fun.

KENT
Briefly, tell us the original storyline of "Shock"?

ANABEL
It was about a young girl, she's in a hotel in San Francisco and she sees a woman get murdered by her husband. She goes into shock. They find out that the man who committed the murder is the house psychologist. As a patient, she is referred to him. He realizes what caused the shock and thinks, "I've got to do something about this person."

KENT
Do you consider "Shock" to be your first big break?

ANABEL
Yes, I guess you could call it that. This was the first time I'd had a lead. The whole thing was a really beautiful experience.

KENT
What was it like filming the dream sequence?

ANABEL
The idea was that this was the night I went into shock. I had these terrible, terrible dreams. I could hear my husband calling me but I couldn't get to him. They had me running endlessly on a treadmill. I practically collapsed when I finished the scene.

KENT
What's in the future for Anabel Shaw?

ANABEL
Great things…I see in the future…acting, acting, acting.

KENT
I guess you'll be acting.

ANNOUNCER
Meanwhile in San Francisco.

NURSE W/GLASSES

Candlestick, candlestick, candlestick.

V.P.

Stuff it.

NURSE W/GLASSES

Wooooo doctor.

SKIP

Doc.

V.P.

Skippy! I'll take over from here.

SKIP

But doctor, you don't know what I was doing.

V.P.

It doesn't matter.

SKIP

Okay.

V.P.

I should short-sheet the bed.

SKIP

Here's the stool sample you ordered.

V.P.

Go stand in the corner.

SKIP

Alright—I'm here.

(SFX: PHONE RINGS)

DR. HARTLEY

Yes Batman, how can I assist you? We've been cut off.
(ECHO)
He must be in trouble.

(SFX: PHONE RINGS)

DR. HARTLEY

Yes, Batman
(or) Batman, thank God.

NURSE

No, it's me. Remember, pick up your wife at Al's Auto Body—they'll be finished with her face lift at 3:00.

NURSE

Well, Dr. Forapain, I've got some interesting news. I believe I've cracked this case wide open. I've got a suspect.

DR. F.

Who is it?

                    D.A.
It was Leonard. I'm positive he was the murderer.

                    DR. F.
No, Leonard's dead. He was the victim. Don't you read the newspaper?

                    D.A.
Oh, I don't believe this. Why don't they tell me these things down at the station? Now I have to start over.
                    (O.C.)
I'll catch my man even if I have to work through dinner.

                    DR.F.
                    (Thought)
What a simpleton.

                    DR. F.
                    (V.O.)
Oh Buddy…You make me want to sing…
You make me want to dance…
You make me want to rev up…and pull down your…
Oh, Latrine.

                    LATRINE
So!

                    DR. F.
I know what you're thinking, but it's perfectly innocent. I came in here to comfort her as her doctor and that's all. I swear it.

(AS NURSE TOUCHES ARM)

Arrrr! My arm! Alright, you've forced it out of me, we've been having an affair, there! I'm glad I said it.

                    ORDERLY
Bedpan races in the hall, better place your bets now.

                    DR. F.
Well first things first. Put four dollars on Mrs. Lundquist for me.

(SFX: WEIRD DOORBELL)

                    DR. F.
                    (Thought)
3:00 a.m. If that's Mom, I'll kill her. Detective.

                    D.A.
What's up, doc?

                    DR. F.
I am now.

                    D.A.

I had to get a second job.

                    DR. F.
As what?

                    D.A.
I'm moonlighting as a door to door salesman.

                    DR. F.
I've got encyclopedias, aluminum siding, brushes and 13 vacuum cleaners.

                    D.A.
But do you have this?

                    DR. F.
What?

                    D.A.
A complete home security system, installed!

                    DR. F.
No one could get into my house.

                    D.A.
Sure they could, I did.

                    DR. F.
That's right.

                    LATRINE
Don't worry about the detective. I know how to relax your pumpkin buns. A couple was necking on Lover's Lane when they heard on the radio about an escaped maniac with a hook for a hand.

                    ANABEL
I think it's time for the home movie.

                    KENT
Already?

                    ANABEL
Here, look at one of these and call me in the morning. It was sent by Geoffrey Lee of Paris, Texas.

                    ANNOUNCER
Across the Barzini Bridge…through the Clemenza Memorial Tunnel…is the nation's highest security prison. This dank cell is now the home of Vic Dalmation, known throughout the nation's prison system as…the Dog Man…of Alcatraz. Once a top mechanic who fixed cars by looking at the dashboard, Dalmation now grows his own beef jerky. But most of his time is spent in the prison yard, doing psychological profiles of cute puppies. These two are suffering from a rare condition that makes them actually think they can breakdance. Often, after lights out, Dalmation has a recurring dream. He's an infant, playing with his first dog, as the

ghost of that dog looks on. Then he dreams that his mother's ghost brings him yet another dog, as the ghost of some other dog looks on…and old cars drive by. Then he—still as an infant ghost—watches the ghost of two more of the cutest dogs you ever saw, playing with the ghost of a ball…as *we* look on. Finally, he—as a ghost—is watching himself as an infant ghost while a ghost puppy plays with the ghost of a ball. Pretty strange, huh?

ANNOUNCER
Meanwhile in San Francisco.

(SFX: BRAKES SCREECH)

PRIVATE PARTS
Uh gee, sorry about your upholstery, doc. I didn't know I'd get car sick.

DR. F.
Hmmm. Still mad at me, Mom?

MOM
Pack it in your shorts.

DR. F.
I guess that's yes.

NURSE W/GLASSES
Good morning, sailor.

DR. F.
I'm a doctor and this is a soldier and you're a…

NURSE W/GLASSES
Candlestick maker.

DR. F.
Go scrub a patient!

NURSE W/GLASSES
Scrub this!

LATRINE
Bend over.

DR. F.
Knock it off.

PRIVATE PARTS
Wake up, wake up, wake up, oh wake up.

PVT.
Why are her eyes closed like that?

V.P.
We have no idea but I will tell you this, Private. It's very dangerous to hover over a sleeping person. They could awaken suddenly and poke you in the eye. Or, they could be dreaming and think you're the boogie-man. And I won't even go into the repercussions of

morning mouth. Do you understand? The worst part is if they wake up screaming, yelling—get me a cup of coffee! Or, "Get out of my way, I have to use the bathroom". We in the medical profession call this condition—crankiness. And by the way, Private, don't do that to your hat.

PVT.

Thank you for explaining that, doctor, but can you explain why my name is on the door?

V.P.

What a dip.

SKIP

I'd like more job benefits.

DR. F.

What do have in mind?

SKIP

Well for one, I'd like a chair to sit on and I'd like to get paid on a regular basis. As a matter of fact, I'd like to get paid. Also, I'd like a ride on a big red fire truck.

DR. F.

Oh I suppose you'll want to make the siren noise too?

SKIP

Thank you, sir.

(O.C.)

Rrrrrrrrrrrrrrrrrrrrrr!

LATRINE

You spoil him. You think I don't know.

DR. F.

Know what?

LATRINE

That Skip's your illegitimate son from your affair with nurse Rachit.

DR. F.

That was during the war.

LATRINE

What war?

DR. F.

All of 'em. Except for the Spanish-American war. I was out of town then. Promise me you'll keep this between you and me.

LATRINE

I promise.

(O.C.)

Hey everybody guess what?

BUDDY

(SONG)
You light up my life.

DR. F.
That's enough of that, get me a hypo.

COMMERCIAL #3/BUMPER #2

ANNOUNCER
Meanwhile in San Francisco.

BUDDY
(SONG)

DR. F.
The hypo didn't work well.

DR. F.
(Thought)
I hate that song.

LATRINE
I hate this tie.

DR. F.
Have to use something stronger.

LATRINE
No, not that, you can't.

DR. F.
Yes, I'm going to give her your coffee.

LATRINE
No, you can't, it's inhumane…

DR. F.
That's not what you said when you gave me some this morning.

LATRINE
There's none left, it was all used to paint the bottom of the space shuttle.

DR. F.
Make some more.

LATRINE
No, you can't make me-neener, neener. Oh look, shadows on the wall. I can do a duck.

DR. F.
I can do a hunchback, look oh wow. You can do a dead woman.

DR. F.
I hope I remember how to eat this. Hold the ice cream cone in an upright position with a firm grip. Placing tongue…

(SFX: KNOCK, KNOCK, KNOCK) (O.C.)

You're under arrest.

                    DR. F.

I guess I'll have to leave my ice cream cone here.

                    D.A.
                 (NODS YES)

                    DR. F.

Alright, but it's gonna drip all over the desk and it'll be on your head.

(SFX: SWISH)

                    D.A.

The squad car's waiting.

                    DR. F.

Well, can I ride in front and make the siren noises? Oh by the way.

                    KENT

Thanks for joining us and I'd like to thank Anabel Shaw for being with us today. See you next time on Mad Movies with the L.A. Connection.

CLOSING CREDITS

PANDA PRODUCTIONS

MAD MOVIES

TITLE: SHOCK PART II

SHOW # 105   DATE: 11/16/85

PAGE 1 of 2

CUE	TITLE	COMPOSER	SOC	PUBLISHER	USEAGE	TIME
BG2	CLIP TEASE	BAKER/NEWLAND	ASCAP	SONGSYNC MUSIC	B.G. INST.	:15
T1	MAD MOVIES THEME				VOC/INST.	:50
BA	MAD MOVIES BUMPER				COMMERCIAL BUMPER	:03
BG1	KENT'S THEME				B.G. INST.	:26
M1	SHOCK II: OPENING MONTAGE					
	A					:15
	B					:14
	C					:41
M2	TRANSITIONAL PIECE	BAKER/NEWLAND	ASCAP	SONGSYNC MUSIC	B.G. INST.	:07
M2	TRANSITIONAL PIECE					:07
M3	A WORD WITH YOU					:08
M4	HAVE YOU KILLED ANYONE					:12
M5	DOES THAT TURN YOU ON					:14
M6	MEANWHILE					:05
M7	FRUIT MEDLY WITH HAM					:49
M2	TRANSITION PIECE					:07
M8	YOU CAN TRUST ME NOW					:28
M6	MEANWHILE	R. BAKER/M. NEWLAND	ASCAP	SONGSYNC MUSIC	B.G. INST.	:05
M9	PHONE CALL FROM MOM					:20
M10	JACK BUMPS					:11
M11	BREAKS OVER					:17
B C	MAD MOVIES BUMPER				COMM/BUMP	:05
B A	MAD MOVIES BUMPER				VOC/INST.	:03
M6	MEANWHILE				B.G. INST.	:05
M12	HOW CAN I ASSIST YOU					:27
M13	I'VE GOT A SUSPECT					:32

PANDA PRODUCTIONS	MAD MOVIES

TITLE: SHOCK PART II

PAGE 2 of 2	SHOW # 105	DATE: 11/16/85

CUE	TITLE	COMPOSER	SOC	PUBLISHER	USEAGE	TIME
M11	OH BUDDY	R. BAKER/M. NEWLAND	ASCAP	SONGSYNC MUSIC	B.G. INST	:06
M1c	OH LATRINE					:14
M10	BEDPAN RACES					:11
M14	PUMPKIN BUNS					:28
HM1	"DOGMAN OF ALCATRAZ"					1:01
M6	MEANWHILE					:05
M2	TRANSITIONAL PIECE					:07
M15	WAKE-UP					:49
M16	MORE BENEFITS					:20
M17	YOU SPOIL SKIP					:24
B B	MAD MOVIES BUMPER				COMM/BUMP VOCAL/INST	:04
B A	MAD MOVIES BUMPER					:03
M18	USE SOMETHING STRONGER				B.G. INST	:29
M10	YOU'RE UNDER ARREST					:08
M19	SHOCK II: CLOSE					:26
T 2	MAD MOVIES THEME	R. BAKER/M. NEWLAND	ASCAP	SONGSYNC MUSIC	SHOW CLOSE VOCAL/INST	1:30

OPENING CRAWL*

SHOW #<u>105</u>

SHOW NAME   <u>SHOCK PT. 2</u>

*Each numbered item as a single page…
Items #1-4: Centerframe
Items #5-9: Lower third of page

1   FOUR STAR
            in association with
            KENT SKOV

2   Presents
            an L.A. Connection
            production of

3   Tonight's Feature

4   Starring

5   Bob Buchholz

6   Connie Sue Cook

7   Stephen L. Rollman

8   Steve Pinto

9   Kent Skov

GENERIC BUMPERS*

SHOW #<u>105</u>

SHOW NAME   <u>SHOCK PT. 2</u>

*Each numbered item as a single page…

1   We'll be right back…

2   Don't Go Away

3   More Mad Movies
          Coming Up

4   Coming Up…
          More Mad Movies

5   Stay Tuned for
          "Your Home Movies"

6   Next…
          "Your Home Movies"

7   Write Us…
          L.A. Connection Productions
          6464 Sunset Blvd., #820
          Hollywood, CA 90028

8   Send Your Home Movies to…
          L.A. Connection Productions
          6464 Sunset Blvd., #820
          Hollywood, CA 90028
          (Include a self-addressed, stamped envelope for return of films)

9   Next…
          Mad Movies takes it to the streets

10   Next…
          A permanent pain killer

CLOSING CRAWL*

SHOW #<u>105</u>

SHOW NAME <u>SHOCK PT. 2</u>

*Each numbered item as a single page...

1	Directed by Kent Skov
2	Written by Connie Sue Cook Steve Pinto Kent Skov
3	Produced by Randal W Ridges
4	Featuring Bob Buchholz Connie Sue Cook Steve Pinto Stephen L. Rollman Kent Skov April Winchell
4a	Special Guest Anabel Shaw
5	Associate Producers (each name single page) Martha Whitney
6	Kent Weishaus (single page)
7	Music Composed and arranged by Richard Baker Mary Newland For Panda Productions
8	Music recorded by Richard Baker
9	Theme performed by Mary Newland

CLOSING CREDIT CRAWL (CONT'D)

10   Research by
      Bob Petrella
      Ken Segall
      April Winchell
      Ted Hardwick

11   Talent Coordinator
      Martha Whitney

12   Associate Director/Stage Manager
      Randal W Ridges

13   Assistants to the Producers:
      Bob Buchholz
      Connie Sue Cook
      Steve Pinto
      Stephan L. Rollman

14   Facilities Provided by
      Hy-Tone Video

15   Lighting and Camera
      Bill Sheehy

16   Production Sound
      Walt Hoylman

17   Gaffer
      Jim Drewry

18   Production Assistants
      Lisa Gougas
      Ted Hardwick

19   Make-Up
      Lora Sanders

20   Wardrobe
      Annie Vicari

21   Production Secretary
      Eloise Gonzalez

22   Post-Production Coordinated by
      Monti Santilli Rainbolt

23   Post-Production Facilities
      Complete Post, Inc.

24   Post-Production Audio by
      Michael Perricone
      Michaele Hogan
      For Interlok Productions

CLOSING CREDIT CRAWL (CONT'D)

25   "Your Home Movies" submitted by
             Geoffrey Lee
             Paris, TX

25   Location Courtesy of
             Bill & Patti Teague
             Studio City, CA

26   Executive in Charge of Production for Four Star Television
             Bob Bosen

27   Special Thanks to:
             Susan Lenti
             Budget Films, Inc.
             Richard Holiday
             Dennis Condon
             Snagglepuss

28   Opening Title Montage by
             Homer & Associates

29   Opening Title Photography by
             Abe Perlstein

30   Post-Production Supervised by
             Randal W Ridges

31   Executive Producer
             Kent Skov

32   "Celebrity Voices and Appearances Impersonated"

33   Copyright 1985 Four Star International, Inc.
             All Rights Reserved

A STAR IS BORN

SHORT RUNDOWN FOR SHOW #103 A STAR IS BORN

Description	In	Out	Seg Time
Show Open	00:00	01:10	01:10
Commercial Break #1	01:10	03:13	02:03
Act I	03:13	10:21	07:08
Commercial Break #2	10:21	12:24	02:03
Act II	12:24	22:47	10:22
Commercial Break #3	22:47	24:50	02:03
Act III/Show Close	24:50	28:00	03:10

MAD MOVIES WITH THE L.A. CONNECTION

RUNDOWN   SHOW #103 "A Star Is Born"

All times are in minutes and seconds	IN	OUT	DURATION
Four Star Logo (slug Black)	00:00	00:05	00:05
Show Open: Clip Tease.	00:05	00:20	00:15
Opening Montage.	00:20	01:10	00:50
Commercial Black #1	01:10	03:13	02:03
Bumper #1	03:13	03:16	00:03
Wrap #1	03:16	03:52	00:36
Movie Segment #1	03:52	10:17	06:25
Bumper #2 (Next…Your Home Movie)	10:17	10:21	00:04
Commercial Black #2	10:21	12:24	02:03
Bumper #3	12:24	12:27	00:03
Man On The Street Intro. (as needed)	12:27	12:36	00:09
Man On The Street or Interview Segment.	12:36	13:29	00:53
Movie Segment #2	13:29	16:36	03:07
Home Movie Intro.	16:36	16:47	00:11
Home Movie	16:47	17:47	01:00
Movie Segment #3	17:47	22:43	04:05

MAD MOVIES WITH THE L.A. CONNECTION

RUNDOWN   SHOW #103 "A Star Is Born"

All times are in minutes and seconds	IN	OUT	DURATION
Bumper #4	22:43	22:47	00:04
Commercial Black #3	22:47	24:50	02:03
Bumper #5	24:50	24:53	00:03
Movie Segment #4	24:53	26:11	01:18
Toss to Preview	26:11	26:30	00:19
Preview	26:30	26:39	00:09
Final Close	26:39	27:07	00:28
Closing Montage	27:07	27:50	00:43
L.A. Connection Logo	27:50	27:55	00:05
Four Star Logo (slug black)	27:55	28:00	00:05

A STAR IS BORN SHOW NUMBER #103

CLIP TEASE

WATSON
What is it, Holmes?

HOLMES
Look Watson, there are people watching. They're waiting for Mad Movies with the L.A. Connection. Do you see them?

SHOW MUSICAL THEME

COMMERCIAL #1

OPENING WRAP

INT. OFFICE

KENT
Hi, I'm Kent Skov and welcome to Mad Movies with the L.A. Connection. This is a video dating service. I'm here because tonight's Mad Movie happens to be about a woman who's searching for Mr. Right and just can't seem to find him. Which is a shame, considering the fact that there are 33,481,381 eligible bachelors. Of course, 10 million of us are probably too old, too young or just boring. So let's follow one woman's search for romance. Tonight's Mad Movie is a classic…the 1937 version of A Star is Born.

ACT I

INT. HOUSE

MOM
Esther! Quit looking at those pictures of naked men. Put that National Geographic away, go out and get yourself a date. Get your butt out that door. If you hang around here too long you'll die a virgin like your grandmother.

INT. OFFICE

"D.A.D. SUPERVISOR"
Esther, at this dating service our operators are standing by 24 hours a day.

OPERATOR #1
"Date A Dude". Can we help you?

OPERATOR #2
Your dude will meet you at 5th and Main for weenies.

"D.A.D." SUPERVISOR
So you see, Esther, it just goes to show you you're not alone. There are a lot of other dull, bulgy eyed, scraggly haired, thin lipped, flat chested, tastelessly dressed, ignorant women out there just like you. And we'll find you a man or something darn close.

INT. HOTEL

                HOTEL CLERK
                  (THOUGHT)
Hmm, a four letter word for hairless.

                ESTHER
Excuse me, is Tom Selleck here?

                HOTEL CLERK
No. He painted the message slots and left. He went upstairs to get some wet paint signs. He's going to hang them on the bannister until it dries.

                ESTHER
Oh, I see.

                HOTEL CLERK
Apparently not too well, you've got paint all over your hands. Oh, here he comes now. Hi, Tom!

                TOM
Is my date here yet? Hmmm.

(SFX—BUZZING NOISE)

                HOTEL CLERK
What, oh yeah, she must be your date. This is Tom Selleck.

                TOM
Hi!

                ESTHER
How do you do?

                HOTEL CLERK
Tom here can burp—in five languages.

INT. BAR

                ESTHER
Two "Skip and go Nakeds" with milk, please.

(SFX: SLURPIN)

(SFX: BONES BREAKIN)

                TOM
Nobody punches me and gets away with it. Next time I'll deck you, understand, Esther?

                ESTHER
Sorry—Cheers.
                (SLURPS)
Whoo! Great stuff. I'd like to get underneath that cow and milk it personally.

TOM
Don't talk dirty around me.
(HITS ESTHER)

ESTHER
I'm paying for this date and I'll talk to you any way I want.

(SFX: BONES BREAKING ON METAL)

INT. HALLWAY

TOM
I'm sorry you broke your hand. I have a metal plate in my arm, from shaving. Please don't cry, that was 20 years ago. Here— When I squat down, I can see right up your nose.

ESTHER
I'm sorry, I guess this date is pretty disappointing.

TOM
As a matter of fact, it is.

ESTHER
Well, it's still early in the evening, is there anything I can do to make it up to you?

TOM
You bet, you can go to bed with me. Right now.

INT. BEDROOM

ESTHER
I don't know what happened.

TOM
It's not your fault. I'm under a lot of pressure. Sure, my name is Tom Selleck, and sure, I look like him but I can't always perform like him.

ESTHER
Maybe we should take our clothes off.

TOM
Good idea, I never thought of that.

ESTHER
Imagine, we could fill the room with Jell-O and dance all around in French Maid outfits.

TOM
French Maid outfit. I just happen to have one right here and it looks like it'll fit you just fine. All we need now is music.

INT. HALLWAY

> **HOTEL CLERK**
> It's 2:30, what you're doing is dirty. I know what's going on, because you're making too much noise and if you don't stop I'm going to call the cops.

> **"D.A.D." SUPERVISOR**
> You weren't that easy to match, why not give Tom one more chance?

> **ESTHER**
> Oh, alright.

> **"D.A.D." SUPERVISOR**
> Why don't you try a little more exotic setting this time?

> **ESTHER**
> Maybe I will. I'll take him bowling.

EXT. HOLLYWOOD BOWL

> **TOM**
> Well?

> **ESTHER**
> This is more fun than licking frozen doorknobs.

> **TOM**
> Gee, that's not 'til next week. Tonight there's a "No Holds Barred" wrestling match between Mario "The Flash" Bonzini and the challenger "Stormin Norman". It sounds like a good fight.

> **ESTHER**
> I can't see.

> **TOM**
> You were the one who picked our seats.

> **ESTHER**
> Oh Tommy, don't say that. People will think that we're in -

(SFX: FIGHT BELL)

> **MARIO "T.F." BONZINI**
> What za matta? You lousy dirtbag.

> **NORMAN**
> Who you calling a dirtbag, you log head?

> **MARIO "T.F." BONZINI**
> Who you calling a loghead? You weasel-brain.

> **NORMAN**
> Who you calling a weasel-brain, you photographer?

> **MARIO**

Nobody calls me a photographer.

> FIGHT ANNOUNCER

And there they go. "Stormin Norman" body slams the camera, Mario "The Flash" Bonzini is stunned and while he's not looking, Norman pulls a gun.

(SFX: GUN SHOT)

The winner and new champion of the world, "Stormin Norman".

> WOMAN

Your fly's open.

> ESTHER

Is shooting legal?

> TOM

No it's not but it's the only way he can win.

> ESTHER

Oh Tom, I've got so much to learn.

INT. BEDROOM

> NORMAN

I got this number off the bathroom wall. I wonder what they meant by a "good time"!

> ESTHER

Hello, what?

> NORMAN

Mumbles.

> ESTHER

Oh.

> NORMAN

Mumbles.

> ESTHER

Oh.

> NORMAN

Mumbles.

> ESTHER

Oh.

> NORMAN

Mumbles.

> ESTHER

Yes…yes I like that, oh thank you.

                    NORMAN
                    Mumbles
                    (THOUGHT)
I finally got a date with a real woman. I'm sorry we're going to have to break up but you can sleep in. I've got morning mouth, the worst breath of the day. We're talking stinko. I could use some gum right now. I stuck some here last week. Damn that maid. Oh, that reminds me, I forgot to tell Esther where I live. Where *do* I live? Let's see Needlebaum, Nishiyama Knackwurst, Norman. Here it is. Hey, I live in a nice neighborhood. That drained me. Move over, Jeannie, I need a nap.

COMMERCIAL #2

BUMPER #1

MAN ON THE STREET

EXT. DAY

                    KENT
The dating scene is a rough, emotional, confusing world where hearts are broken every day. Yet some people still have a dream about their ideal mate. (What is your idea of the ideal mate?)

                    RESPONSES
"One that was out of town alot."
"Female, rich, funny, gorgeous and trustworthy."
"One that cooks, cleans the house, works, takes care of me."
"Um." "Right here what are you talking about." "Right, right."
"Curly hair…critical in a relationship."
"Someone who likes to take their clothes off alot."
"It's kinda hard to say because I might get into trouble."
"There's a nice looking blonde over here."
"You really asked the wrong guy." "What did you mean by that?"
"A woman."
"Richard Gere."
"Joan Collins would be perfect."
"Rambo."
"I prefer Bo Derick."

                    KENT
Any reason you prefer Bo Derick?
"Just for one night."
"A bald-headed man with glasses." "That's me."

ACT II

INT. RESTAURANT

                    BABY CHICK
Cheep, cheep, cheep, cheep, achoo, achoo.

                    MAN IN CAFÉ
Moses, party of 40,000, your table's ready.

BABY CHICK
Glug.

ESTHER
If he tries anything I'll tell him to stick it in his ear and kiss off.

NORMAN
Glug, glug, burp.

ESTHER
(THOUGHT)
I need a new approach. Hi sailor, new in town?

NORMAN
Wanna get lucky?

ESTHER
I'd love to…oh Norman…Did you remember we had a date…did you already eat?

NORMAN
I had a little chicken, but I'm still hungry.

ESTHER
Well, why don't you have a breath mint.

NORMAN
Oh that again, how embarrassing.

ESTHER
It's making my eyes water.

NORMAN
Consider yourself fortunate, you're still alive.

INT. KITCHEN

ESTHER
I thought you were paying for lunch.

NORMAN
No, no, I tried to sneak out the back way, but they caught me, and now we have to do the dishes.

ESTHER
Thanks, creep.

NORMAN
Say…can you see yourself in this plate?

ESTHER
Yeah, I'm a mess.

NORMAN
No, that's just spinach.

ESTHER
On the plate.

NORMAN
No, on your face.

ESTHER
(LAUGHS)

NORMAN
What's so funny?

ESTHER
I was just thinking about last summer, it was so hot the hogs went wild and ate my cousin Willy.

NORMAN
Now I'm afraid of ham.

SCHOOLMASTER
Lesson No. 1, pucker up your lips, put 'em together and make a noise like the toilet backing up.

(SFX: TOILET BACKING UP)

(SFX: SEALS BARKING AND CLAPPING)

TOM

(SFX: HUGE BELCH)

SCHOOLMASTER
That was good but you'll have to watch the spit bubbles.

ESTHER
Thank you. I want to apologize for my hat exploding earlier and blowing your hair off.

SCHOOLMASTER
Now I have to buy a toupee.

NORMAN
Here's a dollar, get something nice.

TOM
I stole this from his safe.

NORMAN
We have to go.

ESTHER
Bye, bye.

NORMAN
Toodle-oo, caribou.

INT. TRAILER KITCHEN

ESTHER

Give me a horse, real big horse, a great big kangaroo and let me wahoo, wahoo, wahoo.

(SFX: BRAKES)

NORMAN
(THOUGHT)

Sounds like a moose.

ESTHER

Wonderful!

NORMAN

Were you calling for me?

(SFX: MONKEY KISS)

Well I think it's time to move on to second base. I'll go in the back and get naked, okay Esther?

ESTHER

I'll join you in a minute. I've got to clean up the kitchen.

NORMAN

Is there someplace private I can undress? I'm kinda shy.

ESTHER

Let's see, not here, oh how 'bout next to the water heater?

NORMAN

Ok, but don't look.

ESTHER

Don't you worry, you get ready and I'll be in in a minute. Oh no, it's all burnt and dirty.

NORMAN

I told you not to look.

HOME MOVIE

KENT

Boy, she's having a tough time. Let's take a break from the movie for a second and watch a Home Movie, sent to us by Stacey Kosmidas from Northridge, California.

ANNOUNCER

This was the thousand year old castle of King Nimrod, a mad tyrant who was said to treat his subjects as if they were farm animals, refusing even to upgrade their outdated transportation system. Nobody complained until one day, as his bodyguards led him down the Royal Stairs, the looks on their faces said that something very serious was about to take place. Of course, the King had no idea that a full-scale rebellion was underway. It started with a brief scuffle in the throne room. The cruel King assumed he had things under control, so he visited the one place he could contemplate his tyrannical rule, the beach. Where the elements of nature always convinced him he was afraid of nothing. He began to harass his subjects by breathing on them at close range. Finally, the palace guards attacked him with everything they had, putting an end to his insane rule. The tyrant was replaced by the Good Queen Anne, a kind-hearted monarch who would gladly gift-wrap presents for her subjects and have lingerie shows every other Tuesday. She gave free medical advice to the poor as well as offering her services as a volunteer fireman. Good Queen Anne…beloved by all.

                    ESTHER

Honey.

                    NORMAN

Pumpkin lips.

                    ESTHER

Oh no, you've been drinking eggs again. It's a disease, darling, you should get professional help.

                    NORMAN

The guys at the garage say you have a lot of hair on your back.

                    ESTHER
              (OBNOXIOUS LAUGH)

                    NORMAN

They were right. We're talking sheepdog.

                    ESTHER

Exciting.

                    NORMAN

Yeah. How 'bout a hickey?

(SFX: SUMP PUMP)

Hey, I'm taller than you.

                    ESTHER

You're wearing my high heels.

(SFX: MONKEY KISS)

MMM mmm mmm.

                    NORMAN

Something the matter?

                    ESTHER

Your suit smells like a sandwich.

                    NORMAN

Geez, that's probably my breath. I'll go gargle with air freshener. I'll be back next week.

ESTHER
Good luck.

MAX
Listen pal, your breath stinks. What the hell are you doing out in public? Didn't you see the no Halitosis sign on the wall. People are trying to smoke in here and some of us are trying to breathe. I ought to report you to the Health Department. Go back to the cesspool where you belong. Haven't you ever heard of a toothbrush?

NORMAN
Mumbles

MAX
That's the worst excuse I ever heard. You're a sorry example of a human being. You ought to be locked up. Don't breathe on that. People eat here and I don't like your hat either.

CROWD
What is that stench? Get me a gas mask. Is the sewer backing up? Nadine, honey is that you? Whew, whew, whew.

NORMAN
Give me a scope, double, leave the bottle here.

VOICE IN CROWD
Did something die back here?

MESSENGER
Package for Stormin' Norman.

NORMAN
What is it?

MESSENGER
It's a case of breath mints.

NORMAN
Wise guy, huh?

MESSENGER
Say please.

NORMAN
Well who sent it?

MESSENGER
The Environmental Protection Agency and not a moment too soon.

COURT CLERK
Court is now in session. Judge Wopner presiding. Next case, State vs. Stormin' Norman. State calls first witness, Foster Brooks.

JUDGE
State your case.

DRUNK
Norman breathed on me.

JUDGE
That's not a crime, be more specific.

DRUNK
I'm only nineteen. I was a hunk 'til he walked by.

JUDGE
You remind me too much of my wife. Mr. Eisenhower, take him away. Stormin Norman, approach the bench. Lizard Breath, stop right there, that's close enough. There's no penalty for bad breath, so I'll have to let you go.

ESTHER
Please, wait. Listen Judge you're running for reelection. I think you should reconsider.

JUDGE
What do you mean?

ESTHER
Put him away.

JUDGE
Do you realize what you're asking? This man's not really a criminal.

ESTHER
Please judge, you've got to understand, I've been dating this man for a while. You don't know what it's like to kiss a man with bad breath.

JUDGE
Yes I do, but that's a different case. Do you realize if I convict him he'll be put away for life? Well do you, do you, do you?

ESTHER
I do.

JUDGE
I should have brought a lunch. Lock him up.

ESTHER
Thank you. Good bye, Norman.

IKE
You can stay with Mamie and I.

PIERRE
Hello, Mon Cheri.

BALIFF
State vs. Fernando Valenzuela.

JUDGE
Mr. Valenzuela, you've been charged with dancing and twirling in the park.

FERNANDO VALENZUELA
I'm a ballerina.

ADOLPH
Hello Esther, this is Pierre. I'm the man who gave you a ride home form court yesterday, and would you like to go out to a very formal event? That's right, Pierre, the one with the fake moustache. I'll pick you up in five minutes.

MAKE UP MAN #1
Esther says she is going to a very highbrow affair. I'll take care of that.

MAKE UP MAN #2
She doesn't appreciate our work.

MAKE UP MAN #1
I know.

MAKE UP MAN #2
I'll make her smile.

WOMAN IN CROWD
Look! Esther has two dates.

ESTHER
A funeral is your idea of a formal date?

VOICES IN CROWD
How was the limo ride? What's Tom Selleck really like? Sign my yearbook.

(SFX: PARTY NOISES)

2ND WOMAN IN CROWD
Where did you go for dinner?

3RD WOMAN IN CROWD
Do you think I look like Eleanor Roosevelt?

4TH WOMAN IN CROWD
What's the number for Date-A-Dude?

TOM
Quit pushin' me, Esther, or I'll deck you.

5TH WOMAN IN CROWD
Say Esther, how do you like your dates?

ESTHER
AAAAAAAAAFUL—EEE!

COMMERCIAL #3/BUMPER #2

GRANDMA
Darling Esther, don't be discouraged. There are a lot of young men out there who will love you. I should know. I had 'em. Just last weekend I had a wonderful experience. I took on the entire football team at Bob's Jr. College. Wowwie-wow-wow—Get a young one—they're the best. Get off my lap—you're hurting me. Here's a buck.

MOM
You two were out late again tonight.

ESTHER
C'mon, Mom, we're on our honeymoon.

KID
Mother-In-Laws, hmmph. Say Esther, go fix me some weenie surprise.

ESTHER
Sure, Alfalfa.

KID
I think a woman's place is in the kitchen. Isn't that right, old man?

DAD
Well I…

ESTHER
Don't encourage him. I wish I'd been like grandma and never married.

KID
No wife of mine is going to read National Geographic.

GRANDMA
Shame on you, Alfalfa. I'll teach you a lesson; you're going to bed early.

KID
Esther, aren't you coming with me?

ESTHER
Not tonight, I have a headache.

KENT
Well, that makes one less eligible bachelor and I'm glad of it. You know, every day a star is born and by golly, the next one could be you. So send us your home movies. Now let's see a preview of our next Mad Movie.

KENT
Hi, my name is Lance. I'm 6 foot, 4 and worth well over 10 million dollars. My hobbies are professional football, buying expensive gifts for women, flying my private jet to Hawaii on my lunch hour. I want a date with you baby because I'm so hot…

CLOSING CREDITS

PANDA PRODUCTIONS

MAD MOVIES

TITLE: STAR IS BORN

PAGE 1 of 2 SHOW # 103 DATE: 9/28/85

CUE	TITLE	COMPOSER	SOC	PUBLISHER	USEAGE	TIME
T 1	MAD MOVIES THEME	BAKER/NEWLAND	ASCAP	SONGSYNC MUSIC	MAD MOVIES SHOW OPENER	:50
BB	MAD MOVIES BUMPER				COMMERCIAL BUMPER	:03
BG1	KENT'S THEME				B.G. INST.	:31
M1	STAR IS BORN THEME					:07
M2	DATING THEME					:33
M3	TOM SELLECK	BAKER/NEWLAND				:16
M4	SKIP AND GO NAKED					:38
M5	TAKE OUR CLOTHES OFF					:35
F1	LA DONNA é MOBILE RIGOLETTO	P.D. ADAPTED BY BAKER/NEWLAND AUTHORS: CONNIE COOK STEVE ROLLMAN STEVE PINTO BOB BUCHHOLZ KENT SKOV			FEATURED SONG	:23
M2	DATING THEME	BAKER/NEWLAND			B.G. INST.	:33
M6	WRESTLING MATCH					:08
M7	CALL FOR A GOOD TIME					1:23
BB	MAD MOVIES BUMPER				COMMERCIAL BUMPER	:03
BA	MAD MOVIES BUMPER					:03
M2	DATING THEME					:33
M8	LESSON #1					:36

PANDA PRODUCTIONS

MAD MOVIES

TITLE: STAR IS BORN

SHOW # 103 DATE: 9/28/85

PAGE 2 of 2

CUE	TITLE	COMPOSER	SOC	PUBLISHER	USEAGE	TIME
M9	GET ME A HORSE	BAKER/NEWLAND AUTHORS: CONNIE COOK STEVE ROLLMAN STEVE PINTO BOB BUCHHOLZ KENT SKOV	ASCAP	SONGSYNC MUSIC	FEATURED SONG	:15
BG1	KENT'S THEME	BAKER/NEWLAND			B.G. INST.	:12
HM1	THE REVOLUTION					1:00
M10	PUMPKIN LIPS					:07
M11	HAIR ON YOUR BACK					:13
M12	SANDWICH BREATH KISS					:05
M13	YOUR BREATH STINKS					:44
M14	FOSTER BROOKS					:26
M15	PUT HIM AWAY	BAKER/NEWLAND	ASCAP	SONGSYNC MUSIC	B.G. INST.	:27
M16	DO YOU					:05
M17	THIS IS PIERRE					:18
M18	HIGH BROW AFFAIR					:16
M19	FUNERAL					:33
BA	MAD MOVIES BUMPER					:03
M20	DARLING ESTER	BAKER/NEWLAND				:41
M21	STAR IS BORN: CLOSE					:20
BG1	KENT'S THEME					:18
T2	MAD MOVIE THEME	BAKER/NEWLAND	ASCAP	SONGSYNC MUSIC	MAD MOVIES SHOW CREDITS VOC/INST.	:56

OPENING CRAWL*

SHOW #<u>103</u>

SHOW NAME   <u>Star Is Born</u>

*Each numbered item as a single page…
Items #1-4: Centerframe
Items #5-9: Lower third of page

1   FOUR STAR
                in association with
                KENT SKOV

2   Presents
         an L.A. Connection
           production of

3   A Star Is Born

4   Starring

5   Bob Buchholz

6   Connie Sue Cook

7   Stephen L. Rollman

8   Steve Pinto

9   Kent Skov

GENERIC BUMPERS*

SHOW #<u>103</u>

SHOW NAME   <u>Star Is Born</u>

*Each numbered item as a single page…

1   We'll be right back…

2   Don't Go Away

3   More Mad Movies
         Coming Up

4   Coming Up…
         More Mad Movies

5   Stay Tuned for
         "Your Home Movies"

6   Next…
         "Your Home Movies"

7   Write Us…
         L.A. Connection Productions
         6464 Sunset Blvd., #820
         Hollywood, CA 90028

8   Send Your Home Movies to…
         L.A. Connection Productions
         6464 Sunset Blvd., #820
         Hollywood, CA 90028
         (Include a self-addressed, stamped envelope for return of films)

9   Next…
         Mad Movies takes it to the streets

10   Next…
         Esther Gets Married

11   See you next time.

SHOW #103

SHOW NAME   Star Is Born

*Each numbered item as a single page…

1   Directed by
    Kent Skov

2   Written by
    Connie Sue Cook
    Steve Pinto
    Kent Skov

3   Produced by
    Randal W Ridges

4   Featuring
    Bob Buchholz
    Connie Sue Cook
    Steve Pinto
    Stephen L. Rollman
    Kent Skov
    April Winchell

5   Associate Producers (each name single page)
    Martha Whitney

6   Kent Weishaus (single page)

7   Music Composed and arranged by
    Richard Baker
    Mary Newland
    For Panda Productions

7a Music Recorded by
    Richard Baker

8   Theme Performed by
    Mary Newland

CLOSING CREDIT CRAWL (con't)

9		Research by Bob Petrella Ken Segall April Winchell Ted Hardwick
10		Talent Coordinator Martha Whitney
11		Associate Director/Stage Manager Randal W Ridges
11a		Assistants to the Producers: Bob Buchholz Connie Sue Cook Steve Pinto Stephen L. Rollman
12		Lighting and Camera Steven Hirsh
13		Video Technician Bob Thorndike
14		Grips Scott Steele
15		Production Assistants Lisa Gougas Ted Hardwick Monti Santilli Rainbolt
16		Make Up Lora Sanders
17		Wardrobe Annie Vicari
18		Production Secretary Eloise Gonzalez
19		Post-Production Facilities Complete Post, Inc.
20		Post-Production Audio by Interlok Michael Perricone Michaele Hogan

CLOSING CREDIT CRAWL (con't)

21   "Your Home Movie" submitted by
Stacy Kosmidos
Northridge, CA

22   Executive in Charge of Production for Four Star Television
Bob Bosen

23   Special Thanks to:
Susan Lenti
Budget Films, Inc.
Richard Holiday
Dennis Condon
Snagglepuss

23a   Opening Title Montage by
Homer & Associates

23b   Opening Title Photography by
Abe Perlstein

24   Post-Production supervised by
Randal W Ridges

25   Executive Producer
Kent Skov

26   "Celebrity Voices and Appearances Impersonated"

27   Copyright 1985 Four Star International, Inc.
All rights Reserved

THE STRANGER

With the

SHORT RUNDOWN FOR SHOW #115 THE STRANGER

Description	In	Out	Seg Time
Show Open	00:00	01:48	01:48
Commercial Break #1	01:48	03:51	02:03
Act I	03:51	12:12	08:21
Commercial Break #2	12:12	14:15	02:03
Act II	14:15	20:09	05:54
Commercial Break #3	20:09	22:12	02:03
Act III/Show Close	22:12	28:00	05:48

MAD MOVIES WITH THE L.A. CONNECTION

RUNDOWN   SHOW #115 THE STRANGER

TIMES IN MINUTES AND SECONDS	IN	OUT	DURATION
FOUR STAR LOGO	00:00	00:05	00:05
OPENING CLIP TEASE	00:05	00:21	00:16
OPENING MONTAGE	00:21	00:49	00:28
OPENING WRAP	00:49	01:19	00:30
CLIP #2	01:19	01:42	00:23
WRAP #2	01:42	01:48	00:06
COMMERCIAL #1	01:48	03:51	02:03
BUMPER #1	03:51	03:54	00:03
TOSS TO FEATURE	03:54	04:02	00:08
FEATURE SEGMENT #1	04:02	11:34	07:32
TOSS TO TEASE	11:34	11:50	00:16
CLIP TEASE #3	11:50	12:12	00:22
COMMERCIAL #2	12:12	14:15	02:03
BUMPER #2	14:15	14:18	00:03
FEATURE SEGMENT #2	14:18	20:05	05:47
BUMPER #3	20:05	20:09	00:04

MAD MOVIES WITH THE L.A. CONNECTION

RUNDOWN   SHOW #<u>115 THE STRANGER</u>

TIMES IN MINUTES AND SECONDS	IN	OUT	DURATION
COMMERCIAL #3	20:09	22:12	02:03
BUMPER #4	22:12	22:15	00:03
FEATURE SEGMENT #3	22:15	25:02	02:47
HOME MOVIE INTRO	25:02	25:19	00:17
HOME MOVIE	25:19	26:25	01:06
CLOSING WRAP	26:25	26:57	00:32
CLOSING CLIP	26:57	27:31	00:34
CLOSING MONTAGE	27:31	27:50	00:19
L.A. CONNECTION LOGO	27:50	27:55	00:05
FOUR STAR LOGO	27:55	28:00	00:05

THE STRANGER SHOW NUMBER 115

(INT. CLOCK TOWER)

> ROBINSON
> Listen, I know my daughter invited you to watch Mad Movies with us, but for some reason, she put the tv up on the roof and the antenna in the living room. Why?

> LONG
> I think you get better reception that way.

> ROBINSON
> Yeah, I guess you do, see.

CREDITS

(EXT. NEWSTAND)

> HOST
> Hi, I'm Kent Skov and welcome to Mad Movies with the L.A. Connection. We've just shown you a clip from our version of "The Stranger," originally about a war criminal hiding from the law. But we've changed all the dialogue, and now it's about one reporter's search for an unusual story. It just so happens that our reporter works for my favorite magazine. A respected journal of total integrity.

(PACK OF NEWSPAPER MAGAZINES THROWN AT HOST'S FEET)

> Ah, here's the latest issue now.

HE BEGINS OPENING THE STACK OF "PEEP-HOLE" MAGAZINES WITH THE HEADLINE, "Whatever Happened to the Quasimodo Family?"

V.O. OVER CLOSE-UP: Here's a clip of what's coming up.

(EXT. SIDEWALK)

> BOY
> Hey, Quas, you lost a couple of pounds?

> BOY #2
> We're going girl watching.

> BOY
> Wanna come?
> (BOYS WHISTLE)

> BOY
> Well, we're done.

> Q
> Gee, that was fast. Not like when I was a kid.

> BOY
> We haven't reached puberty yet.

                              BOY #2
           I'm the cute one.

                                Q
           What the heck does that mean?

(EXT. SIDEWALK)

NEWSTAND

                              HOST
           In a moment, we'll be right back with the L.A. Connection's Mad
           Movie.

COMMERCIAL #1

(EXT. NEWSTAND)

                              HOST
           Well, as I promised, here's the L.A. Connection's version of "The
           Stranger."

(EXT. CHURCH)

(SFX: BAD CHIMES)

(INT. CHURCH)

                             PRIEST
           Do you Quasimodo the IV take this woman Esmeralda?

                            QUASIMODO
           I might.

                             PRIEST
           Do you Esmeralda take this man Quasimodo the IV to be your
           awfully wedded husband, for better, for worse, for richer, for
           poorer, in sickness and in health, in Minneapolis, in St. Paul?

(EXT. WOODS)

                            PAPER BOY
           Extra! Extra! Read all about it! Hunchback marries today and my
           Mom got me this job.
                         (LAUGHS HYSTERICALLY)

(INT. CHURCH)

                             PRIEST
           In sandals and in dress shoes; in drive thrus and in fancy, expensive
           restaurants; for thinner for fatter; for Cheech or for Chong.

(EXT. WOODS)

                            PAPER BOY
           Get your newspaper! Weeeeeeeeee!

(INT. CHURCH)

PRIEST
In regular or decaffeinated, in "Good Times" or in "Happy Days" or 10,000 miles, whichever comes first.

ESMERALDA
What?

(INT. BEDROOM)

SHADOW (V.O.)
Bernstein, I've got a story.

EDWARD G. BERNSTEIN
What is it?

SHADOW
It's about Quasimodo, he's up to no good.

E.G.B.
Who knows what evil lurks in the hearts of men.

SHADOW
The shadow knows.
(LAUGHS)

(INT. HOUSE)

QUASIMODO
Everyone left the reception early.

ESMERALDA
I ate all the Früsen-Gladje.

QUAS
Oh, wow.

(EXT. WOODS)

PAPER BOY
Special edition in 35 sections.
(LAUGHS)

BOY #1
Let's nail him. He's ripping up all our newspapers.

BOY #2
Let's grab his bag and kick him in the classifieds.

(INT. CONFERENCE ROOM)

E.G.B.
What about this guy Quasimodo?

EDITOR #1
He used to play Hunchback for Notre Dame, but he doesn't have his hump any more.

EDITOR #2

He sold it at a yard sale.

EDITOR #3

As a punch bowl.

EDITOR #2

I went to that yard sale, bought a nice hand.

EDITOR #1

They make good soap dishes, don't they?

E.G.R.

What's the matter with you mugs? NYHHH…what kind of a story is that? This is Peephole magazine. We got our finger on the pulse of America. Inquiring people want to know about this man and… I'm gonna tell them. Don't interrupt me, I'm on a roll, just sit there. I don't need you goons. See, I'll get the story myself. While I'm out I'll get a new pipe.

(EXT. SIDEWALK)

BOY #1

Quasimodo. Quasi.

Q.

Hi boys, you're all dressed up, huh?

BOY #2

We caught up with the paper boy.

BOY #1

We saved the comic strips.

BOY #2

Hey, you look great Quasimodo, you've lost a couple of pounds.

BOY #3

We're going girl watching.

BOY #2

Wanna come?

(BOYS WHISTLE)

BOY #2

Well, we're done.

Q.

Gee that was fast, not like when I was a kid.

BOY #2

We haven't reached puberty yet.

BOY #3

I'm the cute one.

                        Q.
                  (Thought)
What the heck does that mean?

(INT. STORE)

                   FAT MAN
That's the funniest hat I've ever seen.

                   E.G.B.
So what?

                    DAD
                 (Thought)
That's not such a bad hat. I kinda like it.

                   E.G.B.
My hat.

                   FAT MAN
Last time I had a hat like that I had hair.

                    DAD
                 (Thought)
I wonder where I could get a hat like that. I'll let my fingers do the walking.

(FAT MAN LAUGHING)

                   E.G.B.
                 (Thought)
This guy's a wacko.

                    DAD
Let's see, jalapenos, here it is…hats 748-1868, 784-1868, 874-1688.

KEEPS REPEATING DIFFERENT NOS.

                  CUSTOMER
Stiffed you again, Pops.

                    DAD
Excuse me. I'll trade you this suitcase here for a pencil.

                   FAT MAN
Is that yours? That's the funniest looking suitcase I've ever seen. Last time I saw a suitcase like that I had hair.

                   E.G.B.
Say, wise guy, I work for this magazine, Peephole, see? How come you don't sell it here?

                   FAT MAN
We used to have a newsstand down the street, but the reflection off my head set it on fire.

                          E.G.B.
Yeah.

                          FAT MAN
And that's the funniest looking pipe I ever saw. Last time I saw a pipe like that I…

                          E.G.B.
Yeah, I know you had hair.

(EXT. SCHOOL)

                          DAD
This is the last place he'd look for me.

                          E.G.B.
                         (Thought)
Hmmm, where's the last place I'd look for him? Ah ha! I know, I got to sneak up on him, see. Yeah, yeah, see.

(INT. SCHOOL GYM)

                          DAD
Nice wood.
                         (Thought)
When are these people gonna learn there's no smoking in here. Hey, don't walk on the gym floor with those hard shoes. I hope he doesn't drool on the floor. The janitor will get him in the morning. He should have read the warning sign on the door. 784-6688.

(INT. HOUSE)

                          ESM
What's up, Dad?

                          DAD
There's a reporter from Peephole magazine pestering me about your husband.

                          ESM
You just have a seat here in your favorite chair.

                          DAD
Thank you, Esmeralda.

                          ESM
You look all nice and comfy.

                          DAD
It's just gas.

                          ESM
Are you gonna stay very long, Dad?

                          DAD
Mmmm.

ESM

I'm sorry I can't let you sit in the living room, Dad. But last time you were here you did a naughty on the carpet and we just now had the drapes cleaned.

DAD

It was the dog.

ESM

Oh Dad, come on, we've never owned a dog. Unless of course, you count the time…oh, never mind.

DAD

Um mmm, I'm having trouble with my hemorrhoids. I can't sit too long without my donut.

ESM

I had some dry toast. The bakery is open 'til 6:00.

DAD

Alright.

ESM

Get me a bearclaw.

ESM

Quas, honey, come down from the bell tower. Stop ringing your chimes.

Q.

I can't. It's in my blood.

ESM

Honey, I've got an idea. Let's have a dinner party. It'll be fun. We'll invite the neighbors and that nice reporter who's been asking about you all over town. It'll be fun. We'll have peas on toast.

Q.

Peas on toast for dinner? You're crazy. You're nuts.

ESM

Well it doesn't have to be peas on toast. It could be broccoli on toast.

(SFX: BIRD DROPPING)

MAN

Ow. My eye.

WOMAN

Hey, my hat.

VOICES
(People scream)

Q.

Those birds are good shots. Alright Esmeralda, you can have your dinner party on one condition.

        ESM

What's that?

        Q.

No soup.

        ESM

Alright.

(INT. DINING ROOM)

        MAID

Soup's on!

        RICHARD

I've never had cream of weasel soup before.

        ESM

It's my favorite.

        E.G. BERNSTEIN

They made Weasel a la King when I was in the army.

        ESM
        (Loud Slurp)

        Q.

What'd you say?

        MAID

We're out of napkins. How about a sponge?

        Q.

No.

        FRAZIER
        (Loud Slurp)

        ESM
        (Loud Slurps)

Quasi helps me out around the house. I thought it would be hard once we were married. (Loud Slurp)

        Q.

I beg your pardon.

        ESM
        (Loud Slurp)

        E.G. BERNSTEIN

I think I'm missing something.

        ESM
        (Loud Slurp)

FRAZIER
Excuse me, would you mind repeating that?

Q.
(Loud Slurp)

FRAZIER
I still couldn't hear you.

(EXT. WOODS)

DAD
Please do the interview. Think of my daughter. Don't be afraid of Peephole magazine.

MUSIC CUE

(BACKGROUND CHORDS)

WHEN YOU STROLL THROUGH THE PARK.

Q.
Oh no, please not again.

DAD
Keep your eyes open wide.

Q.
Stop!

DAD
And don't be afraid of the…

Q.
I asked you nicely.

DAD
Daaaaaarrrrrrkkk!

(EXT. NEWSTAND)

HOST
(READING "PEEPHOLE" MAGAZINE.)
"Man comes back from the dead to file tax returns."
"I saw Bigfoot kissing Santa Claus."
You know these stories are pretty strange. But not as half as strange as our Mad Movie. Here's a little of what's coming up next when our reporter discovers he has psychic powers.

(INT. ROOM)

EGR
I'll tell you what's in that suitcase.

FAT MAN
Ohh, okay. This oughta be more fun than smashing someone's hand in a car door. Okay, I'm ready.

> EGR
> Well, to start with, it's a pair of underwear, Tuesday's, some pants, and a towel, and a canister of plutonium stolen from the Serafin Hotel.

CHYRON…"WE'LL BE RIGHT BACK."…

COMMERCIAL #2

(INT. STORE)

> E.G. BERNSTEIN
> What can you tell me about this Quasimodo guy, see?

> FAT MAN
> Nothin'. Say, we're having a special on ants, you interested?

> E.G. BERNSTEIN
> Hmm.

> FAT MAN
> I got some giant reds from the desert. We have mosquitos too, but they're not on sale.

> E.G. BERNSTEIN
> How much do the ants run?

> FAT MAN
> About a mile a day.

> E.G. BERNSTEIN
> I don't want that one, I meant what's the price?

> FAT MAN
> If you have to ask you can't afford 'em.

> E.G. BERNSTEIN
> I see.

> FAT MAN
> Since you're a stranger, I'll let you have them for a buck a dozen. Just like the sign says. You get one on your forehead. That's a freebie.
> (LAUGHS)

> E.G. BERNSTEIN
> I'll take a dozen.

> FAT MAN
> Okay.
> (Mumbles)
> 2…4…6…8…10, 11. Gotta make a living somehow.
> (Laughs)
> It's cheaper if you bag 'em yourself.

(EXT. AT THE PARK)

       E.G. BERNSTEIN
Why does your brother-in-law, Quasi, spend so much time up in that tower? Does he like the bells?

       RICHARD
No, not really. He's practicing to get on the Gong Show.

(SFX: BELL CHIMES)

       E.G. BERNSTEIN
It's cancelled.

       RICHARD
Oh gee, I like Chuck Barris a lot. I wish I could have been more help with your article, Mr. Bernstein. But I want you to know I appreciate this nice balloon.

       E.G.B.
Yeah, see, it's filled with helium. You can suck on it and make your voice sound like Alvin and the Chipmunks. Yeah.

       RICHARD
       (Thought)
I like Simon.

(INT. LIVING ROOM)

       ESM
       (On Phone)
Yes, the party's at 7:00 and it's bring your own chair.

       Q.
       (O.C.)
Aw, darn it!

       ESM
What's the matter? I'm on the phone.

       Q.
Another mouse ran up the clock.

       ESM
Cut off its tail with a carving knife.

       Q.
You're not making that cream of Mouse Tail soup, Esmeralda. And get off the phone. I'm expecting a call from Ed McMahon with Publisher's Clearing House.

       ESM
I've got to hang up.

                              Q.
Who was that?

                              ESM
Ed MacMahon. By the way, I invited Mr. Bernstein from Peephole.

                              Q.
He's a jerk.

                              ESM
Jerk…he'll get drunk and make rude noises with his armpits.

(INT. LIVING ROOM PARTY)

                              MAID
Wipe your feet.

(SFX: FEET SQUISHING)

                              E.G.B.
Ezzie baby, thanks for inviting me to the party.

                              ESM
Oh sure. What's in the bag?

                              E.G.B.
I brought some slides from Yosemite.

                              RICHARD
I'm going there. I'll take 'em back for you.

                              E.G.B.
Who asked ya, see?

                              E.G.B.
What do you have to do to get a drink?

                              ESM
Look around.

                              FRAZIER
I'll get you one.

                              E.G.B.
I'll take this.

                              FRAZIER
That was his drink.

                              E.G.B.
You're a swell pal.

                              PROFESSOR
And then the little train said wooo wooo.

ESM

I'll try to get him to leave.

LADY IN LACE VEIL

I wish you would.

SITTING LADY

Ow, my foot.

ESM

Oh sorry. Can I take your cup?

PROF.

No, I'm keeping it.

MRS. PROF.

We have almost a whole set now.

(INT. FOYER)

ESM

Goodnight.

MAN AT DOOR

We just got here.

ESM

Get out.

Q.
(O.C.)

I thought they'd never leave.

ESM

Ah, I'm caught in the door.

Q.

Can I help you?

ESM

No. It's all your fault.

Q.
(Thought)

Oh wow.

(INT. HOTEL ROOM)

BERNSTEIN
(Thought)

Yeah my deadline's tomorrow. There's the church, there's the steeple. I gotta get this story ready for Peephole. I wish I had more time…that positive thinking course is working out. My mind is more powerful than I thought. I'll try it out on something else.

(INT. STORE)

BERNSTEIN
Get that suitcase down and I'll tell you what's in it.

FAT MAN
Alright, this sounds like more fun than smashin' someone's hand in a car door. Hee hee…okay. Go ahead.

E.G.B.
To start with there's some underwear, Tuesdays, some pants and a towel and a canister of plutonium stolen from the Sheraton Hotel.

FAT MAN
What else, Bub?

E.G.B.
Howard Cosell's tap shoes and odor-eaters.

(EXT)

E.G.B.
I'll give you some gum for some info. It was stuck to my shoe. But it's still good.

RICHARD
I have braces. I'm not allowed.

E.G.B.
Yeah, I'll save it for myself, you ungrateful mug.

(INT. MOM'S HOUSE)

ESM
Mom, I've got to go.

MOM
Please wait…you hardly ever visit.

ESM
Mom, I've been here six days. And I only live next door.

MOM
I took care of you and changed your diapers for 18 years. Ever since you've been married to Quasimodo, you spend more time with him than with me.

ESM
He's my husband.

MOM
If you go I'll just die.

ESM
Be serious.

(SFX: MOM FALLING)

MOM

                                ESM
Ah.

                                ESM
Mother.

                                MOM
Aarrgg.

                                ESM
What is it?

                                MOM
You've got your knee in my spleen.

                                ESM
Oh.

(INT. PHONE BOOTH)

                                Q.
Oh dear, I'm teaching that class on how to tell time and I need directions to Paul Bunyon Junior College. Right on Board Walk, left on Park Place. Do not pass go, do not collect $200 dollars. Free parking at Marvin Gardens.

                                ESM
Yes, that's right.

                                Q.
According to this, I'm already there.

(INT. SCHOOL)

(STUDENTS MUMBLE AS THEY COME IN)

                                Q.
                              (O.C.)
Ladies and gentlemen, please be seated. Thank you for being here. Now if everyone could reach in your pants and pull out their watches and repeat after me. The time now is 2:30.

                             STUDENTS
2:30

                                Q.
Good, class dismissed. Hello, Hon? How do I get home from here?

(INT. HOUSE)

                                ESM
                             (Thought)
Oh no! I forgot my line. Maybe I should go back and try again. It's too late. Oh darn it!

CHYRON OVER BELL TOWER…NEXT…QUASI PLAYS HIS HUNCH

COMMERCIAL #3

(INT. HOUSE)

              ESM
           (Thought)
I think I've got it. Oh, I forgot again.

              DIRECTOR
              (O.C.)
Just come through anyway. Hurry up. Time is money. C'mon.

              ESM
Alright.

(INT. STORE)

              FAT MAN
You wrote a grocery list just to remember one item? What the heck is the matter with you?

              FAT MAN
What did you say?

              Q.
I'm sorry.

              FAT MAN
What's that?

              Q.
It won't happen again.

              FAT MAN
You bet it won't happen again. You're lucky I waited on you this time. Did you see my sign out in front? It says no shoes, no pants, no service.

              Q.
I was in such a hurry to buy this cholesterol I forget to put my shoes on.

              FAT MAN
Your shoes!

              Q.
Yeah.

              FAT MAN
What about your pants? The last time I saw underwear like that I had hair.

              Q.
Oh wow.

(INT. HOUSE)

              E.G.B.

                    Listen sister, I'm not going to ask you again. I want that interview with your husband. See. I want you to put some pressure on him.

                              ESM
                    I don't weigh enough.

                              E.G.B.
                    You want your arm twisted, sister?

                              ESM
                    You can do anything to me you want as long as it's...

                              E.G.B.
                    As long as it's what?

                              ESM
                           (Thought)
                    I forgot my line again.

                              E.G.B.
                    I got some pictures of your father, naked with a hooker. Well, he's dressed and the hooker's gone. But you get the idea. We're going to put them up on every laundromat and bulletin board in town. See? Understand? You get the picture?

                              ESM
                    No. I have the negative.

                              E.G.B.
                    Don't you get smart with me.

                              ESM
                    I'm not getting smart, I'm too stupid.

                              OLD MAN
                           (Thought)
                    Why's he lookin' at me, I don't have a line.

(INT. BELL TOWER)

                              Q.
                    Blabber mouth, you've been talking to that reporter, Bernstein. You told him where to find me.

                              ESM
                    No, darling I...

                              E.G.B.
                    Yoo-hoo. See.

                              Q.
                    Bernstein.

                              E.G.B.
                    Edward G. Bernstein.

                              ESM

                    Q.
Put down that knife.

                    Q.
It's a gun.

                    E.G.B.
Quit whining.

                    Q.
I will not whine before my time.

                    E.G.B.
Tell me, what's it like coming from a long line of Hunchbacks? What are your turn ons? Your turn offs? What are your hobbies? Have you ever slept on uncooked noodles? Do you know the way to San Jose?

                    CROWD
                  (Musically)
Whoa-whoa-whoa, etc.

                    E.G.B.
Listen to that crowd. Who loves you, baby?

                    CROWD
What advice does he have for a young Hunchback just starting out?

                    Q.
The first step's a dewzy!

                    CROWD
Jump! Jump!

                    Q.
Hey, I can see my house from here.

                    STATUE
Coming through.

                    CROWD
Jump!

                    Q.
Time flies when you're having fun. Arg! Heads up!
                  (Throws statue)

(SFX: Statue smashing)

                    FAT MAN
That was a close one. You okay?

                    E.G.B.
Thanks. I'm just fine. You can't hurt me. I've got a steel plate in my head. I got my story, and you can read about it in Peephole.

                    FAT MAN
Send us a copy. Last time I read a magazine I had hair.

                        (LAUGHS)

                         E.G.B.
        Yeah, see!

"THE END"

(EXT. NEWSTAND)

                          HOST
        Well, you've just seen what new dialogue did to The Stranger. And
        now here's a look at what the L.A. Connection can do to your home
        movies. This footage was sent in by Sidna and Ruby Ubach of
        Downey, California, and we've turned it into a story of a place
        where it's Christmas every day. Here's ChristmasLand.

FOUR SECOND CHYRON OVER PIX..."CHRISTMAS LAND"

                          V.O.:
        This is the tiny village of Kringle, where Christmas is celebrated
        365 days a year. It's easy to run out of gift giving ideas when
        hundreds of gifts are under the tree each morning. And what a tree
        it is. Trees flocked with cement stay fresh looking year after year.
        And every morning at 4:30, children who receive every toy ever
        made by the time they're five years old are dragged from their beds
        to visit with a physically exhausted year-round Santa. What'll it be
        today? Yesterday he got shirts. And it's shirts again today. This time
        with a matching sweater. And it's freeze dried fish for the girl who
        has everything. How many kids can you get on dad's lap? 2? 3? 4?
        No, just 3. Of course, a Christmas party every night has its
        drawbacks. You can't get too far from a toilet seat drinking all that
        eggnog. And it's tedious posing for holiday portraits.

                          MAN
        Waaahhhh! But Christmas is a time for children, and these
        youngsters are off to bed, because tomorrow morning, bright and
        early, the festivities start all over again.

                         SANTA
                        (TIRED)
        Ho, Ho, Ho.

(EXT. NEWSTAND)

                          HOST
        If you'd like your home movies made into Mad Movies, send them
        to the L.A. Connection,

(OVER ADDRESS)

        6464 Sunset, Suite 820 Hollywood, 90028.

(EXT. NEWSTAND)

HOST
You know, since you been watching that tv show, I've been reading this magazine. And quite frankly, I'm really beginning to wonder about the credibility of some of these stories. Listen to this one…"T.V. Show Hosts are Disappearing." Now who do they think they're kidding?

HOST FADES OUT OF PICTURE. OVER NEWSTAND

See you next time for more Mad Movies.

(EXT. WOODS)

DAD
Hey, I know you. You're a famous actor. You were in Citizen Kane. And you were in something else too. Ahhh…

(OVER CREDITS)

Ohh It was just on, too. What was the name of that…It was a tv show, it's just on…what was the name of it…ahhhh, don't tell me…don't tell me…ahh, it's on the tip of my tongue,…uh…

WELLS
Mad Movies.

DAD
No, that's not it.

HOST V.O.
Additional voices by Doug Requa.

OPENING CRAWL*

SHOW #115

SHOW NAME   THE STRANGER

*Each numbered item as a single page…
Items #1-5 Centerframe
Items #6-10 Lower third of page

1   FOUR STAR
         in association with
            KENT SKOV

2   Presents
         as L.A. Connection
             production of

3   MAD MOVIES WITH THE L.A. CONNECTION

4   Tonight's Feature   THE STRANGER

5   Starring
                 the
                Voices
                  of

6   Bob Buchholz

7   Connie Sue Cook

8   Stephen L. Rollman

9   Steve Pinto

10   Kent Skov

GENERIC BUMPERS*

SHOW #<u>115</u>

SHOW NAME   <u>THE STRANGER</u>

*Each numbered item as a single page…

1   We'll be right back…

2   Coming Up
      More Mad Movies

3   Stay Tuned for
      "Your Home Movies"

4   Send Your Home Movies to…
      L.A. Connection Productions
      6464 Sunset Blvd., #820
      Hollywood, CA 90028
      (Include a self-addressed, stamped envelope for return of films)

CLOSING CREDIT CRAWL (CONT'D)

10	Research by Bob Petrella Ken Segall April Winchell Ted Hardwick
11	Talent Coordinator Martha Whitney
12	Associate Director/Stage Manager Randal W Ridges
13	Assistants to the Producers: Bob Buchholz Connie Sue Cook Steve Pinto Stephan L. Rollman
14	Facilities Provided by Hy-Tone Video
15	Lighting and Camera Bill Sheehy
16	Production Sound Mark Hanes
17	Gaffer Jim Drewry
18	Production Assistants Lisa Gougas Ted Hardwick
19	Make-Up Lora Sanders
20	Wardrobe Annie Vicari
21	Production Secretary Eloise Gonzalez
22	Post-Production Coordinated by Monti Santilli Rainbolt
23	Post-Production Facilities Complete Post, Inc.
24	Post-Production Audio by Michael Perricone Michaele Hogan For Interloc Prod. Studios

CLOSING CREDIT CRAWL (CONT'D)

25   "Your Home Movies" submitted by
    Sidna and Rudy Ubach
    Downey, CA

26   Location provided by

27   Executive in Charge of Production for Four Star Television
    Bob Bosen

28   Special Thanks to:
    Susan Lenti Dennis Condon
    Budget Films Snagglepuss
    Richard Holiday

29   Promotion by
    Dan Acree

30   Opening Title Montage by
    Homer & Associates

31   Opening Title Photography by
    Abe Perlstein

32   Post-Production Supervised by
    Randal W Ridges

33   Executive Producer
    Kent Skov

34   "Celebrity Voices and Appearances Impersonated"

35   Copyright 1985 Four Star International, Inc.
    All Rights Reserved

THIS IS THE ARMY

With the

SHORT RUNDOWN FOR SHOW #116 "This Is The Army"

Description	In	Out	Seg Time
Show Open	00:00	02:01	02:01
Commercial Break #1	02:01	04:04	02:03
Act I	04:04	11:29	07:25
Commercial Break #2	11:29	13:32	02:03
Act II	13:32	20:29	06:57
Commercial Break #3	20:29	22:32	02:03
Act III/Show Close	22:32	28:00	05:28

MAD MOVIES WITH THE L.A. CONNECTION

RUNDOWN SHOW #<u>116 THIS IS THE ARMY</u>

(ALL TIME IN MINUTES AND SECONDS)	IN	OUT	DURATION
FOUR STAR LOGO	00:00	00:05	00:05
OPENING CLIP TEASE	00:05	00:24	00:19
OPENING MONTAGE	00:24	00:53	00:29
OPENING WRAP	00:53	01:18	00:25
CLIP #2	01:18	01:46	00:28
WRAP #2	01:46	02:01	00:15
COMMERCIAL #1	02:01	04:04	02:03
BUMPER #1	04:04	04:07	00:03
FEATURE SEGMENT #1	04:07	10:52	06:45
TOSS TO CLIP	10:52	11:14	00:22
CLIP #3	11:14	11:29	00:15
COMMERCIAL #2	11:29	13:32	02:03
BUMPER #2	13:32	13:35	00:03
FEATURE SEGMENT #2	13:35	20:25	06:50
BUMPER #3	20:25	20:29	00:04
COMMERCIAL #3	20:29	22:32	02:03

MAD MOVIES WITH THE L.A. CONNECTION

RUNDOWN   SHOW #116 THIS IS THE ARMY

	IN	OUT	DURATION
BUMPER #4	22:32	22:35	00:03
FEATURE SEGMENT #3	22:35	25:17	02:42
HOME MOVIE INTRO	25:17	25:36	00:19
HOME MOVIE	25:36	26:39	01:03
CLOSING WRAP	26:39	27:01	00:22
CLOSING CLIP	27:01	27:17	00:16
CLOSING MONTAGE	27:17	27:50	00:33
L.A. CONNECTION LOGO	27:50	27:55	00:05
FOUR STAR LOGO	27:55	28:00	00:05

THIS IS THE ARMY SHOW NUMBER 116

    OPENING CLIP...

> SGT.
> The sergeant is sitting at a bar with two pigs on his lap, and a bartender says, hey, you can't sit there with those pigs on your lap. So he says, those aren't pigs, they're my privates.
>
> SHOT OF SOLDIERS
> Aahhh, what a stupid joke, etc.
>
> REAGAN
> Let's get out of here, Mad Movies is about to start.

CREDITS

(EXT. ARMY CAMP)

> HOST
> Hi, I'm Kent Skov and welcome to Mad Movies with the L.A. Connection. The clip you just saw is from our version of "This is the Army." It was originally an Irving Berlin musical about soldiers who stage a show during World War II, and it starred Ronald Reagan. Now we've taken the liberty to tell a new story by changing the dialogue. In our story Ronald Reagan makes an impromptu visit to check out the condition of the Army.
>
> OFFICER
> Time for the hand touching contest.
>
> HALE
> I won.
>
> OFFICER
> I wasn't ready.
>
> HALE
> Let's do it again.
>
> OFFICER
> Alright, Sgt.
>
> HALE
> You know, Captain, it's not as much fun with just two people. Why don't we find someone else to join us, huh?
>
> OFFICER
> Mmm, how about you, Lieutenant?
>
> LT.
> Alright, I win.
>
> OFFICER
> He cheated. He didn't wait for us to say "go."
>
> SGT.
> The scum.

                                OFFICER
            You came in second. Congratulations.

                                HALE (SGT.)
            Let's do it again.

                                OFFICER
            It was a tie.

(EXT. ARMY CAMP AND JEEP)

                                HOST
            We're here at the American Heritage Museum, and this is an actual
            military jeep for government use only.

(PHONE RINGS)

            Oh, excuse me.

(ANSWERS PHONE)

            Hello.

(INT. CAMP)

                                REAGAN
            Get out of the jeep, now!

                                HOST
            Oh, we'll be right back with our Mad Movie.

COMMERCIAL #1

(EXT. CAMP)

                                HOST V.O.

(OVER OPENING TITLE)

            And now here's the L.A. Connection's version of "This is the
            Army."

(EXT. CAPITOL) MUSIC ONLY

(INT. OFFICE)

                                RADIO VOICE
            Also in the news conference yesterday, President Reagan denied
            reports that he was contemplating a return to his show business
            career.

(REAGAN IS SEEN READING VARIETY)

            In other news, a giant cabbage rolled thru Omaha killing…

(SFX: CLICK)

LILAH

Hi, Ron.

REAGAN

Hello.

LILAH

Darling.

G. BUSH

Sweetheart. You know my secretary, don't you? This is a suitcase. I bought it for you at a yard sale. You put clothes in it.

(INT. LIVING ROOM)

REAGAN

So that's how Dad was framed, huh, Mom?

MOM

That's right, son. If you're going to join the army, don't bring your laundry home to me anymore.

REAGAN

What about lunches?

MOM

Forget it, and I'm renting your room too.

REAGAN

But Mom…

MOM

Oh dear, I'm sorry. I know you have to enlist to show the whole world that there's really no corruption in the army. But while you're there, would you stop by the PX and pick up a six hundred dollar coffee pot, and I could use one of those fifteen hundred dollar toilet seats. Your father was so rough on the old one.

REAGAN

Is your shoulder still sore from re-roofing the White House?

MOM

It only hurts when you touch it.

REAGAN

Oh sorry. You did one heck of a job.

MOM

Thank you, son, but putting up the gutters was the hardest part.

REAGAN

Yeah, but your muscles are bigger.

MOM

Remember, the army's not just a career, it's an adventure.

REAGAN

Bye, Mom.

MOM
(Thought)
Where did I go wrong?

(INT. OFFICE)

NANCY
Here's your pizza. Hold it flat.

MAN
Thanks. Hot pizza coming through.

REAGAN
Gettin' cheese on your shoes. Say Nancy, notice anything different about me?

NANCY
Ronnie. Uh? You shaved your chest.

REAGAN
Yes and I joined the army.

NANCY
You dipstick!

REAGAN
It beats fighting congress.

NANCY
Well, maybe they can keep you awake.

REAGAN
As President I can get an inside look at the army. And look, they gave me got a groovy Rambo watch with to go my uniform, so let's go out and celebrate.

NANCY
But wait. I can't just march out the door. Who can we get to run the pizza parlor?

REAGAN
You can always get George Bush. He never has anything to do.

NANCY
Oh, wait, my hat…I need it.

REAGAN
There's toilet paper stuck to it.

NANCY
I know.

(INT. RESTAURANT)

NANCY

Ron, I don't like your boots.

REAGAN
You should have worn your own shoes.

NANCY
Ow.

REAGAN
Sorry, it's dark in here.

MAN AT TABLE
Can we have the check, waiter?

WAITER
No, but I can let you have the Hungarian busboy.

M.C.
And now ladies and gentlemen, Olivia Newton and the Johns.

REAGAN
(Thought)
I forgot my money. I hope Nancy brought a credit card.

OLIVIA

(SINGS)

Aaaaaa.

(APPLAUSE)

Thank you.

REAGAN
I'm sorry, Nancy. I had to join.

NANCY
Why now?

REAGAN
Good career opportunities.

NANCY
What about us?

REAGAN
Well…we'll still be together.

NANCY
I don't see how.

REAGAN

Remember when I was a big movie star and you were nothing, and do you remember when I was out on location and you weren't? Gosh, I was good.

NANCY

How can you say that?

REAGAN

Remember "Death Valley Days"?

NANCY

I think we better go. Last time we discussed that…things got real ugly between us. You want to join the army…go ahead. If you think the security of the entire nation is more important than me, then fine!

REAGAN
(Thought)

Wow, how am I going to pay the bill?

(INT. BARRACKS)

(ARMY MEN GROWLING)

G. BUSH JR.

You guys keep squinting…it makes you look tough.

ABNER

Do I look tough?

G. BUSH

I'm squinting so hard I can't even see myself in this mirror. You're going to have to look for yourself, I'm going back to bed.

(MEN GROWL)

SGT.

You guys kept me up all night with your squinting. Now get up. President Reagan is coming today.

G. BUSH JR.

I'll let him wear my zebra costume, and he can share my bunk.

SGT.

Yeah, he's had enough of your bunk, Junior. Now get up. It's time for the earthquake drill. I'm giving you a 6 point 5 on the Richter, and you a 3 point 2 on the Richter Scale, and what about you, a 6 point 8. Now get up.

(INT. CAPTAIN OFFICE)

CAPTAIN

Sergeant, is this true that you've been harassing the men again and short sheeting their beds?

SGT.

No sir.

CAPTAIN
What's this I hear about you always saying to the men, "I can't hear you. I can't hear you." Don't you know that it's your responsibility to clean your own ears?

SGT.
Well, yeah.

CAPTAIN
Now go get a bucket of water and put out my hand. I'm burning.

SGT.
I'm sorry, I can't hear you.

CAPTAIN
I'm on fire.

SGT.
I won.

(INT. BARRACKS)

(BACK STAGE)

G. BUSH JR.
Hey, Yip. Yip, quit writing your name on the walls. That recruiting sign needs a splatter design, so take your brush and do this, putt, putt, putt. That ought to make 'em join, huh? Great! Shoot him later.

(INT. BACKSTAGE)

TWO SOLDIERS
We give up, we give up.

BUSH
Don't surrender so easily. First poke 'em in the eye then kick 'em in the shin. And then you surrender.

DUDLEY

(SFX: KNOCKS)

Hi, I'm Dudley.

G.B. JR.
Doright?

DUDLEY
Yes, this is my weapon.

CROWD O' SOLDIERS
Let me see. Let me see. Let me see.

G.B. JR.
Wait a minute, that's the nuclear powered blowgun, isn't it?

DUDLEY

>   I bought it from Snidely.
>
>   G.B. JR.
>   Cost 7 million dollars?
>
>   DUDLEY
>   Yes, without tax.
>
>   G.B. JR.
>   Go ahead and show us your weapon, we'll put a target up over here. We'll use the mess hall menu.
>
>   CROWD O' SOLDIERS
>   Yeah, we're having spaghetti.

(INT. CAFÉ)

>   ABNER
>   Hi, Junior.
>
>   G.B. JR.
>   Oh, I got my knee caught in the potter's wheel in ceramics class. I'll have a root beer.
>
>   ABNER
>   It's diet.
>
>   G.B. JR.
>   Say, what's with him? How'd he get that clay all over himself?
>
>   ABNER
>   He made an ashtray and put it in the kiln too soon. It blew up in his face.
>
>   G.B. JR.
>   He looks better.
>
>   SGT.
>   Laugh if you want. I have to hold a bedpan on my head.
>
>   DUDLEY
>   Oh, what's that smell?
>   (Gets kicked)
>   Ow!
>
>   G.B. JR.
>   Oh, that. I'm not sensitive about that. I haven't changed my socks since I was 12 years old. Oh, by the way, I got this weird letter from my Mom today. Listen, to what she says: "Dear Son, I've missed you so much, I let the pig eat at the table."
>
>   ABNER
>   Your father!

(INT. BACKSTAGE)

>   PVT.

Sergeant, I got my shoe dirty when I went out on manures.

SGT.
You idiot! I told you to go out on maneuvers!

(INT. THEATRE)

CROWD V.O.
Alright men, fall out for the potty break.

MISC. MEN'S VOICES
Yeah, let's go. Finally. Woowee.

ROSEMARY
They won't all fit in the bathroom.
(O.C.)
Oh, they're gonna trample him…that was close. They just missed him.

(SFX: MONKEY KISS)

Oh dear, let me go with you.

G.B. JR.
I can't, it's the men's bathroom.

ROSEMARY
Well…use a sani-seat. And remember, I love you.

(EXT. ARMY CAMP)

HOST
The vehicles here at the American Heritage Museum were used on several movies and tv shows, including Mash and Amazing Stories. In fact since 1955, every military show shot used a vehicle from this location. It was here that several important battles were mapped out, such as "Battle of the Network Stars," and "Family Feud." And here's what's being mapped out next on our Mad Movie.

(INT. CAMP)

HALE
Gentlemen, the president of the United States.

BUGLE SOUND

HALE
Sergeant Shriver, take your fingers out of your nose.

REAGAN
I just wanted to say that now I'm in the Army, I want you to treat me like a regular guy. Just pretend I'm not even here…just like they do in Congress.

CHRYON…WE'LL BE RIGHT BACK…

Okay, shoot the bugler.

(GUN SHOT)

COMMERCIAL #2

(EXT. STREET)

        V.O. UNCLE SAM
It's impolite to point. Do not try this at home.

        WACK
Hey, hey can't you see we're trying to have a parade here. Get out of the way or I'll have these Forest Rangers force you to move. I've been standing here, smiling and waving on this float for six hours. And this polka band behind me is driving me nuts. Move it.

(EXT. STREET—VENDOR STAND)

        ABNER
Bye, Dad. Goin' back to the base. Gettin' ready for the President. It's a hot day, Dad…take off that disguise. The army wouldn't take you anyway.

        DRAG DAD
You wouldn't lie to me, would you, son? They're changin' the laws all the time.

        ABNER
Even if they did, Dad, you're too old for the army. Besides, they got rid of the draft. See, you have to enlist now. So you have nothing to worry about.

        DRAG DAD
Son, take this.

        ABNER
Get out of my pocket.

        DRAG DAD
Stop him! He stole my watch.

INSERT—SOMEWHERE IN FRANCE

(INT. DANCE HALL)

        MADEMOISELLE STAR
Mademoiselle, mademoiselle, Frara Jacque, Jonte allouette, si vous plia.

        MADAME LACE
Yoplait!

        M.S.
Uh-huh.

        M.L.
Vinegarette, vichyssoise, se moi.

        M.S.

Moi!!!!!!! Croissant, Maurice Chevalle, Citroen le crepe suzette.

(INT. BARRACKS)

SENATOR MONDALE
Say, Mr. Bush, there goes the helicopter taking Reagan to the base.

BUSH
Good.

SEN. MONDALE
Yeah.

(Laughs)

BUSH
With Reagan away in the army, I guess that makes me acting President.

JUSTICE CHUBBS
One acting President was bad enough.

BUSH
Did you see him with that monkey?

SENATOR BALDY
Hey, it's too bad he didn't join the space program, we could have sent him to the moon.

BUSH
Speaking of moons...

(INT. MEETING HALL)

SGT.
Gentlemen, the President of the United States. Sergeant Shriver, take your fingers out of your nose.

REAGAN
I just want to say now that I'm in the army, I want you to treat me like a regular guy. Just pretend I'm not even here. Just like they do in Congress. Okay, shoot the bugler.

(SFX: GUN SHOT)

(INT. BACKSTAGE)

BUSH
Hey, Mohammed Ali.

ALI
I whipped Joe Frazier. I whipped George Foreman. I could've beat Jos Louis...I'm the greatest.

BUSH
Well that's just fine. I'm glad to hear that, Mohammed.

SIMMONS
You could beat Billy Martin.

ALI
Float like a butterfly, sting like a bee.

(INT. BACKSTAGE)

(SFX. REPEAT BLOWGUN)

BUSH
I'll give you a buck for that coat.

SOLDIER
Okay.

BUSH
Great deal. Hey Ron, I'm gettin' that coat for a dollar.

RON
Ya think that's a good deal?

BUSH
You bet. Originally that coat cost a thousand.

RON
I'm here to change all that, George. See, when I get rid of the corruption in the army, a coat like that won't cost more than $800.

BUSH
Gee, you're smart.

(INT. STAGE)

ARMY CHORUS

(SONG)
We are young conservatives and we lean to the right.
But we joined the army, we must not be too bright.
When we first enlisted, we took all our clothes off.
Then the doctor told us to turn our heads and cough.
(Cough)

(INT. AUD.)

APPLAUSE

(INT. AUDITORIUM)

MAN 1
Check out that ugly girl up there in the fancy hat.

(INT. STAGE)

LOVER
Say, Petunia, is this a cross your heart bra?

(INT. AUDIT)

MAN 2

That's my boy.

                                MAN 1
Aahh, he's cute.

(INT. BACKSTAGE)

                                JAMES
Mr. Bush…you've got to help me. I didn't know Mr. Reagan was going to be here.

                                BUSH
Chill out.

                                JAMES
I can't find the pearls that go with this dress. What am I going to do?

                                BUSH
Just get a string of cocktail weenies and tie them in a knot around your neck. It'll be fine.

                                JAMES
Thank you.

                                BUSH
Oh, by the way, your slip is showing.

                                GILLIS
Wasn't that guy James Watt?

                                BUSH
Sad, isn't it?

(INT. BACKSTAGE)

                                REAGAN
Say, which one of you guys bought a $75,000 water cooler? Come on, fess up.

                                STEVE
We got tired of drinking bath water.

                                REAGAN
Morons!

(SFX: YELL & BODY FALLS, LAND)

                                BUSH
What's the trouble, Ronnie?

                                REAGAN
I'm no good at this.

                                BUSH
Oh come on…just fake it. You've been doing that for years.

GILLIS
Stop that. Your brain's rattling.

REAGAN
What?

SGT.
Your budget stinks. You won't let us get Barbara Walters pin-up posters.

BUSH
That's right, Sergeant and wait 'til you hear what else he plans to do.

REAGAN
I could cut the army budget in half just by eliminating the food you eat in the mess hall.

SGT.
Huh?

(INT. BACKSTAGE)

REAGAN
Corporal Chipmonk, the French troops have arrived. Go welcome them.

CHIPMONK
Alright, here's a letter for you…hi guys!

VARIOUS FRENCHMEN
Bon jour, allo mon ami, Buenos dias.

DELIVERY MAN
Heavy Moses comin' through.

STEVE
Hey look, it's from Nancy. What's she say?

REAGAN
Dear Ron, I miss you. The garbage is really piling up here at the White House.

DIRK
What? You mean you didn't take it out before you left home? I know I had to.

STEVE
So did I. My wife would have knocked my teeth down my throat if I didn't.

REAGAN
So would I.

(EXT. TRAINING CAMP)

RICH
It's time for the Richard Simmons workout. One, and two stretch, two and three…Reach for the sky and touch your toes, and reach…

ALAN
Oh, I'm exhausted just watching.

REAGAN
Maybe now Jane Fonda will like me.

(EXT. TOP OF PHONE POLE)

SKIPPY
I'm takin' a telephone pole. Where do you want me to put it?

(EXT. BATTLEGROUND)

TANKMAN 1
Hey Johnny, you wanna race?

TANKMAN 2
Oh, no tanks.

(EXT. HAY PILE)

LT.
Private, you'll need more meatballs for that spaghetti.

(EXT. SIGN POST)

BILL
Spaghetti again, yuk.

LT.
We need three volunteers to shoot some meatballs.

(3) SOLDIERS
Yes, sir.

COLONEL
Alright men, I don't appreciate all you men dressing alike trying to fool me. Now I know that President Reagan is in there among you. Since none of you have pointed him out to me, we're going on a 1000 mile hike to the Falkland Islands!

ALL MEN
One.

SOLDIER
Two, three, oh sorry.

ALL MEN
Two, three, four, one, two.

REAGAN

Now pay attention and learn something, men. This is how camouflage works. The General didn't see me 'cause I dressed to match my surroundings.

                SGT.

I knew where you were.

                ROGER

We don't need camouflage.

                STEVE

Yeah, we could hide behind the Sarge.

                SGT.

After dinner I'm taking away your Ding-Dongs.

(EXT. JEEP)

                REAGAN

How do you like the grapes Nancy sent us?

                STEVE

Grapes, I thought they were raisins.

                REAGAN

Yeah, I gotta do something about speeding up the mail service.

                STEVE

Hey Ron, isn't that Nancy over there? Look.

                REAGAN
                (O.C.)

Yeah.

                STEVE

Think I should leave?

                REAGAN

No Steve, stick around. We always enjoy your company.

                NANCY

I'm hot for you.

                REAGAN

Oh, well, ah gee, Nancy. Here Steve, take this and get the heck out of here. G'wan.

                STEVE

I'll go plant these raisins.

                NANCY

They're jelly beans.

                REAGAN

Oh, we knew that. Well let's get out of the way of the jeep. Steve's a wild man.

(SFX: CAR SCREECHING)

Park it! This is wet paint. Nancy, there's something I have to say to you. I've decided to stay in the army.

NANCY

Well, Ron if you think you look so good in khaki green, maybe you ought to wear this cheap ring you got out of a gum ball machine and let it turn your finger a different color.

CHYRON—"NANCY JOINS THE ARMY."

COMMERCIAL #3

(INT. REAGAN ON STAGE)

REAGAN

I'd just like to say whoever drew these hamburgers all over our good curtains is going to pay for it.

(INT. BARRACKS)

DANNY

So Reagan decided to stay in the army, huh? Oh boy am I happy. Oh boy, oh boy, oh boy, oh boy. I could throw up.

(INT. BACKSTAGE)

LITTLE MAN

Hey, dude.

G. BUSH

Well, now that I've assumed the presidency, I demand a little respect. So if you could please just come to attention. Well maybe I'm asking too much too soon. Well alright men, then just a simple little salute would be okay. Alright, maybe you could just listen to me, after all I am the Commander-in-chief. Well, I see you're busy so I'll salute myself and then wait outside.

MEN

Bye, so long, ciao.

ROGER

Say, who was that guy?

ABNER

I don't know…never seen him before in my life.

(EXT. NIGHT OUTSIDE BARRACKS)

REAGAN

One, two, three, five. Hey Nancy, what are you doing here?

NANCY

Well Ron, what do you think? Could you go for a girl in uniform?

REAGAN

Sure, where is she?

                    NANCY
Me!

                    REAGAN
You!

                    NANCY
Oh Ron I missed you so much. Besides, one evening with you is worth two with the Bushes.

                    REAGAN
This is no place for you, Nancy. There's just men here and me. I don't think they'll let you stay. I've only been here a short time. I hate to ask them and impose.

                    NANCY
Ask them nice.

                    REAGAN
Well, I'll see what I can do.

                    STEVE
Let her stay!

                    REAGAN
Wait here, I'll go check on it.

                    NANCY
                  (Thought)
I must be desperate.

(INT. BARRACKS)

                    CORPORAL
Don't do that to your pants. By the way, your wife's outside. She's been waiting here for three days.

                    REAGAN
Oh no, I forgot.

(EXT. ALLEY WAY)

                    CORPORAL
There she is. Recognize her?

                    REAGAN
Nancy!

                    NANCY
This man's been teaching me the hat contest.

                    REAGAN
I won.

                              LT.

But you're not wearing a hat.

                              REAGAN

Since when do I follow rules?

                              NANCY

Forget the game. What's the answer? I've been waiting here for three days. I don't think it's fair you to treat me like this. Now I want an answer and I want it now. What is it?

                              REAGAN

Well, I forgot the question.

                              NANCY

It's whether or not I can stay here in the army with you. Well, can I?
                    (Whines & Whimpers)

                              REAGAN

Don't blow your nose in my pocket.

                              NANCY

Can I stay?

                              REAGAN

Sure, the movie's over and I got the last line.

                              LT.

I'm sorry Mr. Reagan, but I've got the last line.

(O.C. OVER THE END)

                              REAGAN

No, I do.

                              LT.

No, I do.

(EXT. ARMY CAMP)

(OUTSIDE OF TANK)

                              HOST

Retelling old Hollywood films isn't the only genre we've tackled. We also like to add dialogue to your old home movies. Tonight's was sent in from Sylvia Smith from San Jose, California. We've carefully looked at the footage, rearranged it and came up with a vision of the future. Here's Future Wives.

Four Second CHYRON OVER PIX—"FUTURE WIVES"

Studies show that in the future, food will be so scarce that housewives will need high-powered telescopes just to locate a single onion. This specimen is a miracle hybrid, with an outer hide so tough that cooking it will entail the use of giant Teflon spatulas covered on this side—but not on this side—with ionized lard. Housewives on the planet Jupiter will wear flexible shinguards made out of old space waffles…fastened with strips of moon cheese here, here, and of course here—with tiny jet afterburners here and here for flash frying. Jupiter's increased gravity will make it difficult just to slice such an onion, leading to clumsy attempts such as this.

Teamwork will be impossible, as extended exposure to these conditions induces a form of space madness in which housewives will lose all sense of direction…leading to increased hostility, as best friends attempt to trip one another and smash each other's ankles in with their giant space-age utensils. Some women will strike out. But others will join intergalactic bowling leagues and show off their nifty team jackets.

"THE END"

(EXT. ARMY CAMP)

(IN JEEP)

HOST
If you'd like you home movies made into Mad Movies, send them to the L.A. Connection, 6464

(OVER ADDRESS)

Sunset, Suite #820, Hollywood, California, 90028.

(EXT. JEEP)

HOST
You know, we look at several hundred features before we decide on which ones would be good to dub. And you're probably wondering what do we do with all the rejects. Actually, it's quite simple.

(TOSSES CANISTERS OUT OF JEEP).

(SHOT OF TANK TIRES CRUSHING CANS)

See ya next time.

(INT. ARMY OFFICE)

SGT.
I wanna go home now. Mad Movies is over.

CAPT.
I'll let you go home, Sergeant, if you can find out where this smoke is coming from. It's very irritating.

(CREDIT ROLL)

SGT.
It's just your cigarette, sir.

CAPT.
Oh, good. I thought it was coming from my pants.
(SMALL LAUGH)

HOST V.O. OVER CREDITS: Additional voices by Mark DeCarlo.

V. O. OVER CREDITS: REAGAN AND OTHERS ARGUING OVER WHO HAD THE LAST LINES.

Mad Movies with the L.A. Connection

OPENING CRAWL*

SHOW # <u>116</u>

SHOW NAME <u>This Is The Army</u>

*Each numbered item as a single page…
Items #1-5 Centerframe
Items #6-10 Lower third of page

1. FOUR STAR
    in association with
    KENT SKOV

2. Presents
    an L.A. Connection
    production of

3. MAD MOVIES WITH THE L.A. CONNECTION

4. Tonight's Feature   THIS IS THE ARMY

5. Starring
       the
     Voices
        of

6. Bob Buchholz

7. Connie Sue Cook

8. Stephen L. Rollman

9. Steve Pinto

10. Kent Skov

6464 Sunset Blvd., Suite 820 Hollywood, CA 90028 (213) 465-2449

GENERIC BUMPERS*

SHOW #<u>116</u>

SHOW NAME   <u>This Is The Army</u>

*Each numbered item as a single page…

1   We'll be right back…

2   Coming Up
    More Mad Movies

3   Stay Tuned for
    "Your Home Movies"

4   Send Your Home Movies to…
    L.A. Connection Productions
    6464 Sunset Blvd., #820
    Hollywood, CA 90028
    (Include a self-addressed, stamped envelope for return of films)

5   Next…
    Nancy Joins the Army

CLOSING CRAWL*

SHOW #116

SHOW NAME   THIS IS THE ARMY

*Each numbered item as a single page…

1   Directed by
            Kent Skov

2   Written by
            Bob Buchholz
            Stephen L. Rollman

3   Produced by
            Randal W Ridges

4   Featuring
            Bob Buchholz
            Connie Sue Cook
            Steve Pinto
            Stephen L. Rollman
            Kent Skov

5   Associate Producers (each name single page)
            Martha Whitney

6   Kent Weishaus

7   Music Composed and arranged by
            Richard Baker
            Mary Newland
            For Panda Productions

8   Music Recorded by
            Richard Baker

9   Theme performed by
            Mary Newland

CLOSING CREDIT CRAWL (con't)

10	Research by Bob Petrella Ken Segall April Winchell Ted Hardwick
11	Talent Coordinator Martha Whitney
12	Associate Director/Stage Manager Randal W Ridges
13	Assistants to the Producers: Bob Buchholz Connie Sue Cook Steve Pinto Stephen L. Rollman
14	Facilities Provided by Hy-Tone Video
15	Lighting and Camera Bill Sheehy
16	Production Sound Mark Hanes
17	Gaffer Jim Drewry
18	Production Assistants Lisa Gougas Ted Hardwick
19	Make Up Lora Sanders
20	Wardrobe Annie Vicari
21	Production Secretary Eloise Gonzalez
22	Post-Production Coordinated by Monti Santilli Rainbolt
23	Post-Production Facilities Complete Post, Inc.
20	Post-Production Audio by Michael Pericone Michaele Hogan For Interloc Prod. Studios

CLOSING CREDIT CRAWL (con't)

25   "Your Home Movie" submitted by
      Sylvia Smith
      San Jose, CA

26   Location provided by
      American Heritage Museum Park
      El Monte, CA

27   Executive in Charge of Production for Four Star Television
      Bob Bosen

28   Special Thanks to:
      Susan Lenti   Dennis Condon
      Budget Films, Inc. Snagglepuss
      Richard Holiday

29   Promotion by
      Dan Acree

30   Opening Title Montage by
      Homer & Associates

31   Opening Title Photography by
      Abe Perlstein

32   Post-Production supervised by
      Randal W Ridges

33   Executive Producer
      Kent Skov

34   "Celebrity Voices and Appearances Impersonated"

35   Copyright 1985 Four Star International, Inc.
      All Rights Reserved

UNDER CALIFORNIA STARS

With the

SHORT RUNDOWN FOR SHOW # 110 UNDER CAL. STARS.

Description	In	Out	Seg Time
Show Open	00:00	01:10	01:10
Commercial Break #1	01:10	03:13	02:03
Act I	03:13	09:14	06:01
Commercial Break #2	09:14	11:18	02:03
Act II	11:18	20:17	08:58
Commercial Break #3	20:17	22:20	02:03
Act III/Show Close	22:20	28:00	05:40

MAD MOVIES WITH THE L.A. CONNECTION

RUNDOWN

SHOW # 110 UNDER CALIFORNIA STARS

All times are in minutes and seconds	IN	OUT	DURATION
Four Star Logo (slug Black)	00:00	00:05	00:05
Show Open: Clip Tease.	00:05	00:20	00:15
Opening Montage.	00:20	01:10	00:50
Commercial Black #1	01:10	03:13	02:03
Bumper #1	03:13	03:16	00:03
Wrap #1	03:16	03:53	00:36
Movie Segment #1	03:53	09:10	05:18
Bumper #2 (Next…Your Home Movie)	09:10	09:14	00:04
Commercial Black #2	09:14	11:18	02:03
Bumper #3	11:18	11:21	00:03
Man On The Street Intro. (as needed)			
Man On The Street or Interview Segment.	11:21	12:14	00:53
Movie Segment #2	12:14	15:33	03:18
Home Movie Intro.	15:33	15:46	00:13
Home Movie	15:46	16:50	01:04
Movie Segment #3	16:50	20:14	03:24

UNDER CALIFORNIA STARS #110

SHOW INTRO

CLIP TEASE

GUY
Where we can watch Mad Movies?

MAYTAG MAN
Mad Movies? Oh, my wife's going to watch it, but she likes watching T.V. by herself, forget it. It'd out of the question, no way, not today.

LADY
It's going to start in two minutes, darling. Make him an offer.

GUY
I'll give you a dollar.

MAYTAG MAN
A dollar! The T.V.'s over here.

MUSIC INTRO

COMMERCIAL #1

ACT I

SHOW OPEN

(EXT.—RANCH)

HOST
Hi, I'm Kent Skov and welcome to Mad Movies with the L.A. Connection. Tonight's feature stars
(V.O.)
one of America's favorite cowboy heroes. Many of us grew up with him. This fellow claims to be a relative of another star in our movie. Trigger, the Wonder Horse…Our version of "Under California Stars" is about a cowboy who competes at everything from dog racing to arm wrestling. Just like this big fella here. Right, fella?

HORSE
Oh, get on with the movie and get off my fence.

(EXT.—BARN)

MOLLY
(Gasp)
Eeee! It's Ben. It's Ben. Help!

MOUSE (BEN)
(SQUEEK)

(SFX: SHOTGUN BLAST)

ROY
I'll bet there's trouble in the barn, Cowboy Andy.

COWBOY ANDY
Good thinking, Roy.

MOLLY
(Scream)
Help! Who greased the railing?

(SFX: SLIDE WHISTLE)

MOUSE (BEN)
(Laugh)
I did.

MOLLY
(O.C.)
I messed up my hair. He'll never find me up here.

HORSE
She's on top of the hay, Ben.

MOUSE (BEN)
Thanks, pal.

ROY
Hey!

COWBOY ANDY
Yes it is.

MOLLY
I know karate, Ben.

MOUSE (BEN)
So do I, I'm a black belt.

(SFX: GUNSHOT)

MOLLY
That mouse tried to kill me.

COWBOY ANDY
Ben's on another rampage.

ROY
She fell on me.

COWBOY ANDY
That happened to me, now I'm a soprano.

(INT. BARN)

ROY
Get off me, you weigh a ton.

COWBOY ANDY
I bet I can hold her longer than you can, Roy.

MOUSE
Spit-shine, mister?

ROY
We'll just see who can hold her the longest here.

COWBOY ANDY
It's a bet. She's not that heavy.

MOUSE
I'd better buff the tops.

COWBOY ANDY
I guess she weighs about 183.
(SCREAMING)

MOUSE
(Laughs)

(SFX: BUFFING MACHINE)

COWBOY ANDY
Ow, ow, ooh, ow. Timber, Ben. Aah!

(INT.—OFFICE)

COWBOY POP
I'll cover your bet this time, but if you don't pay up, I'll have Cowboy Bob break your legs. Okay Mom, say hi to Dad for me. These collect calls are killing me. I gotta come up with some cash quick.

COWBOY BOB
Why don't you set up a sucker bet with Roy, Cowboy Pop? We'll have him fight a ringer.

COWBOY POP
A good idea. You know people passing by can see you have your hands in your pants.

(INT.—BARN)

VOICES IN CROWD
Alright, yeah, way to go!

ROY
See Cowboy Andy, I told you I could throw a kid across the barn.

COWBOY ANDY
You broke the old record of thirty-five feet.

ROY
You owe me your first born.

                        COWBOY ANDY
Will you take my second cousin?

                        COWBOY KID
That's the farthest I ever been thrown, Roy.

                        ROY
Well, thanks.

                        COWBOY KID
I wish you'd quit throwin' me in the horses stall, tho. Look what I got on my face.

                        ROY
Well Cowboy Kid, it can't be half as bad as the smell coming from your feet.

(EXT. STREET)

                        CROWD
Bonjour, aloha, strosvochek, good murken, yo!

                        COWBOY SHERIFF
You're late, Cowboy Banker.

                        COWBOY BANKER
I stopped for donuts, Cowboy Doctor.

                        COWBOY SHERIFF
I've been here all night holding up this wall.

                        COWBOY BANKER
I appreciate that. I'll hold it from the inside now.

                        COWBOY SHERIFF
Great!

                        COWBOY BANKER
I got it now. Thank you.

(SFX: BRAKES SCREECH)

                        ROY
I parked in a red zone. If the cops come by, here are the keys.

                        COWBOY KID
Can I play the radio? Huh?

(INT.—OFFICE)

(SFX: DOOR OPENING)

                        COWBOY POP
Yuck! When are you going to house break this dog, Cowboy Kid?

                           COWBOY KID
Sorry.

                           COWBOY POP
Hey, Cowboy Kid, this is the third pair of pants your dog's ruined.

                           COWBOY BOB
Does Roy know you're here?

                           COWBOY KID
No, he doesn't, but…what the hell have you got on? I've never seen a cowboy jumpsuit before. Golly, if Cowboy Bob wears that, he'll draw attention to us and ruin your plan. Besides, it's ugly.

(EXT.—STORE)

                           ROY
                         (Thought)
I got my lunch out of the bank.

                           COWBOY KID
                           (O.C.)
Hey, Roy.

                           ROY
What happened to you, Cowboy Kid?

                           COWBOY KID
Cowboy Bob bit me on the leg. Apparently he's more sensitive about his clothes than I thought.

                           ROY
Oh he's wearing that stupid jumpsuit again, huh. Watch your fingers.

(SFX: DOOR SLAM)

                           COWBOY KID
Aaaaaaaaaah! My foot.

(INT. HALLWAY)

                           COWBOY TED
Hey everybody, you're not gonna believe this but we just got a letter.

(EXT.—CAR)

                           COWBOY KID
Slow down, Roy, slow down. You're going too fast.

(SFX: CRASH SOUND)

(INT.—KITCHEN)

                           MOLLY
Roy's home! Look, a real letter. It's the first one we ever got. Open it.

COWBOY ANDY

Yeah, yeah.

MOLLY

Wish I could read.

COWBOY ANDY

Watch out for the paper cuts. Look at those big words.

(SFX: INCREDIBLE PAPER RATTLING)

ROY

"Dear Nancy, I'll be home as soon as the exterminators are through in the oval office. Don't let the horse sit at the breakfast table and put some gas in the pick-up truck. Love, Ron." This was delivered to the wrong ranch. I knew it was too good to be true.

COWBOY ANDY

Can I have your lunch, Roy?

MOLLY

We'll get a letter someday, Cowboy Kid.

ROY

Yeah, and I'm locking my food up so you can't get it...

COWBOY DOCTOR

I'm worried about you, Roy. You entered the bake-off, every event in the Olympics, came in third in the Miss America contest. You competed in the three-legged race by yourself.

ROY

I won—so what's the point, Cowboy Doctor?

COWBOY DOCTOR

You're much too competitive for a normal man. Your blood pressure's too high, your heart rate's fast and your eyes are way too small.

MOLLY

It's not only the competition, but he bets on everything he does.

COWBOY KID

He won me in a poker game.

MOLLY

Shh.

COWBOY DOCTOR

That's right, son. Your Mom and I miss you an awful lot.

COWBOY ANDY

Mmmmmm. I bet you can lick this problem.

ROY

You got a bet, fatty. Tell you what, Doc. I'll race Trigger against anything in town. If he loses, I'll change my ways. If he wins, you owe me three million dollars and a new hat.

                              COWBOY DOCTOR

Read my lips. I hope you get saddle sores where the sun don't shine.

COMMERCIAL #2 BUMPER Next...Your Home Movies

WRAP AROUND

ACT II

                                HOST

Our four legged friend's name is Earl and as I said before he claims to be related to Trigger, the Wonder Horse. Ironically he also is in show business. How did you get into stand-up comedy?

                                HORSE

Well, I kind of got roped into it. I always wanted to be a hoofer.

                                HOST

Were you born and raised in California?

                                HORSE

Na, I'm from Filly.

(HORSE COUGHS A FEW TIMES)

                                HOST

Are you okay?

                                HORSE

Fine, thanks. I had a little colt in my throat. I'm still kind of hoarse.

                                HOST

You may be sick but you look wonderful.

                                HORSE

Actually, I'd like to get into a stable relationship.

                                HOST

And give up show business?

                                HORSE

You bet. Half the time I feel like some kind of ass.

(EXT.—ROAD)

                                TRIGGER

I've got a bet with Roy. Let me win or it's the glue factory for me.

                               COWBOY DOG

Alright, but you owe me one.

ROY
Let me get the cow patty out of the way.

COWBOY ANDY
(Laughs)
That's the third pair of boots he's ruined this week. You'd think he'd learn how to use a rake. He's such a stupid dipstick. Oh hi, Roy. Hide me.

COWBOY KID
Molly, you're not wearing a bra. Let's start the race. Last one in is tonight's supper…run!

TRIGGER
Don't pull a Zola Budd on me.

COWBOY KID
Run.

COWBOY DOG
I'm outta shape.

TRIGGER
I'm sweating like a pig.

ROY
Cowboy Dog is gonna make a good dinner.

COWBOY KID
Roy, I was only kidding.

ROY
Oh, a welcher, eh?

COWBOY KID
I thought for sure he'd win.

ROY
Don't let the dog do that to you. Let me put you up here where it's safe.

COWBOY KID
Ow!

(INT.—BARN)

COWBOY BOB & COWBOY POP
We're cowboys, we're cowboys.
He's a cowboy, I'm a cowboy.
We're all cowboys.

ROY
Great song.

                              POP
Thanks.

                              ROY
Did you write it yourself?

                              POP
Yeah.

                          COWBOY BOB
I helped.

                          COWBOY KID
Still wearin' that ugly suit, huh? Did you guys see the race?

                          COWBOY POP
Yeah and we have a proposal for you.

                              ROY
Great!

                          COWBOY BOB
You haven't even heard it yet. What if I told you that you had to put Trigger there on your head and dance in the moonlight in your underwear?

                              ROY
I've already done that.

                          COWBOY KID
Wait a minute, Roy, Trigger had the underwear on.

                          COWBOY BOB
No, no, no, that doesn't count.

                             MOLLY
In case you were wondering, I'm not Dale Evans.

                          COWBOY POP
Hey, come back with those gloves, you mangy mutt.

                          COWBOY KID
I'll get 'um.

                          COWBOY BOB
Wait Pop, those are Dog's gloves.

                          COWBOY POP
Oh yeah, I borrowed them last month and forget to return them.
                              (O.C.)
Thanks, Cowboy Dog.

(INT.—OFFICE)

                          COWBOY POP
That darn maid straightens up around here and now I can't find a damn thing.

(Horse Enters)

Get that horse out of the living room, you've got assigned parking outside.

COWBOY CLINT

Hi, Pop. I'm Cowboy Clint. I'm that ringer you sent to fight Roy.

COWBOY BOB

Hi everybody, how do you like my new outfit?

COWBOY CLINT

Makes you look fat.

COWBOY BOB

Anyone that calls me fat gets hit in the stomach.

COWBOY CLINT

This stomach.

COWBOY POP

Save it for Roy.

COWBOY BOB

Stomach, chin, they're all the same.

COWBOY CLINT

Yeah.

COWBOY BOB
(O.C.)

That's the dog that plays guitar.

COWBOY KID

Come back with my knee cap!

COWBOY POP

I hate rock 'n roll.

COWBOY BOB

You keep your mouth shut to Roy about the ringer we brought in for the fight.

COWBOY KID

I won't tell him you're cheating, but it'll cost you.

COWBOY BOB

Here's my gallstone.

COWBOY KID

Come on, Cowboy Dog.

COWBOY POP

Hey, come back here with my breakfast. That dog stole the dry toast and that's my favorite part.

COWBOY BOB

It's not dry any more, it's got dog spit all over it.

(INT.—BARN)

COWBOY LEONARD
I know you guys think I should've gotten a horse with legs, but I never hit my head on a low branch.

VOICE
(O.C.)
Got any queens?

COWBOY LEONARD
(Holds up seven)

HORSE
That's a queen.

COWBOY LEONARD
Argh!

HOME MOVIE INTRO

HOST
Some wagon, huh? You know, some things that were made years ago can never be replaced. Just like your old home movies. Tonight we have a vintage home movie from the 1950's sent in by Cecil Santilli from San Francisco, CA.

HOME MOVIE

NARRATOR
This is the giant. This is the house he built, and these were some of the states which were completely covered by that house. The giant enjoyed teasing dinosaurs. He alone controlled the airways, as well as the shipping, and all the train travel for miles around. These are the giant's friends. Sometimes he wrestled with them for exercise, but when they lost, they didn't like it. The giant turned one of his old belts into a bridge. *This* bridge. Then, from the smoke stack of the Queen Elizabeth 2, he pulled a giant cat. *This* was the cat. This was his dog. And this was the camera he used to film them when they did *this*. When the giant got bored, he liked to play golf…with the *moon*.

(INT.—BEDROOM)

ROY
Goodnight, pooch. Sorry. Didn't mean to spit on you. Put your foot on my butt and make a wish.

COWBOY KID
It didn't come true.

ROY
Try again.

COWBOY KID
It didn't work, you're still here. Bet you can't read my palm.

ROY

You lose, I'm part gypsy. Say, let me show you something. See this line? It says you'll have lots of kids. This line? It says you'll have lots of paternity suits.

COWBOY KID

What kind of suits did you say?

ROY

Paternity. Sorry, didn't mean to spit on you.

(INT.—OFFICE)

COWBOY POP

Here's six dollars.

COWBOY CLINT

That's ok for now but, when do I get the other half of my money? Cowboy Pop!

COWBOY POP

When you win your fight with Roy. And you better win, Cowboy Clint.

COWBOY BOB

What are you going to do with all that money?

COWBOY CLINT

Start a flower shop.

COWBOY BOB

What would you sell?

COWBOY CLINT
(Thought)

Idiot.

COWBOY POP
(O.C.)

Don't shut the door, it turns out the light.

(INT.—HOUSE)

ROY

Like a virgin. Yeah. Gotta go.

MOLLY
(Thought)

Seventy dollars for a new scarf and he didn't even notice...Roy, wanna have some fun?

ROY

What is it?

MOLLY

I bet you'd like to pull my fringe off one at a time.

ROY

I'd take that bet, but I have to be alone for a while.

MOLLY
I'll go with you.

ROY
No, uh, being alone means by yourself.

MOLLY
That's not necessarily true. That's just an old wives' tale. Come on, I'll show you.

(INT.—ROOM)

ROY
Molly tried to hit on me in the house.

COWBOY ANDY
She did? I didn't know you were lookin' for a boyfriend. I'm a great date and a fabulous dancer. I swear, Roy.

ROY
But you've got two wooden legs.

COWBOY ANDY
(Whines)

ROY
And there's a dwarf sawing on your ankles.

COWBOY ANDY
Oh no, timber!

MOLLY
Oh, you squished the dwarf! Did you all hear his little head pop?

(INT.—LIVING ROOM)

COWBOY FLIP
Say, Roy, you're late for the big fight. Better put a wiggle on it.

ROY
Where are you going, Cowboy Andy?

COWBOY ANDY
If I don't get to the bathroom real soon, I'm gonna wet my pants.

ROY
There's no time.

COWBOY ANDY
Well then I'll just bring my hat. You know there's no outhouse on the range.

ROY
Good idea.

COWBOY ANDY
Maybe we should bring some newspaper.

(EXT.—HOUSE)

       ROY
Someone give Cowboy Andy a boost.

       VOICE
       (O.C.)
That's too dangerous, let him use a ladder.

      COWBOY ANDY
Is this the steel-reinforced horse?

       ROY
Hi ho silver, away!

      COWBOY ANDY
That's the Lone Ranger, Roy.

       VOICE
Last one there has to help Cowboy Andy off his horse.

(EXT.—FIELD)

      COWBOY CLINT
Where've you been, punk? I had to start without you.

       ROY
We stopped for gas.

      COWBOY CLINT
You're too late. My horse and I need a nap.

      COWBOY ANDY
Hey everyone, adjust your shorts. I gotta empty my hat.

      COWBOY CLINT
Ahchoooo!

(FIGHTING)

      COWBOY ANDY
Cowboy Clint, how many fingers am I holdin' up? You got a rope on your back, Roy.

       ROY
Once, twice, three times a lady.

      COWBOY KID
C'mon Roy, sing "Penny Lover".

      COWBOY BOB
I hate that song.

      COWBOY AL
Down in front! I can't see.

ROY
Your shirt is getting dirty.

COWBOY BOB
You're going to have to pre-soak.

COMMERCIAL #3

BUMPER Trigger Sings.

(INT. LIVING ROOM)

ACT III

CROWD
That was some fight. Roy was really something. Where *is* Roy? He's parking the horses out back.

COWBOY DOCTOR
Oh no, look at this. Say Roy, someone ate your lunch. They even ate the carrot sticks.

MOLLY
Try to be brave, Roy.

ROY
That's easy for you to say. They didn't eat your jelly sandwich. All they left was some shredded wax paper.

(INT. SINGING HALL)

ROY
We're gonna have a telethon now to raise money to get me a new sandwich. I'm gonna sing.
Had a sandwich,
Jelly sandwich,
I made it on rye.
Had a sandwich,
Lost my sandwich,
What a sad guy am I?

COWBOY KID

(SFX) FINGERS GETTING CUT OFF

Ow!

COWBOY ANDY
Here, have a thumb.

(SFX) APPLAUSE

COWBOY RED
That's enough, Roy.

ROY
Had a sandwich,

Jelly sandwich,
And a fresh rhubarb pie.

(EXT.—TRUCK)

TRIGGER

Had a sandwich,
Jelly sandwich.

(INT.—HOUSE)

COWBOY AL

Hey everybody, Roy taught his horse that stupid song.

COWBOY ANDY

What'd you say, Cowboy Al?

COWBOY AL

Look.

COWBOY ANDY

Oh no.

COWBOYS

We're in trouble now.

COWBOY ANDY

Ah, c'mon, Cowboy Luciano, let's all sing a song and drown him out when he comes in.

COWBOY LUCIANO

Let's sing that cowboy song. O.K?

(EXT.—BARN)

TRIGGER

Had a sandwich,
Lost my sandwich.

(INT.—LIVING ROOM)

COWBOY LUCIANO

When it comes to competition, you ain't heard nothin' yet. Roy's got the gambling bug, there's not a match he's met. Your turn.

COWBOY ANDY

Everyone has heard the rumors that Roy is wearing bloomers. In fact, he won them from his mother on a bet.

COWBOY LUCIANO

Hold it!

ROY

                    (THOUGHT)
Oh Man! That sounds awful. Sounds like a cow giving birth.

                    COWBOY ANDY
Where'd Roy go? I could've sworn he pulled in. I guess he must've left.

                    ROY
I came in through the back door, Cowboy Andy.

                    COWBOY ANDY
You didn't happen to see an elephant in the driveway, did you?

                    COWGIRL MANDY
Yoo hoo.

                    ROY
Who the hell is that?

                    COWBOY ANDY
That's my twin sister from the circus.

                    COWGIRL MANDY
Roy, Roy! That Roy won't come out and kiss me.

                    ROY
Oh, that cures me of betting.

                    COWBOY ANDY
She was caught in a tornado and now she wears her bra down here.

(SFX) UPCHUCKING, HEAVING

                    ROY
Your sister's making everyone sick.

                    COWBOY ANDY
She has since she was little.

(INT.—BARN)

                    COWBOY KID
Gee Roy, we just wanted to have a barbeque to celebrate you winning the fight and quitting gambling, but the lighter fluid got out of control and I'm sorry about the barn burning and most of the house.

                    ROY
Don't worry about it, Cowboy Kid, it's the thought that counts.

                    COWBOY ANDY
Do you want me to shoot him, Roy?

                    COWBOY KID
Shoot the dog, he knocked the lighter fluid over.

                    ROY
Aw! Shoot 'um both.

(EXT. RANCH)

                    TRIGGER
Watch out for the speed bumps…ow!

                    COWBOY ANDY
Geez, I should have brushed my teeth. Thanks.

                    MOLLY
I can't believe Roy got a gig in Vegas.

                    COWBOY DEREK
It wasn't Roy that got the job. Trigger was the one they hired to do the singing.

(INT. CAR)

                    ROY
Had a sandwich.

                    COWBOY KID
I gotta go.

                    ROY
Shoulda gone before we left.

                    COWBOY KID
Owh!

                    ROY, COWBOY KID, COWBOY ANDY
Had a sandwich,
Jelly sandwich,
I made it with rye.

                    CROWD
Bye, bye.

THE END

PANDA PRODUCTIONS   MAD MOVIES

TITLE: UNDER CALIFORNIA STARS

PAGE 1 of 2   SHOW # 110   DATE: 11/2/85

CUE	TITLE	COMPOSER	SOC	PUBLISHER	USEAGE	TIME
T 1	MAD MOVIES THEME	RICHARD BAKER/ MARY NEWLAND	ASCAP	SONGSYNC MUSIC	SHOW OPEN VOCAL/INST	:50
L01-M2	UNDER CAL. STARS WRAP				B.G. INST	:37
M 1	UNDER CAL. STARS: THEME					:17
M 2	TROUBLE IN THE BARN					:15
M 3	THANKS PAL					:09
M 4	COVER YOUR BET					:25
M 1	COWBOY BANKER					:17
M 5	COWBOY KID					:43
L01-M2	WE GOT A LETTER					1:42
B B	MAD MOVIES BUMPER				COMM/BUMPER VOCAL/INST	:04
B A	MAD MOVIES BUMPER					:03
L01-M2	EARL THE HORSE WRAP				B.G INST	:53
M 2	START THE RACE					:15
F 1	WERE COWBOYS	COMPOSERS: R. BAKER/M. NEWLAND AUTHORS: CONNIE COOK STEVE PINTO STEVE ROLLMAN BOB BUCHHOLZ KENT SKOV R. BAKER/M. NEWLAND			FEATURED SONG	:10
M 4	DARN MAID				B.G INST	:25
M 6	GUITAR PLAYING DOG					:03
M 4	I WONT TELL					:25
HM1	"THE GIANT"					1:04
M 5	NIGHT POOCH					:30
M 6	PIANO CUE					:05
M 7	I'LL TAKE THAT BET					:28
M 8	LATE FOR THE BIG FIGHT					:24
M 9	GIVE ANDY A BOOST					:15

PANDA PRODUCTIONS   MAD MOVIES

TITLE: UNDER CALIFORNIA STARS

PAGE 2 of 2   SHOW # 110   DATE: 11/2/85

CUE	TITLE	COMPOSER	SOC	PUBLISHER	USEAGE	TIME
M10	START WITHOUT YOU	R. BAKER/M. NEWLAND	ASCAP	SONGSYNC MUSIC	B.G INST	:35
B B	MAD MOVIES BUMPER				COMM/BUMPER VOCAL/INST	:04
B A						:03
F 1	JELLY SANDWICH SONG	COMPOSERS: R. BAKER/M. NEWLAND AUTHORS: CONNIE COOK STEVE PINTO STEVE ROLLMAN BOB BUCHHOLZ KENT SKOV			FEATURED SONG	:35
F 2	WHEN IT COMES TO COMPETITION	COMPOSERS: R. BAKER/M. NEWLAND AUTHORS: CONNIE COOK STEVE PINTO STEVE ROLLMAN BOB BUCHHOLZ KENT SKOV			FEATURED SONG	:17
M11	WHERE'D ROY GO	R. BAKER/M. NEWLAND	ASCAP	SONGSYNC MUSIC	B.G INST	:40
M12	JELLY SANDWICH: CLOSE					:28
L01_M2	RANCHO MAD MOVIES: WRAP				SHOW CLOSE	:40
T 2	MAD MOVIES THEME				VOCAL/INST	:59

OPENING CRAWL*

SHOW #<u>110</u>

SHOW NAME   <u>Under California Stars</u>

*Each numbered item as a single page…
Items #1-4: Centerframe
Items #5-9: Lower third of page

1   FOUR STAR
    in association with
    KENT SKOV

2   Presents
    an L.A. Connection
    production of

3   Tonight's Feature

4   Starring

5   Bob Buchholz

6   Connie Sue Cook

7   Stephen L. Rollman

8   Steve Pinto

9   Kent Skov

GENERIC BUMPERS*

SHOW #<u>110</u>

SHOW NAME   <u>Under California Stars</u>

*Each numbered item as a single page…

1   We'll be right back…

2   Don't Go Away

3   More Mad Movies
    Coming Up

4   Coming Up…
    More Mad Movies

5   Stay Tuned for
    "Your Home Movies"

6   Next…
    "Your Home Movies"

7   Write Us…
    L.A. Connection Productions
    6464 Sunset Blvd., #820
    Hollywood, CA 90028

8   Send Your Home Movies to…
    L.A. Connection Productions
    6464 Sunset Blvd., #820
    Hollywood, CA 90028
    (Include a self-addressed, stamped envelope for return of films)

9   Next…
    Mad Movies takes it to the streets

CLOSING CRAWL*

SHOW #<u>110</u>

SHOW NAME   <u>Under California Stars</u>

*Each numbered item as a single page...

1   Directed by
        Kent Skov

2   Written by
        Connie Sue Cook
        Steve Pinto
        Kent Skov

3   Produced by
        Randal W Ridges

4   Featuring
        Bob Buchholz
        Connie Sue Cook
        Steve Pinto
        Stephen L. Rollman
        Kent Skov

5   Associate Producers (each name single page)
        Martha Whitney

6   Kent Weishaus (single page)

7   Music Composed and arranged by
        Richard Baker
        Mary Newland
        For Panda Productions

7a   Music Recorded by
        Richard Baker

8   Theme performed by
        Mary Newland

CLOSING CREDIT CRAWL (con't)

9	Research by Bob Petrella Ken Segall April Winchell Ted Hardwick
10	Talent Coordinator Martha Whitney
11	Associate Director/Stage Manager Randal W Ridges
11a	Assistants to the Producers: Bob Buchholz Connie Sue Cook Steve Pinto Stephen L. Rollman
12	Facilities provided by
13	Lighting and Camera Bill Sheehy
14	Gaffer Jim Drewry
14a	Production Sound Mark Hanes
15	Production Assitants Lisa Gougas Ted Hardwick
16	Make Up Lora Sanders
17	Wardrobe Annie Vicari
18	Production Secretary Eloise Gonzalez
18a	Post-Production Coordinated by Monti Santilli Rainbolt
19	Post-Production Facilities Complete Post, Inc.
20	Post-Production Audio by Michael Perricone Michaele Hogan For Interlok Productions

CLOSING CREDIT CRAWL (con't)

21   "Your Home Movie" submitted by
Cecil Santilli
San Francisco, CA

21a   Location Courtesy of
Cathy Ebsen and Meta Lyons
of the Circle 7 'E' Ranch, Agoura, California

22   Executive in Charge of Production for Four Star Television
Bob Bosen

23   Special Thanks to:
Susan Lenti
Budget Films, Inc.
Richard Holiday
Dennis Condon
Snagglepuss

23a   Opening Title Montage by
Homer & Associates

23b   Opening Title Photography by
Abe Perlstein

24   Post-Production supervised by
Randal W Ridges

25   Executive Producer
Kent Skov

26   "Celebrity Voices and Appearances Impersonated"

27   Copyright 1985 Four Star International, Inc.
All Rights Reserved

ZORRO'S FIGHTING LEGIONS

With the

SHORT RUNDOWN FOR SHOW #122 ZORRO'S FIGHTING LEGIONS

DESCRIPTION	IN	OUT	SEGMENT TIME
SHOW OPEN	00:00	02:01	02:01
COMMERCIAL BREAK #1	02:01	04:05	02:03
ACT I	04:05	12:30	08:25
COMMERCIAL BREAK #2	12:30	14:33	02:03
ACT II	14:33	20:59	06:26
COMMERCIAL BREAK #3	20:59	23:02	02:03
ACT III/SHOW CLOSE	23:02	28:00	04:58

RUNDOWN

MAD MOVIES WITH THE L.A. CONNECTION

SHOW #122 ZORRO'S FIGHTING LEGIONS

All times are in minutes and seconds	IN	OUT	DURATION
Four Star Logo	00:00	00:05	00:05
Clip Tease #1	00:05	00:34	00:29
Opening Montage	00:34	01:01	00:27
Host Intro and Preview Clip	01:01	02:01	01:01
Commercial Black #1	02:01	04:05	02:03
Bumper #1	04:05	04:07	00:02
Movie Segment #1 (includes Host Toss)	04:07	11:53	07:46
Host and Preview Clip	11:53	12:30	00:37
Commercial Black #2	12:30	14:33	02:03
Bumper #2	14:33	14:36	00:03
Movie Segment #2	14:36	20:55	06:19
Bumper #3	20:55	20:59	00:04
Commercial Black #2	20:59	23:02	02:03
Bumper #4	23:02	23:05	00:03

MAD MOVIES WITH THE L.A. CONNECTION

RUNDOWN, Pg 2

SHOW #122 ZORRO'S FIGHTING LEGIONS

	IN	OUT	DURATION
Movie Segment #3	23:05	24:27	01:22
Host Intro to Home Movie	24:27	24:50	00:23
Home Movie (includes Billboard at tail)	24:50	26:04	01:14
Host Wrap-up	26:04	26:35	00:31
Clip Tease #2	26:35	27:08	00:33
Closing Montage (includes L.A. Connection logo)	27:08	27:55	00:47
Four Star Logo	27:55	28:00	00:05

ZORRO'S FIGHTING LEGION SHOW NUMBER 122

CLIP TEASE

(EXT. CAVE)

ZORRO

My name is Zorro. I am the star of tonight's episode of Mad Movies with the L.A. Connection. I know that you would all like to see it, but I also know that you are a poor people with no tv sets, so you may all come to my house.

MEN CHEER

ZORRO

Wait! You must all bring refreshments. I cannot feed all of you. All I have is some leftover Halloween candy. It's a little stale, but it's still edible.

MEN CHEER

ZORRO

Wait. Before we leave, who has to go potty, raise your hand.

MEN RAISE HANDS...

ZORRO

Thank you.

MUSIC THEME

(EXT. NEWSPAPER RACKS)

HOST

Hi, I'm Kent Skov and welcome to Mad Movies with the L.A. Connection. We've just shown you a clip from our version of Zorro's Fighting Legion, originally an action packed movie serial from the forties. We've taken a few episodes, changed all the dialogue and changed it into a story about a consumer vigilante.

CLIP

(INT. LIV. ROOM)

CUBBY

What's going on, Zorro?

ZORRO

Cubby, I've told you never to call me Zorro until I put my mask on.

CUBBY

I forgot, Floyd.

ZORRO

It's your turn to bring refreshments to the Zorro club.

CUBBY

I'll meet you at the clubhouse.

                    ZORRO
Now you can call me Zorro.

                    CUBBY
Bye, Floyd.

                    ZORRO
Argh.

(EXT. BALCONY)

                    ZORRO
I'm afraid of the staircases. I'll take the swashbuckling exit. Argh.

(SFX: BIG CRASH)

                    VINCENT PRICE
Zorro hit another tree.

                    SOLDIER
OH!

(EXT. NEAR NEWSRACKS)

                    HOST
You know we would have loved to have Zorro on the show today, but as you know he's a pretty elusive character, and so hard to catch up with. In a moment, we'll be right back with our Mad Movie.

COMMERCIAL #1

ACT ONE

(EXT. NEAR NEWSPAPER RACKS)

                    HOST
While I keep an eye out for Zorro, here's the L.A. Connection's Mad Movie.

(LOOKS AROUND FOR ZORRO STANDING BEHIND HIM)

TITLES

ARROW FIRES (OINK SOUND)

(EXT. TRAIL)

                    LT. O'FACIAL HARE
And on your left is our family tree.

(SFX. TWANG, SCREAM)

Someone hit grandpa. Darn those kids.

                    KID
Hee! Hee!

                    LT. OFH

(O.C.)

Okay men, let's get 'em! Hey, where everybody go?

(INT. OFFICE)

LT. OFH

One of the kids tried to shoot me and missed. I had to pull this out of grandpa's trunk.

GENERAL SHORT

I had one in my hat and after it rusted people thought I was a weather vane.

LT. FALK

A thing like that could put someone's eye out.

LT. OFH

So I had an uncle who once put a cat out with one of those things.

GEN. SHORT

I believe the transverter King is responsible. He's the one who can transform himself into anything from a space shuttle to a BLT.

MR. GORDO

I have something important to say! One of you took my parking space again this morning. I pay 35 dollars a month to park downstairs and I'm sick and tired of someone else taking my space.

LT. OFH

Why are you wasting your money? You don't even own a horse.

MR. GORDO

Was it you, you, you? One of you is guilty.

GEN SHORT

I did it because I'm in charge and I can do anything I want.
(O.C.)
Besides, you have more hair than I do.

MR. GORDO

I can't take it out on any of you 'cause you're my superiors. But you work for me. C'mon.

(INT. CAVE)

TRANSVERTER

Bring in that lousy salesman. You haven't met your quota of selling pointy things to the children. I should fire you.

TRANSVERTER

If you don't sell more, I'll transform myself into a dump truck and haul you outta town.

TRANSVERTER

Wait. Don't anyone move. I lost my contact lens and you gotta help me find it.

KIDS

I don't see it. Nope.

(SFX: GLASS CRACKING)

I found it.

(EXT. STREET)

(SFX: SOUNDS OF BAD GUITAR MUSIC)

        MEN
Knock it off! That's enough! I'll give you a gold piece just to stop. That's bad.

        GUITARIST
Hey, who put this mothball in here?

(INT. BEDROOM)

        CUBBY
What's going on, Zorro?

        ZORRO
Cubby, I've told you never to call me Zorro until I have my mask on.

        CUBBY
I forgot, Floyd.

        ZORRO
It's your turn to bring refreshments to the Zorro club.

        CUBBY
I'll meet you at the clubhouse.

        ZORRO
Now you can call me Zorro.

        CUBBY
Bye, Floyd.

        ZORRO
Argh.

(EXT. BALCONY)

        ZORRO
I'm afraid of staircases. I'll take the swashbuckling exit. Wheee, Argh!

(SFX: BIG CRASH)

(INT. ROOM)

        PRICE
Zorro hit another tree.

        SOLIDER

OH!

(EXT. CAVE)

ZORRO
Where are our masks, Cubby?

CUBBY
Apparently, the Lone Ranger club took all the ones the store had in stock.

MAN
Did you bring the refreshments?

CUBBY
Nachos.

MEN	ZORRO	MEN
Not again!	Boo!	Oh! Ooo!

ZORRO

(SFX: HORSE'S NAY)

Darn it. I should never have bought this horse from a circus. Listen men, we've got a job to do. We've got to find the Transverter King and stop him from making pointy toys. Now on the count of three, let's have a rousing cheer. One, two...

MEN
Yay!

ZORRO
Wait! Wait! I didn't say three. Now let's try it again. This time get it right. Ready one, two...

MEN
Yay!

ZORRO
Forget it. I'm gonna find some men who can count to three.

(INT. OFFICE)

MILTON
Gentlemen, I've heard rumors, there's a tv actor who's been sitting in on all our meetings. His name is Peter Falk. Which one of you is it?

(SUSPENSE MUSIC)

I'll find out. Even if I have to call Columbo.

(INT. BEDROOM)

ZORRO
Hey Cubby, that's mine. What are you doing?

CUBBY
I'm gonna borrow your mask. My mom's taking my picture on a pony.

ZORRO
That's mine, come back. I need that. It's the only one I've got!

(INT. CLUES)

BUBBA
Lunch wagon! Everyone, the lunch wagon's here!

JOSE
I'm glad you're here. I'm really hungry. You got any sloppy joes?

JOE
No, I fired them.

JOSE
What about dessert?

JOE
I'll tell ya, but first you two gotta take a shower.

V.O. (MAN)
C'mon guys, let's clear the table. It's almost time for lunch. We're having tongue in the basket.

JOE
Did you wash your hands for lunch?

V.O. (MAN)
Yes, we did.

JOE
Ok.

ZORRO
Play it cool. Let me do all the talking.

JOE
(THOUGHT)
These guys are overdressed. Hello.

ZORRO
Hi. I'd like a table for two in the no smoking section, please. I'd also like a table near the window.

JOE
If you can find a window, you can sit next to it.

ZORRO
Alright, I'll have a scotch on the rocks while I'm waiting.

BUBBA
It's Zorro.

ZORRO
No, I'm Floyd. Move your ass. Let me explain this to you. When I have this mask on…

BUBBA
Whoop, whoop, whoop…

JOE
Don't back up, severe donkey damage.

ZORRO
Joe, I'll trade you suits if you help me.

CUBBY
The transverter's men.

ZORRO
Ah-ha. Let's go, you don't have a chance. I'm the best swordsman in the world.

BAD GUY
I'm the best shot, Zorro.

ZORRO
No, I'm Floyd. You see when I'm not wearing the mask…

BAD GUY
Oh shut up. Get back along the wall, let's compare their hats.

(SFX: BONK)

ZORRO
You wanna play see-saw?

MEN
We rather play hide & seek.

CUBBY
Get up. You're getting your suit all dirty.

ZORRO
That's one down.

JOE
This man should be punished.

CUBBY
Let's make him go to the dentist, listen to musak, read old magazines and get a tooth pulled.

JOE
Or else make him eat a rock.

(EXT. TRAIL)

>   Z-MAN
>   (Thought)
> I can't see where I'm going.

(EXT. TRAIL-COLOR)

>   ROY ROGERS
> Hey, sounds like a mask hit the ground. Wonder if it's over here. Nope, no, don't see it. Well, I better get home, Dale's cooking me dinner.

(INT. HOUSE)

>   MOTHER
> Yes, General Short, the mole on your head does look a lot like the Brooklyn Bridge.

>   TUREEN
> I noticed we're the only women in town.

>   GENERAL
> Except for Raoul, but we don't talk about him.

>   TUREEN
> I'm staying till I get married.

>   MOTHER
> Me too.

>   GEN
> Um...er...good luck.
>   (THOUGHT)
> Someone should call an animal shelter.

>   CUBBY
> Hi, you must be women and that's a door.

(INT. CURTAIN—"MY FAV. BRUNETTE")

>   HOPE
> No, this is curtain number three. If you want what's behind it, Let's Make A Deal. After all, I'm not Monty Hall.

(INT. HOUSE)

>   ZORRO
> Ziegfried, take these boxes of masks up to my room. I borrowed them from Batman.

>   ZIEGFRIED
> Siiii.

>   ZORRO
> Well, what do you know...women.

                    MOTHER
Hello handsome, this is my daughter, Tureen. She's desperate. If
you're single we want you now.

(SFX: MONKEY KISS)

                    LT. FALK
I noticed she didn't tell him her daughter eats gravy with her hands.

                    CUBBY
Excuse us. We gotta get this brown stuff off our lips.

                    MOTHER
Sorry about that.

                    TUREEN
He probably thinks I'm a slob.

                    MOTHER
He's no charmer either; he spit all over my hand.

                    ZORRO
I suppose it's all my fault the Transverter King moved his hideout
somewhere else. Go ahead, say it.

                    GEN SHORT
Alright my friend, it is your fault.

                    ZORRO
But you're the only one who thinks so.

INSERT

                    OTHERS
No, I agree. It's your fault alright. That's true.

                    ZORRO
Okay, so I was wrong. So sue me.

                    GEN SHORT
You bet.

(EXT. HOUSE)

                    ZORRO
Did I see you take some silverware?

                    CUBBY
No, not me.

(SFX: CLINKING)

                    ZORRO
You're not lying to me?

CUBBY
No.

(SFX: SILVERWARE FALLING)

ZORRO
Look.

(EXT. "LITTLE PRINCESS")

TEMPLE
Don't they know it's impolite to point?

MAN
Yeah, so what? What are you getting at?

TEMPLE
Now I see why all the women left town.

MAN
Let's go to a commercial.

(EXT. NEAR PHONE BOOTH)

HOST
Well, I got a hot tip on how to get a hold of Zorro. But don't get your hopes up. He's probably very busy anyway. Out righting some wrong or parking his Z someplace. Anyway it never hurts to try. Who knows, we may just run into him

(TURNS TOWARD BOOTH)

Ah, just my luck. Somebody's on the phone. Well, while I'm waiting, why don't you guys see what's up next with our Mad Movie.

(TURNS AGAIN).

(EXT. WOODS)

ZORRO
You lost your mask again, didn't you? That's the ninth one this week.

MAN
No, it's at the cleaners.

ZORRO
He's lying.

MAN
If I'm lying, may I be struck dead...
(ARROW HITS HIM)

CHYRON..."We'll be right back..."

COMMERCIAL #2

(EXT. HOUSE)

         ZORRO
Oh no, what's that?

         CUBBY
A parking ticket.

         ZORRO
I tell you, I never saw that fire hydrant. Oh, there goes my insurance rates. Come on, we must find the Transverter King.

(INT. CAVES)

         TRANSVERTER
Tell us where Zorro is.

         MUMMY
Mmmmmmmmmm.

         LT. OFH
That mummy stole my hat.

         TRANS.
That's your problem. Where's Zorro?

         ZORRO
Right here. Stick 'em up.

         MEN
Zorro!

         ZORRO
We finally meet mask to mask. Picking on a poor defenseless mummy.
         (O.C.)
Don't do it, Bubba.

(SFX: GUNSHOT)

         TRANSVERTER
Nice shot.

         ZORRO
I was aiming for his hat.

         LT. OFH
I think this is dangerous.

(SFX: SWORDS)

         MEN
Hee-ya! Ho ho! Wee!

LT. OFH
I gotta find a bathroom.

ZORRO
This is fun. I wish I had my camera.

MUMMY
Wait a minute! What the heck am I fighting for? Bye, Zorro.

ZORRO
Hey! That's my wallet and my gun!

MUMMY
(Mumbles)

ZORRO
You ungrateful mummy.

TRANS
Zorro dropped a nickel over there.

MAN
A nickel…huh…beat you to it.

ZORRO
Gotta go. My mummy's calling me.

(MAN W/GUN FIRES SHOT, HITTING MAN ON HORSE)

(EXT. COLOR)

MAN ON HORSE
Ohhh…

MAN W/GUN
Whoops, excuse me.

(EXT. WOODS)

ZORRO
Oh, those kids are after me now.

INDIANS
INDIAN SOUNDS

ZORRO
Olga, olga, olga.

ZORRO
Faster boy, faster.

EXT. COLOR TANKS

EXT. WOODS B&W

ZORRO

Oh, they're going to catch up after me. Darn circus horse.

EXT. COLOR INSP. GENERAL

MEN YELLING

EXT. WOODS B&W

        ZORRO
Oh, the road repair crew hasn't come. Whoa, whoa, choo. Aaahhh…

        INDIANS
Ah, mama mia, that's what I call a pothole.

        ZORRO
Wait until I tell the guys about this.

(INT. OFFICE)

        LT. FALK
It was nice of you guys to remember my birthday.

        GEN. SHORT
Why don't you blow out the candle. Sorry about the cake, but we ate it all. It was good.

(INT. ROOM)

(SFX: KNIFE THROW)

        JAKE
        (O.C.)
This cheese is hard.

(SFX: BAD GUITAR MUSIC)

        SLAPPY
That dude plays bad.

        JAKE
Let's get out of here.
        (THOUGHT)
Before I go, I'll cut the cheese.

        ZORRO
You lost your mask again, didn't you? That's the 9th one this week.

        LT. OFH
No, it's at the cleaners.

        (O.C.) V.O.
Liar!

        LT OFH
If I'm lying may I be struck dead.

        ZORRO

Men, go check out the dry cleaners. Now that they're gone, I'll take his coat.

CUBBY

But there's a big hole in it.

ZORRO

I know. I have a wart on my back and it will fit over it just fine. Has anyone ever told you that you have a resemblance to Ken Barry?

(INT. CARD TABLE)

BAD GUITAR PLAYING

V.O.

Oh no, not him again.

MAN

Oh, let's go.

LYNDE

Oh, forgot about him. I'll show a card trick. The next card I turn over will be the ten of diamonds. Watch.
(ACE OF SPADES)

MAN

Whoa, that's pretty good. Now if he can only make an arrow go through it, he'd be great.

LYNDE

Oh, it would be great.

ARROW HITS CARD

(EXT. CAMP)

SOLDIER

99 bottles of beer on the wall, 99 bottles of beer, take one down, pass it around, 98 bottles of beer.

(INT. OFFICE)

JOE

On the wall.

ZORRO

98 bottles of beer on the wall.

JOE

98 bottles
     (pause)
of beer
     (pause)
you take one down, pass it around,
     (pause)
97 bottles
     (pause)
of beer.

                    (O.C.) V.O.
Shut up!

                    ZORRO
Oh no. What happened after 97 bottles? He's the only one who knew.

(EXT. BALCONY)

                    ZORRO
I gotta get that Transverter King. Oh, I'll never do that again.

                    CHICO
Hey, Groucho…
I found another Easter egg.

                    BOSS
Never mind that.
                    (O.C.)
Zorro and his men are heading for the Transverter King's cave.
                    (ON C.)
Hey Harpo, take a look. I didn't call you Chico.

                    ZORRO
I'm going to enter alone. I want you to create a diversion by slitting your throat.

                    KEN
What? I…uh…

                    ZORRO
Then while they're watching you die, I'll enter the cave. Let's go.

                    KEN
But -

(EXT. ELEVATOR)

                    LEROY
This job's got me going in circles.

                    BOSS

(SFX: LUNCH WHISTLE)

Go ahead, boys, take a full six minutes for lunch.

                    BERNIE
Hey, Skippy. What are you doing on break?

                    LEROY
I have to do my laundry. Bernie, I haven't had a shirt to wear in weeks.

                    BERNIE

Yes, I'm tired of wearing these shanties.

ZORRO
(Thought)
I wonder what kind of bleach they use.

BOSS
Now remember, don't wash your whites with your red or your underwear will come out pink.

ZORRO
(Thought)
Now's my chance to try out an elevator.
(O.C.)
Oh wow, I got the shaft again.
(Sliding down cable)

V.O.

(SFX: ELEVATOR BELL)

Third floor, ladies lingerie, second floor sporting goods, first floor, rocks and dirt.

ZORRO
It's dark down here. I'll use my light saber.

(SFX: STAR WARS SABER SOUND)

Ah, that's better, someone left the hot water on.

TRANS
Zorro! Leave at once or I'll transform myself into a lawnmower and chew your grass.

ZORRO
You don't frighten us. Who will help me destroy him?

VARIOUS INDIANS
Me gotta go burp my papoose. Me gotta vacuum my teepee. I gotta scalp some tickets.

(SFX: LAWNMOWER RUNNING, BREAKING DOWN)

ZORRO
(O.C.)
We're outta gas?
(ON C.)
I filled you with leaded.

TRANS
Gun? Ha! I have only one vulnerable spot...

(SFX: SHOOT)

Oh that was it!

ZORRO

King, take a powder. It's not safe here. Have your parents pick you up out front. Ah, this place is gonna blow.

      ZORRO

There goes the bike rack.

      TRANS
     (Painfully dying)

Ah-choo-arg.

(INT. COUNCIL CHAMBER)

      KEN

I'm not able to read the minutes of our last meeting. My dog chew'd 'em up.

      LT. FALK

No, I did it, sorry.

      GEN SHORT

What is it?

      MESSENGER

The Transverter King is dead.

      GEN SHORT
      (gasps)

You mean…

      MESSENGER

Yes sir. Here's the last pointy thing.

      MAN AT TABLE
      (gasps)

Be careful.

      ZORRO

Now the kids won't get in trouble for scratching the furniture or leaving bodies all around.

      GEN SHORT

Yeah, that's right. Now the children will have safe toys to play with.

      ZORRO

Our homes will be safe…thanks to Zorro.

(EXT. TRAIL)

      MALE CHILD

Say, how do you throw these things?

CHYRON…NEXT…ZORRO'S HOT UNDER HIS CAPE…

COMMERCIAL #3

(INT. GEN OFFICE)

COL. CORN
Well General, what do we toast to today?

GEN SHORT
I don't know, what do you say we toast to Danny Kaye?

(INT. COLOR—INSP. GENERAL)

HALE
Ah, to Danny...Ah, heads up, ah-ha...

BEARDED MAN
He's a great guy, but I think we should toast to Ronald Reagan.

GROUP WITH REAGAN
WELL...

LT. FALK
I have an idea, what do you say we toast to oil companies?

INT. OUTPOST IN MOROCCO...

MEN SLURP AND BURP

LT. FALK
Ah, let's just drink.

(EXT. HOUSE)

ZORRO
Whoa, Whoa, Dumbo...

TUREEN
Zorro!

ZORRO
(Thought)
Darn circus horse.
(dialogue)
I'm setting up a celebration dance.

WOMEN
A dance!

ZORRO
I want you to invite all your friends so there'll be plenty of women to dance with.

TUREEN
But we're the only women in town.

ZORRO
In that case, we'll have to call Raoul.

TUREEN
Don't invite Floyd. Oh Floyd. Um... nice mask, bye...bye.

                    ZORRO
I have one more thing left to do.

(EXT. STREET)

(BAD GUITAR MUSIC)

                    ZORRO
Ah-ha! You there!

                    GUITARIST
Uh-oh.

                    ZORRO
Gimme that guitar!

(SFX: GUITAR SONG)

Ha, ha.

                    MILTON
Who was that masked man?

CHYRON: THE ENDS

(EXT. PARKING LOT)

                    HOST
Well, I hoped you enjoyed our version of Zorro's Fighting Legion. You know, it's not just Hollywood movies that get the L.A. Connection Treatment. We can do the same thing to your home movies. Tonight's was sent in Arlene O'Neil of San Gabriel California. We call it Zombie Kids.

(TURNS TO CAR)

Oh, a parking ticket. It's just not my day.

CHYRON OVER LITTLE BOY—"ZOOMBIE KIDS"…

How ya doin? Lemme tell ya about these zombie kids. First, this here zombie kid come crawling out of the ocean one day. Soon, all these other little zombies were marchin' around town actin' like they didn't know each other, even when they met head on. Then one of 'em walked right into my movie camera and busted it…stinkin' little zombie. Three big scientists came down from Vienna to run tests on 'em in the lab. These boys was real smart—this one here's from France—but the zombie kids caught on and got all jacked up and tried to fly away. When that didn't work a lot of 'em took off by theirselves and tried to get a little shut-eye. At first we thought they was drunk, but when we asked 'em they said naw. Are you drunk? Naw. Then the zombies started fighting among themselves. Soon they lost their coordination…and before you knew it they was hoppin' back to the beach the same way they come in. When that last zombie boy crawled back in the water, all the men in town had a party…but Wayne here didn't tell his wife. Take it easy.

(EXT. BUILDING)

> HOST
> If you'd like you home movies made into Mad Movies, send them to the L.A. Connection,

(OVER ADDRESS)

> 6464 Sunset Blvd., Suite 820, Hollywood, California, 90028.

(EXT. WALKWAY)

> HOST
> Well, thanks for joining us today. I'm real sorry I couldn't talk to the star of today's feature, but you know how things go.

(ZORRO BEHIND HIM, CONSTANTLY PATTING HIM ON THE SHOULDER)

> Not now, I'm busy. Anyway, I was saying, Hollywood's an unpredictable place, but you can't always count on things to happen. Not now, I'm on television.

(ZORRO JUMPS TO OTHER SIDE)

> Boy, I can't believe how pushy some people are.

(ZORRO PLACES Z. ON HOST)

> Well, anyway, see you next time with more Mad Movies.

(EXT. WALKWAY)

HOST WALKING AWAY WITH VISIBLE "Z" ON BACK SIDE. HE CHECKS FOR "CHANGE" IN PHONE BOOTH, CONTINUES WALKING.

CLIP TEASE

(INT. OFFICE)

> ZORRO
> I'll give you your pet spider back if you do a short scene for our acting class. They're anxious to see your work. I don't understand you. You're supposed to be a great actor.

> MAN
> I am. I'm better than him, and him…and him. I am a lot more animated and I got a lot more energy than anyone here. I was going to do a death scene…

(SHOW OF ARROW)

> but I was just waiting for the right moment. I'm ready…

(ARROW HITS HIM)

> GROUP OF MEN
> Ah, wonderful,…wonderful death scene…that's incredible…That's fantastic.

CLOSING CREDITS...

HOST V.O.
Additional voices by Mitch Watson.

###

OPENING CRAWL*

SHOW #<u>122</u>

SHOW NAME   <u>ZORRO'S FIGHTING LEGIONS</u>

*Each numbered item as a single page…
Items #1-5 Centerframe
Items #6-10 Lower third of page

1   FOUR STAR
in association with
KENT SKOV

2   Presents
as L.A. Connection
production of

3   MAD MOVIES WITH THE L.A. CONNECTION

4   Tonight's Feature ZORRO'S FIGHTING LEGIONS

5   Starring
the
Voices
of

6   Bob Buchholz

7   Connie Sue Cook

8   Stephen L. Rollman

9   Steve Pinto

10   Kent Skov

CLOSING CRAWL*

SHOW #122

SHOW NAME   ZORRO'S FIGHTING LEGIONS

*Each numbered item as a single page…

1   Directed by
            Kent Skov

2   Written by
            Bob Buchholz
            Stephen L. Rollman

3   Produced by
            Randal W Ridges

4   Featuring
            Bob Buchholz
            Connie Sue Cook
            Steve Pinto
            Stephen L. Rollman
            Kent Skov

5   Associate Producers (each name single page)
            Martha Whitney

6   Kent Weishaus

7   Music Composed and arranged by
            Richard Baker
            Mary Newland

8   For Panda Productions
            Music recorded by
            Richard Baker

9   Theme performed by
            Mary Newland

GENERIC BUMPERS*

SHOW #<u>122</u>

SHOW NAME   <u>ZORRO'S FIGHTING LEGIONS</u>

*Each numbered item as a single page…

1   We'll be right back…

2   Coming Up
           More Mad Movies

3   Stay Tuned for
           "Your Home Movies"

4   Send Your Home Movies to…
           L.A. Connection Productions
           6464 Sunset Blvd., #820
           Hollywood, CA 90028
           (Include a self-addressed, stamped envelope for return of films)

5   Zombie Kids   (Homemovie Title)

CLOSING CREDIT CRAWL (CONT'D)

10	Research by	
	Bob Petrella	
	Ken Segall	
	April Winchell	
	Ted Hardwick	

11   Talent Coordinator
Martha Whitney

12   Associate Director/Stage Manager
Randal W Ridges

13   Assistants to the Producers:
Bob Buchholz
Connie Sue Cook
Steve Pinto
Stephen L. Rollman

14   Facilities Provided by
Hy-Tone Video

15   Lighting and Camera
Bill Sheehy

16   Production Sound
Eric Zeehandelaar

17   Gaffer
Jim Drewry

18   Production Assistants
Lisa Gougas
Ted Hardwick

19   Make-Up
Lora Sanders

20   Wardrobe
Annie Vicari

21   Production Secretary
Eloise Gonzalez

22   Post-Production Coordinated by
Monti Santtilli Rainbolt

23   Post-Production Facilities
Complete Post, Inc.

23a   Editor
Brent Carpenter

24   Post-Production Audio by
Michael Perricone
Michaele Hogan
For Interloc Prod. Studios

CLOSING CREDIT CRAWL (CONT'D)

25   "Your Home Movies" submitted by
           Arlene O'Neil
           San Gabriel, CA

26   Location provided by

27   Executive in Charge of Production for Four Star Television
           Bob Bosen

28   Special Thanks to:
           Susan Lenti   Dennis Condon
           Budget Films   Snaggelpuss
           Richard Holiday

29   Promotion by
           Dan Acree

30   Opening Title Montage by
           Homer & Associates

31   Opening Title Photography by
           Abe Perlstein

32   Post-Production Supervised by
           Randal W Ridges

33   Executive Producer
           Kent Skov

34   "Celebrity Voices and Appearances Impersonated"

35   Copyright 1985 Four Star International, Inc.
           All Rights Reserved

www.ingramcontent.com/pod-product-compliance
Lightning Source LLC
Chambersburg PA
CBHW080401300426
44113CB00015B/2376